San Francisco's Forgotten Jason

SAMUEL BRANNAN

AND

THE GOLDEN FLEECE

A BIOGRAPHY · BY REVA SCOTT

NEW YORK · 1944
THE MACMILLAN COMPANY

SET UP BY BROWN BROTHERS LINOTYPERS
PRINTED IN THE UNITED STATES OF AMERICA
BY THE AMERICAN BOOK—STRATFORD PRESS

SAMUEL BRANNAN

About 1852

To
Omer Winfield
and
Ronald LeRoy

Author's Foreword

SAMUEL BRANNAN was a vivid personality. His quest for romance and adventure started when he was a little boy and ended only with his death as an old man. In the tapestry of California history he emerged vividly to assist in founding an empire. As the years passed, his thread was lost. A younger generation has never heard of him. All that remains to remind San Franciscans of their most illustrious pioneer, the man to whom they owe most, is an obscure street in the industrial section.

Acknowledgments

IN DEPARTING from the narrative form of writing, I have been forced in this biography to take some liberties where detailed scenes are involved, but the story itself is based entirely upon historical fact and every incident has been verified. The material was gathered over a period of ten years, from newspapers, Mormon church records, periodicals, Sam's personal letters, and interviews with his relatives. I am especially indebted to the following persons and agencies:

The California Historical Society. I have quoted from the *Quarterly* in many places. The society has been very generous in opening its files to me.

Edna Martin Parratt, of the Bancroft Library. She has been of invaluable assistance in hunting out material.

Bancroft Library and its entire personnel.

Mrs. Maude Pettus, herself a writer of distinction, who has allowed me to consult all papers in her possession. The letters from Sam to her father, Alexander Badlam, Jr., have made it possible to piece out the last ten years of his life. Without her help Sam's story could not have been written.

Alice M. Rich, for information concerning the affiliation of Alexander Badlam, Sr., with the Mormon Church.

The California State Library: Miss Mabel Gillis and Miss Caroline Wenzel in particular. The index and file at the State Library is a joy to work with.

The Society of California Pioneers.

Mrs. Sophie Brannan Haight, a woman of remarkable memory who died a short time ago in her eighty-fifth year.

Fred M. DeWitt, for his constant encouragement.

Harold Holmes, for every assistance he has given me.

Illustrations

SAMUEL BRANNAN

AND

THE GOLDEN FLEECE

Prologue

SAN FRANCISCO, which until the year before had been the village of Yerba Buena, lounged in an unusually warm May sun, that year of 1848; for warm days were rare in this land of ever-present wind and summer fogs. Several men idled on the dusty *plaza*, the same plaza upon which every important drama of San Francisco was usually played. They spoke with appreciation of the warmth. The little square lay on the side of the hill above Kearny Street, and all around it the village spread its hundred or so adobe and log houses over dusty sand hills in every direction. Most of the hills had clumps of scrub-oak clinging to their sands, but the plaza had no vegetation and no buildings other than the squat adobe custom house on the lower eastern corner, where it crouched under a high flagpole from which floated in the constant wind the Stars and Stripes.

Robert Parker, who kept a store on Dupont Street, stopped to exchange a few words with George Winner, a first-class pilot. Their attention was distracted after a time by the arrival of the *Dice Mi Nana*, Sutter's little sailing launch from the fort up the Sacramento River. They watched with interest as it came to anchor in Yerba Buena cove, which danced and dimpled in the sunlight below them. Many an emigrant-train traveler arrived on that boat from the fort, at the end of a long trek from the States. The arrival of the launch was always an event. George shaded his eyes against the brilliance of the sun-dappled water and watched intently for a few moments, then exclaimed, "Why, Sam Brannan's getting off. I'd know his walk at any distance. He's stoppin' to talk to them fellers hangin' around the landin'. He's showin' them somethin'. Look how excited they seem to be gettin'! Now Sam's walkin' along Montgomery toward Washington Street. Now he's comin' up this way and they're follerin' him." George paused, eagerly tense, watching. "He's got somethin' important on his mind! I can tell by the way he walks. And look at the bunch of men follerin' him. Every man they meet starts taggin' after the crowd. Sam's got news! Wonder what it is—"

Parker squinted in order to see better. The two men stood silent, impatiently watching the swift-moving figure as it strode up the hill, followed by a ragged queue of men and boys. The other idlers on the plaza gathered around George and Parker, awaiting the arrival of the tall, vigorous man whose very movements bespoke a message of importance. Sam was lost to view for a few moments as he went around the old Mexican-built custom house, but when he rounded the end of it and climbed the incline they had come to meet him. He faced them dramatically, a half-smile on his face. They saw a tall man, darkly handsome, whose hair fell in soft brown waves to his shoulders from under a broad-brimmed beaver hat. Here was no rough frontiersman in dirty boots and sweaty flannel shirt, but a neat businessman dressed in black broadcloth, with a brocaded vest across which ran a heavy gold watch-chain—his only departure from formality being a Mexican carved-leather holster which held a pistol and a bowie knife. He was young, not yet thirty; slim, and solidly built. His lips were full and passionate, his eyes romantic, his bearing self-assured, almost debonair. He had the fair skin of the Irish, through which his closely shaved whiskers showed blue-black.

He flung up his hand, showing a tiny bottle which gleamed yellow. "GOLD! GOLD FROM THE AMERICAN RIVER!" he shouted at the top of his powerful and compelling voice. The crowd around him went crazy. Shopkeepers a block away heard the persuasive voice and came running from far and near, bringing their friends. Men fought to secure for a moment the precious little quinine bottle filled with gold flakes.

"It's true then!" Parker exclaimed as he rolled the bottle back and forth in his hand before "Kanaka" Davis rushed up to snatch it for a moment's study. "All them rumors about a gold strike in the mountains was true," he said to Davis, who nodded in agreement. Parker fought through to Sam Brannan.

"Where'd you get that sample, Sam?"

Sam answered a dozen men at once when he replied, "I got it up at my store at Sutter's fort. The Mormon battalion men Sutter's got working for him at the flouring mill at Brighton have made a newer and richer strike than the one up Coloma way. That was a rich one, but this one's better!"

While young men clasped hands and danced in crazy circles of excitement and older men gathered in knots to babble over this wonderful development, for a few welcome minutes Sam was left to himself. He was filled with satisfaction. He had planned this moment for two months and it had come off even better than he had hoped. As long ago as March, Sam had been told by the Willis brothers that they had found gold just a few miles above the site of the flour mill they were helping to build for Captain Sutter at Brighton. They told him that Marshall had found gold in January at the sawmill site at Coloma, and it had turned out to be a rich strike. It was in March that Sam had visited the Mormon find at the place they called Mormon Island, and he then and there entered into an agreement with the Willis brothers to grubstake them for a one-third interest in their claim. After that, the men from the Mormon battalion had made a practice of bringing their sacks of gold to Sam's store to be put in the safe until called for.

Again in April he had visited the settlement at Mormon Island and had made arrangements to build and operate a store and boardinghouse for his fellow Church members. Mounting his horse, he had ridden on up to Coloma to choose a site for a store. There in the evening he had talked to Smith and Bigler, Mormon workmen, who showed him where Marshall had made the original discovery of gold in the tailrace. They took him up the American River a short distance and showed him how they dug pure gold out of the crevices of the rocks with their jackknives. Then Sam returned to the Fort Sutter settlement and made arrangements with Captain Johann Sutter to have lumber hauled to the *embarcadero* on the river, two miles from the fort, so that a huge wooden warehouse could be built to take in the shiploads of merchandise which Sam would be constantly sending up to the region when the gold rush began. A storeship already rode at anchor in the river at the embarcadero, but it was not large enough to stock three stores.

As Sam watched the frenzied antics of his friends and neighbors he felt almost as if he were God, pulling the strings and making the puppets dance.

The air became filled with an electric tension. The bottle of gold flakes had set off an explosion which was turning the sleepy little Mexican village into a madhouse, and would eventually ignite the rest of the world. Man after man told him, "I'm going to the gold fields in the morning, Sam." The gold rush had begun.

Robert Semple, a California giant who towered six feet eight inches above the earth, strode into the square and grinned down at Sam, who was a foot shorter.

"You pooh-poohed me when I published in my *Californian*, just after I brought it down from Monterey, that gold had been found at Coloma. What was your reason, Sam Brannan?"

Sam grinned impudently. "You let the cat out of the bag before I was ready, Semple. I had my reasons for wanting the news kept quiet till now. And bein' as I'm the only man in San Francisco that runs back and forth between here and the fort quite regular, you'll admit that I was in a spot to make people believe what *I* said."

"You was that," Semple agreed, and drifted after the bottle of gold which was still making the rounds. George Winner drew Sam to one side. "What's the chance of me staking a claim up at Mormon Island?" he asked.

"You got a good chance," Sam replied and lowered his voice for George's ears alone. "George, you round up all our Mormons and tell them to come to your house tonight. I got word for them from the battalion men." George asked a few questions, then darted away.

As the hours passed, the excitement of the villagers increased. There were three times as many men in San Francisco as there were women, and women seldom ran about the streets. But this day was different. Women came with their men, trailing children behind them. Sam grew weary at last, and decided to go up the hill to the office of his newspaper, *The California Star*. The crowd followed him and people crammed themselves into the little adobe office, which occupied one corner of the Brannan yard. The acting editor, Edward Kemble, a handsome youth of eighteen, looked more like the son of a Spanish nobleman than of a Troy, New York, newspaper editor, which he was. He stood at ease beside his assistant, John Eager. Both boys beamed with pleasure when Sam entered but their expressions changed to surprise as the unexpected crowd poured noisily after him into the room.

"I brought some gold samples!" Sam bellowed, and handed the bottle to Edward. The youth rolled it in his hand, watching with excited eyes the sparkle on the moving flakes. Finally he handed it to John Eager.

"Look, John. Here's something worth looking at." He spoke to Sam, who stood watching him with a pleased expression. "That's prettier than it looked in the rocks and crevices when I was up at the gold field last month. I kept it quiet, though, like you told me to. But this sample here'll start a stampede—or is that what you want?"

Sam nodded. "Yep, let 'er rip now. I got my stores all set and claims staked. The greater the gold rush, the richer I get in a hurry. In the issue of April 22 that I got out while you was gone, I admitted that gold had been found and said I'd seen samples, but nobody got excited. But just show 'em the stuff and they go crazy. Look at 'em fighting to get hold of that bottle, now they've got it away from John!"

"I think I'll strike out for the gold region!" John exclaimed excitedly.

"You and the rest of the town," Sam said drily.

Sam, fearing that the bottle of gold dust might get lost, secured it from the crowd and placed it in a cupboard behind glass doors. During the rest of the afternoon he presided over it proudly while a constant stream of people poured through the little room to inspect the miracle of the day.

At dark, Sam shooed the remaining enthusiasts out of his office and locked the door. He crossed the yard, mounted the steps to the porch of his story-and-a-half redwood house, crossed it, and entered the parlor. His wife, the dark-eyed, dark-haired Ann Eliza, darted out of the kitchen to confront him belligerently. She was small and pretty, but there was a petulant look about her mouth and eyes. "Home's the last place you ever come," she accused him. He ignored her remark and leaned to kiss her upon compressed lips. "I guess you never would have come home if you hadn't got hungry," she went on as he straightened up.

Three-year-old Sammy came running to be thrown into the air. He screamed—half in fear, and half in delight—and Ann Eliza scolded her husband in the usual way until the lad was safely on the floor again. Grandma Corwin, Ann Eliza's mother, came to the door of the kitchen; when Sam looked at her and said "Howdy, Grandma," she began as if upon a signal.

"My land, you did remember you got a home! We was beginning to think you'd forgot you had one."

Sam turned to hang his hat on a peg by the door. "No danger," he said lightly, "not with you womenfolk to keep reminding me. But I guess neither of you wanted to see me very bad or you'd have come on over to the office."

Fanny Corwin made a gesture of distaste with both hands. "Land sakes! We didn't aim to go and get killed in that mob. I guess we're just about the only two people in all of San Francisco that ain't been in that office today."

Sam fished the gold sample out of his pocket and handed it to Ann Eliza. "I should think a sight of this would have been worth coming after." Fanny quickly joined her daughter to peer at the fascinating spectacle. At last Ann Eliza lifted her eyes to Sam's face.

"It's the real stuff all right, just like you been telling me about for the last two months." Her eyes grew remote and she spoke as if dreaming aloud, "I'm going to buy me all the pretty clothes I've wanted all my life. I'll have patterns sent from New York City and silks from China. You can pick the best when the next China shipment comes in, and save it for me. Then I'm going to have a new house—a fancy new house—and furniture for it from New York. It will have to come around the Horn, but I'll be the envy of every woman in San Francisco when I get all the things I want."

Sam put his arm around her shoulders and guided her toward the kitchen and the tantalizing odors of Grandma's cooking. "Sure, Lizzie, you can have everything your heart desires, but take it easy. Wait till I get a lot of money in hand first." He stopped and turned her so that she faced him. "I'm going to buy the world and give it to you for a plaything," he promised solemnly. She searched his eyes, trying to make sure that he meant what he said, and was at last convinced. She hugged him tightly around the waist and lifted her lips to be kissed. This time she kissed him.

Sam sat down heavily at the table, for he was tired. He watched impatiently while Ann Eliza put Sammy in his chair. Fanny was taking up the food and in a moment she set a steaming dish of beef stew in front of Sam.

As he was scouring off his plate with a piece of bread he said suddenly: "Oh, I almost forgot. You folks get your wraps on. We're going down to George Winner's house for a last meeting with the Saints."

Fanny's back stiffened. "Just what do you mean by a 'last meeting' I would like to know."

Sam grinned good-naturedly. "Just what I said, Grandma. After this meeting tonight with the Mormons I'll never meet with them again. I'm through with them and the Church for good."

"Why? What's the Church done to you?" Fanny persisted.

"Plenty. I took the leadership of this group of Saints, brought them out here on a ship all the way around the Horn, and practically wet-nursed a lot of them, and what thanks did I get? I'll tell you. When I went last year to meet the pioneers on the westward trail and tried to talk them into not settling in that Godforsaken Salt Lake Valley, Brigham Young got ornery. He tried to make me eat crow. He thought that if he could make me knuckle to him he'd feel a lot more important. But I wouldn't do it. I told him to his face what I thought of him. Never a word of thanks or praise did I get from him for all I'd done for the Church. All I got was a kick in the backside." He paused dramatically. "Well, if the rest of you folks want to be bossed around by the likes of him and told what to eat and where to live and when to go to the privy, it's all right with me. But I don't like it. Not Brigham Young, nor no other man, is going to tell me what I've *got* to do!"

"You're a strong-willed man, Sam Brannan—too much so for your own good," Fanny burst in. "You'd do better to listen to counsel and pray for a more humble spirit. If you keep on this way you'll rush headlong to perdition and drag your wife and child after you. You've taken to evil ways since you came back from the Great Salt Lake Valley last fall. Many's the time I've smelled liquor on your breath, and if the gossip I hear is true you've been known to do worse than drink."

Ann Eliza looked questioningly at Sam. It was plain that she had heard this from her mother before now and that she wondered about these vague rumors. Sam flushed, his temper touched. "Gossip! Gossip! If you listen to gossip, you'll have nothing but trouble. Come on you two, get up and get ready. It's getting late and we've got to go."

Fanny arose, still irate. "It won't be my last meeting with our Mormon folks, I can tell you that."

That evening Sam looked into the faces of the old friends whom he had led and advised on the six months' journey around the Horn. The original company had numbered more than two hundred; now there were left only about sixty faithful members. A hard-working, sincere group they were, much respected by their non-Mormon neighbors. Many had come from New England, some from New York State, and the rest from various other states on the eastern seaboard; farmers and artisans they were for the most part.

"Folks," Sam began, "our brethren who marched out here as proud members of a Mormon battalion to fight in the Mexican War—which was over before they got here—have added another exciting chapter to their lives. They have made a rich new gold strike above the site of the flouring mill they've been building for Captain Sutter, at a place they've named Mormon Island. They want you San Francisco Saints to come up and join them. Every man-jack of you can have a claim eighteen feet wide on the American River and running back as far as you want. They think that if our Mormon brethren hang together you can keep out ruffians and live at peace among yourselves. Now, most of you have been staying on here in San Francisco because of the epistle the Twelve Apostles sent you by me last fall, telling you that the valley in the mountains could furnish no food and that the thousands then pouring in there might face famine. You were supposed to wait until word comes that it's safe for you to migrate there. Well, my guess is that the first year's crops won't be much good and you won't be able to go in there before this fall, anyway. You might just as well go on up to Mormon Island with your families and dig for gold as stay here waiting."

"Is it safe for our families?" George Winner asked.

"Why, sure it is! There's a few bears up there, but with a lot of you in a community they won't bother you. It's beautiful country, all filled with pines and fresh mountain streams full of trout. It's a fine place for your families."

He talked on at great length, answering questions as they arose. In closing he warned his friends to be sure and stock up at his store at Sutter's fort before they went into the mountains, for there would be no way to get provisions after they got there until later, when Sam opened his projected other stores.

When Sam and his family started home they were stopped at every few steps by some villager who wanted firsthand information about gold from Sam. Eventually Ann Eliza and Fanny drifted on home with the sleeping Sammy.

It was late when Sam crawled between the covers over the straw tick. Ann Eliza did not stir when he put his arms around her. He was tired, and settled himself for sleep. But sleep eluded him—he found his brain engrossed with dreams of the future. He saw himself as the richest and most powerful man in the San Francisco of the time to come. He had predicted in one of his newspaper editorials that their city would one day be the Liverpool of the western world. This he believed implicitly. When that time should come, when San Francisco should become a city of thousands—yes, even of hundreds of thousands; when argosies from the far ends of the earth should lay their gleaming cargoes upon San Francisco docks—Sam would be master of that domain. For hours he pictured himself in scene after glorious scene, until at last his weary brain gave way to sleep. He saw the smiling, gentle face of his dear old mother, long since dead. He was back again in his boyhood home at Saco, Maine.

"I'm going to be rich and famous, Ma," he told her. She put her finger to her lips to hush him.

"Your Pa's been drinking overmuch today and he's nodding in his chair there by the fireplace. If he hears you talking so big he's liable to thrash you."

"I'm not afraid of Pa now," Sam replied, somehow getting his present self mixed up with his little-boy self. "I always have been afraid of him, ever since that night he beat John the last time—but now I'd give him as good as I got."

His mother's eyes grew misty. "Poor John, such a young lad he was to go running away. I think of him all the time and worry. If only he'd come home or write so that I'd know he was all right, I could die in peace."

"John's all right," Sam assured her.

"I hope so. I do hope so!" She turned anxious eyes upon Sam. "Don't you ever run away and leave your old Ma, will you, Sammy-boy?"

"No, Ma, I won't never run away," he promised, and the sound of his voice awoke him from his sleep. He pillowed his head on his crossed palms and was lost in memories of his childhood.

Book One

Chapter I

As FAR BACK as Sam could remember [1] his father had been an old man, a gnarled old man who leaned on a cane and spoke with an Irish brogue. He spent hours every day sitting in the wooden armchair beside the great fireplace in the kitchen of his farmhouse at Saco, Maine. Usually he was bemoaning the vagaries of the modern world and deploring its wickedness.

" 'Tis a wicked gineration we're raisin', Sara," he said often to his half-Irish second wife.

On a spring evening of 1827 he sat thus in his chair to settle his supper, and while his daughter Mary Ann washed the dishes at the long kitchen table he took his pleasure by nagging at her in his indirect way. "When I was a boy in Waterford, Ireland, I was not always seekin' after the pleasures of the flesh' like young people be after doin' all the time any more. We worked for what we had. I worked from the time I were a little lad and when I come to this country in '75 it were my own savings I used to buy my ticket. I was not begging it from my father like my boys are always after trying on me. I was never a burden in my father's house, neither."

"And who's a burden on you, might I ask?" Mary Ann demanded, turning her irritated glance upon him.

Thomas leaned forward to rest his chin on the back of the hand his cane supported, and pretended innocence while he looked up at her from under his bushy brows. "I'll be accusing no one," he said in mock mildness, and added, "But I ain't meaning your half-brothers Rufus or Thomas, nor your half-sister Nancy."

"Then you must mean me," she sputtered and went on, shaking her finger at him. "Let me tell you, Pa Brannan, that I more than earn my keep in this house. I work from sunup till sundown with never a minute's rest. But that's the least I have to put up with. Listening to you growl all day is worse. I don't stay here because I like to."

Thomas grinned as he looked up into her face. "Never was a truer word uttered, daughter. 'Tis only the chance you'd be needing to be leaving." He shook his head sadly, "With your lack of looks 'tis not likely you'll ever be after marrying."

Mary Ann looked at him with mixed emotions and then burst into tears and fled up the stairs. Thomas grinned after her fleeing figure; rising, he hobbled to the door, pulled on his greatcoat with the cape—for the evening was chill—adjusted his muffler and his cap and went out. A nondescript hound belonging to John and Sam jumped on him eagerly and the old man beat him off with muttered curses; he turned and called to one of the two boys who were playing in the yard. "John, lock yon cur in the barn afore·I come home, or I'll be after killing him. 'Tis a good for nothing hound he is!" He clumped off down to the tavern, not waiting for a reply.

"You boys lock Rover in the barn," Sara, their mother, said as she came out of the milk cellar. Fourteen-year-old John and his eight-year-old brother Sam followed her instruction, and Rover made little protest for he knew how to get out again when he was ready. When they came back to the house Mary Ann had finished the dishes, and their two older brothers, Dan and Tom—seventeen and nineteen, respectively—were playing checkers on the kitchen table by the light of the oil lamp. John fetched a partially completed ship's model from the mantelpiece, and while he carved young Sam watched with eager and interested gaze, now and then asking a question or making a suggestion. Mary Ann brought her knitting within the halo of light cast by the lamp, and the frail and aging Sara sat rocking gently, a crocheted shawl about her shoulders.

Sara watched her children with quiet pride. Mary Ann was the oldest—poor lovable, homely Mary Ann, who would be twenty-one in a few months and thereby a confirmed old maid. Tom, named for his father and also for an older half-brother, was tall and earnest. Dan and Little Tom, as they called him to distinguish between the half-brothers, were much alike in disposition. They did the farm work, now that their father was an old man, and co-operated to make life hard for John and Sam, the babies. Sara thought back over the years to the time when she had married Thomas Brannan, a widower of fifty with two sons then about the ages of Little Tom and Dan. She had been the widow Emery for over a year, then, and Thomas had lost his wife, Mary Goodrich Brannan, but six months earlier. When he suggested that Sara marry him, it had seemed to her indecent haste, but the nine-year-old Nancy decided her. Tom did not know how to take care of the girl and she looked so forlorn and neglected that Sara Knox Emery yearned to give her a mother's love. And so she had done from the day she married Thomas Brannan. Sara stirred faintly and sighed. It had not been a particularly happy marriage, though she had born him five children on whom she doted. Thomas' drinking had been a cross to bear; at first she had borne it with the thought that as he grew older he would become more temperate. But the Irish in him had gone just to the reverse. The older he grew, the harder he was to live with—more contrary and set in his ways.

A little after the clock struck nine they heard his faltering step and the tapping of his cane as he hobbled up the walk. The older boys rose and put the checkerboard away, and John hastened to set the ship's model on the mantelpiece. One never knew what old Thomas would do if he came home in a temper. They heard him stumble up the porch steps and then there was the sharp yelp of a dog. With stricken eyes Sam looked at John, who waited anxiously for the door to open. Their ears caught the thud of Tom's cane on flesh and bone and the sound of the dog's yelping as he ran away from the house. The door was thrown open and Tom stood angrily on the threshold, his cap and muffler awry. Little Tom jumped forward to help his father into the room, but Thomas lifted his cane and cracked the lad over the wrist with it. The boy exclaimed with pain and turned back into the room; Dan motioned him to come upstairs and they ascended the worn steps, Little Tom holding his arm in great pain and his brother trying to help him. John attempted to dart past his father after the dog, to see how badly he was hurt, but as he passed, the old man put out his cane and tripped the lad so that he fell headlong. Sara cried out in anxiety when she saw Thomas lift his cane to strike the fallen boy. "Don't hit him, Pa! He ain't done nothin'!"

Sammy had retired to the fireplace corner to watch what went on and be out of harm's way. Mary Ann ran forward to help John to his feet, but Thomas motioned her back and leaning over he dragged the boy to his feet and cuffed him on the ear. "I'll teach ye to leave that cur underfoot after I've told ye to get rid of him," he bellowed and pushed John ahead of him into the room.

"I locked him up like you said," John replied, defensively.

"Talk back to me, will ye?" Thomas shouted, and raising his cane he struck the boy again and again on his backside. At first John permitted the blows, but as his temper rose he turned swiftly and jerked the cane out of the old man's hand.

"You'll not hit me again!" John shouted and threw the cane into the far corner of the room. "I told you a day or so ago that if you ever hit me with that cane again, I'd leave home for good! And I meant what I said! You're not going to beat me every time you get in a temper—I'll not stand for it!"

He turned and ran up the stairs. Surprised, Thomas stood looking after the lad. Then he laughed shortly and said to Sara, "I'll take care of him in the morning." He paused. "The lad's got spunk. He's got the old Brannan temper." His glance fell upon Sammy.

"Fetch me my cane, Sammy, and then get to bed afore I whale the tar out of you too."

Sammy did his bidding and then scurried upstairs. Behind him came Mary Ann, carrying the lamp; and Sara, urging Thomas's uncertain footsteps up the steps, followed.

Sam found John in their room gathering up his few belongings and tying them into a kerchief.

"What you doin'?" he asked.

John spoke with bitterness, fighting all the while to keep back the boyish tears. "I'm going to run away, Sammy. I told that old fool I would if he hit me again, and now he's gone and done it. I'll show him! Tonight's the last time he'll ever hit me—yes, or ever lay eyes on me again."

Sam looked at him with big eyes. "Golly, John, ain't you scared to run off by yourself?"

"Scared? What's there to be scared of? I'm big enough to take care of myself. I'll go to Boston and go to sea as a cabin boy. I'll support myself, and if I never see or hear of this farm again it will suit me."

Sammy was suddenly overcome with a feeling of utter lonesomeness. "Don't you ever want to see me or Ma or Mary Ann again?" he asked forlornly.

John seemed to be swallowing a lump. "Well, yes," he began, hesitating, and added more hurriedly, "of course I do." Then he finished angrily, "But I'm never coming back as long as he is alive."

"I wish I could go with you," Sam said hopefully, scared of the idea even while he was expressing it.

"Naw, you're too little. Maybe someday, after I get to be a captain or something, I'll come back and get you, though."

"Will you, Johnny?"

They heard their mother's furtive footsteps on the bare boards of the hall, and hurriedly John slipped under the covers—clothes, kerchief bundle, and all. Sammy began quickly to undress. Sara came into the room and looked uncertainly at John, who lay pretending to be asleep. She went over to the bed and stood looking down at him, and sighed a deep, revealing sigh which spoke of heartbreak. Then she pushed the hair back from his forehead and kissed him lightly. He opened his eyes, then, and looked up into her face. She saw the tears and asked anxiously, "Are you all right, Son?"

"Yes, I'm all right," he whispered.

"You won't hold no hard feelings agin your Pa for what he done tonight, will you? He'll be sorry in the morning when he's sober, even if he don't say it to you or let on like he is."

John made no reply, and at last she said, "Well, good night. Sleep tight and we'll iron things out tomorrow."

Still John made no reply, and as Sara moved to the door she admonished Sammy. "Hurry up, lad, and slip into bed. You oughtn't to dawdle so."

As soon as she had closed the door after her, Sammy jumped into bed. He talked to John for a time and determined to lie awake with his favorite brother until the house grew quiet, but presently he fell asleep. He dreamed that someone kissed him on the cheek, but it did not waken him. When morning came, John was gone.

When they were all seated at breakfast, old Thomas looked down the table at John's place. "Where be the lad?" he yelled. Sara turned to Sammy. "Go tell Johnny to hurry down," she said.

Sammy held the spotlight and made the most of it. There was

something of the actor in his makeup and he could not resist this opportunity to create a dramatic scene.

"He ain't upstairs," Sammy said.

"Where is he?" Sara asked.

"I don't know."

"Where did he say he was going when he first got up?" Sara persisted.

"I'm after having enough of this foolishness," Thomas roared. "Speak up, Sammy, and be saying where John is. I'll whale the day-lights out of him when I get me hands on him, being late for his meals and making us all be waiting."

"I don't know where he is," Sammy said loudly to be sure that his father heard every word. "He's run away. He went last night. He said he would never come home again so long as Father was alive. He was mad because you caned him again and he run away like he promised he would."

"Oh, he did!" Thomas roared. "I'll find out about this. I'll be after having him brought back and put in chains, that's what I'll be doing. Fine country this is, where a lad can talk back to his father and then up and run away!"

He got up from the table, put on his cap and coat, and went stump-ing down the path. Sara ran after him to find out where he was going, but all he would say was that he was going to get a marshal to fetch his unruly son home.

When Little Tom and Dan went to the west field to work they took Sammy to help with the hoeing. As the sun rode high the day grew warm, and the small boy began to fall behind. From time to time either Dan or Tom would throw a rock or a clod at him to prod him into more activity, but eventually they got so far ahead on their rows of beans that they grew tired of urging Sammy and left him behind. When it seemed that it must be around noon, Sammy sneaked away and ran up the road until he came to a side road, which he fol-lowed down to his half-brother Rufus's farmhouse. He waited until he saw Rufus come up from the field with his children, some of whom were older than Sam. When he ran to meet them Rufus stopped and waited.

"Hello, Son," he said. "What you doin' over here at this hour?"

"I come to tell you about John," the boy replied.

"I know about him. Mary Ann was over this morning. Can't say as I blame him. I hope he gets clean away. Pa don't treat him right."

"It's kind of lonesome without him," Sam said. Rufus patted him on the head and motioned toward the house.

"I guess it is, all right. Come on in the house and have some dinner. That'll make you feel better."

"No. I guess I'll run on home. Ma'll be feeling bad and she'll be needing me to comfort her."

Rufus, tall and dark, like all the Brannans, looked down into young Sammy's face and there was a new expression in his eyes. "Yes, I calc'late she will be needing you, Sam. You're all the child she's got left. See that you don't ever go breaking her heart," he said.

"I won't," Sam promised, and hurried across the nearest field toward home. Dan and Tom had not yet come in from the fields and old Thomas was still in town. Sam wondered if he would come home dragging John. Mary Ann was cooking dinner, and when Sam asked where his mother was she pointed upstairs with her fork. Sammy ran up the stairs and into his parents' bedroom. Sara was lying on the big four-poster, her eyes red from weeping. Sam went on diffidently into the room until he stood beside her.

"Crying about John?" he asked. She nodded, and reaching up took one of his hands and clung to it.

"Don't you ever run away and leave me, will you, Sammy-boy?"

"No, I won't, Ma," he promised. She pulled him down so that he sat beside her on the bed. It was plain that she wanted to talk to him.

"I can't say that I blame John much for what he's done, but still and all he didn't have a right to run away. I loved him—we all did. And he's hurt me and the rest of us more than he's hurt Pa. He didn't have a right to be so selfish. We need him here to help with the farm work, and besides, he's too young to be out in the world alone. I'll never draw a contented breath again until I know he's safe. How could he do this to me? That's what I'll never understand. And he never let on about it last night when I was talking to him!"

She wept for several moments, and Sam felt guilty, for he had known John's deception and had held his tongue. At last he patted his mother's hand awkwardly. "Don't feel so bad, Ma. You still got me. I won't never do nothing to hurt you."

She smiled at him tremulously through her tears and patted his cheek tenderly. "I know you won't. You're the last of my flock, but you're the most loving, too. I sometimes think that you was sent to comfort my last days, and I have a feeling that you'll do more to make the name of Brannan live than all the rest of them put together."

Sam said nothing. He was embarrassed by the emotionalism of the scene and wanted desperately to get away.

"Well, I guess dinner must be about ready," Sara offered, wiping her eyes. "You better go and eat and then go back to the field and work like a good boy to help your brothers. You'll have to work hard to make up for John."

"Why don't Pa ever have to work in the field like the rest of us?" Sam asked, aggrieved.

"Because your Pa is an old man. He's done his share of hard work and now he's entitled to take it easy while his boys support him. He does what he's able."

"You mean taking eggs and stuff down to the market-place to sell?"

"Yes. After all your Pa drives a sharp bargain."

"Are you all right now?" Sam asked, and when Sara nodded he said, "Then I'll go eat and go back to the field like you said."

She nodded, and he got up and ran downstairs. Dan and Little Tom had come in and were eating.

"I ought to give you a licking for running away this morning," Little Tom threatened.

Mary Ann set a steaming bowl of potatoes in front of Sam, and wiping her hands on her apron she sat down. Dan always echoed Tom when they were deviling Sam. "Yeah, and I'll give you a kick in the backside if you don't get a move on you this afternoon."

This was too much for Mary Ann. "You're brave, you two. Always picking on a youngun. Go on now and get your dinner and shut up. Just let me catch either one of you laying a hand on Sammy and I'll take a broom handle to you both, big as you are."

In spite of Mary Ann's protection, Sammy took his share of tormenting from his older brothers whenever he had to work with them, which was every day. And so it was on this occasion.

One day, when he was in his twelfth year, Sam found Mary Ann crying in the orchard. He approached her cautiously and sat down beside her.

"What you bawling for, Mary Ann?"

She raised tear-wet eyes. "Nothing in particular, Sammy. It's just that I'm discouraged. I just come back from Molly's wedding. All my friends are married and gone and here am I still an old maid." She made a gesture of futility. "I guess I'll never get married. I'm just too homely."

"Naw, you ain't either, Mary Ann. When a body gets used to you, like I am, you look all right. I love you no matter how you look."

She put her arm across his shoulders and gave him a quick squeeze. "You ain't very flattering, Sammy Brannan, for a fact, but I know how you mean it and it helps an awful lot."

A year later Alexander Badlam came courting. He was dark and curly-haired and there were those in town who said he was lazy, but Mary Ann saw qualities in Alexander that others did not see, and when after a year's courtship he proposed, she accepted him with alacrity.

The day before their wedding Alexander drove a covered wagon, all loaded and ready for the journey to Ohio, into the Brannan yard and left it. Mary Ann was busy the whole day getting her clothes ready for the wedding and packed. That night she was packing her linen chest, when Sara led Sam into her little attic room. Mary Ann was sitting on the floor folding a pile of linens and laying them neatly in rows in the chest, her voluminous skirts spread fanwise about her. Sara sat down on the little rocker near the chest, and Sam stood on one foot and then the other while he wondered why his mother had brought him here. He looked at Mary Ann's sleekly combed hair and a lump came into his throat. He was going to miss having her around.

"Mary Ann, I been thinking," Sara began. "I been thinking a lot about Johnny and now I've made up my mind what I want to do about Sammy. I want you to take him away with you."

Mary Ann looked at her with unbelieving eyes and said nothing as Sara hurried on. "Pa's old now and hard for young folks to live with, especially when he's in his cups."

"Which is every night," Mary Ann said drily.

"He is drinking overmuch for a man of his age, but then, every dog to his poison. But what I'm getting at is that now that Sammy's fourteen, Pa's picking at him just like he did at Johnny. I worry that Sammy will run away. I worry so that I can't sleep some nights. If that was to happen, I just couldn't stand it. That's why I want Sammy to go with you. I know that you'll look after him good and I think Alexander likes him, and he'll probably be a better father to him than Pa is now. I know he won't run away from you."

Mary Ann protested, "We'd like nothing better than to take Sammy with us, but I don't think he ought to go. After all, you're getting old, too, and you need him. Sammy can put up with Pa a few more years for your sake. Can't you, Sammy?" she appealed to the lad.

Sam's eyes were shining with the vision of a far, unconquered land where Indians lurked behind every bush. But when Mary Ann appealed to him he looked at his mother and knew instantly that if she wanted him to stay he would. "Yeh, I can stand it till I'm grown. I wouldn't run away and leave Ma." He tried to be manful about his statement, but there was an undercurrent of disappointment in his voice.

. Sara shook her head. "No! You two ain't going to talk me out of this. I know what I'm doing. I ain't saying that it won't just about kill me to lose both of you at the same time, but it's best that way. I've lived my life and it's been a full one. Now you children have got to be considered first." She pulled her purse from her apron pocket.

"I've got some money here that belongs to me. It was left me by my first husband, and I've saved this much of it all these years for just such a time as this. I want you to take it, Mary Ann, and buy Sam an apprenticeship with a printer. He's a smart boy, the brightest in his school—whenever Pa will let him go to school. He's slight built, not heavy enough for farm work. It would be a shame to waste such a keen mind on plowing and harvesting. If he wants to be a somebody, he's got it in him. If he'll apply himself to learning printing, he'll end up being somebody important. I know that 'way down deep inside me."

Tears filled her eyes but she quickly, almost angrily, wiped them away. Sammy swallowed a big lump. He wanted to hug her, but somehow he just couldn't show his feelings any more. It seemed unmanly. "I'd better stay here with you, Ma. I can learn the printing business here just as good," he protested.

"No, no," she objected quickly. "I don't want your Pa to know about this money. If he knew I had it he'd take it to build a new barn or something. No sir, I want it for you, Sammy, and the only way you can get the good of it is to go with Mary Ann."

"Oh," he said shortly, and Sara hurried on.

"You go on with Mary Ann like I want you to. You work hard and hold that devilish Brannan temper in check, and you'll end up famous. I know you will! You're thoughtless and impulsive now but you'll get over that when you get older, and there ain't a more worthwhile or lovable boy on the face of the earth. If you wasn't so worth while I wouldn't be sending you away like this."

Sam felt a glow 'way down inside himself. His mother believed in him and somehow he must meet her challenge. "You won't never be sorry you sent me away, Ma, I promise you that. Before I die, I *will* be famous. Every person in this country will know who Sam Brannan is."

"I hope so," Sara said softly, and added, "Son, put your hand on this Bible, here on the washstand, and say after me, 'I will not smoke nor drink nor carouse around. I will work and study and strive to be somebody my mother can always be proud of.'"

Solemnly Sam repeated the words.

The next day relatives came from far and near. The wedding ceremony was at six in the evening, in the parlor. Afterward the guests sat at two long tables in the kitchen and ate the festive wedding supper.

The following morning Alexander and Mary Ann climbed up to sit on the seat at the front of the wagon, while Sam was stationed in the rear where he could watch the load. Thomas was unwell after

the festivities, so that only Sara and Dan and Little Tom were there
to wave the travelers good-by. Alexander clucked to the horses and
they pulled the wagon out into the long lane. Sam waved to his mother
from halfway down the lane, and just before the wagon turned onto
the highway he waved again. He saw her lift her hand and wave, and
suddenly her figure became distorted in his tear-washed eyes and he
slid down in the bottom of the wagon-box where no one could see,
and wept.

All the way on that long trip to Ohio, Sam had visions of the new
home Mary Ann and Alexander would build in the wilderness. Indians lurked constantly behind the trees and he and Alexander frightened them away by their expert shooting. But when the dust-covered
wagon drew into the outskirts of Painesville, their destination on the
shore of Lake Erie, Sam was disappointed to find that this was but a
New England town transplanted. Square, white-painted houses with
well-kept lawns and flower gardens and elm-shaded streets filled the
main part of town. Sam felt sure that there had been no Indian raids
here for a long time. He did see some log cabins on the edge of the
settlement and one or two in the town itself, but the farm grounds
which surrounded them were well kept, the outbuildings whitewashed, and there were no woods near by in which Indians could
lurk. A tidy church dominated the residential part of town and tolled
its message on Sunday mornings, bringing the faithful to worship—
most of them from New England or New York State, dressed in their
Sunday best and promenading just as people did in Maine. Except
for the lake which dominated all phases of town life, Painesville
could have been any conservative eastern community.

Mary Ann and Alexander bought a farm on the edge of town,
and while they camped in a tent to await the building of their house,
Sam was left pretty much to his own devices. He found to his joy
that Painesville was at heart a pioneer town in spite of its conservative
appearance, for this was the supply center for trappers who gathered
furs along the lake. They came into town in fringed buckskin suits
and coonskin caps to buy supplies, get drunk, and to release a fund
of profanity which only a good trapper could muster. As with mariners

of old, there was always one among them who loved to tell tall tales, and Sam was drawn to these men as by a magnet. Eventually, after listening to hair-raising accounts of trapping, Sam decided that he would become a trapper instead of a printer. He asked Lem Hawkins's advice, as they squatted in front of one of the general stores one afternoon. Lem spat a stream of tobacco before he made answer.

"Naw, I don't think you're cut out to be a trapper. You maybe could set traps and gather in the animals, but you wouldn't have the guts to knock 'em in the head if they was still alive." He spat again. "Hell, it takes a he-man to be a trapper, not no lily like you. You can't swear like a man or drink like a man."

"I could learn." The boy said it eagerly.

"I doubt it. Let's hear you swear a string."

Sam swore every oath he had heard the trappers utter, and soon a little group of them collected around him and suggested new words for his vocabulary. Finally they laughed and said he couldn't swear "no better than a woman."

"Let's see what you can do with brandy, Son," Lem said, and held out his bottle while he winked broadly at his associates. Sam shook his head. "Uh-uh. I don't like it."

Lem laughed, wiped the mouth of the bottle, and took a goodly swig. "That's just what I thought. You got the beginnings of a mustache but you're still tied to your Ma's apern string."

"I am not!"

"Go on with you—you are, too! If you ain't, let's see you take a man-sized gulp of this."

With a gesture of reckless defiance Sam grabbed the bottle and tipped it up. The raw spirits strangled him, and he coughed, but in a manner of braggadocio he continued until he had emptied the half-filled bottle.

When he was next conscious, he was lying on his bed in the Badlam tent and Mary Ann sat on a stool beside him, wiping his face with a damp cloth. She looked at him with reproachful eyes.

"What happened?" he asked and tried to sit up, but the top of his head felt as if it might fly off, so he quickly sought a horizontal position again.

"How could you, Sam Brannan? How could you disgrace us all by getting drunk in front of the store that way, and you only fourteen?"

"Drunk? Did I get drunk?"

"Did you get drunk?" she repeated angrily, "You was a sight to see, laying in the street dead to the world and horses picking their way around you, and all them dirty trappers standing around laughing fit to kill. Alexander had to take the buggy and dump you in it to get you home at all. I'm so ashamed, I'll never be able to look my neighbors in the face again! And you promised Ma on the Bible that you'd never do no such thing."

Sam sighed and put out his hand toward her. After a long time she took it, and then began to cry in long racking sobs. "I'm sorry, Mary Ann," he consoled her. "I'm awful sorry. I didn't go to do it. It'll never happen again, I can tell you that. If you only knowed how I feel, you'd know that I'll never do it twice."

"Well, I hope not," she said at last, drying her eyes. "You're an awful bad boy sometimes, but a body can't help loving you anyway. You'll break some woman's heart someday."

Sam pressed her hand and closed his eyes. "I won't never try to break nobody's heart. I'm always sorry when I do bad things. And I'm awful sorry now."

"I can't blame you too much," Mary Ann said at last. "We been neglecting you lately. But Alex is out now taking care of that. He's arranging with printer Jenkins to start your apprenticeship right away. That ought to keep you out of mischief."

Sam's new boss, printer Jenkins, was a slave driver. He had Sam working soon after daylight and kept him busy until dark. Sam was often too tired when he went home to Mary Ann's at night to do more than fall into bed after a warmed-over supper.

A few months after settling in the white-painted frame house, Alexander decided that he could not make enough at farming and began looking for a job in town. He secured a position as clerk in one of the stores. In 1833, the year after Sam began his apprenticeship, little Mary Ann Badlam was born. She was a pretty baby, much loved by them all.

There were times in the next two years when Sam often felt like deserting his job. But he remembered the promise he had given his mother and the sacrifice she had made for his opportunity, and remained resolute.

Sam's mother wrote regularly. Things were as monotonous as ever in Saco; old Thomas was gradually getting more feeble and crippled with rheumatism. Little Thomas married first and moved to his own land. Dan remained at home, running the farm which now barely supported them. In 1833 old Tom was fading. They did not think he would outlast the spring.

In 1835 a boy, young Alexander, was born to the Badlams. When Sam got home early enough he loved to hold the baby in his arms and rock him to sleep. The child was fair and lovely and more than ordinarily intelligent. As young Sam held the baby and looked into its eyes, he could not know that this tiny fragment of humanity was eventually to be the only living relative who would love and cherish him when by all the rest of the world he was forsaken.

That same year Dan married and brought his wife to live on the farm, Ma said in a letter.

In 1837 the year before Sam's apprenticeship was completed, Sarah Badlam was born; she who was to become the toast of San Francisco because she was so beautiful; the one person who was to cost Sam everything he held most dear. Destiny set her lovely feet upon a path of selfishness the day she was born, one which would lead her and all whose lives touched hers to destruction.

A month after Sarah was born came word that old Thomas had died, in his eighty-second year. When his estate was settled, Sara sent money to Sam and Mary Ann—their share of the estate after the land had been sold. Sam held the gold pieces which were his heritage in his hand. These would buy his freedom.

"Better give me that money and let me invest it along with Mary Ann's," Alexander suggested.

Sam shook his head. "Nope. I'm going to buy up the year that's left of my apprenticeship, and the rest I'm going to invest in Ohio land. They say you can make a fortune overnight if you get in on this land scheme."

"Those land sharks will skin you," Alexander warned, and his voice changed to a pleading tone. "Mary Ann is going to give me her money to invest in a little store of our own. Let me have yours too, Son, and you can help me with the store. We'll be sure of a steady profit even if it is small."

Sam shook his head again. "No, Alex. I can't see that. I want to make a lot of money fast—money I don't have to work for."

"You can't get something for nothing!" Alexander insisted, but Sam laughed at him. In a few months he found himself but one of thousands of investors who had lost everything in the Ohio land frauds of '37. He was eighteen now, a failure as a big business-man.

However, while he still had money he had bought himself a new suit, cut in the latest style, and he was a handsome figure. When he found himself without funds or a job he took stock of the situation and came to a quick decision.

"I guess I'd better get out and find a job," he told Mary Ann one morning as she changed the diapers on the baby. "Ohio's broke after these land frauds and I'll have to go somewhere else to get work as a printer."

"My land, you don't want to leave home when there's a panic on everywhere. I don't ever remember times being as hard as they are now."

"But I can't stay here. There's no work in Painesville—you know that."

"You could work in the store with Alex. He's asked you to, times enough."

"No, I don't like clerking in a store. I don't want to spend my life with an apron on. I want to get out and see the world. I've got a good notion to work my way on the boats up home and see Ma. After that I can go on down to Boston or New York and get work at my own trade."

Mary Ann sighed resignedly. "Well, I can't make you do what I think's best. You're a grown man now and I guess you'll have to do as you please. You won't listen to me any more, anyway. While you was waiting around to make millions on Ohio land, you was hanging around with a pretty wild bunch of fellers. Alex says he saw you smoking a cigar one day when you was coming out of the ale-house.

Next thing, I guess you'll be chasing women. And that, after all your fine promises to Ma."

Sam grinned down into her face. "Yeh, Sis, I'm growing up now. I made a promise to Ma when I was a little boy, and I'll keep it. I said I wouldn't drink or smoke or carouse around. What she meant was that I wasn't to make a habit of doin' them things. Well, I won't. But I got to do the things other men do, or I'll never be a man."

"Oh, you!" Mary Ann said, bristling impotently. "Ma didn't mean no such thing. She meant not to do them at all and you know it."

"Well, I'm not tied to any woman's apron string, and what's more I never will be. I'll live a good life as I see it."

She shrugged. "I suppose you will. But it's hard for womenfolks to sit by and see their menfolks start on the road to perdition and not warn them."

Sam patted her on the shoulder. "I'm a long way from perdition, and I wouldn't worry if I was you."

Chapter II

IN THE SPRING of 1838 Sam boarded a boat, later transferring to an Erie canal-boat, to go to New York City. He stayed in the metropolis for a few days to take in the sights, then sailed up the coast to Maine. He arrived at the farmhouse in Saco on an April afternoon. The house was quiet. He tiptoed into the kitchen. His father's old wooden armchair with the uneven cushion stood in its accustomed place by the fireplace, and Sam for a moment almost expected to see the old man sitting there. All the unpleasantness which revolved around his father was forgotten and he remembered only the pleasant things, such as the stories about bygone days in Waterford his father had told him, on warm Sunday afternoons when the old man had been in an expansive mood. Suddenly he wished that his father were there again, tapping out his pipe against the cobbles of the fireplace. The house seemed deserted. Sam wandered up the stairs searching for Sara. He pushed open the door into his parents' bedroom, and there she was, lying asleep. He hardly recognized her, she was so old and shrunken and faded.

"Ma," he whispered, joyful at seeing her again and filled with pity at her condition.

Her eyelids flew open and she looked at him. It was plain that she did not believe her eyes, for she said "Sammy?" as if she feared he was only a dream.

"It's me, Ma," he said and plunged across the room to seat himself on the edge of her bed. She raised her arms weakly, and he put his arms about her and held her close for a long moment. She clung to him and patted him and felt him, and cried a little with joy. "It's my baby," she kept saying over and over. "I thought I was going to die without ever seeing you again."

At last she held him away while her faded old eyes took in every detail of his appearance. "You've growed up," she said with conviction. "You went away a boy, and you've come back a man." She looked at him a long time and added, "You're a fine-looking man, Sammy."

He blushed with embarrassment and asked quickly, "Where is everybody? You ain't living here all alone, are you?"

"Oh, no. Dan and his wife live here. She's gone over to Nancy's house this afternoon. I told her I'd be all right here alone. She gets so tired being tied up with me here all day. And Dan's down in the field, working. What about you, lad? Have you got located yet?"

"No," he admitted. "I'm going out to look for work now, but I thought I'd come home and see you first."

"You done right, Son. I don't think I'll live much longer and I did want to see you before I go. How is Mary Ann and all the younguns?"

They talked for a long time about his sister and her family. Sam told her all there was to tell about himself and the Badlams, and how lively the children were; then Sara winked her eye at him in her pert way.

"I got a nest egg put away for you, Sammy. When you're ready to go I'll give it to you. I want you to promise not to invest this in no get-rich-quick scheme. That's gambling. What I want you to do with this money is, use it as a nest egg, save up more to go with it, and buy yourself a press. Then you can set up in business for yourself. Will you do it?"

He nodded, his thanks in his eyes, and she seemed content. Sam got up and began to wander around the room looking at all the familiar objects—playthings of his own and of the other children; faded and old-fashioned they were, but still treasured by Sara. He picked up his father's cane, leaning in the corner, and examined its polished surface.

"It seems funny. Pa not being here, don't it?"

She nodded. "Yes, I miss him. He was a trial the last year, but I used to feel about him like I always felt about one of you younguns when you was mean. I got awful mad at him but I went on loving him just the same. I'm glad I'm going to go and be with him soon."

Sam thought that his mother might die at any time and so remained long past the day when he had planned to leave. But he did not get on well with Dan and was soon anxious to be gone. Sara sensed it in him and at last she spoke.

"You want to go, don't you, Sammy?"

"In a way, yes. But I'll stay as long as you need me, Ma."

Her eyes filled with tears, but she smiled. "There's nothing you can be doing for me, so you'd just as well get started if you want to. Fetch me that box out of my top bureau drawer and I'll give you the money I promised."

Sam told her that he would stay and pretended not to believe that she was dying, as she insisted; but she had her way at last. He brought her the box and she gave him the envelope that had her gift in it.

As he stood with it in his hand he looked down into her troubled eyes. "I'll do with this just what you want me to, Ma. And I will amount to something before I die, just like I promised you a long time ago."

"I know you will, Son," she said in a steadfast voice. He stooped then and kissed her on the forehead and went swiftly from the room.

The next day he took the coach to Boston. Here there was no work to be found, so he worked his way to New York on a boat. The metropolis was still paralyzed from the panic of the year before, and thousands walked the streets hunting for employment. Sam used a little of his precious hoard to ride down to Washington, but could find no opening there, either. He drifted from place to place and finally got work on a boat going to New Orleans. He found that in the lovely old city the worst effects of the depression were not present. New Orleans carried on a lively commerce with the old world and seemed at a glance more European than American. Sam wandered up Canal Street carrying his bag, fascinated by the color and movement of this strange environment. Then he turned and went back down the street to rest in the park across from the French market. He had never before seen such a place as the old French town, and his Gaelic blood responded to everything about it. Down Bienville he finally took his way to the old French quarter, where he found lodgings.

By the end of the week he had a job as a printer's "devil" on a small trade sheet. Soon he was adding regularly to the money his mother had given him. During his free hours he explored the old-world city. He was fascinated by the dark elegance of the creole ladies he saw riding in their liveried carriages. He envied the handsome young dandies who rode so insolently on their thoroughbred horses up to the entrance of the magnificent St. Charles Hotel. He watched them stride across the wide, pillared portico to be met by beauties dressed in the latest Parisian creations. Two well-known young bloods he saw one night consorting with octoroons, near Rampart Street. This seemed strange to Sam. He had no respect for men who crossed the color line, and said so to his fellow "devil" the following morning.

"You No'the'ners are snoopers," the other replied hotly. "Why do y'all come down heah if you don't like the way we act?"

"We-all go where we want to," Sam imitated him. "This is a free country and an American can go any place in it he wants to. You folks don't own the South even if you did get here first. New Orleans is the prettiest city in the world. They ain't nothing wrong with it except the people that live here."

"We're better than any stinkin' thing that comes out of the No'th," the local boy replied.

"Like hell you are!" Sam said violently. "The men down here go around talking about how they respect all women. They spend most of their time worrying about the virtue of the women in their families, but I've got to see the first one of your men that won't take somebody else's sister the first chance he gets. Yes, and then go around bragging about it. I saw two of your young bloods fooling around with some black women on Rampart Street last night. They treat 'em like dogs and then go to bed with them. Where 1 come from we really respect our women but we don't talk about it all the time. We act decent because we're born decent."

"Then go on back whe' y'all come from," the Southern lad shouted and hit Sam a sudden blow on the chin. They fought and panted and wrestled until they were parted by the boss. The next day Sam started looking for another job.

He secured one as a grocery clerk and smiled to think that he had refused to do such work for his own brother-in-law. One evening he came upon a mob which was manhandling a dark-clad young man. As Sam reached the scene, a giant seaman lifted the youth high and threw him into the canal at the far end of Canal Street. The victim struck the lower bank and rolled into the water. He went under, and a moment later came to the surface. With a desperate cry for help he went under again. Sam could not swim, and he watched the helpless man with a feeling of panic.

"Save him!" he shouted to the man nearest him.

"Save him? What fur? We want him to drown, the darned fool."

"What's he done?"

"Aw, he's one of them danged Mormons. He says that all the churches in the world are bastards except his'n. He says Joseph Smith is a prophet, the only true prophet on earth today. He's lucky we didn't lynch him."

"A Mormon?" Sam echoed. "They're kind of crazy, ain't they?"

The stranger nodded. "Yeh, teched," he replied.

A big negro woman had come out of a ramshackle building on the far side of the stream, and when she saw the man drowning she slipped and slithered down the bank, and lying on her stomach, reached out her hand. The sinking man grasped for it and took hold. The crowd roared with disappointment, and men began to bellow at her to hit the fellow and drown him. She pulled the dripping creature up on the bank. He tried to get to his knees, but it was plain that his back was injured for he sprawled helplessly on the muddy ground. The black woman dragged him up, lifted him in her massive arms, and carried him into her house while the crowd howled with disappointment.

When the magnolia trees bloomed along St. Charles Street and the walks were sun-dappled, Sam walked in paradise.

By accident one day he came upon the slave market. Fashionable carriages and thoroughbred mounts were tied to the hitching rail along one side, while farm wagons and work horses lined the other. Sam went inside. Men sweat-stained and soiled stood on one side of the auction block while dandies and conservatively dressed businessmen stood opposite. Sam watched the auctioneer sell slave after slave. The sleek, healthy ones were bought at high prices by the rich; the

bewildered, underfed ones, more cheaply by the farmers. The auctioneer treated these black people as if they were animals. An attractive,
light-skinned girl was put on the block. A young blood went up, spoke
to the auctioneer, then walked all around the girl. He pinched her
buttock and felt her breasts. Others of the businessmen followed suit.
When bidding was opened the price was high. There was no doubt in
Sam's mind what these men wanted the girl for. Perhaps one of these
very men was her own father; some white man was, for she was
more than half white. A man in his sixties finally led the girl away.
Sam felt that he would enjoy committing wholesale murder. On that
day was born his hatred of slavery and for any man or woman who
condoned the practice.

In December, when the weather was cold and the rains depressing,
a letter which had taken two months to come told him that Sara had
died peacefully in her sleep on one of the beautiful days of Indian
summer. Sam wept that night because he would never see his mother
again.

Two years passed. Sam bought a press and started a little literary
journal which hardly paid its own expenses. He lived in a hotel in
the French quarter and was well taken care of by the French proprie-
tress, who had a homely daughter. Sam fell into the habit of talking
over his business problems with the Frenchwoman, for she had
shrewd business sense. One evening in the winter of 1841 he sat beside
the stove in the little parlor, figuring up his debits and credits. He discovered that he was losing money. In spite of working from daylight
until dark he was going into debt. He could not get enough subscriptions and advertising to keep the paper going. When Madame Drollet
came in, she found him looking dejectedly out of the window.

"I can't make it go," he said.

The fat woman put her hands on her hips. "You can make it go
if you can stay with it till spring," she assured him.

"But I can't stay with it till spring. I'm going in debt now. If I
get in any further I'll lose my press. And that I'll never do."

She shrugged and spread her hands. "You have the answer. You
marry with my daughter. She will have a dowry big enough to make

you the success with your journal. I have watch you and I tell you, you will make the success someday. I know it. Yvonne knows it. You are the kind of man I want for my daughter to marry with."

"But I'm not in love with Yvonne," he protested.

The Frenchwoman threw back her head and laughed. "But what has the love to do with this? I make you the business proposition, and you talk of love! Yvonne, she helps you with the money, you make the success, and she is happy. When you are in the family, I help with the money. When I am old, you will take care of me."

Sam would not consider the proposition and said so. Madame Drollet told him that he was very naïve and would get over his foolish ideas about love. "Every man has the wife for business reasons and the mistress for love," she assured him; but Sam was shocked and said he had been raised in a good moral home where such goings-on would not be tolerated.

That night he walked back and forth in his room. He knew that if he persisted in publishing the journal he would lose his press for debts. "I can't do it!" he told himself. "Ma went without things she needed to get me that money. I've worked like a dog to add to it. I'll keep that press if I have to starve to death. If I stay here I'm liable to let that whiskered old Frenchwoman talk me into marrying her homely daughter," he summed it up. "So the only answer is to put my press in storage and take out for some other place where I can make a living with it." On the morrow he took a river boat north.

Chapter III

SAM DECIDED to take this opportunity to see a little more of the world. He worked his way on the river boat for two days, then stopped to work on a farm in order to earn enough to keep going farther. In the next few months he drifted from one city to another, making his way by any kind of labor available. Eventually he had visited most of the states then included in the Union. His wanderings came to an end in Indianapolis, where he secured a job the day he arrived. He had gone into the office of the *Gazette*, which he had heard was in favor of abolition. He asked for a job as printer. The editor asked him how he stood on the question of slavery.

"I say, down with slavery!" Sam replied.

"You're hired," the editor and publisher replied, "but you won't get much pay. The businessmen in this city are mostly in favor of slavery and they're making it hard for me to make this paper profitable."

"If I can earn enough to pay my rent and have something to eat, I'll be satisfied."

Sam worked hard in the weeks that followed, but he and the editor and the "devil" were fighting a losing battle. The creditors descended upon the office one day and hauled the press away to pay the publisher's debts. This was a challenge to Sam, who straightway sent for his own press. Thus it was that he became publisher and editor of the *Gazette*, a venture which lasted less than six months. When the debt for newsprint began to look dangerous, the *Gazette* silently closed its doors and Sam had his press shipped home to Painesville. Being only one state removed from Mary Ann and his only real home, Sam turned his steps toward Ohio. On his way he took time to go to Madison, Indiana, to see a train. As the engine puffed in front of its wagon on the narrow track, Sam looked it over in wonder and was much impressed. "I'd like to own one of them myself," he exclaimed under his breath.

When he arrived in Painesville he walked with his vigorous, quick-moving stride down the streets, passing many a familiar face, but unrecognized by his former acquaintances. He had gone away five years before a stripling, and now returned a well set-up, bearded man. He wore a suit of the latest style with a skirted coat and looked like a prosperous young businessman. Only a few golden leaves still clung to the shivering branches of the bare trees. Sam noted as he came up to the Badlam house that an addition had been built on recently, and the verandah now ran around three sides of the house. He mounted the steps, crossed the porch, and knocked on the door. There was a flurry of footsteps and a moment later the door was opened by the prettiest little girl he had ever seen.

"Well, what's your name?" he asked smilingly.

"Sarah," she said with dignity, not smiling. "I'm five."

"Five? Well, what do you think of that! You're a mighty big girl for five." He removed his beaver hat and stepped into the front hall. Mary Ann came running from the back of the house. When she recognized Sam she stopped short and shrieked, "Sam Brannan, is it really you?" He held out his arms and she rushed into them, hugging him tightly and kissing him on the cheek.

When she drew away she motioned toward the kitchen. "Come on in where it's warm. My lands, but Alexander is going to be surprised to see you when he comes home!"

"How's he making out with the store?"

"All right. My land's sakes alive, I can't believe it's you! It sure seems good to have you home." She opened the door into the kitchen and gathered up a year-old toddler from the floor. "This is Ezra, one of the twins. Emma died when she was just a few months old, like I wrote and told you."

Sam nodded and pulling up a chair sat down by the table. "How's Alec and Mary Ann? They must be pretty good-sized now."

"Oh, they are. You'll like those younguns. They're awful good children. And are they going to be glad to see you! They're always talking about Uncle Sam."

There was a certain substantial pleasure to Sam in being in the bosom of his family again. The children were dear to him. He always had time to help Alec or Mary Ann with their lessons or to romp on the floor with Ezra, or to hold Sara in his lap and tell her stories of his travels. His only discomfort was the new religion that Alexander and Mary Ann had embraced. Near-by Kirtland was the Mormon Zion, to which the faithful were flocking from all parts of the Union. It did not seem strange to Sam that Painesville should be overrun by Mormon missionaries from Kirtland, nor did it seem strange that the townspeople should often become impatient with the exhortings of these religious fanatics and pelt them with eggs or overripe fruit, and set dogs on them to run them out of town. But it did seem strange and unfortunate to Sam that Mary Ann and Alexander gave ear to these advocates of a new religion.[2]

"I don't see how you can swallow the stuff those fellers preach," Sam said to his sister in remonstrance. "It sounds like nonsense to me, all this about Joseph Smith being a prophet of God, the only true prophet, and him being the only one that's got the true religion."

"It's true, though," Mary Ann said firmly. "You just drive over to Kirtland with us on Sunday and listen to Joseph Smith preach, and you'll believe just like we do."

"I doubt it," Sam replied, but upon their insistence he went with them to listen to the handsome, magnetic Joseph. He soon became interested, too. He began to listen to the preachings of the missionaries and within a month was converted.

On a sunny day in December he and Mary Ann drove to Kirtland in the light cutter, skimming over the snow with exhilarating speed. She had made him start early so that she could visit the colony of Friends from Pennsylvania who had been baptized into the Church of Jesus Christ of Latter-day Saints, in a body, by their leader Sidney Rigdon.

"I've heard so much about their neatness and their communal way of living that I want to see their little village with my own eyes. I hear they have a common storehouse and everybody puts all they got into it and draws out what they need," she said.

Sam nodded as he flicked the horse lightly with the end of the whip. "Yep, I hear that Joseph Smith is much taken with the idea and purposes to try out the scheme among our people. He calls it the 'United Order.'"

"Why, I think that would be a good idea. It would make us live

more for our religion and less for selfish purposes." She was silent
for a moment. "We'll only stop in the Friends' village for a few
minutes. You've got to get early to the temple to get dressed for your
baptism."

They visited the prim houses of these former Quakers and were
impressed by the spotlessness of homes and farms, and by the industry
of all members of the village. Then they drove straight to the white
stone temple which dominated the town by its single spire. On the
ground floor Sam was ushered into an anteroom where he was told
to change into his white clothes. When he emerged into the baptismal
room in the steamy basement hall, he saw the font, resting on the
backs of twelve oxen carved out of oak. A dozen other men and
women were waiting about, dressed in white even to their stock-
ings. An Apostle with flowing robes and a beard entered, and climbing
the steps to the font, stepped down into the water, which was waist-
deep. One by one the converts were sent up the ladder by an elder.
After the Apostle said the proper prayer, he put his left hand over
the nose of the disciple, his right hand under the disciple's neck and
swiftly dipped him into the warm water. The neophyte then climbed
down the steps and another convert ascended.

Riding home, Sam felt a glow of satisfaction. He had lived a wild
life, he told himself; he had drunk strong spirits, and he had known
woman carnally; he had sampled all the vices. It was good to know
that now his sins were all washed away and that henceforward he
could fill his record book with only white marks.

At a special conference called by Joseph Smith a few Sundays
later, Sam met his destiny. While the handsome Joseph was telling
his devoted followers that they must prepare to pull up stakes in
order to move to the new Zion, located at Nauvoo in Illinois, on the
banks of the Mississippi, Sam was watching out of the corner of his
eye the plump, pretty blond girl who sat next to him. The temple
was filled with an eager throng, anxious to hear the words of their
prophet. When Joseph Smith had completed his address, the congregation arose to sing. Sam offered his hymnbook to the pretty girl, and
with a shy little gesture she accepted a corner of it. He smiled boldly,
and she blushed and looked away. She had a clear, sweet voice when

she sang. Sam listened for a few moments and then nudged Mary Ann in the ribs and indicated the girl with a jerk of his head.

"Do you know who she is?" he whispered in his sister's ear.

Mary Ann looked around him at the girl and nodded, while the singing continued. After a prayer the meeting was dismissed. Mary Ann leaned over Sam and touched the girl on the knee.

"I want you to meet my brother, Samuel Brannan," she said, and to Sam, "This is Harriet Hatch. She lives in our town."

"I'm certainly pleased to meet you," he smiled, and his eagerness gave truth to his words.

"How do you do?" she said in her flustered way, and waving toward a middle-aged man with a straggly mustache who was just then arising, she said, "This is my Pa." Sam put out his hand and shook the limp one of Mr. Hatch, and then Mary Ann leaned across holding out her own. "Well, Mr. Hatch, good morning. It's nice to see you again." He grinned in a sickly way and turned to leave the hall. Outside the two members of the Hatch family and all the Badlams gathered in a group.

"We could make room for you in our sleigh going home," Sam offered to the girl, but she shook her head.

"Pa wouldn't like to make that long drive alone, would you, Pa?"

"Nope. But this young feller can go with us if he wants to. Kinda like to have some one to talk to—you're always so gosh-darned quiet." So Sam rode home with Mr. Hatch and the daughter he called Hattie.

A week later he escorted her to a cottage meeting. Soon it became an accepted fact that Hattie and Sam were going steady. One Sunday afternoon Sam took Hattie for a roundabout drive after church, and in a country lane he stopped the horse and sat looking at her with hungry eyes. Immediately she was frightened, and when he tried to take her in his arms she fought and struggled and finally burst into tears. The more timid she became, the more desirable she seemed to him. In a frenzy to have his own way he lifted her chin and kissed her long on her quivering lips and pulled her body close against him. She fought him then, hammering at his chest and face, and finally broke away, weeping bitterly.

"Oh," she panted, "I hate you, Sam Brannan! Don't you dare treat me like that kind of a woman!"

"Like what kind of a woman?" he asked in surprise.

"You know what I mean," she flared. He had never seen this meek girl angry before and he thought her sudden vitality irresistible. It was just what she needed to make her pallid beauty come to life. "The idea of you, a good religious man acting in such an awful way," she added.

He laughed into her angry face. "Religion don't stop a man from falling in love."

She sat in a far corner of the seat away from him, straightening her cap and her jacket. "I don't mind you're falling in love, but you ain't going to kiss me yet. I'm a good, clean, decent girl and I intend to stay that way until after I get married."

"How are you going to know whether you'll love a man enough to marry him if you don't kiss him first?"

"Well, you ain't going to kiss me—not that way, and neither is any other man—not till he's married to me. I trust the Lord will pick me the right man and I won't need to go lallygagging around to be sure he picked right."

Sam gathered up the reins and clucked to the horse, who started to move. "You got a lot to learn about life," he said slowly, "and it looks like I'd just as well start teaching you."

Although he did not speak to her again until he said good-by at her front gate, he was aware of every feminine gesture she made. She was a fever in his blood, and he knew that he would never be content until he possessed her.

A week later he asked her father for her hand. Mr. Hatch was delighted to have his daughter make such a good match, and when, in the parlor, Sam asked Hattie to be his wife, she dissolved into emotional tears and clung to him for the first time. Two weeks later they were married by Joseph Smith in the temple at Kirtland.[3]

Chapter IV

Since Hattie kept house for her widowed father, the most logical thing for the newlyweds was to make their home with Mr. Hatch. This they did. Sam had secured a job with the local printer—the man he had trained with—and although his salary was small they managed to live comfortably.

The first month of Sam's marriage was ecstatically happy, for he reveled in the physical delights of his union with Hattie. Her plump, soft body aroused him to a passion he had never known before, and although she was so prudish that she would not allow him to see her unless she was fully clothed, still she passively allowed him to fondle her in the privacy of their bed, and unwillingly endured what seemed to her an over-affectionate nature. For that first month she passively gave him his own way and he was not chilled in his quest of love, but as the weeks passed she became impatient with his continued caresses and his seemingly never-satiated passionate desire. She grew plaintive and querulous.

"I wish you would quit pawing me every minute, Sam. My lands, a woman gets tired of having a man kissing her and hugging her every minute. I never was a one for much lallygagging and I'm free to own it turns my stomach sometimes."

"What did you get married for if you don't want to be loved?" he demanded, out of patience at last.

She flushed, "Well, certainly not to be standing around kissing all the time." He looked at her angrily for a moment and then flung out of the house.

One evening she sat down on his knee, and thinking that she was at last learning to love him, he drew her close. She lay against him for a moment, then stirred.

"Sam," she said in a husky voice, "I got a secret for you."

"What?" he asked quickly.

"We're going to have a dear little baby."

"Baby!" he repeated. Rising abruptly, he almost dumped her onto the floor. "Already?" he demanded, looking into her bewildered eyes. "Why, we've only been married six weeks. You kind of rushed it, didn't you?"

"*I* rushed it?" she burst out, her eyes filling with tears. "I didn't have anything to do with it. It's all your fault, and now you blame it on me! You make me sick! All men make me sick," she blubbered and ran from the room.

Mr. Hatch came from the kitchen, his pipe in his mouth, and looked questioningly at Sam. "What's the matter with her?" he asked, and Sam shrugged and slammed his way out of the house.

After this his marriage became a dispiriting ordeal, for Hattie was sick much of the time. She moped around the house with her hair unkempt, full of complaints. All the beauty and youth were gone, blotted out by coming motherhood. Her skin became blotched and her body swollen, and Sam began to wonder what had caused him ever to fall in love with her at all. At the end of a few months he was firmly convinced that he had made a terrible mistake. He had married Hattie so that he could possess her body, but having possessed he discovered that the pleasure had been mostly imaginary, for Hattie had never answered to his passionate love-making. She had been repelled and frightened by his hunger and had given at best only passive acquiescence to his demands. He began to be filled again with his old wanderlust. He spoke several times to Hattie of giving up his job and traveling about the country as a journeyman printer.

"No," she said firmly. "You'll stay here where you got something sure. Now that I'm in the family way you're not going to up and leave me here alone. This is your baby as much as mine and you got to stay here and face your responsibilities."

Sam did not argue, but he did a lot of thinking privately. He attended church regularly with Hattie and on several occasions was induced to preach the sermon. The elders of the Church, after hearing him speak, realized that this ardent, eloquent young Irishman was a potential missionary of more than average ability. Joseph Smith approached him one Sunday and suggested that he should undertake a mission. As Sam listened his eyes lighted up with enthusiasm. Here was the solution to his problem. A mission would give him a chance to travel and get away from Hattie's clinging fingers. Sam agreed. When the letter of authority came to him from Apostle Woodruff, he showed it to Hattie. She wept and pleaded with him not to go until after the baby was born, but Sam insisted that Joseph had requested him to go just before setting out for Nauvoo the last time; and a request from Joseph Smith was tantamount to a command from God himself.

"All us Mormons got to be ready to sacrifice everything for our religion at any time," he pointed out to her. "Your Pa'll look after you while I'm gone and there's no good reason why I shouldn't go now." Reluctantly at last she consented.

"Mary Ann will come over when the baby's born and take good care of you. You're part of our family now and there's not a better nurse lives than Mary Ann," he said to console her.

He was ordained and set apart for his mission at Kirtland. He did not go far, his field of endeavor being mostly in Clinton County, Ohio, and the surrounding territory. The more he preached to "gentiles" and tried to convert them to Mormonism, the more converted he became to it himself. They did not all listen to him meekly. Sometimes he received a barrage of eggs and overripe tomatoes; sometimes he was forced to swim a canal with dogs at his heels, and one night he was dipped in warm tar, rolled in feathers, and placed on a fence rail which the citizens carried to the edge of town; from there he was chased by dogs until he was exhausted. But he persisted in proselyting in spite of these ordeals and succeeded in baptizing many people in the little Ohio streams. After months of labor in the missionary field he wrote to Apostle Woodruff to report his progress:

Waynesville
Dec. 5, 1843

DEAR BROTHER WOODRUFF:

On my arrival at Clinton County, the adjoining one to this, I had the happy fortune of meeting with Elder Ball, who was lifting a warning voice to the inhabitants of that region, which induced many to come forward and renounce the world, and be buried with Christ by baptism for the remission of sins. They now number between 60 and 70 in good standing. Elder Ball and myself commenced laboring together, in the adjoining region of country, and "God give the increase" twelve more were immersed for the remission of sins, and are now rejoicing in the truth with their faces Zionward.

There being quite a manifestation of feeling in this place by some of the citizens, and having received a special invitation from them I came to this place and commenced preaching the word, and soon the seed sprouted and needed watering. I was joined by Elder Elliott, from Cincinatti, who laid hold of the work with undaunted courage, and through many struggles of debate and refutation of lies and slanders, we have been enabled, through the grace of God, to plant the standard of truth, in defiance of all opposition of men and devils—for truly we have been visited by both. The faithful in this region number about twenty-two, and there are many more that will obey from the heart that form of doctrine which we have delivered unto them.

I remain yours truly,

S. BRANNAN.[4]

Wherever Sam preached he found willing converts in the women, which did not displease him. He sometimes went in company with another elder but very often traveled alone, trudging the frozen roads through sleet and storm in the winter that was upon the land; carrying neither purse nor money and obliged to beg his food at the houses where he stopped to proselyte. It was at a convert's house in a county adjoining Clinton that he awoke one morning with a feeling of great lassitude. He rose and ate breakfast with the farm family, but afterwards grew sick to his stomach and went outside to relieve himself. When he returned he was white and weak, and one of the boys helped him back to his bed on the floor. By nightfall he was raving in delirium. His bed was moved to the floor of the parlor, and there he lay for two weeks and struggled for his life, while the kindly family ministered to his wants as if he had been one of their own. It was late in January of 1844 when he arose and took a few staggering steps. All the spare flesh was wasted from his six-foot two-inch frame; his neck looked scrawny in the size fifteen collar, but he still had a forty-inch chest expansion, as he discovered when he drew in his first breaths of fresh outdoor air. He peered at himself in the wavy mirror in the kitchen and saw that his skin was yellow and dry, the luster gone from his eyes. Even his usually glossy black hair looked discouraged. As soon as he was able to walk about freely he packed his little bundle and started for home. His farmer host made him ride for five miles on one of the farm horses, but after that Sam walked over the frozen roads, getting only an occasional sleigh ride between towns.

He was not a beautiful sight when he panted up the snow-covered walk to Mary Ann's porch, and without knocking, went in. He was sick and tired and he needed Mary Ann; she could send for his wife later. A baby was crying in a protesting scream as he pushed into the hall which led to the kitchen, and when he opened the door into the warm room, the startled faces of Mary Ann and Hattie looked up at him.

Hattie rose and ran to him, "Sam you're back! We never dreamed you'd be back so soon. You look awful! Here, sit down in my chair by the stove."

Sam dropped into the chair and Mary Ann handed him a bowl of warm stew which she had dished up while Hattie was greeting him. "Here, this will fix you up. You look half dead. How long you been on the way coming home?"

Sam took the bowl and the spoon she handed him and began busily shoveling the food into his mouth while he answered, "Over a week. Stop that baby crying! It's splitting my ears."

Hattie went to the cradle, picked up the crying baby, and brought it to show to Sam. "It's our baby," she said proudly. "This is your Pa, Almiry." The baby had stopped crying the moment her mother took her up, and she looked at Sam now with wet eyes, then turned restlessly again to her mother.

Sam finished the bowl of soup and set it on the table and then held out his arms for his baby. She was afraid of him and whimpered when he held her close. The whiskers on his face seemed to alarm her, and she cried when he kissed her dimpled neck. She was blond and chubby, with more of a Hatch appearance than the black Brannan look, yet there was something about her eyes that reminded Sam of his mother. She kept on crying, so Sam handed her back to Hattie and relaxed in his chair.

"Sister Evans wrote that you had western fever but we didn't know how bad you was," Mary Ann said as she stood looking down on Sam with eyes which were filled with pity and love.

"I was pretty bad, I guess, but I'll get over it with a lot of your good food and plenty of rest."

"Oh, Sam, ain't you coming home with us?" Hattie asked quickly.
He nodded wearily. "Yeh, I guess so. But Mary Ann will come down

and cook for me every day, won't you, sis?" Mary Ann nodded happily.

Sam had not yet finished his mission, and a letter from the General Authorities of the Church at Nauvoo arrived, notifying him that he was to hold himself in readiness to complete his mission as soon as his health would permit. He lounged about his home, sometimes playing with the baby but mostly resting, for the slightest exertion wearied him. After a week or so his restless spirit grew discontented and he longed to be well and strong again and about his work.

With the first thaw came a second letter from Nauvoo. He was commanded to report there for orders—if he was well enough—concerning the completion of his mission. Sam read the letter to Hattie and her father that night at supper.

"Religion is all right," the old man grumbled, "perviding it don't take a man away from his duties. You got a wife and a youngun now, and they're what should concern you most. Let someone else do the preaching and you stay home and support them. It ain't my job."

Sam spoke hotly. "If everyone felt like you do there'd be no one out spreading our gospel. I guess if I can go out in sleet and snow and cold to spread the word, you can sacrifice a little to take care of my family, especially when it's your own flesh and blood."

At Nauvoo Sam stood presently at the opposite side of Joseph Smith's desk awaiting the words of his leader. Joseph arose in a leisurely fashion. The sunlight fell upon his burnished fair hair. There was manliness in his tall body, warmth in his blue eyes, and assurance in his proud erectness. "Brother Brannan," he began, "the assembled Apostles have discussed you, and we have decided that you are both intelligent and ambitious. We think that you will work to amount to something. We are, therefore, sending you up to Connecticut and the New England states to finish your mission. You will labor there a few months until we complete a favorite plan we are considering. We hope ultimately to establish a newspaper in New York City, and you are just the man we will need to publish it. We will need a press. Have you got one?"

Sam nodded. "Yes, a Washington Hoe. It's in storage at Indianapolis. I could have it shipped to New York if I had sufficient funds to pay up the storage charges and the freight."

Joseph began to walk back and forth thoughtfully, his hands clasped at his back. "I think the Church could arrange to do that," he said slowly, "providing that you dedicate this press to Church work. Through it you could spread the gospel." He turned suddenly. "You journey on up to Connecticut and preach the word until our plans are ripe, and we will send word to you when to go down to New York." He looked at Brannan closely. "Do you feel well enough to go on? You still look pretty yellow."

Sam nodded. "I'm not well yet, but I can manage to get out and work until my strength comes back." He paused for a moment. "Brother Joseph, I would like to ask your advice about something that is troubling me. I've been married a little over a year now and—well, I'm not exactly satisfied. Hattie and me don't have the pleasure in each other that I thought we would have."

"Few of us do have the things in life we've dreamed of. No man's marriage turns out what he thought it was going to be." Joseph sighed.

"Well, I guess there's nothing to do but make the best of things." Sam sighed also.

They fell to discussing other subjects and at last Joseph smiled and held out his hand across the desk top. "Well, goodbye, Brother Brannan, we look for much from you."

"I will remember," Sam replied as he shook Joseph's hand.

Sam set forth for Connecticut. In the small town which he finally selected as his headquarters, a Mrs. Frances Corwin—widow and recent convert to Mormonism—ran the boardinghouse. Fanny Corwin took an immediate liking to the handsome young missionary and invited him to stay with her. "I can't bear the thought of you young fellers going hungry while you travel without purse or script, spreading our gospel," she said. Sam accepted her generous hospitality and soon came to love the motherly, middle-aged woman. Her dark-eyed, pretty, vivacious daughter, Ann Eliza, who sometimes condescendingly waited on table, he found attractive too.

Ann Eliza had a way of wearing clothes which set her apart from the others. She had style. Her wavy dark brown hair set off intelligent dark eyes. Her skin was fair and her coloring vivid. She was small and alert, the exact opposite of Hattie. Sam soon discovered that she had ambition, too. She told him that first evening, as they sat on the porch steps, that she wanted to get away from her small town and travel.

"What for?" Sam asked.

"I want to live different than my Ma has. I don't want to live where everybody knows your business. I want to maybe marry a rich man and live in a fine house—and maybe even someday go to Europe."

Sam looked at her admiringly. "You're pretty enough to do it. I wish I was rich. I'd like to do all those things with you."

"I guess we're both just daydreaming," she laughed. "I don't suppose I'll ever get to go anywhere, and your chances of ever being a rich man are pretty slim."

Sam laughed at the idea, too. He was still sallow from the fever but he had begun to regain some of his lost weight. He tired easily and found that he could not get about the countryside as rapidly as he had done the previous fall. He was neat in his apparel, although he could not indulge his taste for fancy dress while wearing the dark clothes of a missionary. But Ann Eliza seemed to find him attractive.

The next day he went, as missionaries are supposed to do, from door to door, trying to arouse an interest in the gospel among the housewives of the town. Some listened; some slammed the door in his face. Some set the dogs on him or called husbands from the fields. Sam always had a head-start on husbands armed with pitchforks, and made notes not to return to that particular home again. When, rarely, he found a man or woman who would listen, he gave them copies of the *Book of Mormon*, which he had been obliged to purchase with his own money—money sent to him by Alexander and Mary Ann. Among those who accepted copies of the *Book of Mormon* he often made converts, and many of these he baptized himself in the small brooks of the locality. From his headquarters he branched out into adjoining towns, walking sometimes on the dusty highways, sometimes cutting through the fields and woods; he was forced to depend for food mostly upon the kindness of strangers who lived in the houses along his way. When he returned from these forays footsore, weary, and dusty, Fanny would cluck over him like a mother hen and then like Mary of old would bathe his tired, swollen feet. Ann Eliza felt it was not proper for a young lady to see a young man's bare foot, and she always absented herself on such occasions. There were many things she felt were not proper for her to do; waiting on table and washing dishes, or setting the tables, were among them. While her mother and the hired girl washed the supper dishes, Ann Eliza usually sat in a secluded corner of the front porch apart from the boarders, and there Sam was apt to seek her out in the cool of the evening.

When Sam realized that he was in love with Ann Eliza, he began to search for a way to solve the problem which this complication presented. During one anguished night he walked the floor until dawn, pondering all the angles of his life. At one moment he would tell himself that he must leave his love unspoken and go away; yet in his innermost heart he knew that he would never do so. Then he would decide to tell Ann Eliza about Hattie and his baby daughter, and to ask her to be just a dear friend. "That's the decent thing to do," he said aloud to himself. Then he struck the fist of his left hand into the palm of his right and exclaimed, "But I can't do it! I've got to have Ann Eliza." He was pulled and torn between his desire and his conscience. His mind fought valiantly to maintain the values of his New England upbringing by a puritanical mother, but his love for Ann Eliza and his desire to marry her constantly battered down his conscience. At dawn he came to a decision. He would simply take advantage of Joseph Smith's permission to take a second wife, never revealing the truth either to Ann Eliza or to Hattie. To make sure that Ann Eliza should never know, he would destroy the few letters he had from Hattie and then would write to her no more; taking care that she should not know where he was so that she could not hunt him out. He hoped that he would never have to see either his wife or his child again. Before he crawled into his bed he wrote a letter to Joseph Smith telling him what he had done and requesting that his forwarding address be given to no one except the Church authorities.

He did not write to his sister, Mary Ann. Good old Mary Ann would know that he was all right, and he would get in touch with her again when he got around to it. Meanwhile she would have no address to give to Hattie.

The next evening, after his missionary chores were done for the day, Sam suggested to Ann Eliza that they walk down by the brook. They sat on the grassy bank and Sam took her hand in his.

"We've not known each other very long," he said after a long silence, broken only by the rippling waters of the little stream, "but I've known you long enough to know that I never want to go away from you."

She lifted her head suddenly. He could see her in the growing lightness which presaged a rising moon. "I like you, too," she said positively.

"Do you think you could give up your dreams of marrying a millionaire to marry a poor missionary?"

She laughed lightly, as if relieved. "I guess so," she said, "if the poor missionary looked to me like a man that might amount to something in the future."

Sam's eyes drank in the lovely curve of her retroussé nose and the graceful line of her neck against the sky. "Well, do you think I might amount to something in the future?" he demanded anxiously.

She nodded her head slowly. "Yes, I've thought so from the first minute I laid eyes on you. There's something about you that shows you're full of push and ambition. I guess maybe it's your eyes. You always seem so enthusiastic about everything. When you talk, you convince a person against his own will."

"Then you will marry me," he said quickly, with a sigh of relief.

"You'd have hard work stopping me," she smiled as she looked at him expectantly. He pulled her to him and kissed her hard on the lips until she cried out for him to stop.

"You're mussing me all up and hurting me," she said, drawing away. "Goodness, you're not so weak!"

He jumped to his feet and pulled her up and crushed his lips against hers. "No, I'm not too weak to kiss the girl I love. We're going to be awful happy, Lizzie girl."

She gave herself to his kiss, but when she drew away there was petulance in her tone. "Sam, you're not to call me Lizzie. My name is Ann Eliza and if you don't mind I'd like to be called Ann."

He laughed and pulled her arm through his as they started back to the house. "Lizzie, it's no use putting on airs with me. I'm free to own that I like Lizzie and that's what you'll always be to me. Let's go back and tell Ma Corwin that we're engaged."

She laughed happily as she hurried to keep up with his long-legged stride. "Ma's going to be surprised, us getting engaged so soon. But please, Sam, don't make a spectacle in front of everyone. Let's be sure to tell Ma when she's in the kitchen by herself."

"All right," he agreed. When they went up the back steps and entered the kitchen, Fanny was alone; the hired girl was in the dining room setting the table for breakfast. Sam blurted out the news. Fanny looked from one to the other for a moment and then burst into tears. Sam put his arms around her and asked why she was crying, and she dried her eyes on her apron and looked up at him fondly.

"I don't know, Brother Brannan. I just guess it's 'cause I'm happy. You're a good religious man; the kind I've always hoped Ann Eliza would marry, but never thought she would. I declare, I've got so fond of you since you been living here that I love you like you was my own."

Sam and Ann Eliza were married a few days later by Sam's missionary companion in the little front parlor of the boardinghouse, under a bower of honeysuckle which Fanny and the hired girl rigged up. The marriage had been rushed so that Ann Eliza could go with him whenever he was transferred. Less than a week after the ceremony a letter came from Nauvoo instructing him to go down to New York City, where a bank draft on the Church awaited him to pay the storage and shipping fees on his press. When Sam went to break the news to his new family, Fanny was peeling potatoes and Ann Eliza was filling the sugar bowl.

When Sam told them, Ann Eliza began to dance around the room. Fanny sat as if stunned and slow tears ran down her cheeks. "I can't let you go," she said at last. "Ann Eliza's all I've got in this world."

"We have to go, Ma," Ann Eliza put in quickly. "Sam promised the Prophet he would go down to New York when they told him, to start that Church paper. And where Sam goes, it's my duty to go, too."

Sam looked from one woman to the other and the Irish heart of him could not but pity the grief in Fanny's face. "There's no reason why you can't come with us, Ma, if you want to," he suggested.

"Oh, I couldn't do that," she said quickly. "This house is all I got to support myself with. 'Course, I got a little in the bank, but I want to keep it for my old age."

Sam stroked his chin thoughtfully. "You could sell the house— I guess if I can take care of me and Lizzie, I can take care of you."

"More likely I'll be taking care of you," she retorted, wiping away her tears with the back of her hand. "A man on a mission is in no position to take care of anyone, including himself."

"Well, let's put it like this," he went on. "When we get down to New York we're going to have a hard time to make a living. The Church will partly support the paper; the rest we'll have to get from donations and subscriptions of our members. I doubt whether there'll be anything left to live on. You sell this house and all the belongings you don't want to keep, fetch your savings, and come along. Your money can support us until I fulfill my mission, and after that I'll support you the rest of your life."

Fanny thought over his words for several moments before she spoke. "I hate to give up this old house. My grandpa built it and I was born here. Me and Ann Eliza's pa spent a few of the happiest years of our lives here, before he died. It's full of memories that I hate to leave behind." She lifted troubled eyes to the young faces and added more brightly, "Still, I wouldn't want to live on here all alone." She went on speaking as if she were thinking aloud. "I've always sort of hankered to see a big city like New York and to travel a long ways on a boat. I guess this is my chance. It'll be a sort of mission for me, too."

Fanny sold the boardinghouse without much difficulty, for it was good income property. Then for three days she and Ann Eliza and the hired girl packed and cleaned and oversaw the crating of their furniture. It was the first of May when they reached New York. Sam rented a small house near Chambers Street, and while the women were busy getting themselves settled in it Sam looked for a location for a newspaper office and waited for his press to arrive from Indianapolis.

Book Two

Chapter V

THE CITY was a fascinating place to Sam with its constant movement and colorful commerce, for ships from all over the world berthed along the waterfront. Sailors in pigtails and shiny hats, Hindus in turbans and beards, Chinamen with flowing sleeves and queues, all mingled in the human galaxy which made up life along the wharves, and Sam strode its interesting thoroughfares aware of all the movement and noise. Horsecars clattered over cobbled streets and drays loaded with merchandise from all the world moved in every direction away from the water. Further uptown, men and women of fashion drove in carriages which were the last word in style—themselves resplendent in clothes so extreme as to be fantastic. A few of the younger men appeared with coats checkered in blues and greens, over very tight pantaloons. Women carried tiny parasols held high above the head to protect the towering arrangements of their hair.

The steam press had come into its own, and New York had six daily newspapers, hawked by dirty little' boys, impudent and self-sufficient, the like of which Sam had never seen anywhere else. His own press worked in the old ball-and-pad manner, by hand.

At 102 Nassau Street, just behind the old Park Theater which fronted on Chatham Street, Sam finally rented a room to house the press. While the teamsters dragged it into place in the back of the room, Sam printed by hand a sign which read, "Printer's Devil Wanted." The first applicant was a handsome lad of perhaps fifteen, with dark eyes and hair. He said his name was Edward Kemble and that his father was editor of a newspaper in Troy, New York; that he had learned his trade from his father. After questioning the lad fully, Sam hired him, with a warning that the pay would be small and sometimes uncertain. The boy took off his coat and joined Sam in his efforts to get the jumbled type in order.

An hour or so later William Smith, brother of the prophet Joseph Smith, arrived with a boy of about eighteen whom he introduced to

Sam as John Eager. William was president of the Atlantic States Mission, with headquarters in New York.

"This is the widow Eager's son, John. Lucy Eager and her two sons and two daughters are faithful members of our little band. John wants to learn the printing business, and I thought it would be a good idea if you took him on as helper."

Sam looked the boy over. He was a nice quiet sort of lad, but seemed to Sam to lack initiative. At last Sam nodded slowly.

"I guess we could do that. It would save hiring another lad," he said to William, who nodded pompously. Sam turned to John. "You'll have to work long hours with no pay," he said.

"I know. Brother Smith told me."

"As a usual thing an apprentice has to pay to learn a trade," Sam reminded the youth, who shifted his weight uneasily.

"I know, but I've got no money and I've got to learn a trade so's I can help my family."

"Well, this being a Church paper, we can afford to be a little charitable," Sam said. "Take your coat off. I guess we won't kill you." The young man moved with alacrity, and when he had passed down the room to the press and had been taken in charge by Edward, William smiled.

"Thank you, Brother Brannan. I appreciate this."

"Oh, it's all right," Sam said, and again began searching his mind for the reason he did not like the big, handsome man. William lacked the magnetism and sincerity of his brother and somehow Sam distrusted him a little. He had heard that William was the black sheep of the Smith family and had been sent on this mission, after being made an Apostle, with the hope that it would steady him.

"When you get things straightened out, and the press ready, I will come in and write the editorials and a letter or two to the Saints abroad in the world," William said. Immediately Sam spoke his mind.

"I know you are in charge here, Brother Smith, but you'll not write all the editorials. After all, I'm publisher of this paper."

"With the assistance of the Church," William reminded him. "We will both write the editorials, Brother Brannan," he said firmly, and walked out the front door.

On May 9 Sam and the lads worked hard all day, and Sam took the horsecar home early in the evening to clean up for a giant mass-meeting which was to be held in town that night. While he changed his clothes, Ann Eliza followed him about asking questions.

"Have you got the press set up yet?"

"No. It will take at least another week to get both it and our copy ready to roll."

"Why don't you ever come home and spend the evening with Ma and me?" she asked petulantly.

He stopped knotting his tie to gather her up into his arms and squeeze her. "'Cause I don't have time," he laughed. "But I will have, pretty soon."

She pursed her lips for his kiss and he gave her a hearty one. "Stay home tonight. Why do you have to go down to listen to Wendell Phillips and Garrison rave and rant about slavery?"

He let his arms drop as he completed his dressing. "Because I'm interested in slavery. I want to see it stopped, and it's mass meetings like this that will rouse the public to the crying need for action now."

She sighed and turned away. "I never saw a man that had so many irons in the fire: Mormonism, slavery, newspapers—everything except a little time for me. I wish you'd stop trying to be a public figure and be just my husband."

He spoke a little crossly at this. "If I did, you wouldn't like me near so well." Kissing her quickly on the lips and calling a goodnight to Fanny, he was away.

He sat in the midst of the packed hall and heard Wendell Phillips recite the evils of slavery; he listened while Garrison pounded his fist on the table and declared that if slavery could not be stopped the Union must be dissolved. But this Sam would not accept. He took issue with his neighbor in the next seat when the meeting was finished, and while the other gentleman insisted that it was better to dissolve the Union than put up with slavery in the Southern states, Sam shouted back that it was more important to lash the Southerners into line. "They are offspring of the Devil and we should run them all into the ocean!" he bellowed. Fists flew before the argument was settled, but Sam, though forced to leave without landing a decisive blow, was destined never to change his mind about the people of the South.

On May 18, 1844, Samuel Brannan and William Smith stood side by side as Sam lifted the first printed sheet of *The Prophet* from the press and held it up for inspection. In a little box on the left-hand upper corner was the title of the paper, and underneath it, "published and edited by Samuel Brannan," with a further announcement that the paper would appear regularly every Saturday morning.

When he made his rounds of the business district and the water-front, gathering news items, he often stopped to listen to the soapbox orators; his especial delight was an earnest man who was always advo-cating that women be given the vote. He usually picked a spot at the crossing of Pearl and Whitehall, where the sailors loved to heckle him. He never seemed to realize that they were making light of him, and would expound carefully some disputed point until they laughed and walked away in the midst of his argument. Sam listened to all the earnest men who had new panaceas to offer, but his own preaching he confined to church services, and there was seldom a Sunday on which he did not preach at morning or afternoon service.

Ann Eliza and Fanny went faithfully to church with him and reported their reaction to his sermons. If they sometimes felt his preaching was not up to standard, there were other fair listeners who did not agree, and these would crowd around Sam after meeting to touch his coat or pat his arm and tell him with adoring eyes and flat-tering tongue how inspiring he was. Sam loved this adulation, and if he could avoid the watchful eye of Ann Eliza, he was not above retiring into a corner to pour compliments into some particularly attractive ear. However, Sam was a family man as yet, and although he might flirt by word or side-glance, he was never unfaithful to the wife he adored and who was carrying his child. Now that he was older and had more judgment he welcomed a baby, especially if it were to be a son to carry on his name. His reckless youth, in which he had experimentally drunk and smoked, was past. Now he was a good, moral man, building for a solid future.

On Sunday afternoons he sometimes took his wife and mother-in-law for little outings after church. One such excursion took them on a horsecar which ran on rails out to the Bowery. They watched these

New Yorkers who were so different from any type of human being they had ever seen before. The "boys" and "girls" of the Bowery worked hard in factory and shop on weekdays, but on Sunday they dressed in an extreme style of their own and promenaded on the main street. The boys and men, a few of them, gathered in knots on vacant lots to throw horseshoes or to wrestle, but the girls paraded past the boys until one of them was chosen as a Sunday partner.

Another trip took the Brannans to Greenwich Village, which had at last become a part of greater New York. A few short years earlier it had been a rural village frequented by New Yorkers who fled there' in summer to escape the heat and epidemics which often swept the city. Sam and his family found it a quiet, pretty place, but too far from the city for convenience.

One day in June Sam was writing an editorial for the *Prophet* when John Eager came hurrying in with white face and wide eyes and thrust into his hands the latest copy of the *Sun*. Sam looked wonderingly at the page until a familiar name caught his eye. "*Joseph Smith Killed by Mob at Carthage, Illinois*" the small headline said. Sam read it through with a feeling of stupefaction. This could not be! The Prophet was a man of God, and no ignorant mob of gentiles *could* kill him. But as he read the account of the march of armed men who converged upon the jail at Carthage to shoot down, in cold blood, four unarmed prisoners on the second floor of the inadequate jail-house, he realized that it was true. The door opened and William Smith came in. On dragging feet he approached the table at which Sam was sitting.

"They've done it! They've killed my brother!" he cried out, and even as he spoke the tears streamed down his face.

"Yes, the forces of evil are filling the world," Sam said slowly.

William sat down on the edge of the table, bent his face into his hands, and wept as if he had been a child again. After a time he lifted his head and, looking at Sam, exclaimed, "Joseph knew he would die this way! He always said that he would be made a martyr."

Sam nodded gloomily, "All I can say is, it's a day of doom for our people."

William dried his eyes and sat down in a chair at the end of the table. The two lads were busy at the press and the clacking was so great that they were not aware of what went on between the older men. William leaned forward as he addressed Sam. "This is the beginning of chaos in our Church, Sam. Brigham Young, the arch-pretender, will try to grab the reins of leadership while our people are still stunned by my brother's death." He clenched his fists and spoke between taut lips. "But he'll not have his way. I'll fight him to the last ditch. Joseph always told us at home that Brigham was too big for his pants—that he yearned for power—and he warned us not to let him ever get it. He said that Brigham would lead our people astray if he ever got the chance." He struck the table with his fist for emphasis. "But I'll make it my business to see that he never gets the chance."

"Oh, I think Brigham's all right," Sam began in a conciliatory tone. "I've met him. He's impressed with his own importance, but he's always been faithful to Joseph. I think we could do worse than Brigham. After all, he *is* the head of the Quorum of Twelve, and as such he is the logical leader, now that Joseph has been taken from us."

"Yes, he is the head of the quorum, but only by accident. One Apostle died and one apostatized, and both at such a time that Joseph had no opportunity to rearrange the seniority rights in the quorum, which leaves Brigham there very much by accident."

William stood up suddenly and pounded the table again with his fist. "I want the Church to be kept intact. I think that we should appoint the members of the Smith family to act as a board of trustees to keep the Church organization in trust until such time as Joseph's son comes of age and can take over the presidency."

Sam rubbed his chin. "Well, I don't know. You talk as if you thought the Church was a kingdom to be handed down from father to son. It's not that kind of an organization at all. It's supposed to be a democracy."

"In some ways, yes. In other ways, it's the peculiar result of my brother's work and vision. I think we should protect what he built up and not let some tyrant come along and grab it off for his own glory—and that's just what Brigham will do. I warn you!"

"Well, what do you suggest?" Sam asked.

"I think that Emma Smith, Joseph's widow, and myself and Hyrum should act as a board of trustees to administer Church affairs until the boy grows up, and then we can turn it over to him. Will you back me if I start a fight to accomplish this?"

"Did your brother Joseph want it that way?"

"Yes, he did. Many's the time I've heard him say so."

Sam was thoughtful for some moments and when he spoke it was gravely. "It seems logical, and if you give me your word that Brigham was distrusted by Joseph and Joseph wanted it this way, then I see no reason for not backing you."

"I do give you my word. Brigham Young is a tyrant. I'd rather see the Church destroyed than become his instrument."

Sam stood up and thrust out his hand. William wrung it. "Thank you, Sam. I appreciate what you are doing. We will have much trouble before we have our way."

The following Sunday Sam preached an eloquent sermon [5] setting forth the principles of Joseph Smith, and in finishing warned his listeners to be on their guard against Brigham Young and to vote against him if his name were brought up as the new leader.

"I tell you this because I want to save you and save the gospel we believe in. Brigham Young is an ambitious man and he will stop at nothing to make himself all-important. Our Church, our gospel, our priesthood, were all given into the hands of our Prophet because he was the right man for the job. God has never given any revelation to Brigham because he is a worldly and greedy man. If our Church now becomes a Brighamite Church we will have become a bastard Church, departed from our original principles. It was Joseph's wish that his son take over the reins when he was called home, and I tell you now that it is your duty to vote for a trusteeship of the Smith family which will guarantee that the principles set forth by Joseph Smith will live on into eternity.

"I have not wanted to tell you what I tell you now. But in order that you may be on your guard I am forced to." Sam paused and looked calculatingly at his audience, then he continued: "Brigham Young is a polygamist. Nobody knows how many wives he has. If we elect him our new leader the first thing we know he will be telling all of us that we've got to take plural wives. Do you want that to happen?"

The congregation stirred and whispered, and he heard a few answers of "No." He felt that he had made his point and after a few more admonitions he sat down.

In the days that followed he was sent by William to the various branches of the Church on the Atlantic seaboard to repeat his warning sermon, and while he was away on this task he always took the opportunity to stop in the market places of small towns to proselyte from a box or the steps of a public building. The citizens did not take kindly to his exhortations and were vociferous in their objections. Usually they set the dogs on him or sent a group of small boys to throw rocks until he took shelter. In some sections they pelted him with eggs or mud, so that the kind ladies of the church had to help him to remove the dirt from his clothes before he departed.

As soon as Sam returned from his short mission, William Smith left for the New England states to promote his scheme to oust Brigham, and Sam was left to get out the paper with the help of the two "devils." But at the end of a month they found that their scheme had failed. In a mass meeting at Nauvoo, Brigham had been voted into the leadership of the Church by an overwhelming majority. This caused a peculiar situation in the branches of the Church under William's leadership. Those who came faithfully to church, and the number had become small, were ready to back William in his fight. Those who stayed away were either devout followers of the gospel and willing to back Brigham in anything, or out-and-out apostates, driven away by the fear of polygamy. All that William had really accomplished was to reduce the number of Mormon believers, for few remained. The *Prophet* began to feel the results. Subscriptions fell off; donations were almost impossible to obtain.

At this crucial moment word came from Nauvoo that the Governor and politicians of Illinois were determined to expel the Mormon population from the state while the faithful were still disorganized by the death of their leader, who had held a solid block of ten thousand votes and had thus been able to throw votes to either Whig or Democratic machines in order to gain what he could for his own people. Joseph had held the balance of power between the two parties. Now that he was gone, the political powers of Illinois were determined that no other Mormon leader should ever again hold such sway. They were bringing every pressure upon Brigham and his followers to get out of the state at once. At first they had merely suggested, then they had urged, and finally insisted. This pressure was taking the form of mob violence—night-riders descended upon small settlements of Mormons and destroyed their crops, killed or wounded their men, and mistreated their women. Nauvoo was facing panic.

In January of 1845 Sam looked up one day as the door opened to admit a flurry of snow and a heavily built man buttoned into a black overcoat. The man put his strength against the wind-pushed door and latched it before he turned around. The big-bellied stove in the middle of the room interfered with Sam's clear view of him, but in a moment he came around it and removed his fur cap. He was a big man with a wide brow over intelligent grey eyes, and there was in his face a quality of lovableness, humility, and good humor, all mixed together, which attracted Sam to him at once. The stranger held out his hand as he advanced, and Sam arose and took it.

"My name is Pratt, Parley P. Pratt. I've been sent by the Twelve Apostles in Nauvoo to take over the presidency of the Atlantic States Mission." [6]

Sam smiled broadly, "I've heard wonderful things about you, Brother Pratt. I'm sure glad to meet you." They shook hands, and then Sam asked, "What about William Smith? I thought he was the president of this mission."

"He was," Pratt said gravely, "but not any longer. My orders are that he is to return immediately to Nauvoo to stand trial for treason to the Church. It seems a pity that at a time like this in Nauvoo an Apostle should take it upon himself to stir up dissension within the Church itself." He paused and looked sadly at Sam. "I understand you have been a party to this plot of his." Sam started to protest, but Parley held up his hand and continued. "Yes, it is a plot, Brother Brannan, by which William meant to gain power for himself. We have had letters from the faithful in this mission telling us the stories that you two men have told about Brigham Young, and they are lies. Why have you told our people that Brigham is the man who started polygamy? You know that is a falsehood. You know that Joseph was the one who had the revelation, and although a few of our Apostles and elders are allowed to practice celestial marriage, it is not a practice that anyone can indulge in, nor will we ever force any man to take more than one wife if he don't want to."

Sam sat down and tapped his pencil on the table beside him before he answered; his words were apologetic. "Well, I'll tell you, Brother Pratt. William Smith is an Apostle and the brother of our Prophet, and as such I look up to him. He told me that Joseph had never wanted Brigham to take his place, and William himself said that Brigham was not the right man for the job. If what he says about Brigham is true, then Brigham is certainly not the man to be our new leader, and I myself still think that the Smith family should carry on the principles that Joseph set forth. They are the logical ones to do it. The only reason we brought up polygamy was to scare people into doing what we thought was for their own good."

Pratt was taking off his greatcoat. He pulled up a chair and sat down. "Well, you have certainly been misled by William," he said. "Brigham may not be the man I would have chosen either, but he is the man all our people have voted in as their leader. We are bound to respect their wishes. After all, the Smith family does not own the principles of Joseph, and I don't know that they are better qualified than any one else to carry out his ideas. As far as William is concerned, I know that he is not the one. He has always been wild, and not over-intelligent. I would not trust him, and neither should you. As far as polygamy is concerned, you had no right to mention it. Joseph gave no one permission to tell of the revelation abroad, and I fear that you have gotten yourself into serious difficulties by breaking that rule. The next question is, are you going to work with me to bring the faithful back into the fold, or are you going to keep on causing dissension within our ranks until the Church is forced to put you out, as it undoubtedly will put William out if he persists?"

"I don't want to be cut off from the Church," Sam said quickly. "I want to assure you that what I have done, I have done in good faith. I do not think that Brigham is the best leader we could have chosen, and I have said so. But I do still believe in the principles of the gospel, and if I have to swallow Brigham to hold my principles, so be it. I have no choice."

Parley smiled suddenly. "Well," he said, "now that we understand each other, let's get to work. I want to write a letter to all the members of this mission, to be published in our next edition. It will inform our local members of the change we are now instituting. By the way, where is William now?"

"He's up in Maine. I am expecting him back on the boat today."

"He will be surprised to see me," Parley said grimly, and added, "He will take it hard, having his wishes crossed. He was a wilful boy and he is a selfish and irresponsible man, but he is most certainly going to meet his match shortly. Now, suppose you show me where you keep things around here."

Chapter VI

SAMUEL ARRIVED at the office one morning to find Parley writing an editorial letter for the *Prophet* which was to be copied from its pages by the Mormon publication in London, the *Millennial Star,* and by *Times and Seasons,* Church vehicle in Nauvoo. John Eager was putting coal on the fire in the stove and Ed Kemble was standing at ease. Sam was glad to shut out the gloom of the overcast sky, and as he hung up his cap and coat he noticed that the night's snow lay in drifts along the window ledge. He walked slowly to Parley's side and stopped, then spoke.

"I've just been down to see William Smith off. He feels very bitter towards you and the other Apostles."

Parley sat back and looked up into Sam's face, nodding understandingly. "Yes, I guess he does. He was very angry the day I gave him his marching orders and he has not spoken to me since."

"He swears he never will," Sam put in. "He left breathing fire and brimstone, swearing that he is going to start a new church of his own, patterned after his brother's ideas, and he says he will call it the Josephite Church to distinguish it from the Brighamite Church. He says he will travel far and wide to tell the gentiles how wicked the Brighamite Church has become."

Parley sighed and went back to his composing. Sam watched him for a moment and then remarked, "You work too hard, Brother Parley. I'll bet you've not even taken time to see any of our famous sights."

Parley hesitated in his work, passed his hand wearily over his forehead, and sat back again to listen to Sam. "No, I haven't," he agreed.

"Well, say, you ought to go to the American Museum and see Barnum's petrified mermaid."

Parley grinned and shook his head. "Oh, no. Phineas is a foxy old bird with such things as petrified mermaids. We all know there ain't no such animal, and I certainly don't intend to put out what little money I've got to see a fake."

Sam grinned right back. "I paid mine and I'm satisfied. It may be a fake, but it looks real."

Parley shook his head. "If I had money to spend on amusement I'd go to the Park Theatre and see Wallack in 'Hamlet.' When I was in London on my mission—that was when I began the *Millennial Star*—I went to see a few of Shakespeare's plays. They're wonderful. I'm something of a poet myself, but I worship at Shakespeare's shrine, who could write such magnificent verse. Wonderful!" He sighed. "But who am I to think of such light things in times as troubled as these? It takes all we can rake and scrape together here in this branch to get this paper out every week. We've succeeded in coaxing some of our members back, but not the number I had hoped for. You and William did a thorough job of getting rid of church members. It's no easy task to get money from our dwindling membership. With the situation getting more tense in Nauvoo every day, and the authorities constantly begging money from every member of every branch so as to get the Church ready for its exodus next year, it leaves us too little to carry on our work here. I fear me sometimes that we will not survive."

Sam nodded and sat down on the edge of the table. "Why don't you write a letter to the authorities in Nauvoo and tell them to stop their constant appeals for money from our branches? Each branch has got all it can do to take care of its own members. After all, we've got to join this exodus when it takes place, and that's going to take money for outfits and food and other necessities. We're behind on our rent here and for our hall, and if something is not done pretty soon we'll die for lack of nourishment, just as you say."

"I don't want to write to Nauvoo until I have to," Parley replied.

Later in the morning Edward Kemble brought the mail from the post office. Parley tore the cover off the Nauvoo paper, the *Times and Seasons*, anxious to read the news from home. After a few minutes he let out a whistle of surprise and turned to Sam, who was working at the case.

"You're in for it, Sam. You've been disfellowshipped for your part in the William Smith plot, it says here."

Sam went swiftly to his side and read the article over Parley's shoulder. When he had finished he sat down suddenly in a chair. Funny, but he still got tired easily, and a shock like this made him feel weak and ill. He wondered irritably if he was ever going to get over the effects of the fever. Let's see now, if he was to be disfellowshipped it would mean that he would have to give up the newspaper and try to start making a living where jobs were practically non-existent; he would no longer be a leader among his own people —only a nobody in a hostile world; he would be denied the right to preach sermons in which he could express his absolute belief in the gospel. No, this must not be! He believed his religion. Already he had suffered for it; he had a wife who would be no wife at all if he were suddenly thrust into the outer gentile scheme of things. True, there was no law against bigamy as yet, but outside the Mormon orbit this might cause him trouble. He wanted most earnestly to remain a Mormon leader, and to become eventually a great power in the Church which was growing so fast. After the exodus into the west, in a new Zion where there would be tens of thousands of followers, he might become one of the Apostles. He did not wish to lose all these advantages because he had used bad judgment. At last he looked up into Parley's face.

"What shall I do?" he asked.

"There's only one thing you can do: Drop everything and head straight for Nauvoo. Ask for a Church trial, and when you get it admit your error in humbleness and beg for reinstatement. The Church needs men like you, and we need you here, desperately."

"You mean, I ought to leave right now?"

Parley nodded. "Immediately."

"I don't see how I can," Sam remonstrated. "Ann Eliza's time is nigh and I might be gone a month or more. I ought to be with her at a time like this."

Parley nodded his head sympathetically, "I know. But after all, Sister Fanny Corwin will be with her and she can take as good care of her daughter as you can. If you tarry here you will delay your chance of reinstatement, and in the meantime you will not be allowed to go on with your work here on the paper and in the branch. We cannot carry on without you. Other than myself there is no man capable of carrying on the work alone. When I take my trips to the other states I have to leave you in charge to call meetings, to preach, and to attend to all church business in this branch. If I were to lose you now it would seriously cripple my work. No, Sam, there is no time to waste. When the Lord calls we must drop everything and go. Would you believe it if I told you that I have got up from a sickbed and left an ailing wife, destitute of home or money, to set forth on a mission? And that when I came home everything was in good condition?"

Sam shook his head. "I don't see how you dared. I'd be afraid to do a thing like that, even though I knew that the Lord would look after my affairs while I was away."

"The Lord does not fail those who believe in him," Parley replied, and added, "By the way, Sam, I have a letter here from my family in Nauvoo. One of my wives says that she has been asked to get word of you—says that you have a wife in Painesville who has written to friends in Nauvoo asking where you are and wondering why you do not write. She says your sister is anxious also. Why is this?"

Sam flushed. "Well, I have not written on purpose. As you probably know, Ann Eliza is a plural wife; but I don't want her to know it. You know how women are. I thought it was just as well not to keep in touch with my folks in Painesville, to avoid trouble."

Pratt spoke reprovingly, "I can understand your taking a second wife and not telling her she is a second wife, but you have no right to desert your first wife. If you don't love her and don't intend to go back to her, write and tell her so. She has a right to know. And your sister has a right, also, to know that you are well."

Sam laughed. "That's what I'll be in for if Ann Eliza ever hears about Hattie." He raised his hands and added, "God forbid!"

At noon the others went away early to lunch, and it was while Sam was putting on his cap and coat that he noticed a letter written in Edward's boyish scrawl lying on the mail table. Sam picked it up idly and noted that it was addressed to the boy's father. The letter was not sealed and Sam, curious, opened and read it. He chuckled over the first part, which set forth Edward's impressions of the metropolis. But when he came to where the boy described Sam himself and the office, he did not find it particularly amusing.

Sam Brannan is a tall man, awful thin with kind of a hard look about his face. He's just getting over the effects of a spell of western fever and his skin is still yellow and he is pretty weak yet. When he does move, he is sort of quick and nervous-like but he works hard even when he don't feel like it. He has got a good head on him and is easily the leader of the Mormons here in New York City. I went to hear him preach last Sunday, just out of curiosity, and he sure does carry a fellow along with him. He made me want to get out and fight the Gentiles that have been persecuting his people but afterwards when I was walking by myself, I felt different. The reason he is the leader here is because most of the people that belong to the Church are uneducated and kind of simple. Mr. Pratt, an Apostle that just come out from Nauvoo, is a bright man, though. He's been to Europe and all over on missions and he treats me nice.[7]

Sam was not interested in the rest of the letter, so he put it back in the envelope and left it lying on the table. When he went out into the street he caught his reflection in a small window-pane and stopped to take stock. Perhaps he was still sallow; he couldn't be sure from the poor reflection in the window. But what the boy said about his face being hard rankled. It didn't seem hard to Sam. True, his eyes did glitter with restless energy and his face was bold of outline, but surely it was not hard-looking. He determined to grow a pointed beard which would soften the lines of his rugged jaw. He had always felt that Edward liked him, but the letter left him uncertain. At last he sighed and decided to put it out of his mind. He liked the boy and would do the best he could for him, and perhaps in time the lad would become less critical and return his genuine affection.

A few days later Sam set out on an Erie canalboat for Nauvoo. After days of travel he approached the goal of his journey from upstream on the Mississippi River, which made a wide arc around the Mormon Zion. Sam caught his breath as the city slowly came into view. The white marble temple on the hill which crowned the site seemed like a dream temple. There was a fairylike beauty to this city, which grew on all slopes of a gentle rise of land, surrounded on three sides by the Mississippi. The tree-lined streets ran at right angles to each other up and down the hill, and now that spring was come flowers made the gardens of the homes flame with brilliance. Red-brick houses surrounded by neat picket fences stood next to white frame houses bordered by log railings; altogether the city had a neat appearance. Sam was amazed at the size of the place, which had been only a village when last he saw it. A magic wand had turned it overnight into a community of breath-taking beauty.

When he disembarked on the busy wharf he made his way straight to the old Mansion House, which had been Joseph Smith's home and also a sort of hostelry. Emma Smith, Joseph's widow, rented Samuel a room and warned him, as she led the way down the hall, to beware of Brigham Young and the wickedness he was bringing upon the Church.

"Are you an apostate?" Sam asked.

"From the Brighamite Church, yes. But we are starting a new Church which we will name after Joseph," she replied. Sam felt chilled by her manner and determined to seek other lodgings immediately. The next day he rented a room in a private home.

It was a matter of days before his hearing on a charge of Church treason came up before the Apostles. Sam admitted his error as the half-dozen bearded men looked at him from the far side of the table. They allowed him to tell his story in his own words and then consulted among themselves. Eventually they decided to admit him back into fellowship and he was free to return to New York. Before he took ship again he wrote a long letter to Hattie, saying that he did not love her and did not intend to return to her. He explained that he was still on a mission and short of funds, but that when he had an income again he would provide for her and the child Almira. Meanwhile, if she wanted a divorce she was free to go ahead. He knew she would not do this, but wanted her to know that he would not object if she did. He did not mention the fact that he had married again. She did not answer his letter.

Back in New York, Sam ran from the horsecar stop to his home. When he threw open the door into the parlor, Fanny was walking back and forth with a crying baby. Sam dropped his bag and rushed to her side, lifting the baby awkwardly into his arms. "What is it— a boy or a girl?" he asked.

Fanny smiled fondly at the baby. "A boy, of course. We've named him Samuel, Junior, after you. He's going to be christened at church next Sunday."

Sam joggled the baby for a moment and then handed him back to his grandmother. He hurried in to see Ann Eliza, whom he found sitting up in bed, her hair in two braids over her shoulders. He took her in his arms and held her close while she clung to him.

"Did it come out all right in Nauvoo?" she murmured into his neck, and he nodded and asked, "Did you have an awful hard time?"

She nodded gravely. "Awful. I hope I'll never have to have another baby."

He kissed her and fondled her until she became restless and pulled away. "How are things in Nauvoo?" she asked to distract his mind. She did not like him to be affectionate; she hated being rumpled. He sat back on the foot of the bed and hooked his hands around his knee. "Bad," he said. "The governor of Illinois keeps telling our people that they've got to get out of Nauvoo or they'll be driven out by gentile mobs. Brigham and the Apostles don't know where to turn. It's not easy to uproot a city full of people and send them out into the wilderness just because someone says they've got to go. Brigham sent a man to Washington to ask President Buchanan for help, but I don't look for any help from those Washington politicians. Meanwhile the Saints are worried sick; they go about their tasks with a feeling of dread, never knowing what will happen next. In the outlying districts it's a common thing for night-riders to swoop down and burn their houses and crops, and abuse or kill the farmers and their families. It makes you so mad you could fight, to hear about it."

She shuddered. "Don't tell me any more. I'm not well enough yet to hear such bad news. I think I'll take a little nap, if you don't mind."

"No, go ahead," he said and arose. "I've got to go down to the paper and help Brother Pratt. I'll be home early, though."

On the morning of July 19, 1845, Sam was awakened before

daylight by the sound of fire bells. In the darkness he dressed hurriedly and ran toward town, where the flicker of flames could be seen against the whitening dawn. At Chambers and Broadway he stopped to locate the position of the fire, and then hurried on until he reached New Street, where a guard stopped him. Several still forms lay huddled on the ground beneath a tarpaulin, and the air of the oppressive July morning was heavy with the odor of burnt flesh.

"How'd it start, and where?" Sam asked the guard. As they talked, a half-dozen newcomers surrounded them.

"Broke out in the warehouse across the street, and the fire company had it almost out, when an explosion started it all over again. That's when these fellers got killed." The guard waved him down the street. "Better get down there in one of them bucket brigades and help. All the fire companies are working like mad, but the fire's still spreading."

Sam ran down the street and took his place in a long line of men which stretched from a tank to the nearest blaze. Hour after hour he handed buckets from the man on his left to the man on his right; as the flames leaped the dampened patches the brigades changed their positions. By midmorning the fire had spread erratically into fresh areas, so that sporadic fires were breaking out constantly. But by noon the fire-fighters had won. Sam walked away, surveying the burned section with a feeling of pity. Practically every building between Exchange Place and Stone Street, and from Broad to Broadway, was gone, and parts of many another block completely destroyed.

He walked up Nassau Street, weary and blackened, and when he came to the newspaper office went inside and dropped into a chair. The boys, hearing him, came out from the back. "We've been pouring water on our building all day so that no sparks would light on it," Edward said.

"Good boy!" Sam responded, and laying his arms on the table he put his head on them and fell into sleep.

A week later Parley left for Nauvoo. All the Apostles were being recalled to Nauvoo so as to assist in finishing and furnishing the temple and in giving temple ordinances before they were forced to leave the new building and the city. Word had come that the

Church might move to the Rocky Mountains. In Parley's place came the younger Pratt, Orson, who was not at all like his brother either in looks or disposition. Orson was only thirty-three—seven years older than Sam. He was small and handsome, with the dreamy eyes of an idealist and one of the sharpest brains of his day. This was the person Sir Frederick Burton, the scholar, was one day to call a "well-educated, though self-educated, man."

Orson and Sam stood side by side in front of the worn steps of the old Park Theatre one day, reading the announcement that Charles Keen and Ellen Tree were shortly to arrive from England to present their repertoire.

"I saw them once in London. Parley and me went," Orson said wistfully. "I wish I could afford to see them again."

"If they would leave that Shakespeare stuff alone I'd like to see them too, but I don't like plays I can't understand."

Orson smiled tolerantly and they went on to the office. Orson had objected from the first to "The Prophet" as a name for the Church paper. "It sounds like a Church paper. How can you expect to entice new readers when you tell them to begin with that it's a Mormon paper we're printing?"

"What would you suggest?" Sam asked.

"I've given it a lot of thought and I think 'The Messenger' is better. We'll be able to get a few readers then that won't know what they're getting until after they've read it."

And so, in July, the paper appeared under its new name. But even the *Messenger* had a difficult time. Every penny that could be begged from the faithful went to Nauvoo.

"I'll have to put a stop to that," Orson said firmly. "If this keeps up, our branches will have to quit working for lack of funds. I'll write right now to Apostle Hyde and tell him to cease these constant solicitations."

"I tried to get Brother Parley to do it, but he just never got around to it," Sam said.

So Orson wrote the letter, and within a few weeks the New York branch began to feel the difference as lifeblood flowed back into it.

Sam and Orson were now happier in their work, for it was no longer a hopeless and losing fight. They preached every Sunday at the New York branch or in one of the small outlying towns, and Sam seemed to grow ever more glib in citing the scriptures, and ever more fanatic in his faith.

The *Times and Seasons* brought a message that Governor Ford had set the final day by which the Mormons would be allowed to leave Nauvoo peaceably, as February 1, 1846. After that time they would be driven out if they still remained. The Mormon press carried an editorial on this edict and a letter which Governor Ford had addressed to Brigham Young on April 8, 1845. It said:

> . . . If you can get off by yourselves, you may enjoy peace; but surrounded by such neighbors I confess that I do not foresee the time when you will be permitted to enjoy quiet. . . .
>
> I would suggest a matter in confidence. California now offers a field for the prettiest enterprise that has been undertaken in modern times. It is but sparsely inhabited, and by none but the Indian or imbecile Mexican Spaniards. I have not inquired enough to know how strong it is in men and means: but this we know that if conquered from Mexico, the country is so physically weak and morally distracted that she could never send a force there to reconquer it. Why would it not be a pretty operation for your people to go out of the vacant country and establish an independent government of your own, subject only to the laws of nations? You would remain there a long time before you would be disturbed by proximity of other settlements. If you conclude to do this, your design ought not to be known, or otherwise it would become the duty of the United States to prevent your emigration. But if you once cross the line of the United States territories, you would be in no danger of being interfered with. . . .[8]

Sam read the article and turned to Orson. "In other words, Governor Ford is willing for us to go anywhere and take any risk, even to breaking the law of our country, as long as we get out of his state. Why are the politicians in Illinois so determined to get our Mormon population out of there? While Joseph was alive we did not have this trouble."

"No," Orson agreed. "I will tell you why. Joseph dabbled in state politics. With a solid block of ten thousand votes, he held the balance of power between the Whigs and the Democrats. Any politician who wanted to get office had to make concessions to Joseph or he couldn't win. Now that Joseph is dead, they want to spew us out before we get another strong leader and continue to dominate state politics."

"Oh, 1 see," Sam exclaimed. "Then their fight against us is political, and not religious?"

"You are absolutely right," Orson said.

In the early part of November a letter came to Sam at the newspaper office from Parley P. Pratt. Among other things it said:

> Our Apostles assembled in meeting have debated the best method of getting all our people into the far west with the least possible hardship. We have read Hasting's *Account of California* and Frémont's *Journal of Explorations in the West* and we have concluded that the Great Basin in the top of the Rocky Mountains where lies the Great Salt Lake, is the proper place for us. Frémont visited this place and he says that the soil is fertile and traversed by many mountain streams. This will make it possible to irrigate during times of drought. And so, it looks as if we will head for the mountains where Joseph so longingly turned his eyes during his life. I inclose to you a letter of instructions from the Apostles, authorizing you to lead the group of Saints in its exodus from New York City and the Atlantic seaboard. Brother Brigham is, this day, sending a letter to my brother Orson directing him to call a conference of all Saints in your mission to lay before them the plan to emigrate by water from New York.

When Sam had finished reading the letter he handed it to Orson. "I have my instructions here about the conference," Orson said after reading it. "Set up a notice to go in Saturday's edition calling all Saints to a conference in American Hall on November 12."

When the conference[9] was called to order, Orson Pratt and Sam Brannan sat side by side on the speakers' stand and surveyed the packed hall. People had come from the New England states, from New Jersey and other states adjoining New York. Although these Mormons had not been subject to mistreatment by their neighbors, they made common cause with their mistreated brethren in Illinois. In Washington, the President had refused the Mormon envoy, saying "Your cause is just, but I can do nothing for you,"—and so saying, had set every Mormon's hand against him.

Orson arose and called the meeting to order. Sam offered a prayer and the congregation sang a hymn as prelude to the main address by Orson, who exhorted the listening people to make ready to leave the confines of a Government whose servants had been so consistently unfair to them. "Three times," he said, "we have been driven from communities where we have bought land and improved it, and built up a worth-while commonwealth. We have been driven out by lawless mobs, backed by those in power. Now it is time to get out of such an evil nation.

"While Joseph lived, he cast his eyes longingly towards the mountains in the west, but he himself felt that he could not move his people so far because of the hardship it would entail. Now we have this hardship thrust upon us, and we are bound to follow Joseph's vision. What I tell you now, I tell you in strictest confidence and it must not be told beyond these walls. Our leaders have decided to settle in the Rocky Mountains on land which is in Mexican territory and will be isolated from gentile neighbors. For you who do not know, I will explain that there is a treaty between this country and Mexico which says that no armed groups from either country shall invade the other. We must arm to go into trackless wilderness, but our Government will stop us if it knows our purpose. We have decided therefore to publish it abroad that we are going to Oregon, which is being disputed with England at this time. There will be no interference with this plan. Make yourselves ready to go west with the main body of Saints. Sell your farm or your business and be ready, so that you can go as soon as the order to move forward arrives. Help the poor among you so that they may go, too. Brother Samuel Brannan has already been appointed as the man to lead all those who leave from the Atlantic Coast. I myself have to go back to Nauvoo to assist in the final ordinances at the temple, which has just been completed. We will have time for our first and last rites before we leave our beautiful temple—deserted while it is still new. Before I go I will have a last message for all of you."

He now launched into his sermon. When he had finished he turned the meeting over to Samuel, who rose with a document in his hands. He began by reading a preamble which set forth that the Mormons had been "sorely persecuted by the Protestant Christian Churches, our houses burned and we disinherited of our possessions, and driven forth upon the charity of a cold-hearted world." The citizens and authorities of the United States sanctioned such proceedings "without manifesting any disposition to sustain us in our constitutional rights, but have rejected our many petitions to judges, governors and presidents."

He drew a long breath and launched into the resolution itself:

"Be it resolved that the Mormons hail with joy this decision to depart."

The congregation made vociferous approval of this statement and Sam continued: "Be it further resolved that William Smith is a wicked, selfish man and we most heartily agree with those who have excommunicated him."

Another demonstration of approval was made by the audience, and Sam added, "We wish to caution all Saints to have nothing more to do with William Smith. He is treacherous. Now lastly, I have one more resolution to read: 'Be it resolved that all branches of the Church shall move west of the Rocky Mountains before the next season, by land or water, and that no one shall be excused except the old, the sick, or those too poverty-stricken.' "

This was approved. Sam laid the document aside and took up a letter. "I have here a letter which has been sent to me by the General Authorities in Nauvoo, directing me to charter a ship, outfit it, and make it ready to sail to the west coast. How far we will be from the Rocky Mountains when we land in San Francisco Bay I don't know, but I don't think it is very far. We will build up a community, and a community farm, on the coast and share with the Saints when they come. If the new Zion is going to be quite a ways from the coast, then we will join it, wherever it is. I want all of you who intend to join this exodus to make arrangements to go on this ship. I've got to know how many are going before I can charter a ship, because if a large number are going we will need a big ship and if not, a small one. So don't forget, before you leave this hall tonight give me your name and tell me you want to go."

On the last Sunday in November, 1845, Orson Pratt made his farewell address to the Saints assembled in New York.

"I grieve to leave so many loyal workers that I have learned to love and depend on but I must go home to prepare our people and especially my own family for the long trek over the Great Plains which now faces us. We must leave by the first of February, in the dead of winter, Governor Ford tells us. I want to warn the poor among you here not to try to go to Nauvoo with the idea in mind that the Church will outfit you for the westward journey. The Church cannot help you. Already we have more destitute there than we can take care of. To the rest of you I want to say that if you have enough means to buy horses, wagons, tents, equipment, and food enough to get you to Nauvoo, then you will have more than enough to pay your passage by water to the west coast and it will be an easier journey. Besides, those of you who go by ship can carry heavy machinery, tons of seeds, and every manner of thing necessary to build up a new commonwealth, whereas we who go by land can take little with us. Brother Brannan is looking for a ship, although he has not found a satisfactory one yet. He will have one, we hope, very soon and we have therefore set the tentative sailing date from New York City for about the middle of January next. If a hundred and fifty passengers can be obtained Brother Brannan can charter a vessel on that basis and your fare will be practically nothing and the voyage will take not more than four or five months. Brethren! Awake! Be determined to get out from this evil nation next spring!" [10]

Sam spoke briefly when Orson had finished. "You folks want to make a trip but you want some one else to do all the worrying and work for you. Two weeks ago I told you that every one who wanted to go had to sign up right away. A few of you did sign up and a lot more said they were going to, but didn't. You know as well as I do, that I can't charter a ship on promises. Make up your minds and come up here and see me. Put down your names and pay a deposit on your passage money and then I'll have something to work on. I can't go out and tell a captain we want a ship and promise him we'll pay him later. I have to have money before we can talk business. Come up now and sign your names and leave a deposit."

That night over a hundred people signed up for the voyage, but only a few paid a deposit. Sam consoled himself with the knowledge he had enough money to begin to put the business on a financial basis.

Chapter VII

As THE WEEKS passed, more and more families decided to sail with the Mormon ship. Men, heads of families, called one after another at the office of the *Messenger* to sign their names to the passenger roll. Most of them paid a small deposit but a few made excuses; among these was Elisha Hyatt. News of the voyage to Oregon went beyond the Mormon group and eventually half a dozen non-Mormons who wished to reach the west coast applied for passage, and these Sam signed up.

While he was busy going up and down the waterfront from one end to the other, hunting for a vessel which would suit the needs of the exodus, the greater share of the responsibility for getting out each edition of the *Messenger* rested upon the two youths, Edward Kemble and John Eager. Young church members fell into the habit of coming in to help in folding the sheets as they came from the press and address them for mailing. Edward Kemble often wrote the editorial, and John Eager put his hand to writing small articles. Every issue carried news of the forthcoming journey and appeals to those who had signed up to bring in the balance of the deposit money. Elisha Hyatt proved stubborn, and Sam finally had to publish his name along with several others who must either pay or give up hope of sailing with the company.

Not being able to find a ship in New York harbor of the right size and necessary sturdiness, at a price he could afford, Samuel took passage up to Boston in the dead of winter to search the harbor there. It was exceedingly cold, now that December held the coast bound in snow and ice, and Sam shivered in his greatcoat as he prowled the Boston water front. At the end of a week he concluded that his trip was useless and returned to New York.

At old Coenties Slip, where ships from all over the world berthed, Sam found at last one shipmaster with the right kind of ship for his purpose, who offered to take the Mormons to the west coast at a price of sixteen dollars a ton, counting their displacement; providing Sam would get him a government mail contract to Honolulu and San Francisco Bay to cover the greater part of the cost of the voyage. This seemed a reasonable idea to Sam, who agreed to go to Washington to ask Amos Kendall, the Postmaster General, for such a contract. He cooled his heels in the Postmaster General's outer office for three days before finally gaining an audience with the great man. He found Kendall not over-friendly and a little impatient at the discovery that Sam was a Mormon. He evidently supposed that Sam had come as a Mormon representative to beg for help in regaining what had been taken from the faithful by the mobs of Illinois and Missouri.

"Well, Mr. Brannan, I must admit you are a persistent man. State what you want as briefly as you can. I'm very busy today."

"I will," Sam said grimly and began. "I am taking a shipload of our people to Oregon to set up a colony. We want to charter a vessel and that will take more money than we have. I have talked to a shipmaster who has agreed to take us at sixteen dollars a ton, counting our displacement, if I can secure from you a mail contract for Honolulu and San Francisco Bay."

Kendall relaxed and leaned back in his chair. "Oh, so you're going to take a shipload of your people to Oregon." He looked intent for several moments and then asked abruptly: "You are sure you don't intend to land upon the shores of San Francisco Bay?"

"Positive," Sam said shortly.

"That is well," Kendall said slowly. "On account of the treaty between Mexico and this country you would not be allowed to land there, you know."

Sam nodded. "Yes, I know."

Amos rubbed his chin meditatively. "I'm sorry, but I cannot give you a mail contract. There is little mail for those ports and what there is has already been contracted for." He leaned forward. "You are positive that you do not wish to make a colony on San Francisco Bay?"

Sam nodded and then looked calculatingly at Kendall with the feeling that there was something behind his question. "Why do you keep asking me that?" Sam asked.

Kendall leaned forward across his table and picking up a pencil began to tap it absent-mindedly on the polished surface. "I have a reason," he said guardedly, and then looking pointedly at Samuel he asked, "If I put a proposition to you and you don't want to consider it, I want you to give me your word you won't repeat it beyond this room."

Sam leaned forward and put his elbows on the table. "I promise," he said.

Kendall took a deep breath and said pleasantly, "If you did want to consider setting up a colony on the shore of San Francisco Bay, I could make it possible for you to go without government interference —for a consideration."

This interested Sam. "We might be interested in doing that. What is the consideration?"

Kendall lowered his voice. "San Francisco Bay is surrounded by some of the richest land in America, I've heard, for agriculture and grazing purposes. I've talked to men who have been there and they swear there's a mint of money to be made out of it. I'd like to set up a colony of my own, but in public life as I am, that would be impossible. War with Mexico is imminent, and if a colony of Americans were established there, when it is taken over by the United States they would have the choice lands before others could get out there. Since I cannot send a colony of people out, I might be interested in backing your people providing you look out for my interests."

Sam's eyes gleamed with excitement. "You interest me very much. What would you want in return for giving us such protection?"

Kendall spoke decisively. "Half of the land you settle. You could cut your colony into lots and number them. The uneven numbers you could keep and improve and live on. The even numbers would be set over to me and my associates. You would improve your land and make it your business to see that the taxes on our unimproved land would be no higher than on your own improved lots."

Sam looked at him quizzically. "My experience has been that you fellows here in Washington have not much use for us Mormons. Would you be content to let us settle land for you and be obliged to do business among us?"

"Yes. After all, it is a business proposition with me. We would not be your neighbors. We would only hold the land as an investment."

Sam was thoughtful for some moments. "The people you would sell the land to would probably be gentiles, and we would be once more in the same difficulty we're now trying to get away from. I don't think I like the idea."

Kendall leaned forward again. "There might be a good deal of money in it for *you*, if you put it through for me."

Sam brightened. "Well, that puts a different aspect on it again." He was thoughtful for a time. "I'll consider it and try to put it over for you, for a consideration," he suggested.

Kendall relaxed against the back of his chair again. "I'm not committing myself at this time," he said. "But if I do enter into such a contract my name must never appear in it. My business friend and associate A. G. Benson of New York City will handle everything for me. You see him when you go back, and if he is interested in my idea we can all meet together in New York and make out papers."

"I'll talk to my own counselors and see what they think of the idea—not mentioning your name, of course," Sam added hastily, "but I've got to tell you right now that I can't sign any papers which will be binding on all our people. If any contracts are drawn up they will have to be signed by the head of the Church, Brigham Young, or they will not be worth the paper they're written on."

Kendall frowned. "When do you plan to sail?"

"Sometime in January."

"This is December." Kendall put the tips of his fingers together, pursed his lips in thought, and finally said, "See Benson as soon as you get back to New York and talk to him. The more I think of the idea the better I like it. If we can make an agreement soon, we must get it to Brigham Young and back before you folks sail, otherwise you cannot get away without government interference. You might be stopped entirely without me to help you."

"You forget that we are going to Oregon," Sam said.

Kendall looked at him obliquely. "That is what you tell us. We may or may not believe it. And if we have reason to believe that you may stop short of your destination and land instead on the Bay of

San Francisco, we will be forced to stop you because of the treaty between our nations."

"I understand," Samuel replied, and arose. Kendall likewise arose, and came around his desk. He held out his hand and Samuel took it.

"Good day, Mr. Brannan," Kendall said, "I'm sorry I can't give you a mail contract. But because we could not give you a contract does not mean that you and I cannot do business together."

Sam nodded. "I will see Mr. Benson, as you have requested me to do," he said stiffly.

When Sam had returned once more to New York he went to the Tontine Coffee House at his first opportunity. The many-mullioned bay windows gave light over the numerous tables and nooks where men sat opposite each other over cups of coffee to discuss maritime business. The waiter spoke to Sam as he came in.

"Captain Richardson of the *Brooklyn* just came in a little while ago. I think his ship might suit you, and he's looking for a cargo."

"Good," said Sam. "I saw the ship a while ago and I'd like nothing better than to see her captain." The waiter showed him into a booth where a tall man with piercing eyes and quick movements of the hands was looking through some papers while he sipped his coffee. He looked up and acknowledged the introduction the waiter made, then motioned Sam to a seat opposite.

"How many tons burthen has the *Brooklyn*?" Sam asked.

"Four hundred and fifty. She's as snug and seaworthy as any fast sailer can be."

"There are nigh onto three hundred of us planning to sail to the west coast in January," Sam remarked, and fell into a long explanation of the voyage and its purpose. At last he asked the Captain what price he could take them for. Richardson was thoughtful.

"Fifteen hundred a month and you to pay the port charges, the money to be in my hands before we start."

Sam whistled. "You're way out of reason, Captain. Come down where we can talk business."

"Take it or leave it. I'm not sailing for my health."

Sam pursed his lips thoughtfully for a time and then he brightened. "Could you take us cheaper if I got you a good cargo?"

The Captain appeared more interested. "Aye," he said. "If you get me a freight cargo for the Sandwich Islands and San' Francisco Bay, I might cut it to twelve hundred."

Sam began to figure on a piece of paper. At last he reached a decision. "We could do it for twelve hundred, but not all cash down. I'll pay you the larger part of it before we leave, the balance to be paid when we reach our destination. I think I know where I can get you a good cargo for Honolulu. If we take your ship can you have her ready to sail by the middle of January?"

"Aye. I could have her ready in a week."

"Meet me here at nine o'clock tomorrow morning and we'll try to make a deal," Sam said.

"Only on my terms," said the Captain imperturbably, and Sam flashed him a quick grin as he strode from the room.

Sam was successful in procuring a cargo of freight to be landed at Honolulu in the Sandwich Islands, as the Hawaiian Islands were then called. A deposit was paid to Captain A. Richardson, master of the *Brooklyn*, and plans went ahead for sailing in the middle of January. Sam had been so busy that he had forgotten Amos Kendall. The Postmaster, however, had not forgotten him. One morning A. G. Benson called at his office. That afternoon Sam went in turn to Benson's office, where the Cabinet member awaited him. They discussed fully Kendall's plan to set up a colony on land adjacent to San Francisco Bay. There were those later who said that Kendall offered Sam inducements to present his proposition to Brigham in a favorable light. In any case, Sam wrote to Brigham that night, but fearing that his letter might not reach the leader he wrote again on January 12, 1846.

BROTHER YOUNG:

I have written you three letters of late from Boston, Washington, and New York and I fear they have been intercepted on the way, and I have thought it prudent to direct this to some obscure individual that it may reach you in safety; I have received positive information that it is the intention of the Government to disarm you after you have taken up your line of march in the spring, on the ground of the law of nations, or the treaty existing between the United States and Mexico. That an armed posse of men shall not be allowed to invade the Territory of a foreign nation.

Amos Kendall was in the city last week, and positively declared that that was the intention of the Government, and I thought it my duty to let you know that you might be on your guard. I declare to all that you are not going to California but Oregon, and that my information is official. Kendall has also learned that we have chartered the ship *Brooklyn* and that Mormons are going out in her, and it is thought that she will be searched for arms, and, if found, taken from us, and if not an order will be sent to Commodore Stockton on the Pacific to search our vessel before we land.

Kendall will be in the city next Thursday again, and then an effort will be made to bring about a reconciliation. I will make you acquainted with the result before I leave. My company now numbers about one hundred and seventy five. I chartered the whole ship here in the market. I have obtained already one thousand dollars worth of freight for the Sandwich Islands and a good prospect for more. I have it now in my power to learn every movement of the Government in relation to us, which I shall make you acquainted with from time to time. God is at work in the East, and so is the Devil, but Moses' rod will be too hard for him. I feel my weakness and inability and desire your blessings and prayers that I may be successful. My cares and labors weigh me down day and night, but I trust in God that I shall soon have a happy deliverance.

All the Saints in the East are praying and crying for deliverance; but I must close now by subscribing myself, your brother in the everlasting Covenant.

S. BRANNAN.[11]

He wasted no time in worry over the Kendall contract but went ahead with his plans to sail. In an open letter to the prospective voyagers he said:

We have now on our books the names of about three hundred saints who wish to go by water, and it grieves us to say that only about sixty out of that number will have means sufficient to carry them through. If some of our wealthy brethren who are now dwelling at ease in the world, would but step forward, and plant this company of poor saints upon the western soil, how soon would it be before they would have it in their power to return four fold?

The passage of each person will be fifty dollars, children over five and under fourteen, half price. Each one will need from twenty to twenty-five dollars worth of provisions; the whole amount, seventy-five dollars. If we obtain two hundred passengers, in all probability there will be a deduction.[12]

Plans being almost complete, the sailing date was set ahead to the last week in January.

On the twenty-sixth of January, 1846, he wrote:

DEAR BROTHER YOUNG:

I haste to lay before your honorable body the result of my movements since I wrote you last, which was from this city, stating some of my discoveries in relation to the contemplated movements of the General Government in opposition to our removal.

I had an interview with Amos Kendall in company with Mr. Benson which resulted in a compromise, the conditions of which you will learn by tending the contract, between them and us, which I shall forward by this mail. I shall also leave a copy of the same with Elder Appleby, who was present when it was signed. Kendall is now our friend and will use his influence in our behalf, in connection with twenty-five of the most prominent demagogues of the country. You will be permitted to pass out of the States unmolested. Their council is to go well-armed, but keep them well secreted from the rabble.

I shall select the most suitable spot on the Bay of San Francisco for the location of a commercial city.

When I sail, which will be next Saturday at 1 o'clock, I shall hoist a flag with Oregon on it. Immediately on the reception of this letter you must write Messrs. A. G. Benson and let him know whether you are willing to coincide with the contract I have made for our deliverance. I am aware that it is a covenant with death, but we know that God is able to break it, and will do it. The children of Israel from Egypt had to make covenants for their safety and leave it for God to break them, and the Prophet has said: "As it was then, so shall it be in the last days."

And I have been led by a remarkable train of circumstances to say Amen,— and I feel and hope you will do the same. Mr. Benson thinks the Twelve should leave and get out of the country first and avoid being arrested. You will find a staunch friend in him, and you will find friends, and that a host, to deliver you from their hands. If any of you are arrested, don't be tried west of the Alleghany Mountains. In the East you will find friends that you little think of.

The Saints in the east pray night and day for your safety; and it is mine first in the morning and last in the evening. I must now bring my letter to a close. Mr. Benson's address is No. 29 South Street, and the sooner you can give him an answer the better it will be for us. He will spend one month in Washington to sustain you, and he will do it, no mistake. But everything must be kept as silent as death on our part; names of the parties in particular. I now commit this sheet to the post, praying that Israel's God may prevent it from Falling in the hands of wicked men. You will hear from me again on the day of sailing, if it is the Lord's will.

> Amen.
> Yours truly, a friend and
> brother in God's kingdom,
> S. Brannan.[18]

Included with the letter was the contract which Samuel had signed with A. G. Benson and Company. The preamble stated that the Saints were seeking liberty and security beyond the jurisdiction of the states and the United States, and to do this it was their plan to set up the nucleus of a city on the shores of the Pacific around which would eventually grow up a new state. They wished to depart in peace without molestation from the Government, which might be under a misapprehension as to their designs. They were loyal citizens. A. G. Benson represented upon his part that it was within his power to prevent the Government from interfering with the plans of the Mormons; that he had access to the President of the United States and could set the matter before him in the proper light. All this being so the Mormons were to reward A. G. Benson by signing over to him one half of all the lands they colonized or might colonize in establishing towns or farms, or any lands which might be included for any purpose. The Mormons were to exercise diligence to prevent the vacant land from being taxed higher than the improved lands which would surround it. The contract stipulated that all even-numbered lots taken up by the Mormons, in groups or as individuals, should be deeded to A. G. Benson and the Mormons were to be allowed to retain the odd-numbered lots for their own use.

Samuel sent the letter and the contract away by the fastest service he could find and then went on with his preparations for departure while awaiting an answer. He prepared an editorial for the *Messenger:*

Our company now numbers over one hundred who have the means sufficient to fit themselves out handsomely and comfortably for the voyage. We would say to all who have any quantity of provisions on hand, such as beef and pork, to fetch it with them. They will also remember that they require no thick clothing on their arrival at the place of destination. Everything that is useful here is useful there, with the exception of thick clothing, stoves and such. Persons having large sums of money had better come to the city and assist in their investment and then there will be no cause for dissatisfaction hereafter.

He continued at great length with instructions about everything, especially urging women in a delicate condition who were coming from afar to arrive in the city several days ahead of the sailing date, so that they could have a long rest before the voyage began. He concluded:

We have chartered the ship *Brooklyn*, from Captain Richardson, of four hundred and fifty tons, at $1200.00 per month, and we pay the port charges;

the money to be paid before sailing. She is a first-class ship in the best order for sea, and with all the rest a very fast sailer, which will facilitate our passage greatly. The between decks will be very neatly fitted up into one large cabin, with a row of state rooms on each side, so that every family will be provided with a state room, affording them places of retirement at their pleasure. She will be well lighted with sky lights in the deck, with every other convenience to make a family equally as comfortable as their own fireside in Babylon.

N.B. Now brethren, remember that there must be no disappointing on the part of any individual that has joined this company. By doing so, it might be the means of stopping the whole company, and that man will be morally responsible for the injury done, and God will require it at his hands. We do not say this because we have any fears on the subject, but that none should have an apology for slackness for we will accept of none.

In his closing line he insisted that there must be no delay in the sailing date; but in spite of him there was one. The day for sailing passed and another was set a week in advance. Sam was determined that they should sail on February 4.

On the afternoon of February 3 he was overseeing the last minute preparations. The old stove was taken out of the galley and a new one, which Sam had purchased with money out of the common fund, was installed. He had just finished interviewing two Negroes, one a cook and the other a cook's helper, who were to be in charge of the galley. Every family was bringing its own provisions, but Sam had foreseen that it would be necessary to have one person in charge of all supplies and another to cook, in order to avoid chaos.

A steady stream of longshoremen walked from the piles of luggage on the wharf, up the gangways and down into the bowels of the ship and back again. There was an ear-splitting din of bellowing and squealing when fifty pigs and two milch cows were hoisted aboard by crane and windlass. Fowls cackled in their pens, which were lashed to the deck. Plows, harrows, and all manner of farmers' tools were stowed in the hold, together with blacksmiths' implements, carpenters' outfits, equipment for millwrights; as well as three grain mills, turning lathes, sawmill irons, grindstones, crockery, stationery, schoolbooks, seeds by the ton, dry goods, copper-, iron- and tin-ware. But these last-minute loadings were the personal belongings of the 230 passengers who were beginning to come aboard. In boxes on the wharf were 179 volumes of Harper's *Family Library*, which I. M.

Van Cott, a lawyer from Brooklyn, had presented to them at a farewell party the night before.

Sam walked back and forth, watching everything, answering questions, and pointing out directions to the passengers coming aboard. He went below with John Eager and his family, which consisted of Lucy Eager, a widow; her two daughters and two sons, of whom John was one. He pointed out to them the long main hall in the center of the ship and the staterooms which lined it on either side. It seemed very snug and cozy to Sam, and the long, rough dining-table would accommodate fifty or sixty people at a sitting. He chatted with the Eagers as they settled in one stateroom. Two boys in an upper bunk, two girls in a lower, and Lucy sleeping in a single cot which the boys would lash firmly to the floor.

Late in the day Sam left the wharf and went back to the newspaper office. It looked empty without the big press.

"I'm glad we set up a heading for our California newspaper and bought all our supplies," he said to Edward, who was cleaning out the last litter from the room. "We can start right in publishing our paper as soon as we land. 'The California Star,' " he said, as if he liked the sound of the words. " 'The California Star'—guiding light in the wilderness."

Edward swept the last pile of dirt out the door and came back to Sam. "My mother and father are here in New York. They've come to see me off tomorrow."

"That's fine, Ed." Sam smiled and asked, "Did any mail come from Nauvoo yet?"

Edward shook his head. "That's bad," Sam muttered. "If that contract don't get back here by noon tomorrow, the chances are we won't sail at all."

Sam took his wife and baby and mother-in-law down to the wharf in a livery rig, and they settled themselves by lamplight. Sam slept lightly, his arms around Ann Eliza, aware all night of the rise and fall of the vessel on the water and the slapping of the waves against its side. At daylight he was up and watching the placing of the food supplies where members of the company could reach them to cook their own meals. At nine, the longshoremen began to carry aboard the last-minute provisions—cheeses, bananas, vegetables, and fresh-baked goods.

At ten o'clock Sam saw Benson making his way up the gangplank. For a moment he was filled with panic, but he stood his ground and waited for the man to approach.

"Has the contract come back from Nauvoo yet?" Benson asked.

Sam shook his head gloomily. Children played everywhere, their shrill cries striking Sam's ears like a whiplash. Women in their best winter coats with quilted velvet hoods trimmed with ostrich plumes stood in cluttered groups, their hands tucked in muffs. Men in fur caps and greatcoats stamped their galoshes on the deck to free them from snow.

"That's too bad," Benson said. "I'm afraid you folks won't be able to sail today, after all. And it's going to be a great disappointment in Nauvoo when the Federal officers ride in to arrest your leaders and scatter your people. I've moved heaven and earth to protect you—because my sympathies are with you. And so has Mr. Kendall." He shrugged. "But without that contract we have no assurance of your good faith."

Sam spoke in sudden anger. "I sent the contract by special messenger. It's not my fault that it's not back yet."

"Well, perhaps Brigham held it awhile to think it over. It will be unfortunate for the Mormon people if he does not see eye to eye with us on this proposition. I'll go on doing all I can to protect him and your people, but if he wants full protection he'll have to co-operate with us."

"Oh, he will. Brigham's no fool," Sam replied, trying to conquer his ire. "I told him the wisdom of signing it and urged him to hurry. I can't imagine what's holding it up."

"I hear that the Government agents have orders to prevent your sailing today. I came down to warn you," Benson said unctuously. "I'll do what I can to protect you but under the circumstances that isn't much."

Sam stood looking at the well-upholstered businessman. "We'll sail out on schedule. If the Government stops us—well, we'll just be stopped."

Benson put in quickly. "And if the Government does not happen to stop you here, Commodore Stockton may be on the lookout for you, and it may be a good deal harder to land on the Coast than it was to sail from New York."

"All we can do is to take our chances," Sam shrugged.

Benson smiled and held out his hand. Sam shook it and the other wished him farewell and walked away. Sam went to find the Captain and repeated his conversation with Benson.

"It looks bad," he added gloomily.

The Captain cast an eye this way and that, and then he said, "We'll go ahead and sail with the tide. I sort of think this fellow is bluffing."

"I hope so," Sam sighed.

Friends who had come on board to wish the voyagers well were everywhere. Sam greeted many of them. John Eager came hunting him to tell him that a special "extra" of the *Messenger* [14] was being published in honor of the sailing by the Saints who remained behind.

At noon the passengers and their guests ate a light picnic lunch at the long table in the hall.

Sam watched the wharf while the Captain kept his eyes cocked towards Governor's Island, whence Government interference might be expected. At one-fifteen all visitors were ordered ashore. Half an hour later the Captain spoke tersely to the mate. "Man the capstan!" the mate bellowed. "To your places!" Sailors swarmed over the deck. The gangplank was pulled up. Orders and movement followed. At two o'clock the *Brooklyn* released her moorings and swung away from the pier into the river.

An involuntary cry of exultation broke from more than two hundred throats. The steamboat *Sampson* came alongside, made fast, and began to pilot the ship down the Narrows. The friends who crowded the wharf waved and called. A few friends and relatives had been allowed to remain on board to return with the pilot. As the ship moved majestically down the stream, her banners waving in the light breeze, Sam stood nervously watching for an intercepting Government boat. Minutes passed. At last the mouth of the Narrows was in sight; no boat had appeared. The *Sampson* paused, and those who had been allowed to remain thus far descended the ladder to return to shore. Sam saw many tearful farewells, but was so filled with worry about the Kendall deal that they did not touch him as they might have done. The last person down the ladder was Edward Kemble's father. Sam saw the lad fighting back his tears. When the last visitor was aboard, the *Sampson* pulled away. Voyagers on the *Brooklyn* still crowded the rail to wave to their loved ones. Sam watched as the tiny tug moved off upstream. Still no sign of a Government boat. With her topsails and jib spread to a NNW breeze, the *Brooklyn* sailed out into the ocean. Sam ran up to the bridge and gripped the Captain's shoulder.

"We're free! They didn't stop us," he exulted.

Richardson cackled in his dry way. "I had that Benson sized up as a big bag of wind, all the time," he said.

Chapter VIII

CERTAIN NOW that the voyage was under way with no possibility of interference, Sam went below to organize his forces. His two counselors, Isaac Robbins and E. Ward Pell, were called into conference and Isaac was given a stack of cards, to be distributed by nailing one on each stateroom door. These were the rules for conduct [15] on shipboard as drawn up by the three men earlier, which Sam had had printed before the press was dismantled. They stated that a bugle would blow at six in the morning, and an officer of the day would make the rounds of the staterooms to make sure that the occupants were arising. Each member must be dressed, washed, and his hair combed, before he emerged into the hall. Although a cook and a cook's helper had been hired to take charge of all meals, volunteer help was to be drafted each day to assist in their preparation. A corporal was to visit the staterooms after they were vacated for the day to make sure that they were clean, and that all clothes had been put in bags and stored away; he would also report those who were too ill to rise. The staterooms must be kept clean by their occupants and must be swept, and the beds made, by seven in the morning.

The women on kitchen duty were to set the long pine table in the hall so that the children could begin breakfast by eight in the morning. They must be through by eight-thirty so that the table could be cleared and prepared again for the adults, who would eat at nine-fifteen while the children played on deck or retired to the staterooms. By ten, breakfast must be finished so that the hall could be cleaned and made ready for whatever purpose it was to serve on that day—such as sewing, quilting, or cleaning. From ten until two in the afternoon the passengers must attend to the work of the company.

At two-thirty another meal was begun for the children, who were to start eating at three and must be finished by four, when the adults would sit down to eat. By five in the afternoon the hall must be clear again. From five until eight the stateroom doors must be left open for airing, and the passengers might gather in groups to sing or play games or "indulge in other innocent amusements." At eight o'clock in the evening a cold lunch would be set out on the long table for anyone who wished to partake, but by nine all diners must have finished and the room be thoroughly cleaned and prepared for the morrow. The preparation of meals was to be supervised by the cook, but the men and women of the company must help, and the women do all the cleaning.

Every Sunday morning, services were to be held at eleven o'clock; on deck, in warm weather, in the hall when it was cold. Every person must attend, dressed in his Sunday best; the men shaved and washed in a manner suitable for worship.

The three leaders were satisfied with their rules. While Robbins went about his task, Sam and Pell consulted as to whom they would delegate to the various duties for the first week, and at last drew up a satisfactory list. When Isaac returned, the three divided the duties among them to make sure that each task should be overseen by one of them. Sam was to confer with the Captain at all times and maintain contact between the ship's crew and the passengers. Robbins was to see that the animal pens were cleaned properly each day—that the animals were fed and the cows milked. He was not to do the work, but to make sure that it was done. Pell was to look after the children—see that they attended classes under the tuition of the elder Eager girl—and to check the work of the corporal and the officer of the day; a new one to be appointed each day.

Sam was here, there, and everywhere that first day, trying to get affairs on board down to a schedule. He had little time to see his own family and his baby son. Fanny Corwin had volunteered for the day to look after the children who were too small for school in one end of the hall; while lessons went on in the other, or rather, preparations were made by the elder Eager girl to begin them.

A pleasant relationship was established from the beginning between the Captain and his efficient first mate, and the voyagers; it continued to the end. The Captain had been wise in making it a rule that none of the crew members should mix with the Mormons, and he was strictly to enforce this rule during all the months of the voyage.

Ann Eliza was looked up to by the other members of the group because she was the wife of the leader, and she made the most of this advantage. She felt herself to be better than the others and held aloof from the beginning. Although she was forced to associate daily with the women of the company and sat with them in the hall to sew, she never joined in their conversations nor did she volunteer service to those who were ill, as the others did; especially Fanny, who was always looking after those in need. When it fell to her lot to do kitchen duty she made it plain that as wife of the leader she felt she should not be called upon for menial labor. Sam was asked to arbitrate the matter one day when it came to a crisis. The officer in charge laid his case before his leader in the hall, in front of all the company. Sam looked at Ann Eliza and waited for her to state her case.

"I am not going to peel potatoes or wait on tables. I never had to do it at home if I didn't want to, and I'm not going to do it here. After all I'm your wife, Sam Brannan, and you are the leader. You don't scrub out pig-pens nor do any other such filthy work. If you don't have to, then neither do I."

Sam looked at his counselors and at the set faces of the other women, who willingly did kitchen duty every day.

"I think you ought to do what the others do," he said.

"I won't," she said stubbornly.

"I don't know what to say," he admitted at last.

Everyone was embarrassed. Robbins spoke hurriedly. "I say, let's excuse Sister Brannan. As she says, she's the wife of the leader and it entitles her to some privileges."

The others agreed hurriedly and Ann Eliza turned and went to her stateroom. After that, she was left alone as much as possible. The other women plainly did not like her. But Ann Eliza didn't care. She didn't like them either.

It was beautiful, sunny January weather as the ship sailed down the coast, but most of these farmers and artisans had never before seen blue water and the motion soon overcame their desire to stay on deck. The children suffered less than their elders; more than fifty of them played about on the chilly deck while their parents lay retching below.

On the second day the bugle sounded an early reveille, and those who were able emerged from their staterooms to begin the regular routine. There were few passengers at meals that day.

On the night of the third day the barometer began to fall and the wind to howl.[16] Before darkness closed in the ship was bucking giant waves. Those on deck were ordered below, the hatches were battened down, and the ship braced herself for a hard blow. Sam remained beside the Captain, his feet steadied against the plunging of the vessel, loving the feel of a contest.

"Get below, Brannan. This is no weather for a bloomin' land-lubber. We'll ship water afore the night's gone," the Captain bellowed against the gale.

Sam laughed in the teeth of the wind, "Don't worry about me, Captain. I'm as good a sailor as you and a good deal less nervous."

"As a usual thing I'm not nervous," the Captain yelled, "but 'tis not my usual practice to carry passengers, and glad will I be when I've got them safe landed. I know what's ahead and you don't."

The scream of the wind increased as the water slapped first one side of the vessel and then the other and the ship rolled and wallowed. The fowl and animal pens had been covered with canvas and lashed more securely to the deck, but the cows bellowed mournful protest and the chickens scolded in discomfort.

The whole crew was on duty, and their orders came so fast that the men were hard put to carry them all out. Sails were furled, rigging tightened, and everything made secure. It was late when Sam went below to find his womenfolk violently sick and little Sammy fretting at the bonds that held him tightly in his bunk.

Sam fell asleep clutching the bar on his bunk so that he would not be tossed about. After he had been unconscious for a time he awoke with a sensation of flying. With a thud he came to a stop against a wall and slid to the floor. A moment later Ann Eliza landed on top of him with a cry of dismay. Sam helped her to her feet and half carried, half pulled her back into her bunk. As he turned around he collided with Fanny, who was clinging to a bunk-post.

"My head's busted wide open," she quavered above the roaring that filled the air.

"Hold on, Grandma, till I light a lamp," he bellowed. He was bumped and knocked in his search but finally managed to light it. He found Sammy still tied down and sound asleep. Then he helped Fanny back under the covers beside the baby and tied her in with a blanket. He was thrown violently against the wall several times before he succeeded in tying up Ann Eliza. Then he blew out the lamp, got back into bed, and fastened the ends of his blanket around him.

He was up early the next morning and found himself covered with bruises; he had also one or two open wounds where he had hit against corners or rough edges the night before. The women lay moaning in their bunks. After he had given each a drink of water he picked up his son, changed the child's wet night clothes, dressed him with difficulty, and took him out into the hall to get some breakfast. Little Sammy was delighted to be taken up, and crowed and laughed and played with his father. Sam found it necessary to resort to a crouch, his arms wrapped around the baby, to keep from being thrown headlong. He opened the stateroom door and made for the hall. There he found only a few young people and William Glover.

"Everyone is down sick this morning except us," William greeted him. "And we're a pretty-looking sight. Look at the bruises and wounds we all got!"

"Well, it could be worse," Sam said, looking over the young girls and lads and a few of the children who were gathered around the long table.

"Where's the cook and his helper this morning?" Sam asked.

"Sick," replied Augusta Joyce, a girl in her teens. "We did try to start breakfast, but nothing will stay on the stove. So we're eating hardtack. Want some?" She pushed the package down the table to him. Sam sent one of the children for a cup of water so that he could soak the hard biscuit for the baby to chew on. As they ate, Sam surveyed the bruised and swollen faces around the table. They all looked disheartened. At last he threw back his head and laughed.

"If you ain't the sorriest looking bunch I ever saw," he exclaimed. "What you all so glum about? Everything's all right."

Augusta Joyce grinned, and then one of the Glover girls poked her father in the ribs and said, "You laugh, too, Pa." Glover grinned in such a sickly way that everyone burst into laughter at his foolish expression.

"I know what let's do—let's sing!" Hettie Pell exclaimed.

"A good idea," Sam agreed immediately. "But first let's have prayers." He bowed his head and the others followed suit. Sam launched into a long prayer in which he reminded God that they were his chosen people, now in danger and needing his special care, and ended, "We know that you are looking after us; that you will not forget us; that you will guide us safely through these troubled waters just as Jesus guided the fisherman when he said to the waves, 'Peace! be still!' and the waters did subside. Our lives are in your hands and if it is Thy will that we reach a new Zion, it will be so. Amen."

The others echoed his "Amen," clinging to the table to keep from being thrown over as the ship rolled. As they lifted their heads they could hear running feet on deck. They had been hearing constant movement up there all night, but this noise seemed more pregnant with meaning than the others.

"What shall we sing?" Sam asked brightly.

" 'We're Going to California,' " Lizzie Winner suggested, " 'cause that is where we are going."

"You start it, Hettie," Sam directed. "Singing was your idea." Hettie started the song, and one after another the others joined in. They were singing lustily when they heard the hatch being opened. A moment later Captain Richardson came down the narrow ladder. He braced himself against the wall and stood facing them. The shriek of the wind outside filled their ears, until the hatch was suddenly closed and the sound fell away to its customary dull roar. They all stopped singing and stood waiting. The Captain's face carried bad tidings; he spoke as if wearied to the point of exhaustion. " 'Tis bad news I have for you. We may not outride this squall. Our ship is taking a fearful beating and I doubt that she can keep it up. I'm not wanting to alarm women and children, but 'tis only fair that you know the worst."

The young people looked at each other with fear in their eyes. The young women broke into frightened weeping, all still clutching the table for support.

Sam Brannan sat stock still, holding his son on his lap. Suddenly he smiled his endearing Irish smile. "Now, now, there's no cause for tears," he said heartily. "The Captain is only doing his duty as he sees it. He don't realize that we are God's chosen people and God is looking after us. Why, we're going on a mission, every one of us, and God would not spoil his own purposes by letting us drown. We have nothing to fear." He looked at the Captain. "Thank you for coming to tell us, Captain, but it was not necessary. You remember that the Lord told the waters to be still for the fishermen and the waves subsided. He will say it for us, too, when he is ready." He paused.

"Come on, all of you. Let's sing the next verse of 'We Are Going to California'! Start it, Lizzie," he said.

Again they broke into song. The Captain, dumfounded, stood watching them for a moment and then clambered back up the ladder and knocked on the door. It was opened for him and he went through, the sound of the wind again filling the room for an instant.

On the evening of the third day the waters began to calm, and by afternoon the ship was once more sailing a peaceful course. At sunset Sam was permitted to come up on the bridge with the Captain, who had just returned to duty after his first sleep in three days. He was searching the ocean with his long glass when Sam joined him, and handed the glass to Sam, pointing to a far speck on the eastern horizon. "Look yon where I'm pointing, Brannan. Do you see what looks like a far island?" Sam focussed the glass before he agreed that he could see what seemed to be a peak. "I'll wager you can't guess what land that is," Richardson said and Sam agreed that he couldn't.

"That's the Cape Verde Islands off the coast of Africa!"

"Africa!" Sam exclaimed. "You mean to tell me we were blown that far off our course?"

"Aye."

Sam looked long before he handed the glass back to Richardson. Then he plunged his hands deep into his pockets and stood surveying the majesty of this black ocean that swelled and streamed with the color of the storm still upon it. Sam studied the sturdy spars, which stood out like skeletons against the dark sky as the ship rose and fell. The scene was supremely beautiful and the Irish in him responded to its beauty. "I feel like the king of the world," Sam told himself, and exulted in the knowledge that puny men could conquer this savage force that moved and swelled about them.

The next day routine was resumed. Seasick people began to recover and came clamoring to the hall for food. Meals were served on schedule as the Negro cook and his helper once more took charge. Sam and his counselors, Robbins and Pell, spent the greater part of the day supervising the cleaning up of the passengers' section of the ship. Staterooms were inspected by the officers and ordered to be scrubbed; fresh straw was placed in the animal pens, and the canvases removed. The voyagers were ordered to keep out of the way of crew members who were cleaning up the debris left by the storm. Children played happily on deck again in a sun which became increasingly warm as the ship moved southward toward the summer waters of the southern hemisphere.

After the first week Sam ceased to eat at the community table. He joined the Captain's mess so that they could confer.

On Sunday Sam preached a sermon, and on the many Sundays that followed he alternated with his counselors and William Glover, Barton Mowry, and George Winner, or other members of the company who could and would deliver some sort of sermon.

The birth of a baby boy on board was an event for rejoicing, and when Sam performed the christening in an impressive ceremony on deck a few Sundays later, he solemnly named the child Atlantic.

Although Sam was willing that his two counselors should have a certain authority, he did not feel that either had the right to dictate policy, and when after a few weeks he discovered that Pell and two other men of the company were openly advocating the introduction of polygamy into their numbers, Sam took a firm stand. He called Pell—whose wife and two almost grown daughters accompanied him on the voyage—into council with Isaac Robbins.

"Pell," he said, "I told you before we started this journey that we would never have polygamy among us. I hear that you no longer agree with that decision and are using your influence to convince the members of the company that we should start practicing it. I forbid you to do this any more. I said we were not going to have any polygamy either on shipboard or when we get to our destination, and I meant it."

Pell looked at him for several moments and it was plain that he did not like Brannan's tone. Finally he spoke in suppressed anger, "Brannan, you may be the leader of this company; but, by God, you're not going to tell me what I can or can't do with my private life! If I want to talk polygamy or take a plural wife, it's none of your goddamned business. If polygamy was good enough for the Prophet it's good enough for me."

Sam looked across the table-top at Pell, who faced him in the small stateroom. "I said, no polygamy for you or anyone else. While you are a member of this company you'll do as I say, and you won't start polygamy among us because I won't let you. Joseph Smith never openly practiced polygamy, but even he couldn't stop the whirlwind that blew our people out of their homes when it was whispered that polygamy was part of our creed. We're having to make an exodus into the wilderness right now partly because some of our people were bound they would practice polygamy openly, against his advice. If we start it in this group we will be sowing the seeds of our own destruction. You know that as well as I do. Therefore, Brother Pell, you will cease this agitation or find yourself in trouble." Pell glared at him for a moment and then, rising, left the room.

Robbins looked anxiously at Brannan. "I don't think Pell will give in to you on this," he said nervously.

Sam laughed sharply. "He will," he said, and his lips were grim. "He will because I'll make him."

"I have reason to believe that the widow Eager, John's mother, has been listening to Brother Pell, and that she wants to become his second wife and let one of her daughters marry either Orrin Smith or Ambrose Moses," Isaac said. He added, "It would break their wives' hearts if either Moses or Smith done such a thing."

"Well it won't happen. You can set your mind at rest on that point," Sam said.

"What are we going to do about Elisha Hyatt and James Scott and Isaac Addison?" Robbins asked, turning to another vexation.

Sam's anger went down before this new problem and he rubbed his chin reflectively. "I don't know, Brother Robbins. Hyatt has been a thorn in my flesh since the first day I ever laid eyes on him. When we started signing up for this voyage he was among the first to put down his name and the very last to pay. He wouldn't have paid then if I hadn't publicly called him to account. He is a born hoodlum. He browbeats his wife and everyone else who will let him, and he hates the sight of work. He and Scott and Addison have been caught by the Captain twice playing cards with the deck hands. They won't work, and they've been drunk several times." He sighed.

"We ought to cut them off from the Church," Robbins suggested.

"Not yet awhile. I'll talk to them and labor with their rebellious spirits. For the sake of their families I'll try to be patient."

In April scurvy began to appear among the passengers. Each family had furnished its own food, but being land folk they had not known how to buy wisely for an ocean voyage and as a result the Mormon stores were sadly lacking in scurvy-resistant foods. The Captain had provided lemons and plenty of the necessary vegetables for himself and the crew, so that they did not suffer from the disease, and Sam, eating with them, was also spared. Elias Ensign was the first to fall ill; within a week he was dangerously infected. Eliza Ensign was next to contract the dread scourge. The two Ensigns died within a few days of each other and were buried at sea.

One after another the travelers began to show touches of scurvy, until almost everyone had it in some form. Six small children died, one after the other, as the ship neared the Horn.

The vessel ran up to the cape with a fair wind, then the great white sails took a west wind and ran to 60° south latitude in four days. Then the ship took a south wind. Sam had heard many a varied tale of the terrors and difficulties of rounding the Horn, and it was with a sense of dread that he awaited the ordeal. He stood beside the Captain day after day and watched the barometer and thermometer. It was mild on board at all times, the temperature registering no lower than 50° above zero. Daily the children came to their school in the hall and played on deck during their hours of leisure. They looked fairly well, except for the victims of scurvy in its more severe forms.

The *Brooklyn* took a south wind until she had made the proper longitude west of the cape, then with a fair wind she cut through waters which were neither dark nor cold nor dangerous. Far off on two different days they saw huge floating islands of ice, and in the vicinity of icebergs Sam noticed that the air was chill, while the temperature dropped to 30°. One morning, he was assured by the Captain that the Horn was safely passed. They had met no difficulties. With a fair wind the little ship sailed down the Pacific. Except for Silas Aldrich, near death from scurvy, and the wife of Isaac Goodwin, who was also very ill, everyone was happy in the expectation that they would land at Valparaiso within five days or so to go ashore, take on fresh food and water—of which they were so sorely in need—and rest their sea legs.

Though the water tanks were getting low, on the morning of the first of May Sam called all the company together on deck and apportioned out to each family a pan of water so that they might wash before landing among strangers. No laundering of clothes and little bathing had been possible since the ship had sailed three months earlier, and the voyagers welcomed the water and made a little celebration out of its use.

Sam walked about among the various groups, dropping a word here, a suggestion there. "The natives of Chile are sure going to be surprised to see such a fine-looking lot of Yankees show up among them," he said to John Eager, laughing.

"They sure will," the lad responded, vigorously scrubbing his ears, which were almost hidden by hair that came to his shoulders. "Outside the scurvy we look fairly well."

At mention of the scurvy Sam's eyes were troubled. "Silas Aldrich is dying," he said. "I don't suppose he'll last till sunset. Prudence Aldrich and their son and daughter are down too, and the way they worry about Silas isn't helping any of them. Too bad! If only we could get to land and have some fresh food we might save them. Sister Goodwin is getting worse, too, poor soul." He was thoughtful for a time as he looked far off over the water. Suddenly he leaned forward anxiously and pointed. "Look, John, there to the south it looks like another storm's brewing."

John whirled quickly and searched the blackness on the horizon. "It is, Sam. It is!"

With sunset a howling wind came upon them from the south. The *Brooklyn* was unable to keep her course with safety. She bucked and shifted, dipped and rose, fighting always away from the land to avoid the reefs. Everyone was locked below except Sam, and in one of the short intervals when he was allowed on deck during the three days the gale lasted, he opened the door of the Captain's cabin a crack to find giant green waves breaking over the small craft until it seemed as if she must surely founder. He saw three members of the crew wait for an interval between waves and then rush across the open spaces. Sam himself tried to make it to the galley and had just reached the safety of its refuge when the next enormous wave broke, all foaming and snarling. After that, Sam was content to stay below until such times as the Captain sent for him upon matters of business.

At the end of the third day the Captain retired to his cabin for the first time in many hours, and there he found Sam awaiting him in answer to his summons. Richardson sank wearily to a stool and passed his hand across his eyes.

"Aye, and I'm tired. Not one night's rest in three have I had."

"You look tired to death," Sam said. "Is the worst over yet?"

"Aye, the wind has hauled to the east. But we'll not be making the port of Valparaiso. We're too far off our course to land there like we planned."

Sam groaned. "Silas Aldrich has just died and Sister Goodwin will probably die this day. Six younguns have died of that cursed blight. If we don't make land soon, many another will die."

The Captain motioned him to silence as he leaned to search the chart, which lay spread on his desk. He laid a stubby finger on a spot on the map, north and west of the cape. "We'll likely make land tomorrow at this spot. We're nigh this group of islands."

"What islands are they?" Sam asked, as he leaned over the chart.

"They're the Juan Fernandez group that belongs to Chile. If you ever read the book *Robinson Crusoe* you've heard of these islands. That was where he was supposed to be shipwrecked."

Sam let out a sigh of relief. "Well, if it was good enough for Robinson Crusoe it ought to be good enough for us. At least it means that we'll find fresh water and food." He smiled suddenly. "That takes a load off my mind." He wasted no time in carrying the good news below.

At noon the next day the lookout shouted "Land ahoy!" from the crow's-nest, and the passengers scanned the horizon eagerly, to discover a distant blue cloud which, as the day passed, proved indeed to be land. At sunset the ship approached Cumberland Bay, on the north side of the island charted as Mas-a-tierra. There was the remnant of a once effective stone breakwater, now for the most part a crumbled mass. As the ship moved slowly into the quiet waters its course was held to a snail's pace as soundings were constantly taken. The passengers crowded the rail to see the beautiful tropical land they were approaching. A wide valley spread fanwise behind the harbor to end abruptly at the foot of a sheer mountain, whose topmost peak, El Yunque ("The Anvil"), rose over three thousand feet above the sea. Small streams coursed down its sides, making waterfalls which leaped from ledge to ledge and finally down to where mist-covered tropical greenery grew in tangled profusion. The open spaces on the land reaching back from the harbor were filled with fields of ripening wild oats, interspersed with woods of tropical trees. Ruins of buildings could be seen near the shore, but only a half-dozen human beings could be discerned standing on the beach, and these seemed to be mostly children. Darkness came before the anchor dropped. Early on the morning of May 4 the Captain's boat, with oarsmen, the Captain, the mate, and Sam, went ashore. The passengers were forced to await its return before disembarking. As the boat was pulled up onto the sand by one of the seamen, a dark-skinned man in ragged clothes approached them. In Spanish he greeted them. They shook their heads, and Sam spoke. The islander replied in a variety of English which was difficult for Sam and the others to understand.

Richardson, the mate, and Sam clambered out of the boat and began to ask the man questions. As they did so another dark-skinned man, two women, and four children emerged from a thatched hut in the background and came to stand where they could look and listen.

"Have you got fresh water here?" Richardson asked the man, who nodded eagerly and seemed happy to see them. He motioned toward a spring which was but a short way down the beach. "Spreeng, moch watair," he said.

"Firewood?" Sam asked. The man pointed to the left wing of the mountain as they stood facing it. "Moch wood," he agreed.

"Can we take what we need?" the Captain inquired, and the man nodded in his eagerness until it seemed he would shake his head loose, and he spread his arms wide in a gesture of welcome. The Captain turned toward the boat and motioned his mate forward. "See if you can talk this feller's lingo. I want to find out all I can about this place."

The mate began to speak Spanish and the man answered quickly, showing his teeth in a happy smile. The two talked for several minutes, and Sam and Richardson moved away to look at their surroundings. At last the mate joined them.

"This feller and that other man and their families are the only people that live on this island," he began. "Them and their wives and two children apiece. There used to be a lot of people live here. Then there was a convict settlement with more than two hundred prisoners and a governor and guards to look after them. This place is only twenty days' sail from Fuchywana, or some such funny-sounding place, but it's just a little north of Valparaiso, he says. Two things happened to ruin the island. First there was a great earthquake that destroyed the stone buildings and killed a lot of the convicts. The island sunk and then come up again, about fifty feet all told, he said. Those that lived up in the little valleys at the top of the mountain didn't get drowned and they stayed. Some of the convicts was up on top then, working on that road you can see traces of winding back and forth up the face of the cliff. Some of the people got disgusted and went back to Chile, but a pretty good-sized colony stayed.

"Then about six years ago a flotilla of Peruvians landed and destroyed everything that was left—burned the houses and sunk the canoes in the harbor. They carried away the convicts and scared the settlers so bad that a lot more give up and went home. Another earthquake four years or so ago drove off what was left. These two families live here all alone. They like it here with all this fruit and stuff growing wild. They say it was left by descendants of the people that were brought here by the Spanish when they fortified the island in 1767. They've got melons and apples and cherries and lots of fruit. He says we can have anything we want, from the wild turnips to the fruits and animals, but he says to watch out for the animals 'cause they're dangerous, they've run wild so long." [17]

Sam rubbed his hands with pleasure. "The first thing we got to do is get our folks ashore and let them eat some of this fresh food. That ought to stop the scurvy."

"Aye," the Captain agreed, and turned to his mate. "Go back and order the shore boats made ready and let the passengers come ashore." The mate went to do his bidding.

The rest of the day was a happy one for the voyagers, who wandered about this island paradise and explored its miniature world, which they learned was fifteen miles long and four wide, lying five hundred miles west of Valparaiso. Sam took Ann Eliza with him to examine the hideous ruins of the former prison, and she shuddered as he jumped far down into a hole which had once been a dungeon, where rusted chains still lay fastened to the stone walls.

Captain Richardson had discovered that the bay contained several varieties of fish—sardines and hake being the most numerous. When Sam returned from foraging about with his wife, the two men put their heads together to decide how best to garner food for the remainder of the voyage. Ultimately Sam organized fishing parties to catch fish, which others salted in great barrels. The shore boats traveled back and forth carrying fresh water to fill the two large tanks, and the mate stopped to talk to Sam about the water situation. "Brannan, we were lucky when we landed here instead of at Valparaiso. It costs a dollar for every thirty gallons of fresh water a ship buys from the water boats in the harbor there. You can figger what it would have cost us for this water that we're getting here for nothing."

Sam looked at the mate piously. "I've been telling you fellers for a long time that us Mormons are the Lord's chosen people. He looks after us. He saved us from certain death in that Atlantic storm, and now he's led us to a place where we can get the supplies we so surely need, for nothing."

"Well, I don't know about that," the mate laughed. "But I do know that we'll have eighteen thousand gallons of water aboard when we get through, and getting it for nothing is saving us a pretty penny."

On the second day at Mas-a-tierra Sam had to stop ordinary labors to bury Sister Goodwin, who had finally died from the effects of scurvy. Silas Aldrich had been buried at sea, to the great sorrow of his family, who with other scurvy sufferers were already quickly recovering from the disease now that they had plenty of fresh fruit and vegetables. It was with some sense of relief that Isaac Goodwin and his six children followed their beloved dead ashore, to a known grave.

At the foot of the mountain, in a little clearing surrounded by cork oak and myrtle trees, the Mormons gathered to show the last honors to their sister. Sam Brannan, dressed in his elder's black broadcloth, preached a sermon—it was the first Mormon service ever to be held on a Pacific island.

After the funeral ceremony the voyagers went back to their happy roaming over the valley and lower hills, eating all they could hold of fruits, melons, onions, and turnips. Sickness and death were to be little known on the latter part of the voyage, which from Mas-a-tierra on was more of a pleasure cruise than the stern pioneer undertaking it had been so far.

For almost a week they remained on the island, resting, working, and eating. Sam was everywhere, as usual, supervising the needs of his charges. And when on a sunny day the *Brooklyn* weighed anchor and started slowly out of Cumberland Bay, the island's eight inhabitants stood sadly to watch them depart.

Over a smooth sea, only pleasantly rumpled into lapping waves, the ship traveled before a wind which sent it swiftly toward the Sandwich Islands and Honolulu. Daily the children did their lessons and played on the deck; the men and women went about their tasks, resting in the late afternoon and visiting among themselves. The crew was still kept carefully away from the Mormons, not even being allowed to lounge on deck where they might surreptitiously flirt with a pretty girl.

It was during this peaceful Pacific voyage that Captain Richardson spoke to Sam about his charges.

"Brannan," he said one morning as Sam came to eat breakfast with him. " 'Tis an unpleasant duty I've set myself this morning. Strange things have been going on at nighttime on this ship. The crew is in turmoil. It's undermining their morale."

"What is?" Sam asked.

"The goings on of the Eager woman. She is consorting with Pell and with Smith and with Moses. They meet secretly on the deck and whisper. Aye, and the men on watch report worse. 'Tis a disgrace. I'll not answer for what my men, who are shut up on this vessel without women, will be doing if it is not stopped."

"You mean that the Eager woman is carrying on with three men?"

"I'll not be saying that. But she's hatching a plot with three of them and consorting with at least one of them."

"How long has this been going on?" Sam asked grimly.

"Ever since we left Juan Fernandez Islands. I waited to speak hoping they would call a halt. But there's mischief afoot there."

"I'll stop it," Sam said, "and that right suddenly, or know the reason why."

Sam went down the steep stairs to the hall. Ann Eliza and her mother, with the baby, were at tasks there. He bellowed for Isaac Robbins, and when at last Isaac came running, Sam told him to fetch Orrin Smith, E. Ward Pell, Ambrose Moses, and Lucy Eager. When the four stood before him in his stateroom, Sam lashed out at them with bitter words.

"I stand shamed before you folks," he said angrily. "The Captain tells me that you, Pell—and you, Sister Eager—have gone mad in search of the lusts of the belly. I told you, Pell, that we would have no polygamy in our company, and you have gone against my advice." He glared at all of them, his glance traveling from one face to another. "You, Orrin Smith, with a wife and six children, the last a babe in arms—what right have you got to be casting lustful glances on other women? And you, Moses, with a wife and four children—with two daughters almost grown—you ought to be ashamed of yourself, the lecherous way you've been acting!" He placed his closed fists on his hips. "I tell you here and now, this polygamy business will stop or I'll cut you all off from the Church. I'd do it now except for your families. They'll have suffered enough, with the disgrace you are bringing on them, when the whole company learns the way you've been acting. But just you let me hear of any more of your shenanigans and out you all go, lock, stock, and barrel. Now get out, all of you, before I lose my temper!"

With angry eyes the three men and the woman glared back at him, but none denied his charges. When he ordered them to leave they did so defiantly, and Sam knew when they had gone that he had not yet conquered the problem. This was borne out within a few days, when the Captain exclaimed impatiently, "Blood and thunder, Brannan, can you not handle your own people? By the Lord, you'll do it soon, or I'll do it for you!"

The impetuous Samuel for once counseled patience. "There's little we can do, Captain, while we're all locked together on this ship. I'll speak to them again, but I don't want to cut them off from the

Church and make outcasts of them before we land if I can help it. They've got families, and God knows they're suffering enough without having everyone on shipboard against them. And I have every desire to keep my company a united and happy one."

The Captain turned away grumbling, "Hell's bells, I'll have trouble with my crew if these licentious goings-on don't stop soon!"

Sam smiled impudently. "You can control your crew, Richardson, a hell of a lot easier than I can control three men and a woman or two."

Although Samuel did not officially remove Pell as his first counselor, he no longer consulted with him, and Pell's place was filled by William Glover.

On the twenty-fifth day of June, 1846, a little more than six weeks after quitting Mas-a-tierra, the stout little ship sailed past Diamond Head into the waters of Honolulu Bay. The island of Oahu, King Kamehameha's domain, lay in the vast expanse of the Pacific like an emerald on an iridescent blue curtain.

Gratefully the voyagers again set foot on land. They found that Honolulu was hardly more than a transplanted New England village, for Protestant missionaries had been using it as a proselyting-ground for over twenty years, and they had been successful in covering the beautiful nakedness of a large proportion of the natives, while white men's vices ran rampant in the land. In the harbor were gathered vessels of every maritime nation, the American whaler predominating, for these islanders were natural sailors and proficient at the work a whaler demanded. But the whaling industry was already on the decline.

Sam and the Captain walked up the little main street together, and Sam exclaimed at the beauty of the land. Huge cliffs towered high into the air, topped by crowns of clouds from which misty waterfalls could be seen descending part-way, until they dissolved entirely. Leaving the Captain to report to port authorities, Sam walked beyond the town until he came to a mass of tropical ferns growing amid trees and flowers the like of which he had never seen before. Now and then he met a native—girls in grass skirts with flower leis about their necks, men in loin-cloths and leis, elderly women in Mother Hubbards and leis. It was a long time before Sam returned to the ship, for he was exploring this Eden with a view to the future. "I'll come back here some day to live," he told himself. "This is a garden spot if I've ever seen one, and there's money to be made from it."

When he returned to the wharf he found George Winner and several others of the company talking together in a group as they waited for one of the shore boats, which were plying back and forth with passengers. As Sam came up, George motioned him forward and William Glover spoke up. "I notice that there's almost as many missionaries as natives. There are a few Scotch sugar cane plantation owners that hang around town here, and the businessmen might be anything from French to Swede. There's an American Government hospital over there on the edge of town, too. They tell me it's kept here to take care of seamen on American whalers when they're sick or injured. But whaling is almost at an end now, and a feller was telling me that they ain't had more than a dozen patients a year in there the last few years, but still the Government is keeping that great big place open and paying a staff of doctors and nurses to keep it running."

"What for?" Barton Mowry asked.

Sam laughed. "That's easy to figure out. Wouldn't you like to keep a Government job with big money and live here in this beautiful place, if you could?"

"Well, sure," Mowry replied.

"That's the answer. The people that work here and get paid for it probably send back reports to Washington that they are doing a big business. Washington believes them, or at least pretends to, and keeps sending them funds, and the staff gets to stay."

Barton spat distastefully, "Graft! I believe we got the graftingest nation on earth."

The *Brooklyn* was maintained at Honolulu for a week to permit discharge of the freight she carried for this port; to take on fresh water and food supplies, and to give everyone a complete rest.

The Honolulu newspaper *The Friend* appeared a day or so after their arrival with a flattering account of the visitors. The editor wrote that Captain Richardson spoke well of his passengers; said they were

THOMAS BRANNAN, SR.

A painting of Sam's father in his farmhouse in Maine by Grainger

Courtesy F. C. Deering

"THE LAST MUSTER," BY GRAINGER

It was customary for the militia to get together once every year for drill. There were always food and drink to sell on the side. The old gentleman, half doubled up in the corner, is Sam's father, Thomas.

quiet and orderly and that they were attending daily to their religious duties while in port.[19]

Within a few days a United States frigate, the *Congress*, put into port. Commodore Robert Field Stockton was in command. It was announced that he was on his way to the "Coast," as everyone in the islands referred to California shores. Sam was immediately filled with concern. Did this mean that Stockton would search his vessel and perhaps prevent them from landing where they had planned? No word had reached him as to the fate of the contract that Brigham Young was to sign with Kendall. Well, at any rate they would find no arms, for he had brought none with him for the company. There were many Allen revolvers, but these belonged to individuals and not to the group. Eventually the Commodore sent for Sam, who went to him hoping that the company was not to be turned back at the final stage of its journey.

"I see you fly a flag with the word 'Oregon' on it," the Commodore began. Sam nodded.

"You know, of course, that war is imminent between the United States and Mexico?"

"No!" Sam exclaimed. "Then we can land anywhere we want to, without danger of violating the treaty between our country and Mexico?"

"Yes. And my advice to you would be to land on San Francisco Bay, so that you can take up arms for your country if need be."

Sam rubbed his chin and pretended to weigh the matter. "We might consider it," he said. "I'll talk it over with my company. In the meantime, we'd like to have you visit our ship."

"I intend to. I will inspect every vessel in the harbor," the Commodore said. "That is my job."

On July 3, 1846, Commodore Stockton boarded the *Brooklyn* and talked to the Mormons, trying to ascertain whether they were friendly or treacherous.[20] At last he seemed satisfied that they were friendly and turned to Sam.

"I would advise you folks to arm yourselves before you land anywhere. You seem to have only a few derringers or outmoded arms. I understand there are some condemned army muskets on sale here cheap. Buy them."

Captain Richardson invited the Commodore and Sam to his cabin, where they could talk at length. As the officer sat down he asked Sam what his decision was about landing on San Francisco Bay.

"Well, I've talked it over with our men and they are in favor of the idea. The only thing is, we've been treated pretty unfairly by our Government. We've been chased from pillar to post, and when we ask for justice we don't get it. However, we'd be willing to land at that town on the shore of San Francisco Bay, providing you give us permission to raise the flag when we get there and hold the town for the United States. You see, if we get there first and take the town from the Mexicans in the name of the United States, we'll be the American founders of the town and we'll have a right to dictate policy to them that come after. If we're going to fight to get land for our country we at least want to be in a position to hold it for ourselves, and not have it taken from us by the first rowdy set of gentiles that drifts in there. We want to be in control or we don't want to be there at all."

Stockton nodded. "I see your point, and it is a good one." He paused thoughtfully for a time and then added, "I don't see any reason why, if you folks take the town and hold it in the name of the United States, you shouldn't keep control of it. However, it will take more than fifty or sixty men to hold it for any length of time, for new-comers will be coming in steadily."

"Oh, we'll have reinforcements. The main body of Saints is coming out from Nauvoo; they're on the way right now. They will get there soon after we do, and then we'll have a whole Mormon commonwealth. Our hope is to build up our own colony and make it so strong that the gentiles can't dispossess us again."

"Well, that ought to be possible 'way out in the wilderness. Even if the United States wins over Mexico, which she will, our Government will never have much use for land that is so far from the capital of the nation. All we want it for is its natural wealth and there'll never be any great numbers of people come out there. I see no objection to you folks doing what you plan. The Government won't interfere with you much—if you get there first—if you don't try to set up a nation of your own."

Sam smiled cheerfully. "We've no desire to set up an empire. We only want a home. With my own hands I'll fly the first American flag over that Mexican town."

The Commodore spoke gravely. "I don't think you'll win from the Mexicans if you don't get an army of some kind. Organize your men and start drilling them, and get some muskets for them to use."

"We will. I'll buy the muskets today," Sam said; and he did.

On the Fourth of July, 1846, the newly organized company stood at attention with their muskets, which had cost three and four dollars apiece. Aside from these there were fifty Allen's revolvers. Each man had fixed himself up a military cap, and the women already had material which they planned to sew into uniforms for their fighting men. Robert Smith and Samuel Ladd had had army experience, and they were put in charge of drill. At noon, after ragged maneuvers, the men stood at attention and fired a volley in honor of the national day.[21]

On Sunday, the Mormons repaired to a little clearing beyond the town, and with the blue Pacific gleaming and sparkling behind him, to the music of its rhythmic pounding Sam preached his second sermon on Pacific territory. This was to him only a part of his destiny, this carrying of the gospel into the far corners of the earth.[22]

On Monday he called a conference on deck of all adult members of the company. He outlined to his listeners the program they were to follow, now that they could openly admit their destination to be on the shores of San Francisco Bay—a town whose name they did not even know. He suggested that they form themselves into a company, a plan which was welcomed. One loyal follower suggested that this company be named "Sam Brannan and Company," and by a unanimous vote this was done. It was decided that the company should be arranged in divisions: one group to take charge of all agricultural pursuits; another to take charge of building—to set up mills, stores, and shops, when they had come to their new home; and finally a third section to handle merchandising. All the money belonging to the group was to be kept in a common fund, and Samuel Brannan and his two advisers were to have charge of spending it for the common good.

The proceeds from all labor were to go into the common fund for three years. If any person wanted to withdraw funds for private use he would have to petition for them and secure the whole company's approval of the withdrawal. When the organization was finally completed, Samuel asked the company to approve the replacement of E. Ward Pell as counselor by William Glover, but they were not willing.

"Brother Pell is an able worker and an intelligent man. I'm satisfied with him," John Horner said.

Sam nodded. "What you say is true, Brother Horner, but our next order of business will reveal to all of you why I want to make this change officially, a change which took place unofficially sometime ago. I have put off as long as I could bringing this scandal to your attention because I thought that by keeping it quiet and reasoning with the parties involved I could stop it. But this has not proved to be the case, and so, as I said before, I reluctantly bring it to the attention of all of you." He paused and took a deep breath.

"Three of our members, E. Ward Pell, Ambrose Moses, and Orrin Smith, have all been party to a plot to start the practice of polygamy among us. In fact, one of these men is practicing it. Pell has approached all of you men at one time or another, preaching polygamy, and because you refused to listen to him you believed that the idea stopped there. I feel especially bad about telling you these things today because Brother Orrin Smith and his wife have a very sick baby, and as you all know, we have given them enough money from the common fund to stay here in Honolulu with their baby and the other children until the baby gets well. But the other two brothers are here, and so is Sister Lucy Eager, who has lent a willing ear to their arguments. I have tried to stop them from carrying on with this idea, but I have been unsuccessful. I wish that you folks would now express your feelings about the matter. You have the floor."

George Winner arose quickly and condemned without reservation any acceptance of polygamy among them. William Glover, Jerusha Fowler, the three Kittleman brothers—all impatiently awaited their turn to denounce a belief in the practice of polygamy. At last Pell arose, his face flushed with anger, and Sam gave him the floor.

While Pell tried to justify himself, Moses sat with downcast eyes beside his wife, whose face was filled with suffering. The widow Eager watched them all defiantly.

"Polygamy is part of our creed," Pell began. "Joseph Smith had a revelation about it in Nauvoo, and he himself practiced it and gave others permission to practice it. If you deny us the right to practice it here, Sam Brannan, you deny us the right to live our religion as it was revealed to us by the Prophet before his death."

William Stout was on his feet instantly. "You say that as a fact, but you can't prove it," he shouted. "No man will ever make me believe that Joseph Smith sanctioned any man's living with two or three women at the same time. I'd leave the Church before I'd believe such wickedness."

"Well then, you live your religion as you see it and I'll do the same thing," Pell replied hotly. Sam held up his hands for silence, his voice thundering with authority.

"We are not going to have dogfights here about what our religion is and what it is not. I am leading this company and I will lead it in the way the majority votes to be led. We don't want polygamy among us. If we allow it we will be hounded and persecuted by our gentile neighbors. Therefore we will not tolerate it. For the good of all of us, you who don't want to agree will have to. If you persist in your wicked designs, I will cut you off from the Church. I have the authority to do it, and believe me when I say that I will. Now are you folks ready to confirm my appointment of William Glover as my second counselor? All in favor say aye." The chorus of assent swelled and rolled over the sunlit waters of the islands.

After the meeting had adjourned, as Sam was making his way to go below a young man, a stranger, approached him.

"My name is Henry Harris," he introduced himself. "I am a seaman out of work right now, but I have some money saved up and I want to get to the Coast. Will you let me sail with you folks tomorrow?"

"Why not wait for another boat?" Sam asked inquisitively eyeing the young man, who flushed under his scrutiny. He did not look Sam in the eye as he replied, "Well, I'm kind of stuck on a girl in your company, and if you don't have any objections I'd like to tag along."

Sam laughed aloud as he clapped the boy on the shoulder. "Well, I guess if you pay your fifty dollars into the common fund there won't be any objection to your coming along. Maybe we'll end up by making a Mormon out of you."

"Maybe," the young man said with a sickly grin.

When the *Brooklyn* sailed out of the tropical waters of Honolulu Bay, that nestled beneath the towering peaks of Oahu—fern-covered and beautiful—it left behind the family of Orrin Smith, whose baby was to die within a few days. As the voyagers turned their faces to to the east and north their hearts were heavy with anxiety, for they did not know what awaited them on the Mexican coast. As they watched the daily musket-drill the women sat patiently sewing the uniforms of the *Brooklyn* brigade, and often sighed and longed for the quiet and security of New York or New England villages.

Chapter IX

AFTER TWO WEEKS of bearing toward the coast the voyagers became afflicted with almost uncontrollable uneasiness. They did not know what destiny faced them in possibly hostile Mexican waters. The nearer they came to their destination, the more uncertainty hung in their minds. They had heard that an old Mexican fort faced the strait through which they must pass to reach the Bay of San Francisco, and it seemed possible that they might be blown to bits by its bristling cannon. The only one of all the souls on the *Brooklyn* who never appeared down-hearted or discouraged was Sam Brannan. He was constantly about, stopping to tell a funny story to a group of his devoted male followers, passing the time of day with the women who were sewing, or overseeing the work of the two Negro cooks. He joked with the crew members too, as he passed them at work, and this they appreciated, for he was the only Mormon with whom they were allowed to speak. Finally, he held daily conferences with Captain Richardson, who maintained a continuously pessimistic outlook about the entire voyage. He was not only the last word in authority to his crew, but whenever he felt that Sam was not being firm enough with his followers he demanded a change, and always got it, for on the boat his was the higher authority. One morning at breakfast he hammered the table with his knife-handle in excited indignation.

"Blood and thunder, Brannan! I'm losin' my patience. This Eager widow woman and your Elder Pell are still up to mischief yet and it's got to stop. 'Tis not good for men without women to be subject to the sights some of them have seen."

"I warned them at Honolulu," Sam said, suddenly grim.

"You'll stop them, Brannan, or I'll do it for you."

That afternoon Sam called his counselors and the three recalcitrant members into a stateroom. He motioned Lucy Eager to a bench and the two men to a bunk. He and his assistants sat on a long bench facing them. Sam leaned forward and spoke earnestly, looking into the faces of first one and then another.

"In spite of the warning I gave you in Honolulu the Captain tells me you are carrying on something scandalous; that you are practicing polygamy among us." They looked at him, but none of them made reply. After a moment Sam continued, "My counselors and me have decided to cut you off from the Church. Take notice that you are now disfellowshipped."

Pell arose quickly and spoke. "You mean that we are not going to get a hearing before the rest of the company, and a vote; that you think you can cut us off in this high-handed manner?"

"Exactly. I hold full authority for such an act, and I am the only one who can baptize you into this company or throw you out. I will this day post a notice in the hall notifying the rest of the company of our action."

"I won't be bound by any such action," Pell retorted.

"You'll have to be. On this ship I am the law as far as our company goes. If I tell our folks to have no more to do with you, they'll have no more to do with you. You'll soon find that out."

Moses leaped to his feet. "How about the money I put in the common fund. Do I get that back?"

"No. You put your money in the common fund and you've drawn out whatever you've needed for yourself and wife and half a dozen younguns for months, just like we've all done. No man alive could say whether you've got anything left or not. We now owe and will owe the Captain thousands of dollars yet on our passage fee, and we still have port charges to pay. Whether you're a part of this company or not, you are still an expense to us. When we land we will give you a just share of the provisions that are left. That's all we can do."

"To hell with you and everyone in the whole goddamned Church," Moses said and strode out of the room. Pell followed him without saying another word.

The widow Eager sat with downcast eyes but as soon as the men left she arose falteringly and looked at Sam. "I'm sorry for you, Lucy Eager," he said. "But I'm sorrier for your family. Why you've brought this disgrace on them I'll never understand. Why, with those two lovely girls of yours and two fine sons, I'd have thought you'd have avoided polygamy like the plague!"

Her back stiffened. "The only difference between you and me is that I ain't a hypocrite. I believe in polygamy and I'm willing to practice it free and aboveboard, and I'd have done it, too, if you'd stopped your meddling. Why you done that, I don't rightly know either; for there's them that's told me you've got more than one wife, only you won't admit it."

Sam flushed but sat looking directly into her eyes. "Whoever told you that, Sister Eager, is a liar." He paused and then asked, "Who's second wife are you? Moses', Pell's, or Smith's?"

"It's none of your business," she replied and stalked from the room. Sam sighed and turned to Robbins.

"Go round up Elisha Hyatt, James Scott, and Isaac Addison, and bring them down here. We might as well give them another warning while we're at it."

After a time Robbins ushered the three men into the stateroom. Sam motioned them to the bunk and they sat down awkwardly.

"Men," Sam began, "I've called you down here to try to reason with you. You've been guilty of playing cards with members of the crew strictly against the Captain's orders, sneaking down into the fo'c'sle at night. You've got likker hid some place and you keep guzzling that against all advice and even orders. Not one of you has done your daily stint the way it ought to be done. This is the last time I'm going to talk to you. You'll either mend your ways or we'll kick you out of the Church. You, Elisha Hyatt, have caused me nothing but grief since the first day I ever laid eyes on you. You were one of the first to sign up for passage and the very last to bring your money in, and then only when I chided you in public for your lax ways. You don't obey orders and you treat your family shameful. The other two of you ain't much better. The three of you are a disgrace to our whole company; you give us all a bad complexion with the crew and with the people we've met on this voyage. Either you'll heed this last warning and mend your ways, or when we land we'll have no more of you."

They sat looking at him with venom in their eyes, but none of them replied. "All right, you can go now," Sam said at last, and they got up and ambled from the room, Hyatt muttering under his breath.

During the next two weeks the disfellowshipped members were avoided by the rest of the company; the women would have none of

Lucy Eager, and the men had as little as possible to do with Moses or Pell. The families of these unfortunates, however, were treated as usual. The wives and children of the men came regularly to service and joined in the daily work, and no word of censure was said to them. Lucy tried to keep her little family to herself, but the two youths and two girls, though somewhat bitter at the treatment their mother received, still did not withdraw from the others.

It was warm on deck now, for July was drawing to a close. Sam stood on the bridge with the Captain one morning and looked eastward into a gray haze.

"There's land behind that fog," the Captain said. "But we'll likely not be seeing what it looks like for a time yet."

For an entire day the ship rode north, always skirting the low-lying gray cloud. Now and then the mist would lift enough for them to catch glimpses of cliffs and pines. On the morning of the thirtieth of July they saw a wide break in the fog, and water beyond it. "That's the bay we're looking for," the Captain shouted and gave the order which turned the ship in toward land. As the little ship sailed slowly into the Golden Gate—so recently named by John Frémont—it passed beyond the fog, although long fingers of it moved along the crests of the hills on either side. Inside the ocean belt of fog the land was clear and colorful in the early morning sunshine. The passengers crowded the rail, silently observing the view. To the left of the strait were forbidding cliffs; to the right a curving shore line with rolling hills; and on the point that projected farthest into the strait stood an adobe building. It looked small at this distance.

"That will be the old Mexican fort filled with cannon," Richardson said to Sam. " 'Tis likely they will fire a volley as soon as we pass within range. Get your people below until the danger is past."

Sam went down on deck and herded his charges below. A little frightened, they obeyed his order. Silently the ship slipped through the choppy water. The Captain kept his glass trained on the building watching for signs of movement about it, and Sam stood tensely beside him. Like hours the minutes went by, while they watched for a puff of smoke. The current forced them to pass slowly in front of the building, which loomed massive when the ship was close below it.

" 'Tis strange," the Captain said at last to Sam. "There's no signs of life there at all. I think it's deserted."

Sam breathed a great sigh of relief. "I don't know how God in his infinite wisdom saw fit to remove this danger from our path, but whatever his reason I'm God-awful thankful."

He went down on deck, threw open the hatch and shouted, with joy: "Come on up, all of you! There's no danger after all!"

They crowded on deck and ran for the rail to see what this new land looked like at closer quarters. Ann Eliza, with the baby, came to stand beside Sam as the scene unwound itself before their eyes. The ship moved slowly into the inner harbor. Rounded hills rose, tier on tier, on all sides of the bay. They were brown, in the faded verdure of early autumn, and those on the far horizon seemed to stretch into infinity. The hills near by were bare except for patches of scrub oak and some chaparral, and the sere autumn grass. Long lines of soldier pelicans winged their slow, measured flight above the foamy crests of the waves.[23] In the center of the bay lay a bleak, treeless island shaped like half an egg, and on its top were the graying walls of an old dungeon. When the sheer cliffs of the left wall of the strait were passed, small islands could be seen dotting the sparkling waters of the bay to the north. The ship veered slightly southward to make for Yerba Buena cove, passing the high rounded hill named Loma Alta, and finally commanding a view of the inner harbor. The sight which caught Sam's eye was a Yankee man-of-war, and beyond it on the shore he saw a long adobe building, perched on the side of a hill. In front of it was a tall flagpole. Sam's eyes sought the flag, and in the ever-present breeze he saw—the Stars and Stripes! He stared incredulously for a moment, then turned to his wife. "Do you see what I see?" he demanded.

"The American flag!" she exclaimed.

"Well, I'll be damned!" he exploded. "There's that damned flag!" Turning, he went swiftly to the Captain and with indignation pointed out the flag of his country. The Captain looked, and then grinned. "Well, it's evident that the war is started and the United States has taken possession."

Sam took off his cap and threw it on the deck. "Well, I'll be a son of a bitch," he bellowed. "Commodore Stockton promised me that I could be the first to plant the flag on this spot. If us Mormons could have been the first to run up the flag, we could have had our own way here. As it is, the gentiles have taken over and we'll have to live their way or go off in the wilderness by ourselves. I'm not happy about it, I can tell you that. I'm not happy!"

"Don't take it so hard, Brannan," the Captain urged. "There can't be many gentiles here. This is Mexican land, with likely only a few white men other than sailors and marines. They won't be here long and then you'll have the land to do as you please with. I notice that man-of-war is named *Portsmouth*. Likely it was sent here as part of the fleet to take over for the United States. When their job is done they will no doubt sail back to the states to other business."

Sam felt a little mollified as he slowly picked up his cap and dusted it off before putting it on his head. At that instant he heard an alarming sound. "Listen," he said quickly, "I hear the piping of the bosun's whistle and drums are beating to quarters on that man-of-war. I hope they don't fire on us." They saw the angry muzzles of the *Portsmouth* train upon them, and the men run to their stations. But as the *Brooklyn* continued to move slowly in, the warship relaxed its hostile preparations; the happy faces of their countrywomen had become obvious to these exiled service men. The girls and women waved and called to them, and even the grimness of duty could not prevent the sailors from showing their pleasure.

Slowly the *Brooklyn* came to anchor in company with a gray old whaler, in port to take on supplies—also flying the colors of the United States.

Sam went back to join Ann Eliza, and they stood together surveying the town which was to become their new home. It was an ugly, bleak region of sand hills covered with sparse vegetation.[24] Shacks were scattered over the numerous hills; shacks and shanties which leaned away from the constant ocean wind. The wide arc of the long sandy beach was a lonely place; at one spot lay a stack of hides ready for shipment, while beyond were the skeletons of a few slaughtered cows, whose flesh had probably been used for meat. There were a few adobe cabins and several small wooden buildings, widely scattered and set back from the water. Sand hill after sand hill stretched to the far horizon. A donkey plodded dejectedly along a crooked trail beneath a towering bundle of wood. A few dark-skinned loungers lazed upon the beach and nothing seemed to astonish or arouse them.

On the water front was an old adobe warehouse, almost dipping its toes in the water, and far back on one of the high hills was a giant windmill whose arms flapped with tattered canvas like an aged scarecrow. The shanties and cabins faced in all directions and might have been dropped by a vagrant wind.

Ann Eliza shivered and held the baby close. "I don't think I'm going to like it," she muttered.

"It's not good to look at, that's a fact," Sam agreed, and added optimistically, "Maybe when we get in there and work a little and plant a few seeds, it will look better."

"I doubt it," she said. "I wish we'd stayed in New York and never come on this fool's errand."

At that moment Sam saw a boat putting out from the *Portsmouth*. He watched the oarsmen steer straight for his own vessel. After a time a sailor came aboard and a few moments later Richardson motioned Sam to join them. "Brannan, get your counselors and come with me and the mate. The captain of the *Portsmouth* wants us to explain ourselves."

Sam called Robbins and Glover and they all descended into a *Brooklyn* shore boat and were rowed to the man-of-war. They were taken straight to the captain's quarters. Captain John B. Montgomery rose and shook hands with each of them as they introduced themselves. Then he motioned them to chairs and waited for them to explain their presence in these waters. Richardson showed his ship's papers and referred everything to Sam, who lost no time in telling the purpose of the voyage. Montgomery listened to his whole story in silent understanding, and when Sam had finished he said, "You have my permission to carry out your plans."

"Thank you," Sam said. "There's one thing I'd like to know, Captain Montgomery," he added. "When did you hoist the flag over this town?"

"Three weeks ago. On July 9."

"I'm disappointed," Sam explained. "Commodore Stockton told me in Honolulu that I could be the first American to hoist our flag over this land."

"Too bad," responded Montgomery in a professional tone. "We beat you to it. And by the way, Brannan, you will instruct your Mormon military unit to join our forces here. All your arms and ammunition must be put at our disposal. They will be stored in the armory near the custom house on the plaza. Your men will drill with our regular forces every morning, and if the town is attacked by the Mexicans every man of you will have to fight in our defense."

Sam nodded in agreement. "Yes, I can agree to that. By the way, where are your barracks?"

"On the plaza. We have room there for a few of your single men for a few days, if you have any trouble finding quarters."

"Well, we can certainly use a few extra quarters for our people, from the looks of the town. It don't look like there's enough houses in the whole town for just our company, not to mention the people that are already living in 'em."

"You're right, there aren't," Montgomery agreed.

Richardson interrupted. "There's just one thing puzzling me, Captain Montgomery. Why are there no soldiers at the old Mexican fort? It commands the strait and your forces could hold off any attack by sea."

Montgomery laughed. "We have no fear of attack by sea. You will find the Mexicans poor fighters. We took the town without any firing or bloodshed. We have little to fear in the way of land attacks and nothing at all by sea. Anyway, Colonel John Frémont took it upon himself a few weeks ago to take a company up to the old fort and spike the cannon. We brought them here to Yerba Buena to set up in a garrison to command the inner harbor, but we've found it no easy task to put them in condition again." He arose. "Well, gentlemen, I know you are anxious to land and night is coming on. I think we can say good-day." They rose and shook hands again all round and the little company went back to the *Brooklyn.*

Richardson ordered the shore boats made ready, and when they were manned he and his mate took one of them ashore to present the ship's papers properly at the custom house. The other boat was left for Sam and his group of picked men, who were going ashore to make arrangements for the landing of the whole company on the morrow and also to find what accommodations could be had. Everyone was anxious to land, but as evening would soon be upon them they contented themselves with one last night on board before disembarking.

Sam and his men were rowed past the bow of the *Portsmouth*, to step ashore on the sand at a spot which, in another year, was to become the foot of Clay Street. This was a high-tide landing place. Sam sent Winner, Glover, Robbins, and Stout, to call at the various homes and see how many of the company could be accommodated, while he himself went first to the custom house to assist the Captain with the customs official. Afterward he walked about the streets looking at everything with curious eyes and stopping now and then at a place of business to learn all he could about the town, its inhabitants, and its business prospects. He discovered several grog-shops, four general stores, and a few houses of skilled artisans, such as blacksmith, shoemaker, carpenter, and the like. It was after dark when he rejoined his men and they all returned to the ship. They came with a sense of satisfaction, for they had mapped a plan of action for landing and housing the company.

Sam slept lightly that night, for he was anxious to be up and about his plans. He awoke early and listed over to himself all the things he must accomplish that day, and for a few minutes allowed himself the luxury of musing over the long months just passed. For five months he and his followers had been on the water. Four adults had died during that voyage, and six children. Two babies had been born: a boy they had named Atlantic, soon after the voyage started; and a girl, called Pacific, almost at its end. This day, August 1, 1846—a Saturday —was to see the Mormon emigrants land at Yerba Buena, which would be San Francisco.

Chapter X

SAM WAS ALREADY up and dressing as the bugle blew reveille, and when he went on deck he found the harbor covered by a dense fog. By the time breakfast was over it had lifted, but for the rest of the day there was a high fog which made the atmosphere gloomy. As Sam made ready to go ashore with the first boatload, he stopped long enough to notice the sentry who walked back and forth on the plaza from the custom house to the armory. Off to one side the company of marines and sailors was gathering for morning drill. After landing Sam remained for an hour or so on the beach, directing the coming and going of the three shore boats. The tide was high enough until midmorning for continued landings, and soon the beach was strewn with baggage of every description, including chicken coops and the two melancholy cows, who stood hunched against the wind. As the tide went out, the boats changed their landing-place to the foot of a rocky bluff—later to be named Clark's Point—below the peak of Loma Alta, which was to become famous as Telegraph Hill. Here a wooden landing platform had been built as a wharf, and here landings were made for the rest of the day. There were two or three frame and adobe houses and a store near by—back from the wharf, nestled against the hill.

Sam turned his attention to the setting up of a suitable camping-spot, and this he found on a large lot behind the general store, which fronted on Water Street. The latter was soon to become known as Montgomery Street in honor of Captain Montgomery. On either side of the lot were two lanes, which later became Clay and Washington streets. Other than the general store the lot contained only two build-ings; one, an old mule-power gristmill built a year or so earlier by Nathan Spear, sat in the very center of the lot. Outside its two-story tower ran a crazy little staircase to the upper floor. The other building was an adobe house on the upper, or hill, end of the block. Across the road from this chosen camping site was the grog-shop of J. H. Brown, a gossipy little cockney whom Sam had met on his rounds the night before. Soon the Mormons were spreading their tents over the open space, and by late afternoon the camp ground gave the appearance of a bivouacked army. Sam led his own family up the hill beyond the plaza to the Casa Grande. This was the town's largest structure, built about 1837 by William A. Richardson, founder of Yerba Buena. Nine other families spread their featherbeds and quilts on the floor of the Casa Grande that day in preparation for their first night ashore.

Many of the single men were to lodge with the sailors in the barracks on the plaza, and thither they carried their light baggage. By late afternoon all the passengers were ashore and had their tents set up. A few took lodgings in the one hotel in town, and a few others were taken into private homes of Yerba Buena citizens. On the corner of the camp square was a great pile of baggage, covered before nightfall by tarpaulins. The disfellowshipped members had made a camp of their own across the lane, near the grog-shop.

That first night Sam had a great bonfire built in the center of camp, and soon all the company were gathered around it, shivering in coats which they had been informed they would not need in this land of perpetual sunshine. Fanny voiced the general feeling when she said, "I imagined this place was going to be like paradise, with never any cold. But it's the exact opposite! It's gloomy and ugly and cold, and the fog seems to chill a body to the bone."

Sam leaned forward, holding his hands toward the flames, his face bright with its glow. "Get up on your feet, all you folks, and let's sing a song! How about the 'Old Gray Mare?' " Somebody started it and soon they were all singing lustily, their bodies swaying to and fro to the music and their faces misty in the halo of the fire. Afterward they sat down again on blankets or boxes, and as the flames leaped and crackled George Winner said, "They call this place Yerba Buena. That's supposed to mean 'good herb,' but if anything good will grow here I'm mightily mistaken." He lifted a handful of sand and allowed it to trickle slowly through his fingers. "You can't grow anything in sand," he added. Sam held up a little bunch of a vine that ran rampant over the sandhills. "This is some of the herb this place is named after. The Mexicans make tea out of it. I've got a big kettle setting there on the fire and we've put some of this stuff in it. You've all brought cups like we told you to, and we're going to pass it around to you and let you see how it tastes." Two of the women filled small pails from the kettle and went around the circle pouring it into the cups. They drank and agreed that it wasn't bad. Then Barton Mowry arose. "I got here in my hand a piece of dried beef. The Mexicans call it 'jerky.' They shred beef and dry it so's it'll keep. We're free to buy as much of it as we want. It ain't bad-tasting either. And that reminds me, I found out this afternoon that if we can get horses to ride inland to one of the ranches, we can kill a beef if we want to and bring the flesh back, and it won't cost us a cent so long as we leave the hide hanging on the post so the rancher can find it. They don't care how much of their meat you eat if you leave them the hides. They get a dollar for every hide, but they can't sell the meat."

"Good, Brother Mowry," Sam said quickly. "We'll get inland just as quick as ever we can and get some fresh beef. We sure need something like that, for there's little to buy in the way of food here in Yerba Buena. I've been to every store in town and can't get anything. The storekeepers tell me that they've had no fresh stocks lately —that they can't even sell the whalers the food they want, let alone feed more than two hundred people that just dropped in and surprised them. We've more than doubled the population in one day, and that would be a problem in any small town."

"What are we going to do first in the morning?" Isaac Robbins asked.

Sam was thoughtful for a moment before he answered, "Well, I think the first thing we ought to do, after we get the last of the baggage ashore, is to fetch the press and get it set up. It's going to be no easy task to get that heavy press ashore, but even when we do the worst is yet to come. We're going to set the press up in that old mill, in the top room. The bottom we're going to have to utilize to grind our wheat. I've already bought a mule for power."

Edward Kemble pushed forward and faced Sam. "You mean that we're going to try to get the press up that rickety old stairs to the attic?"

Sam nodded and Edward expostulated, "But Mr. Brannan, do you realize that the press weighs five tons?"

Again Sam nodded and patted the boy on the shoulder. "Don't

worry, we can get it up there all right with the help of the Lord."

"The Lord had better do it all by himself," Edward exclaimed. "Why, when ten men or so get to pushing and hauling a five-ton press up those stairs, the whole thing will come crashing down!"

"Don't blaspheme," Sam said. "We'll get it up all right. You stop worrying. Now to the next order of business: Hyatt, Scott, and Addison, when they landed, made straight for the nearest grog-shop. Since then they have been in all the other grog-shops. This is to notify their families that we will give these brethren just one week to change their ways before we cut them off from the Church. We are living now among gentiles. Any man among us who brings disgrace on us all will be cut off from the Church without much monkey business.

"That reminds me of something else, too. The Pells, the Eagers, and the Moses family are camped across the way. Moses is going to move his family to Mission Dolores settlement, two miles from here, in the morning. Pell has already been promised a job by Mr. Brown, across the street, as inspector of hides. I want all of you to treat their families well. They have as much right to make a fresh start in this new country as we have. Let us do nothing that will bring censure upon them.

"Our next move, as soon as we get settled, will be to find a place to hold Sunday services. We ought to have a meeting tomorrow, being as it's Sunday, but there's so gol-durned much work to be done, I think we'll have to let it slide."

He began to outline the special duties he wished the various members to perform. This done, the newcomers to Yerba Buena sang a hymn, said a prayer, and went early to their beds. As Sam climbed the hill, when he saw the light in Brown's grog-shop he wondered what the older inhabitants of the town thought of this sudden influx. Already he knew most of them by name, and where they lived and something of their history. The gossipy Brown had volunteered all the information he had, which seemed quite complete, when Sam had passed his shop and stopped for a chat that morning.

Early the next day Sam came out on the porch of the Casa Grande and stood surveying the view. From this elevation the town lay spread out before him. He stepped down to the ground, turned, and looked over the adobe building which had housed him through the night, noting its shingle roof and board floor, luxuries which were missing from most of the other houses in town. Then he mounted the steps again and surveyed the town, which lay stretched over the rolling hills that slanted down to the cove. The waters of the bay danced and shimmered in an early morning sun and the *Portsmouth*, the *Brooklyn*, and the gray old whaler seemed to be sitting in molten gold. Across the bay other hills stretched into a vast distance. On his left Loma Alta (Telegraph Hill) loomed over the harbor, covered now with dead brown grass; at its feet the landing which they had used at low tide the day before seemed like a miniature. Back from the weathered little wharf, under the sharp face of Loma Alta were three shacks, of which the principal was "The Beehive"—general store of Dickson and Hay, and one of the four general stores in the town.

Sam's eyes followed the road, which led from the landing around the base of the hill to the town proper. Where Jackson Street would eventually cross Montgomery, when the streets were named, a small bridge spanned a tiny lagoon which spread its marshy borders a hundred feet or so inland. Water Street ran along the cove, and upon it stood several buildings. From the point which would one day be the crossing of Sacramento and Leidesdorff streets, a small stream emptied into a fresh-water pond, and from there the beach swept in a wide arc toward the east, ending at Rincon Hill, where one day a bridge over the bay would touch the land.

Sam could make out, in the west side of Water Street and south of what was to be Washington Street, the home of Victor Prudon, built and still owned by General Vallejo. Next to it was the adobe house of Susana Martinez Hinckley, widow of the smuggler, William Sturgis Hinckley, who had died just a few months since and of whom everyone in town spoke with warm affection. On the corner of the future Clay Street was the store and dwelling of Nathan Spear, now in the Napa Valley trying to regain his health. His nephew, William Heath Davis—lovingly nicknamed "Kanaka" because he had been born during a visit of his parents to Honolulu—occupied the house and carried on the business in the store.

Sam also noted a store and dwelling, located between the future Clay and Sacramento streets, which had been built by Yerba Buena's second settler, Jacob Primer Leese. He had married General Vallejo's sister and had become a Mexican citizen. Sam had heard so many people speak of General Vallejo, who lived at a place they called Sonoma, that he was filled with curiosity to see the wealthy old Mexican Californian. Brown had said that the Hudson's Bay Company had leased the Jacob Leese buildings the year before, but that now the firm of Mellus and Howard occupied them. The last building to the south, on the corner of what were to be California and Montgomery streets, was the house built by the handsome cockney, Robert Ridley, and sold to William A. Leidesdorff. Sam had met Leidesdorff and had wondered about his dark skin; he had asked Brown for an explanation of it. The cockney told him that the Dane had been born in the West Indies of a mulatto mother. He had been United States Vice-Consul in Yerba Buena until Montgomery sailed into the bay and took over. In all the town of Yerba Buena only Leidesdorff's house had a flower garden. Between his house and the cove was the rough board warehouse whose toes had seemed to dip into the salty waters, and which had attracted Sam's attention so forcibly on the night of his arrival. A small schooner was even now taking on cargo from its confines.

Sam's glance turned to the main thoroughfare which led to the town from the high-tide landing place, later to be called Clay Street. On its south side, between what would be known as Montgomery and Kearny streets, stood the saloon of Jean Jacques Vioget, the Swiss adventurer. The saloon had been run until recently by Robert Ridley, who was now languishing in jail at Sutter's fort, Brown had said, because of his excessive patriotism in behalf of the Mexicans when the Bear Flag revolutionaries had invaded Yerba Buena in July of that year. John Henry Brown was now keeping the bar in Ridley's absence, and intended to open part of the building for use as a hotel; already he had a sign bearing upon it the title "Portsmouth House" nailed over the front door.

Where Kearny and Pine streets now cross, an immense sand hill loomed. North of it were three or four small houses, and on the southwest corner of the future Clay and Kearny streets was Leidesdorff's "Big Adobe." Across from it, down the hill directly in front of Sam's point of vantage, lay the plaza, with the old Mexican adobe custom house and the barracks of Captain Harry Watson's detachment of U. S. Marines. Facing the plaza, along what was to be Washington Street, were a few scattered buildings.

On the west side of the future Kearny Street, south of the great sand hill, Sam could make out the beginning of a three-mile trail which led to the mission. To his left, at the corner of Kearny and Washington streets near Dan Sill's blacksmith shop, the trail led over the hills toward the presidio in a northwesterly direction. It went on through a low gap in the hills, along what would one day be known as Pacific Street, to pass the ranch house of Juanna Briones near the corner of the future Filbert and Powell streets. Sam had also heard a good deal about the presidio which lay back of the old Mexican fort, and he told himself that he would go out and see it at his first opportunity. Davis had told him that it was an old Mexican military post:

There were four or five other buildings scattered about the town's outskirts, but these did not hold his interest. Only the town itself seemed important to him—huddled in the lap of the broad slope that extended down from where he stood to the low bank known as the beach; a slope of hard clayey soil, covered for the most part with loose sand. The town of Yerba Buena was bounded by two ravines running back into the hills on about the lines of Jackson and California streets, as we know them now.

Across the street from where Sam stood, just above and back of the custom house, was a neat white-painted frame cottage with a broad verandah. Sam had made arrangements on the day before to rent it for himself and his family. The owner was Stephen Smith, just then living in Bodega. Sam stood looking at it with a sense of satisfaction. Then he prodded himself into action; there were many things to be done before he could get his family settled in the little house this day —furniture to be sent ashore and hauled up, aside from all the other details involved. On his way down to the cove he stopped in at Brown's grog-shop.

"If Hyatt or Scott or Addison come in here today, don't sell them anything to drink. Throw them out on their backsides. For the sake of their families I'd like to get them sobered up."

Brown touched his forelock with two fingers to signify his willingness to do as Sam bade him. Then he spoke, "Mr. Brannan, Hi want to arsk a favor too. See that sign habove my door?" Sam nodded.

"Not long before your ship 'ove hinto view the boys from the *Portsmouth* finished painting and making that sign hand 'ung it there.[25] We be wanting to make a 'ostel of this 'ere place and Hi be needing the services of some good carpenters and the like. His hit likely some o' your company will 'ire theirselves hout?"

"Why, yes. A good many of us will need to hire out as laborers in order to live during the next few months. There ain't no finer carpenters on earth than the Kittleman brothers. I'll send them right over to talk to you."

Brown rubbed his hands happily. "Hand 'ave ye got p'raps some females wot can sew?"

"Sew? Why you never saw such sewing females as we got in our company. What do you want them to sew?"

"Flannel. Hit's got ter be sewed with a seam hup the middle ter make it inter blankets." He was thoughtful for a moment. "Hi don't know wot we'll use for mattresses."

"Mattresses? Why, we've got just the thing. The *Brooklyn's* got a cargo of sea island moss for ballast that we took on at Honolulu after we unloaded our freight. It ought to make fine filling for mattresses."

"Hand so hit will, so hit will! We'll put the women to sewing bags to hold it."

"You ought to have some featherbeds," Sam laughed.

"Wouldn't Hi like to 'ave some, now? 'Ave you got any hin your company to sell?"

Sam snapped his fingers. "There might be some, at that. You better go over to the camp ground and make your wants known. It will save time and get you what you want in a hurry."

"That Hi will and now," the cockney said.

It was afternoon before Sam finished supervising the unloading of several more boatloads of goods from the ship, and started up the hill beside the wagonload of furniture which was being hauled to his new home. For over an hour he worked with the dray man, getting the furniture into the house; and then it looked inordinately bare to him, there were so many things they needed which they had not brought.

But while the women worked at putting things in place, Sam walked over to the Portsmouth House to see how Brown was making out. The Kittleman brothers were sawing and hammering in the lot outside, and Sam stopped to watch them for a few minutes. They explained that they were going to build tables and benches and bunks for the hotel. Sam went inside to find half a dozen women in the back room, sewing with fine stitches on the flannel blankets. Brown set him up a drink of brandy when he came out through the bar. "Him hall set," he beamed. "Lucy Nutting his going to be my waitress, Sarah Kittleman my cook, and Mercy Narrimore, the pretty young widow, his going to be my 'ousekeeper. Now ain't that fine?"

"It certainly is. My people need work and we appreciate your hiring them. But they'll give you good service, too. I'm specially glad about Mercy Narrimore. Her husband died of scurvy on the way and left her with that handsome little boy to support. She'll do your place credit, Mercy will."

"Hi might be hable to make 'er forget 'er sorrow," Brown suggested, but Sam shook his head to indicate that it was no use.

The next morning Sam turned his attention to getting his press ashore. This presented difficulties, since a lighter had to be used; several times it seemed almost certain that the press would slide into the bay. At last it was hauled to the foot of the staircase at Nathan Spear's gristmill. Cables were fastened around it, and while a half a dozen men pulled from above a dozen more took turns pushing it up the uncertain stairs. Before dark it sat in all its efficient beauty in the little room high above the mill proper.

It took the boys a day or so to get things assembled and the press in working order, ready to print blank deeds and other legal forms for which the town was clamoring. Meanwhile Sam was busy with company affairs. He had bought a mule out of the company funds, and had Thomas Eager hitch it to the great stones which must be pulled around and around all day to grind the wheat. This lay on a corrugated stone in the center of the pit. The flour that came out was only half crushed and rather dirty, but the Mormons relished it as a change of diet. The mule stirred up a pungent dust which drifted constantly up into the editorial room, and the noise of the stones was distracting, but John and Edward worked through it all with little complaint. The widow Eager was making plans for opening a small store, and though her sons were still active in the company she was very bitter against the Mormons.

Barton Mowry and his wife proposed to open a coffee and shoe shop, and for this purpose were renting a shack on the beach between what were to be Sacramento and Clay streets. A year's lease was costing them $300.

Sam had sought for a way to build homes for his people, and found the answer in adobe houses. Kanaka Davis led him up to the town's supply of drinking water—springs on the road soon to be called Taylor Street, and another on Washington. The Mexicans there showed Sam how to mix water with the clay adobe soil, together with a little straw, to fashion large bricks. Sam sent up a group of men to make bricks to lie in the sun and dry, so that building could start soon.

The following Saturday two whalers put into port, and the hostelry of J. H. Brown had its christening.

On Sunday the Mormons stopped for a day of rest.[26] Sam had arranged no church service, inasmuch as Captain Montgomery had invited the whole company, earlier in the week, to come aboard the *Portsmouth* for the usual Sunday service there. By ten o'clock the Mormons were waiting on the beach for the shore boats of the man-of-war to pick them up. They could see that the awnings had been spread over the deck against their coming. As they climbed the stairs to the deck they noticed that a great many of the sailors were lounging about to watch them come aboard. The chairs from the ward room and cabin had been placed up front for the women and children, while behind them were capstan bars arranged in seats for the men. As Sam came aboard he heard one old gunner exclaim, "Well, damn my hide, if these here women ain't just like any others." Sam wondered what he had expected. Captain Montgomery greeted the visitors and passed them on to his two sons to be ushered to their seats. When at last the Captain stood facing his audience he explained that it was his custom to read the sermon, as the ship had no chaplain. He had brought a store of printed sermons for such occasions. The Mormons listened politely to his Episcopalian discourse and did not agree with a single word.

Afterward a lunch was served in the dining hall. Then the company was taken on a tour of inspection of the ship. When the ship's boats landed them on the beach, shortly after noon, they went straight to their tents or temporary lodgings, divested themselves of their Sunday raiment, and went back to the work of building homes.

On Monday some of the Mormon men began to build houses out of the adobe bricks; some hauled wood from the hills on carts for heating purposes, some dug wells, and two of them took on the task of procuring water at the springs and peddling it from door to door for domestic use. A small company rode inland to Rancho Las Pulgas ("The Fleas"), owned by the Arguillo family, to procure fresh meat. The rest were busy with individual tasks or with making bricks.

Already a few were falling away from the Church. There were men who did not want to work hard and who resented Sam's continual driving of them. A few, with their families, took passage on the first boat that would carry them back to the States. Sam had been forced to disfellowship Hyatt, Scott, and Addison, in spite of the tearful pleas of their relatives. They were constantly drunk, and such was their behavior that it reflected on every member of the company; Sam had no alternative but to expel them.

On the second Sunday after their arrival in Yerba Buena, Sam arose early to make the Casa Grande ready for the first non-Catholic service the town had ever seen.[27] It was the sixteenth day of August, 1846. Sam swept off the verandah and asked Barton Mowry to help him in preparing the broken bread for the sacrament. Then they set out the two pitchers and the cups from which sips of water would be drunk "in memory of the blood of Jesus," as the cups passed from hand to hand. At ten o'clock Sam took the hand bell from the table inside and carried it out to the porch. He lifted the bell high and swung it with all his powerful might. The clear, sweet tones swept across the plaza and up over the hills. In a few minutes he could see the faithful trooping up the slope, up the streets and across vacant lots, to worship. Kanaka Davis and J. H. Brown came visiting, too, and took up their places at the rear of the congregation, which was forced to stand on the sands, in front of the porch because no house in town was large enough to hold them all. Sam asked Barton Mowry to pronounce the opening prayer. Then the Mormons sang a hymn, led by Lizzie Winner. And Sam Brannan launched into his sermon. Brown declared afterward to anyone who would listen that it was as good a sermon as he had ever heard preached.

Lizzie Winner had wasted no time in falling in love with one of the young service men, and when John Henry Brown heard that an immediate wedding was contemplated between Lizzie and her beloved, Basil Hall, he made haste to offer his hotel as a setting for the ceremony. In a little room in the adobe building which had once been used as a Mexican calaboose, Sam Brannan said the words which made them man and wife. Afterward the guests played games. Sam and Kanaka Davis withdrew to one side to talk. They noticed with amusement that Brown was following Hettie Pell about with dog-like devotion. E. Ward Pell had ignored the wedding, but his wife and Hettie had come, for they were still very friendly with the company of which they had formerly been a part. While Hettie danced with Edward Kemble, Sam called Brown to join Kanaka and himself. "You act like you're stuck on Hettie," Sam laughed. Brown flushed, gulped, and then burst out, "Hi'm gone on 'er for a fact. Hi'd marry 'er tomorrow if she'd 'ave me."

Whether he proposed to her that night or waited till another occasion Sam never knew, but shortly thereafter the two were married. The marriage, however, was destined not to be a success, and Hettie was one of the first women in California to seek divorce as a relief from her unhappiness. Their backgrounds had been so different that they were able to find little in common.

Brown's devotion to Hettie was not, however, the only interesting side-topic at Lizzie's wedding. While Augusta Joyce and Hettie giggled in a corner with the bride, Sam and Kanaka Davis fell into a discussion of the Bear Flag revolt, which had taken place before the arrival of the Mormons.

"I'm not just clear in my mind what it was all about," Sam said to his new friend. "Suppose you start at the beginning and explain it to me."

"It all started with Colonel John Frémont," Davis willingly explained. "He was sent out here by the Government to do some exploring. I have a sneaking suspicion, and so have others I've talked to, that Frémont and his father-in-law, Senator Benton of Missouri, hatched up a plot by which he would take over California in the name of the United States so as to gain some advantage for Benton and his gang in Washington. It's a fact that all the scientists Frémont brought out here with his company were crack shots, and they were all armed with rifles. When they first came into California, the Mexican Governor at Monterey told them to high-tail it out. Frémont pretended to obey the expulsion order but he went on doing as he pleased. At any rate, he brought a picked bunch of men down here to Yerba Buena weeks before ever Captain Montgomery arrived, and they spiked the guns at the old Mexican fort. Later he rode inland and gathered all the trappers and homesteaders that were American, or at least opposed to Mexican rule, and formed them into an army. Then they marched up to Sonoma and arrested General Vallejo, and lodged him in the fort and run up the Bear Flag with the words 'Republic of California' on it. They sent Robert Semple down here to arrest Mexican sympathizers, and he took Bob Ridley in charge. Bob was the feller that run this grog-shop, and it was when he left that his friend Brown here took over. They're both cockney."

"What's this Ridley look like?"

"He's a fine-looking young feller; tall, intelligent, a fine man."

"So Frémont wanted to conquer the Mexicans single-handed, did he?" Sam prodded Davis back to the subject.

Davis nodded. "He took too much on himself, though, 'cause word came to him direct from Washington by messenger to take down the Bear Flag they'd run up in Sonoma and to behave themselves. So Frémont done as he was told, and as I remember it was about three weeks later that Montgomery sailed in here under official orders and took over. Frémont is helping to fight the war, but he's acting under orders of Governor Mason at Monterey now and not being the lord high muckey-muck he'd thought he was going to be. I hear tell that Ridley will be back tomorrow. He's been out of jail for some time, but he's been stopping inland to size up some business prospects."

At midnight the Mormons and the few townspeople who had joined them to celebrate this first Protestant wedding in Yerba Buena stopped to offer a prayer before going home. Next day Brown told all who would listen that it was the finest party he had ever attended in Yerba Buena.

Captain Richardson had allowed his crew to rest for a few days, but more recently they had been hard at work cleaning and caulking the ship and getting her in shape for the home voyage. When everything was in readiness Richardson sought out Sam Brannan. "Have you found a way to pay me the balance of what your company owes me for passage?" he asked.

"Yes, I think we have," Sam said. "If you'll take the men I've organized, on your ship and sail her across the bay to Sausalito, they'll cut you a cargo of redwood logs and saw them on the mill up there." [28]

The Captain beamed. "Redwood, eh? That will bring a good price in New York. Have your men down to the landing early in the morning."

While the lumber crew were absent Sam rented a ship's long-boat and in company with Origin Mowry, Barton's grown son, sailed across the bay to enter the waters of the San Joaquin River, up which they made their way looking for suitable land upon which to establish a community farm.[29] They returned in time for Sam to outline his plans at Sunday meeting, still held at the Casa Grande. Now that some were away and others apostatizing, the company was small enough to be accommodated within the building.

"We've located wonderful land for a farm," Sam told his listeners. "With your consent I intend to use money from the little that's left in the common fund to buy a launch, some oxen, maybe some horses and mules, and a few more seeds than we brought with us. We'll need all these things to get our farm ready. As soon as the boys get back from their work at the sawmill in Sausalito I'll send a company of twenty men or so up the river to get the farm started. We want the crops to be ready when the emigrants come in from the States next year. Now all of you that agree to my plans hold up your right hand." Consent was unanimously given.

Although the press had been set up for some time, Sam had so many other things to attend to that he had been unable to give any thought as yet to starting a newspaper. The press was still printing legal documents and had begun on a book. Governor Mason, the United States military governor of the conquered territory, had compiled a volume of rules which civilians must observe while under military control. This he had sent to Sam to have printed, and the boys spent most of their days setting type for the book, which was destined never to be 'put into use. Today there are few known copies in existence.

Sam, meanwhile, was constantly busy on company affairs. He had had two mills installed on the Jackson Street lagoon, but they were never as successful as the little mule-power mill.

After the men returned from the sawmill at Sausalito, they worked with Sam to make everything ready for the trips up the San Joaquin River to open up their farm. But they were interrupted by a surprising turn of events: Sam was haled into court as defendant by Henry Harris, plaintiff. Harris had tired of following a Mormon lass who would have none of him, and now he wanted back the money he had paid into the common fund. He seemed to feel that by paying his fare he had bought an interest in the company and that whenever he chose to withdraw, the common fund should be divided and his own share paid. Sam lost no time in securing the services of William H. Russell, a Kentucky lawyer and recent arrival in the village. Russell was a man who indulged in spread-eagle oratory upon the slightest provocation, and he welcomed this first opportunity to exhibit his talents.

When Montgomery had become the military head of Yerba Buena he had found it necessary to replace the Mexican magistrate by an American, and had appointed the ship's third lieutenant, Washington A. Bartlett, to the post. Bartlett had taken office on August 26, 1846, and was to remain until September 15, at which time the citizens would be allowed to elect a magistrate. It was early in September when Sam appeared as defendant before Bartlett, who held court in the custom house on the plaza. Bartlett had called a jury together to help him in deciding the case. This was the second jury trial to be held in California.

Sam's followers rallied to his defense. But there were many who took this opportunity to vent their spleen upon him, among them those he had excommunicated and others who had apostatized because they felt he was too arbitrary a leader. Hyatt, Scott, Ambrose Moses, and E. Ward Pell appeared to testify that Sam had been dishonest in his dealings with the company and in his handling of company funds. They all swore that they had put money into the common fund and that Sam had refused to return to them any portion of it. Winner, Robbins, Mowry, and other faithful members of the company, on the other hand, testified that Sam had been absolutely fair and honest from the beginning. They asserted that the company had been organized on an agreement that all members would put the proceeds of their labor into the common fund for three years and would draw from it as they needed funds; that those who would not co-operate should be expelled; and that no provision had been made to divide up the common fund for the sake of those who withdrew. The citizens of Yerba Buena, including Kanaka Davis, Robert Ridley, William Howard, and the Mellus brothers, listened to the evidence and were hard put to decide from the evidence whether Brannan was saint or devil. When Colonel Russell arose, swept his handkerchief out of his back pocket with a flourish, and began to address them, they were lost in admiration of his eloquence; but Kanaka Davis said later that it was hard to pick the truth out of the conflicting stories. When the jury returned from conference they announced themselves as deadlocked. Sam was released.

The next morning the launch, or long-boat, that Sam had purchased left with its first load for the site of the new farm.[30] Small equipment and seeds were carried up on two preliminary trips, and then all was ready for the company to set forth. The launch with a very light load was sent ahead to wait at Marsh's Landing (the future Antioch) for the arrival of Quartus Sparks, who was riding a mule up to Livermore Ranch, where he was to buy a yoke of oxen. These he was to drive to Marsh's Landing to be taken on the launch for the rest of the way.[31] The remaining company of twenty men, headed by Thomas Stout, were to take the team and wagon and follow an old chart made by the trapper Merritt. Two days later they reached the head of navigation and made camp on the east side of the river. A few hours after, the launch arrived with Sam Brannan, Quartus Sparks, Origin Mowry, and the mule and oxen. This launch, or ship's long-boat, was the first sailing vessel to ascend the San Joaquin River, and Sam Brannan was the man who started the first farm in the now famous San Joaquin Valley. The site of New Hope, the Mormon farm, was on the north bank of the Stanislaus River about a mile and a half from the junction of the Stanislaus River and the San Joaquin. Stanislaus City now occupies the old site.

A week or so later Sam rode up to visit the settlement and was much encouraged to find a log house completed. R. H. Peckham, later to become a judge in San Jose, was putting up a sawmill in which the men would cut planks for floors and mill-frames for windows and doors. Already the company were busily at work fencing in fifty acres of land with oak logs, which were rolled into place and covered over with boughs to discourage small animals. Sam stayed one day and then returned to Yerba Buena.

While the company was making preparations to go up the San Joaquin, a grand ball had been held in Leidesdorff's home, and for the first time in its history Yerba Buena had enough women for its men for dancing. There had been a hundred of them to stand up with the officers and big-wig officials. The men of the *Brooklyn* company had for the most part ignored this grand affair—with the exception of Sam, who never missed a party.

But when Sam returned from his visit to New Hope he found that the city elections had been settled. Robert Ridley had contested Bartlett's place as *alcalde* (magistrate), but Bartlett, a favorite with the sailors and marines, who were allowed to vote, had won.

In the last days of September Yerba Buena was all agog over the arrival of the U.S.S. *Congress* and her escort, the U.S.S. *Savannah*. Commodore Stockton was given a rousing welcome by the town which was one day to become famous as "the city that knows how." To make the welcome really formal and official, Samuel ran off the necessary lettering on his press. He secured a heavy grade of beautiful blue satin and printed the programs and badges upon it.

Bright and early on the morning of October 5, 1846, the town was astir for the great event. It was one of the beautiful autumn days for which California is famous. Even the ever-present wind was warm and spring-like. Long before ten o'clock the crowd began to gather at the foot of Clay Street. Captain Watson marched his marines down from

VIEW OF SAN FRANCISCO, FORMERLY YERBA BUENA, IN 1846–1847

A—U. S. S. "Portsmouth." B—U. S. Transport Ships "Leo," "Choo," "Susan Drew" and "Thomas H. Perkins." They brought the 1st Regiment New York Volunteers, Col. J. D. Stevenson, commanding. C—Ship "Vandalia," merchantman consigned to Howard & Mellus.

1. Customhouse. 2. Calaboose 3 Schoolhouse. 4. Alcalde office 5 City Hotel 6 Portsmouth Hotel. 7. Wm. H. Davis' Store. 8. Howard & Mellus Store. 9. W. A. Leidesdorff warehouse. 10. Samuel Brannan's residence. 31. Dr. E. P. Jones' residence. 32. Robert Ridley's residence. 35. Sill's Blacksmith Shop.

* Trail to Presidio. * Trail to Mission Dolores.

RESIDENCE OF SAMUEL BRANNAN, ESQ., IN 1847

This was the house he had built at the corner of Dupont Street (now Grant Street in the center of Chinatown) and Washington Alley. The *California Star* office was built in this yard, and in it the samples of gold were first displayed.

the custom house to act as guard of honor. Frank Ward, one of the non-Mormon passengers of the *Brooklyn* company, was marshal of the day and moved rapidly about making last-minute arrangements. Sam Brannan and his Mormon militia were resplendent in their blue uniforms as they stood about waiting to take their place in the parade.

The ships in the harbor were gay with flags, as were the buildings on shore. Ranking Californians had been invited down from their ranches to take part in the festivities. They had begun to arrive on the day before in their carts with the squealing wooden wheels; the women in mantillas and brilliant-colored silk dresses, the men on gaily caparisoned horses—themselves clad in black velvet and orange and scarlet shirts. Even now they were lined up along the line of march, making bright splashes of color against the somber clothes of the American newcomers.

Shortly before ten o'clock a flotilla carrying the frigate's band and sailors to march in the parade left the *Congress*. The crowd tensed with excitement. At ten, the Commodore's barge in turn left the ship, and when the handsome naval officer set foot on shore Alcalde Bartlett and Marshal Frank Ward stepped forward to shake his hand in formal greeting. The band struck up a martial tune. Marines, sailors, the band, and Brannan's uniformed guards then presented arms. The Commodore was led to the spot where distinguished citizens of the town waited to be formally introduced. When Sam Brannan was presented, the Commodore smiled and remembered their earlier meeting in Honolulu. The introductions completed, Alcalde Bartlett stepped up on the little platform and brought forward Colonel Russell, the speaker of the day. Russell strutted up, took his position, and launched into his masterpiece. The Commodore, standing with his officers at attention before the platform, finally grew restless, but Russell did not abate his flowery oratory. At last he finished with a flourish; then Stockton stepped forward to the platform and made a brief answer.

The parade now formed. Led by Chief Marshal Ward, it was made up of the flagship's band, coming first, then the sailors, the marines, Brannan's guard, Commodore Stockton and his officers, Captain Montgomery and his suite, Alcalde Bartlett and his civil assistants, Colonel Russell; Captain John B. Paty, senior captain of the Hawaiian Navy; Commander Rudacoff of the Russian Navy, Lieutenant Commander Bennet of the French Navy; captains of the ships in port, officers of the late Mexican Government, and finally the citizens of distinction. Up Clay Street these men marched to the music of the band. The parade circled the plaza, already rechristened Portsmouth Square in honor of Montgomery's vessel, and returned to Water (Montgomery) Street, where the Commodore mounted the platform and made a lengthy address setting forth his exploits in the region of Los Angeles and culminating in the occupation of that little town. To Sam his heroic words seemed ironic, inasmuch as word had reached Yerba Buena the day before that the Californians had already repossessed their little city.

That night a grand ball was held again at Leidesdorff's house, and Sam appeared with his wife to dance until midnight. He cut a handsome figure, for he was now entirely over the effects of his fever. At twenty-seven he was distinguished-looking, with a shaggy head of dark hair and alert black eyes. He was taller than the average man, deep-chested, and always well and neatly dressed. In fact, his personal appearance verged upon the dandified. He was smooth-shaven except for side-whiskers low on his jaws and a wisp of hair on his lower lip. His quick intellect and fluent speech, tinged always with forceful profanity, made him an acknowledged leader in the town from the very start. There were señoritas present who found him exceptionally attractive. Nor was Sam blind to their manifold charms.

This celebration for a naval hero aroused the town to feverish heights of patriotism and led to the enlargement of the California battalion which Colonel Frémont was leading in the Mexican War; the struggle flared up at intervals in various sections of the territory. Edward Kemble, J. H. Brown, and the pompous William H. Russell, were the most seriously concerned; they marched away next day to take part presently in the Santa Clara War. Shortly thereafter, Alcalde Bartlett took a group of men inland to round up a supply of beef for the Navy, and was captured by a band of native Californians. Frémont's brave troops came to his rescue, and the Santa Clara War ensued. In less than two weeks all were back in Yerba Buena at their humble tasks.

Chapter XI

SAM WAS MOST anxious to start publication of his paper, but Kemble's absence at war held up his plan for a time. The war seemed to be always interfering with his publication of the California Star.

Brown had sold his hotel to another Kentucky lawyer, E. P. Jones, before he marched away to defend America, and Jones had married the cook, Sarah Kittleman, to insure the continued popularity of the cuisine at the Portsmouth House. When Brown returned, after two weeks of fighting, he found himself without a center of operations from which he could spread gossip, and with no way of making a living. It was at this time that for two thousand dollars a year he rented the Big Adobe, across from the plaza and just a short distance from the Portsmouth House, and began to fit it up as Brown's Hotel, with furniture purchased from the firm of Mellus and Howard, the articles having just recently arrived by ship. John Eager was hired to make the sign for the new hotel; he did himself proud, for Brown said that "few signs were ever gotten up in better taste than this one was."

E. P. Jones, the new proprietor of the Portsmouth House, was a "thin, green-spectacled, bilious-looking man," [32] but he was also a man of education and one who was not afraid to be enthusiastic about things he believed in. Sam was impressed by him almost immediately and lost no time in asking him to become the first editor of his newspaper, when once it should begin publication.

On October 24, 1846, an *Extra in Advance of the Star* was published, but it carried no local news, being given over entirely to "An Account of General Taylor's Victories on the Rio Grande." The Mexican War was being fought on wide and diversified fronts.

In November the whole of Yerba Buena joined Captain Montgomery in mourning for his two stalwart sons, killed while riding in the *Warren's* launch. The Captain never fully recovered from this blow.

Sam grew restive in his desire to begin the publication of his weekly newspaper. Alcalde Bartlett in conjunction with Captain J. B. Hull of the U.S.S. *Warren*, commander of the Northern District, was inflicting an oppressive authority upon the citizens of Yerba Buena, and Sam felt that through the columns of his newspaper he could reach Governor Stephen Watt Kearny and thus bring about repeal of Bartlett's arbitrary and childish regulations. It was irritating to adventuresome men to be herded off the streets at nine o'clock in the evening for no good reason. Hull was even more dogmatic. He made it compulsory for all citizens to report daily at the barracks.

At last Sam had everything in readiness and only awaited the writing of the final articles. Meanwhile he took time to compose a circular letter for general distribution to the Mormons, which outlined the doings of the *Brooklyn* company. It began:

TO THE SAINTS IN ENGLAND AND AMERICA:
BELOVED BRETHREN:

Feeling sensible of the anxiety of your minds to become acquainted with the state of affairs in this country, induces me, at this late hour, to communicate to you this short and feeble epistle. Our passage from New York to this place was made in six months; since our arrival the colony generally has enjoyed good health. In relation to the country and climate we have not been disappointed in our expectations; but, like all other new countries, we found the accounts of it very much exaggerated; so much so, that we would recommend to all emigrants hereafter to provide themselves with thick clothing, instead of thin. There has been no arrival in the country this fall, from those coming by land; but we are anxiously waiting for them next season. They will in all probability winter on the head waters of the Platte, where they can subsist on buffalo meat. We are now busily engaged in putting in crops for them to subsist on when they arrive; I said all, but I should have said all that love the brethren, for, about twenty males of our feeble number have gone astray after strange gods, serving their bellies and their own lusts, and refuse to assist in providing for the reception of their brethren by land. They will have their reward.

We have commenced a settlement on the river San Joaquin, a large and beautiful stream emptying into the Bay of San Francisco; but the families of the company are wintering in this place, where they find plenty of employment, and houses to live in; and about twenty of our number are up at the new settlement, which we call New Hope, ploughing and putting in wheat and other crops, and making preparations to move their families up in the spring, where they hope to meet the main body by land sometime during the coming season. Since our departure from New York we have enjoyed the peculiar care of our Heavenly

Father, everything in a most miraculous manner has worked together for our good, and we find ourselves happily situated in our new home surrounded with peace and security.[33]

This letter was dispatched on the first day of January, 1847.

Eight days later, on January 9, Sam Brannan took his place at the case and with stick in hand began to set type. John Eager served as "ink ball" and with E. P. Jones (commonly called "Doctor") looking on, that Saturday morning Sam pulled the first impression of Volume I, Number 1, of *The California Star*. Edward Kemble missed this history-making event, for he was at that moment away at war. The new paper stated that this weekly would be devoted to "the Liberties and Interests of the People of California"; that its publisher was Samuel Brannan and its editor E. P. Jones. Terms were $6.00 per annum, invariably to be paid in advance.

From the first the *Star* was a liberal sheet, strictly non-sectarian. Although Sam conducted Mormon services every Sunday morning on the plaza, he kept all hint of Mormonism out of his paper. The first page of the first edition was given over mainly to "Progress of the War," and the other pages were filled for the most part with business advertisements.

The Mormons felt the need of a school for their children, and Sam pushed the movement to build a school, in the columns of the *Star*, even going so far as to offer to contribute half of a fifty-vara lot and fifty dollars in cash toward this purpose. The four pages of the *Star*, thirteen by eighteen inches in size, brought the first printed news to the San Francisco Bay region. There was, however, a little rival sheet called *The Californian*, published by the tall Robert Semple at Monterey. Some weeks after publication had begun, Sam received a copy of *The Californian* and with rising wrath read an editorial concerning the *Star*. The sentence which irritated Sam more than any other read, "It is published and owned by S. Brannan, the leader of the Mormons, who was brought up by Jos. Smith himself, and is consequently well qualified to unfold and impress the tenets of his sect." Straightway Sam sat down and wrote an answer to Semple.

We have received two late numbers of the *Californian*, a dim, dirty little paper printed at Monterey, on the worn out material of one of the old California war presses. It is published and edited by Walter Colton and Robert Semple, the one a lying sycophant and the other an over-grown lickspittle. At the top of one of the papers we find the words, "please exchange." This would be considered, in almost any other country, a barefaced attempt to swindle us. We would consider it so now, were it not for the peculiar situation of the country, which induces us to do a great deal of good for others in order to enable them to do a little good. . . . We have concluded to give our paper to them this year so as to afford them some insight into the manner in which a Republican newspaper should be conducted.

Yerba Buena, now that it had become a town, needed to be surveyed and mapped, and to this task Bartlett commissioned Jasper O'Farrell, an Irish surveyor who had come to California by way of South America and Mexico in 1843. O'Farrell hastened to carry out Bartlett's idea, and the foundation was laid for the city of San Francisco.   .

Publishing a newspaper did not take up all Sam's time, and he found himself in the latter part of January the owner of a fifty-vara lot, 137½ by 137½ feet, on the southeast corner of Washington and Stockton streets. He lost no time in hiring a newcomer from the Sandwich Islands, one Seth S. Lincoln, to clear the property of scrub oak and begin the construction of a redwood house, to be built a story and a half high with a generous front porch which would look out over the town below.

Sam had no sooner put his attention to the clearing of his land than Bartlett, the dictator, made a surprise move. On January 28 he brought in a proclamation which he ordered printed in the next issue of the *Star*. Sam was in a fine fury when he read it:

AN ORDINANCE

Whereas, the local name of Yerba Buena, as applied to the settlement or town of San Francisco, is unknown beyond the district; and has been applied from the local name of the cove, on which the town is built; *Therefore*, to prevent confusion and mistakes in public documents, and that the town may have the advantage of the name given on the public map, It is hereby ordained, that the name SAN FRANCISCO shall hereafter be used in all official communications and public documents, or records appertaining to the town.

Wash-ⁿ A. Bartlett,
Chief Magistrate

Published by order,
J. G. T. Dunleavy, Municipal Clerk.

"I'll be cussed if I'll use the name of San Francisco in the place of Yerba Buena. Ed, you see that Yerba Buena stays in the heading of our paper. That goddamned tyrant will find out from me that he can't run things in such a high-handed manner and get away with it."

And the name Yerba Buena appeared weekly on the *Star*. Though Sam was so incensed at Bartlett's move there was purpose in the naval man's maneuver, for Thomas O. Larkin, former U. S. Consul at Monterey, and the lanky Robert Semple, were subdividing a portion of the lands belonging to General Vallejo on the upper bay. The name of the General's wife was Francisca Benicia, and the two promoters planned to name their new town "Francisca" as a compliment to the General. Bartlett's action forestalled them, and the new town became "Benicia" instead.

Although the new year held much of promise to these pioneers in a far wilderness, it marked the end of a tragic ordeal for the Donner party, who had tried to winter in the mountains. News had just sifted down to San Francisco of the plight of the survivors of this company, which had started out from the States early in 1846 to cross the Great Plains by wagon. On the evening of February 3, 1847, a mass meeting was held on the plaza to raise funds to aid the sufferers. W. D. M. Howard, genial partner in the firm of Mellus and Howard, spoke. But it was the eloquence of Sam Brannan which resulted in the collection of fifteen hundred dollars to be sent to Sutter's fort for the rehabilitation of these tragic remnants of a once flourishing group. That night San Francisco came to the realization that no public meeting had any vitality until Samuel Brannan made his appearance.

Life moved swiftly in the rapidly growing little town. In February Bartlett's tenure of office ran out and Edwin Bryant took his place as magistrate. This change did not make Sam Brannan unhappy; at least, not at first. He gave it little attention, for he was intent upon the success of his newspaper. There were those who resented his attacks on their special privileges, and more than once he was offered a bribe. In reply he wrote one day, in an editorial, that the price of the *Star* was six dollars a year, and those who thought they were buying the editor for that price were mistaken.

On March 6 a United States troop-ship appeared in the harbor, and Sam Brannan joined Kanaka Davis and William Howard on the beach to welcome its commander as he came ashore. The latter was greeted by Captain Montgomery and then introduced as Colonel Jonathan Stevenson. Sam was a good judge of men, and he sized up this white-haired, heavily built elderly man as full of braggadocio, but likable for all of that. As Sam shook the Colonel's hand he said, "We're mighty glad to see you, Colonel. 1 hope you have brought a good bunch of men to fight in this war that is practically over with, by now."

The Colonel grinned. "I wouldn't say they are good, but they ought to be able to fight. Most of them come from the Bowery in New York and if you know the 'bhoys' you know just how tough they can be."

Sam laughed. "Maybe they can frighten off the Mexicans by making faces at them."

"We got some that could frighten them without making faces, they're that hard-looking. This ship, the *Thomas H. Perkins*, carries only the first contingent. The rest of my regiment will come in later in the month, on the *Susan Drew* and the *Loo Choo*. You say the war is nearly over?" Sam nodded and waved toward Captain Montgomery. "The Captain is motioning to you. I suppose he wants to discuss military affairs with you. Drop around to Brown's Hotel when you're through and we'll have a drink and get better acquainted." The Colonel nodded and followed the Captain away.

Sam's enthusiasm for this town, which he intended to help build into a great and flourishing city, was boundless. On March 13, 1847, he wrote:

Our town is no doubt destined to be the Liverpool or New York of the Pacific. Her position for commerce is unrivaled and never can be rivaled, unless some great convulsion of nature shall produce a new Harbor on the Pacific Coast equalling in beauty and security our magnificent bay. Without difficulty or danger, ships of any burthen can at all times enter the harbor which is capacious enough to contain the navies of the whole world.

The extensive and fertile countries watered by the Sacramento and San Joaquin Rivers and the numerous navigable creeks emptying into the Bay must, when they are settled upon with an industrious population, pour their products into this place and receive in exchange from our merchants all their supplies of luxuries and manufactures.

The products of gold, silver, copper, iron and quicksilver mines with which the country abounds must be concentrated here for manufacture and export. In a few years, our wharves and streets will present a scene of busy life resembling those witnessed in Liverpool, New York and New Orleans. Mechanics and artisans from all parts of the world will flock here, and we shall be in full enjoyment of all the elegancies and luxuries of the oldest and most polished countries of the globe. This is no fancy sketch but on the contrary all who now read may live to see it fully verified.

On March 20, Sam ungraciously gave in to the Bartlett proclamation which had changed the name of the city. He said editorially: "When the change was first attempted we viewed it as a mere assumption of authority without law or precedent; and therefore adhered to the old name of Yerba Buena." For the first time "San Francisco" appeared in the heading of the *Star*.

Sam spent a good deal of time supervising the carpenters who were working on his house, and he hurried them as much as possible. He wanted it finished so that he could move his family in before starting on his trip overland to meet the pioneer migration, somewhere east of the Rockies. At last it was completed, and they moved into it before the first of April. When winter came on, the Mormons had no longer been able to meet outdoors or crowd into the Casa Grande, so that when Barton Mowry completed his own two-story house on the corner of what are now Powell and Broadway, he left the second floor for the use of his associates until they could build a church. On the last Sunday before Sam left, he outlined his plans to the company and promised to take any letters that they wished carried to friends and relatives.

The next day the men of the company appeared to move the heavy press from the old mill to its new quarters in a little room in the yard east of Brannan's recently finished home. Heavy draft horses drew the five-ton press up the steep hill to Washington Alley, where it was unloaded and set up again. The next issue of the paper carried a sharp editorial by Sam, who was incensed at the tactics of Oregon settlers in turning aside overland immigration on the old Fort Hall road by means of printed circulars representing California to be suffering from famine and bloody war. Sam pointed out that San Francisco was as orderly and quiet as any New England village. Fifty new buildings were proof that the spirit of progress moved among them.

On April 3, 1847, Sam called the two boys and "Doctor" Jones together in the little newspaper office. "Now boys," he began, "me and my three companions are going to leave in the morning to meet the pioneer migration. I'm going to leave Dr. Jones as editor." He turned to Jones. "But Doc, you got to watch your tongue. You get pretty sarcastic sometimes and forget to use good judgment in your editorials. I want you to leave aside all bias while on your 'editorial tripod,' as you so neatly put it one day." Sam turned to Edward. "But if he forgets himself and causes the paper any embarrassment, Ed, I want you to step in."

Jones drew himself up proudly and adjusted his green spectacles. "You mean, Brannan, that this stripling is going to give *me* orders?"

Sam grinned. "Yep, that's what I mean, if you don't behave yourself."

John Eager caught Sam's eye before he spoke. "What about me, Brother Brannan. Am I to stay on?"

"Yes," Sam said slowly. He paused a moment as if searching for words. "John, I feel bad about something you've done and I hardly know what to do about it. I've just found out that you got Washington Bartlett to write a letter to Larkin asking him to give you a job as a clerk. I know you could make more money that way, but after all I resent your going to my enemy for assistance. Bartlett wrote in his letter to Larkin that your absence would kill this lying Mormon paper and its editor both at once. It won't do either, John. We can go on all right without you, but we won't. I sort of think your mother had something to do with that letter and so I'll overlook it. At any rate, you can't get a clerkship with Larkin, so you better stay on with us for a while. I hope you'll be a good and loyal worker till I get back."

"I will, Brother Brannan. I certainly will."

Sam grasped his shoulder for a moment and then smiled his endearing Irish smile. "I think you will, John," he said. Then he outlined the details he wanted his men to follow.

The next morning he kissed Ann Eliza and Sammy farewell and shook his mother-in-law's hand as they stood in the street before the new house. A herd of fifteen horses milled about in the street, kept in control by the three mounted men who were accompanying Sam. All were newcomers to San Francisco who wanted to go back to the States —only one of them a Mormon. This was young Charles Smith who had drifted in recently on a freighter. Sam mounted his horse, waved for a last time to his family, and rode down the hill behind the herd.

Chapter XII

As THE LITTLE PARTY rode down the peninsula to round the southern end of the bay, Sam was filled with exaltation. He was setting forth on another mission. He would picture to Brigham Young the progress the little *Brooklyn* company had made in eight months; would carry news of the colony at New Hope, so auspiciously begun. Then Brigham would be convinced that he should not tarry in the mountains, but should cross them to come down into the fertile valleys of California. There, hand in hand with Brannan, he could establish a powerful Mormon commonwealth in which they would be joint leaders.

Sam and his three companions reached New Hope the next day. They were surprised to find eighty acres of wheat already heading out and fenced. Gardens of potatoes, carrots, tomatoes, and peas, together with other vegetables, were well advanced. The men, under the direction of Thomas Stout, had planted pasture lands along the river with a good grade of redtop grass, ideal for fattening cattle. Sam had been sending up coffee, sugar, and wheat, regularly until such time as the crops should be ripe. He found a group of men grinding wheat on a handmill. Alondus Buckland took Sam down to the river to show him the preparations they had made for irrigating when the dry season should arrive. It was a primitive method of irrigation, by means of a long pole which dipped a bucket into the river, lifted it and dumped the water into an irrigation ditch.

"How's your ammunition holding out?" Sam asked Buckland on the way back to the community house.

"Fine. We still got plenty, and a good thing, too. Out there in the trees and brush there's droves of antelope, elk, deer, and bear. And you should see the swarms of geese and ducks whenever we go out and scare them up out of the swamps along the river."

Stout was waiting for them as they approached the long log house. "You've sure done fine up here, Will," Sam called out to him, and as they came closer he went on, "Brigham Young is going to be mighty pleased with the reports I'll carry with me. As soon as I get back I'll make arrangements to get your wives and families sent up. You'll have crops ready so's you can live comfortable, then."

There was deer meat frying in the skillet when Sam went inside.[34] "What you frying that venison in?" he asked John Joyce. "Bear oil. Finest lard you ever et," the other replied.

The next morning Sam and his companions rode on toward Sutter's fort. The stronghold of Johann August Sutter was situated on a little knoll which commanded on three sides a view of the surrounding oak-covered plains, and of his wide spreading wheat fields on the fourth, where the Sacramento and American rivers joined. The solid structure was built in the form of a rectangle with walls eighteen feet high and three in thickness. The northwest and southeast corners were bastioned, and bristled with cannon. Within the fort ran other thick walls, parallel all the way to the outer ones, but lower, and a slanting roof ran from the outer to the inner, making a long series of rooms around the inside of the fort. Within these rooms were living quarters, shops, and storerooms for the many people who lived there. In the center of the enclosure was a two-story house in which Sutter lived by himself. The main gate opened to the south, and in front of it was the parade ground where, until the American occupation of California, the Captain had daily drilled his uniformed Indian servants. It was through this south gate that Sam and his associates drove their herd of horses one evening. The genial forty-four-year-old Swiss welcomed them. He was a handsome man, now heavy with middle age, with curly blond hair, clear blue eyes which could twinkle at the slightest joke, a blond mustache, and side whiskers. The man was meticulously dressed, carrying as always his silver-tipped cane. Sutter was lonely in spite of the numbers of men and the few women who lived in or near the fort. His own wife and family were still living in Switzerland.

The horses of the party were taken in charge by two Indians, and the three men were invited to Sutter's own table for supper. The others retired early, but Sam and the doughty Captain sat late talking. His host told Sam of the rescue of the survivors of the Donner party.

"Ya, I tell you it vas a terrible t'ing. Dose beople vas got so hongry dey et de corpses of dem dat vas dead already."

He went into detail and Sam shuddered at the thought of the

suffering these people had endured before their rescue from the deep snow in the Snowy Mountains to the east of the fort. At the close of the story Sutter said, "Some of dose beople you vill see here at de fort in de morning and odders lif outside vit families dat got homes clus- tered around dis fort. I tell you ve hafe a fine town here someday. New Helvetia iss growing fast."

Sam arose and yawned. "Well, I guess I better get to bed. We got to get rested up. Crossing those mountains won't be so easy."

Sutter spoke quickly, agitatedly. "Ya, you are right. You better gif up der notion of crossing dose mountains now. You vill get caught in de mountains like dose beople vas, and den ve vill hafe to send a rescue party for you, too."

"Not us," Sam laughed. "I never start anything I can't finish."

"Dere iss a first time for everyt'ing," the Captain said, nodding sagely. "Better you stay here for a liddle while. I tell you vat. You stay till later in de spring. You are a good businessman. You could take ofer my store and run it for me. I don't haf de time to gif it like I should, and I got no one I can depend on to do it for me."

"A store?" Sam asked eagerly. "You got a store here?"

"Ya, a liddle von. I vould like to haf somebody come here and open a good von; somebody who got time to tend to dot kind of pusiness."

"A store—" Sam mused. "I'd kind of like to run a store. You think a feller could make money with a store up here?"

The Captain nodded happily. "Ya, ya. De beople bring in dere hides and tallows and a feller could sell dem a lot of tings dey need. Den you can send de produce down to de bay and sell to merchantmen at a good profit."

"It sounds good," Sam said. "I'll think about it while I'm gone. Maybe when I come back we can make a deal."

It was on the morning of April 26 that Sam's company made its early start for the mountains. In the late afternoon they encountered the last rescue party returning with the final survivor of the Donner group. This was Jacob Keseberg, who had broken his leg the fall before and had had to remain in the mountains until now.[35] The men of the rescue party had little sympathy for him; they told Sam openly, in front of the pitiable creature, that they were sure he had eaten the flesh of the corpses preserved by the extreme cold. They even went so far as to say they believed he had murdered a little boy for food. Sam regarded the man with loathing and was glad when he and his own companions left the party behind.

From Fort Hall, an old Hudson's Bay Company post in wilderness which was one day to be a part of Idaho, he wrote to an old friend in New York.

June 18, 1847.

BROTHER NEWELL:

Once more I take my pen to drop a few lines and let you know of my whereabouts. I left Capt'. Sutter's post in California, on the 26th day of April last, and arrived here on the 9th inst. I am on my way to meet our emigration; I am now a thousand miles on my road, and I think I shall meet them in a couple of weeks. I shall start on my journey again in the morning with two of my men and part of my animals, and leave one man here and the rest of the horses to recruit until I return, and then it is my intention to reach California in twenty days from this post. We crossed the Snowy Mountains of California, distance of forty miles, with 11 head of horses and mules, in one day and two hours, a thing which has never been done before in less than three days. We travelled on foot and drove our animals before us, the snow from twenty to one hundred feet deep. When we arrived through, not one of us could scarcely stand on our feet. The people of California told us we could not cross under two months, there being more snow on the mountains than had ever been known before, but God knows best and was kind enough to prepare the way for us.

We passed the cabins of those people that perished in the mountains, which by this time you have heard of. It was a heart rending picture, and what is still worse it was the fruit of idleness, covetousness, ugliness, and low mindedness, that brought them to such a fate. Men must reap the fruit of their folly and own labours. Some of the particulars you will find published in the Star.

I suppose you will not believe me if I should tell you I can sit down here and eat three or four pounds of roast beef at one meal; it is a fact. A man cannot know himself until he has travelled in these wild mountains. We killed a bullock this morning, and we are now roasting one side—the ribs—for our dinner, four in number. It is most astonishing the amount of food the body demands in this region. But away with the roast beef and let me come to our mental wants. Remember me to Mr. Davids and family and tell them I should have written to them half a dozen times before this, and so would Mrs. B. but we could not recollect Mr. Davids given name or their number in the street.

Remember me to Mr. A. G. Benson and Company and all the good Saints in

New York. May God and angels guard you and bless you, is the prayer of your unworthy brother,

as ever yours in love,

S. BRANNAN.[30]

Sam Brannan was the first man to carry the tale of the Donner catastrophe beyond the limits of California to the east, and his paper was the first to tell the gruesome details. It was the story of eighty persons who had been caught in the top of the Sierra Mountains by an early November snow. Thirty-six of them perished from hunger and cold. More than half the men died, and a fourth of the females, and those who finally got through to the fort with news of their plight had suffered severely from freezing as well as hunger. And it was Sam's paper which carried the news back to the States.

It was the thirtieth day of June, 1847, when Samuel Brannan and his two companions and their herd rode into the camp of the pioneer company headed by Brigham Young, on the shore of the Green River just a few miles from the junction with the Little Sandy.[37] The company was delighted to see them.

As Sam swung down from his mount Brigham came forward and wrung his hand. "Well, well, Brother Brannan, I'm mighty glad to see you. I don't know any one I'd rather see at this moment. Come on over to my tent. There are a lot of things I want to ask you."

"I'll tend to my horse and then come right over," Sam replied, pleased by his cordial reception. After he had removed the saddle and put the horse to graze, Sam went toward Brigham's tent. He was intercepted by Orson Pratt, who came running up. "Brother Brannan!" he exclaimed. "I was down the trail working with my instruments so I missed you when you rode in. How have you been?"

"Fine! We got a fine colony started in California, too. I'm mighty glad to see you with this company, although I hardly expected you. What's your job on this journey?"

"I'm charting the way for those that follow, making scientific observations, mapping, and keeping a record of altitude and weather conditions. It keeps me mighty busy."

"I guess it does," Sam smiled. It was heart-warming to meet this old and respected friend, who seemed not to have grown a day older since they had last met. Sam nodded toward two women who were cooking over an evening fire. "I see you brought a few women along on this trip. I didn't think Brother Brigham would do anything that foolhardy. After all, crossing the Great Plains on foot is a job that's hard on weather-seasoned men, and certainly risky for women."

Orson nodded. "They can stand a good deal more than a body would expect them to. At first Brigham swore no women would be allowed on this trip of exploration, but Aunt Harriet Young was sick and she kept complaining that she didn't want to die until she'd seen Zion. So at last Brother Woodruff offered to fetch her in his buggy. Then Brother Brigham gave in. As soon as the wives of some of our pioneer scouts heard that Aunt Harriet was coming, they insisted that they wanted to come, too, so we ended up with quite a few—more than we wanted." Sam nodded absent-mindedly, his thoughts already leaping ahead to questions his mind was hungry to have answered.

"Wasn't it pretty hard on you people when the United States recruiting officers went into your camps at winter quarters—Mount Pisgah and those other places—and took all your able-bodied men to march to California to fight in the Mexican War?"

Orson nodded his head violently. "It certainly was. When Colonel James Allen first came and suggested that we should send five hundred of our best men to fight in the war, I was against it. But Brother Brigham talked it over with us Apostles and we decided it was the cheapest way to get a large body of men to California. The Government promised to pay them wages, outfit them, and allow them to keep their arms at the end of a year's enlistment. So Brother Brigham went with Colonel Allen and advised our boys to sign up. They did, and when they marched out of Council Bluffs last July our Mormon battalion was as fine-looking a bunch of soldiers as I have ever seen."

"They didn't march into California until sometime in January of this year," Sam said. "I've had word of them now and then, being as all the news comes to my paper in San Francisco. The whole battalion is stationed in or around Los Angeles. The war was over with, so far as active fighting was concerned, before ever they got to the coast. By the way, has Brother Brigham decided to settle our people on the coast, where they can join our boys of the battalion?"

Orson shook his head. "No. Brother Brigham's heart is quite set on settling in the upper regions of the Rocky Mountains. He's talked of nothing else for months. He wants our people to live where we will be isolated. He says that if we can keep to ourselves for ten years we'll be so entrenched that no group of gentile mobsters can hunt us out again. We all think his idea is the wisest. Day before yesterday we met the old trapper, Jim Bridger, on the shore of the Little Sandy. Brother Brigham asked him what kind of country there was around the Great Salt Lake. Bridger says he's trapped its shores for years—that it's a fertile valley but dry in summer. We asked him if the land could be irrigated, and he said it was possible because there's hundreds of mountain streams flowing through different valleys surrounding the Great Salt Lake; but it's his opinion that while it's feasible, it would take too much work to get the water where we might want it. He offered to pay a thousand dollars for the first ear of corn ever grown in the valley of the Great Salt Lake."

"A thousand dollars!" Sam exclaimed. "Why does he think corn can't be grown there?"

"Because the summer is short and the winter's very cold. He says the valley around the lake itself is barren and dry, filled with sagebrush and greasewood, and not a fit place for people to live. He did say, though, that there was a valley to the north of the Great Salt Lake Valley that is filled with timber and brush, with plenty of streams, where we could likely build up a prosperous settlement. But Brother Brigham says we won't go there. He says we must go to the valley of the Great Salt Lake because it is the Lord's will. He's got his mind set on the Great Salt Lake because it is like the Dead Sea of the Bible. We will be the modern children of Israel, carrying out the prophecies in the Scriptures."

At that moment Brigham Young came to the opening in his tent and called impatiently to Sam. The two men parted abruptly as Sam answered the summons.

Brigham sat down on a box and motioned Sam to another. "I see you brought young Charles Smith with you," Brigham said. Sam nodded. "Did you know that he was a member of the firm of Jackson, Heaton and Bonney, who were counterfeiters in Nauvoo?"

"No," Sam said honestly and added, "But it wouldn't have made any difference to me if I had known. Charley is a good friend of mine. I like him."

Brigham made a gesture of distaste with his hand and let the subject drop. "How are our sisters and brethren making out on the coast?" he asked abruptly.

"Just fine. We have a community farm at New Hope, as I wrote you. We got eighty acres of wheat planted and already heading out. There are several houses that will be done there when we get back. It will be a good nucleus for a great Mormon commonwealth, for the land is fertile and the climate mild. In San Francisco we have already built fifty new homes, and we'll build more just as soon as we can buy enough lumber. Most of our houses have had to be made of adobe because lumber is scarce and hard to get in San Francisco."

Brigham leaned forward. "Adobe? What is adobe?"

Sam was all enthusiasm as he described the making of the big clay bricks and their use, and ended with what seemed to Brigham a fantastic statement. "Why, I can put up a thirty-foot house of adobe and put a family in it in two weeks. We did it for our newspaper office." [38]

Brigham laughed indulgently. "That sounds like an exaggeration, Brother Brannan."

"It's the truth," Sam insisted. His versatile mind flew to another idea. "I hear our battalion boys had a hard time of it marching to California."

Brigham nodded his great head sadly. "Yes, they did. They marched out of Camp Leavensworth last July in rags. The only friend they had in the Army, Colonel James Allen, had just died. A Captain Smith took over until they reached Santa Fe. There Colonel Doniphan gave them a hundred-gun salute of welcome, and that's a hundred guns more than he gave the Missouri mobocrats when their unit marched in a few days later. Our boys made good soldiers. At Santa Fe a good many of them took down with fever and diarrhea, and about fifty were left under command of one of our own boys, James Brown. That company wintered at Pueblo with a company of Saints from Mississippi, who stopped over there to wait and meet up with us somewhere on the trail this spring. We've been expecting to meet scouts from that company any day now."

Brigham's voice grew tense as he remembered the struggles of the last year. "I tell you, after five hundred of our youngest and most able-bodied men marched out and left us. we knew it was hopeless for us to plan to cross the Great Plains last year.[39] So we made ready for an early exodus this spring. Thousands of our people gathered at winter quarters this spring, and probably hundreds are following us a few weeks behind. At least that was the plan when our pioneer company left."

"I came as quickly as I could so that I might lead this pioneer company on to the coast," Sam said.

"Then you come on a sleeveless errand," Brigham said in his positive way. "We are going to settle in the Great Basin, in the valley of the Great Salt Lake."

"I think I can change your mind if you will listen to me first," Sam insisted.

"You can talk and I will listen, but I warn you, there's no hope of changing my mind."

Sam talked then, drawing a picture of the beauties of the land along the coast—of the mineral wealth, and the unlimited agricultural possibilities—and when he had at last exhausted his powers of persuasion he waited for Brigham to speak.

"I don't doubt a word of what you tell me, Brother Brannan, but the more you talk, the more I know our people must not go to such a place. We *must* have our Zion in a remote place which the gentiles will not covet while we are developing it. That is why we are going to settle in the land of the Dead Sea."

"But how in God's name are you going to reach it?" Sam burst in excitedly. "It's likely only a mule trail. How are you going to get heavily loaded wagons into a mountain valley where it may be impossible to take wagons?"

"That is Brother Orson's problem; his and the Lord's. We are going into that land. We are going to settle on soil that is now wilderness. We are going to make the desert to blossom as the rose."

Sam's enthusiasm was somewhat dampened and he felt a little aggravated at Brigham for his stubbornness. "I doubt it," he said sourly.

Instantly Brigham was aware of his antagonism, and he seemed to seek a way to put Sam on the defensive. "By the way, Brother Brannan, what personal reasons did you have for sending me that Kendall contract and urging me to sign it?"

"None," Sam said hotly, and rose to his feet.

"None, you say, and yet you urged me to sign a 'covenant with the Devil,' as you put it, and the Lord was to deliver us from it. You look like an intelligent man, Brother Brannan, yet if you make covenants with the Devil expecting the Lord to deliver you, then you are a bigger fool than you look. I was angry with you for ever listening to their words and sending me such a villainous document. Nothing could have made me sign it, to deliver my loved ones into the hands of greedy politicians."

"They told me that our signing that contract was the only way of delivering our people out of bondage; not only us in New York but all of you in Nauvoo."

"They could have told you anything, and I suppose you would have believed them—?" Brigham shook his head; as he talked he slowly paced the ground inside his tent, his hands locked behind him. "Oh, no, Brannan, you didn't believe them. You only pretended to because you had something to gain by favoring their little scheme. I thought so from the first, and I still do. When you sailed from New York, you were not stopped by the Government, which is proof that they were only trying to use you." He turned and shook his finger at Sam. "The trouble with you, Brother Brannan, is that you are too ambitious. I am not blind to the reasons why you wanted me to sign that contract, nor to the reasons why you want the Saints to go on to the coast and settle where you are already an established leader. You want to further your own ends. You want to share authority with me, and maybe eventually to take my place. But it will never be so. You are too ambitious for your own good, and I think that before you leave us we will teach you something about humility."

Sam clenched his fists involuntarily and found himself suddenly disliking the man. "I am ambitious," he retorted aggressively. "Any man worth his salt is. But I doubt that you or any other man can make me humble."

"We shall see," Brigham said. Sam turned and strode from the tent.

The next morning the camp moved on, Sam riding beside Orson Pratt. He was much interested in the handsome young man's readings of the barometer and his computing of the miles from a meter which two inventive brothers had placed upon a wheel to measure the distance traversed by the company.

On July 7 they set up camp outside of Fort Bridger, which was little more than a small stockade of logs pounded into the ground. The wall was eight feet high. The whole was built upon a small island, one of many formed by the branches of Black's Fork River. There were two adjoining log houses with dirt roofs—one was the trading post, the other Bridger's living quarters. Bridger was now on his way east with a pack of furs for sale. Inside the stockade, Sam soon learned, lived perhaps a dozen people—white men with Indian wives and half-breed children. Near by on another island were nine Indian lodges occupied by squaw-men, trappers, and hunters.

Sam was accosted, as soon as he entered the enclosure, by a tall man in a leather-fringed suit. "Are you Brigham Young?" he asked.

"No, I'm not. He's directing the men that are setting up camp outside. He directs everything."

"Will you lead me and my companions to him?" The stranger waved toward three men who stood in the background.

"I guess so," Sam said and turned back to the gate. The tall man fell into step beside him and the others followed.

"We're scouts sent on ahead of Captain James Brown's company from Santa Fe. We got a detachment of fifty men, half a dozen women, and quite a few children, on the way to meet your company. We've been wintering in Pueblo."

Sam stopped and held out his hand. The other shook it as Sam introduced himself.

"I'm sure glad to meet you," the tall stranger added. "My name is Crow. These are my three brothers. We got quite a family of us, what with the Mississippi company that was wintering in Pueblo when the stragglers of the Mormon battalion come over to join us."

Next morning the camp moved on a few miles before a halt was called by Brigham, who called his counselors into a meeting with the advance guard of the Brown company. The messengers explained that none of the men in Brown's company had received any pay since they had fallen ill and had been left at Santa Fe by the Army.

"What will they have to do to get their discharge and pay from the Army?" Brigham asked, adding, "All the boys are going to be discharged in July, but I guess them in California have had no trouble getting their pay."

"Why, as I understand it," the spokesman for the Crow family explained, "some of the men from the battalion will have to get power of attorney from the others to ride on to California to Captain Kearny, who will give them the money and the discharges."

Sam, as an authority on coast affairs, had been asked to the meeting and now he spoke. "Captain Kearny is stationed at Monterey. That means that the company that goes to the coast will have to carry powers of attorney for each man, a muster roll, and authority to carry back their pay and discharges. When I go back to the coast I can lead such a company."

There was a babble of voices as everybody began to talk at once. Brigham carried on a whispered conversation with Orson Pratt for several moments, then turned to Sam. "Brother Brannan, Brother Pratt and me think it would be a wise idea for you and Thomas Williams to go back and meet the Brown company and show them the way we are going.[40] The trail will be easy to follow, once they come to it. You can explain the California coast situation to Captain Brown and decide among you what is best to be done about these discharges."

"I'm agreeable if Brother Williams is," Sam said quickly.

Two days later Sam and Tom Williams met the Brown company and led them to the camp ground near Fort Bridger. As Sam and the company of fifty-odd men, a few women, and several children moved along to the southwest, they could see the snow-capped Unitah Mountains ahead. They kept following the trail which had had been blazed for them a few days earlier by Brigham's group. Later they learned that Orson Pratt, the leading spirit in building this road into a wilderness, had thus far followed the trail cut by the Donner party in 1846, whose leaders had departed from the old Fort Hall road to California and had cut instead a dangerous and costly route across the valley of the Great Salt Lake. They had been led on by the work of Lansford Hastings, who had been to the coast earlier and on returning to the States had published a booklet giving a map of a shortcut through the Great Salt Lake Valley; a route which he had never seen. Thanks to his directions, the Donner party had cut a difficult trail over the mountains and through the valley, to reach the Snowy (Sierra) Mountains late in October; there they were caught in an early snowstorm and thus met disaster and death. The few of the original party from St. Joseph who kept to the old Fort Hall road reached the coast early in the season in safety.

It was now July, and the Mormon stragglers from Santa Fe, led by Brannan and Williams, made no attempt to catch up with the pioneer company, being content to wait until their final destination was reached before seeing them. Later they were to learn that when Brigham came down with what the Saints termed "mountain fever," Orson was sent on ahead with a scouting company to blaze the trail. Brigham and the main part of the company meanwhile remained in camp for two days. But even this two days' delay of Brigham's party did not permit the Brown company to catch up with him.

Weber Canyon, down which Sam led the Santa Fe company, showed traces of the passing of the Donner party the year before, and also of the more recent passing of the pioneers, but it was plain that this year Orson was not following the Donner trail all the way. The Donner party, according to the signs, had gone down into the riverbed many times for easier passage, but Orson—evidently because of higher water this year—had been forced to cut a wagon road over steep and dangerous terrain.

Sam and his company found it necessary at times to hitch on logs at the backs of the wagons to trail on the ground, in order to hold them back on the steep grades. Even double-locking the wheels did not hold them. At one or two places the wagons had to be lowered by chains over abrupt, rocky precipices.

On the twenty-seventh of July Sam and Thomas Williams rode out of the mouth of Emigration Canyon ahead of the others, and reined in their mounts to look out from this benchland over the valley of the dead sea which lay in the bosom of the Rockies. Like a long elliptical bowl it spread out before them, surrounded by mountains on all sides, even beyond the silver expanse of water on the far horizon which was the Great Salt Lake. The sun beat down upon their heads and they panted in the sudden heat, for within the canyon it had been cool, green, and beautiful. Out here it was dry and grayish, and very dusty. Miles of silvery sage filled the floor of the valley. In only one place could they discover anything green, and that was on the shore of a tiny creek which wound out of the mountains to the north. On the edge of it they could see a camp.[41]

"This is surely not a land for God's chosen people," Sam said suddenly. "This is the land that God forgot."

"It sure is ugly," Williams said slowly. A few minutes later the rest of the company came out to surround them, and men and women stood looking down upon this barren desert. They seemed stunned by what they saw. Little was said. At last Sam nudged his mare gently and she moved down the trail to the northward which led to the floor of the valley. James Brown rode up beside him. Sam was irritated by the place, and as the mare brushed through the sage a pungent dust arose which stung his nostrils. "Brigham Young is crazy if he thinks he can settle our people on this spot," Sam burst out. "Why, if he had any sense he'd come on out to the coast like I been coaxing him to. There our folks could live in green, fertile, beautiful valleys. Anything will grow with little effort. We could build up a commonwealth there without killing ourselves, and in a few years we would be prosperous and happy."

Brown nodded grimly. "Prosperous and happy. You're thinking of our purses. Brigham is thinking of our souls. I'll stake my life on anything that Brigham recommends. He's got more sense in one little finger than the rest of us got in our whole bodies."

"He's not got any sense, not even in his little finger," Sam retorted. "If he did, do you think he'd settle thousands of people on a desert like this?"

"It looks like desert, all right," Brown agreed, "but there's water here. And where there's water you can irrigate. And if you can irrigate you can have gardens and farms. What more do you want?"

"I want to make a living without killing myself. While I'm worrying about my soul, I don't want to have to kill my body. I say the soul will thrive if the body does."

"I don't agree with you," Brown said. "Brigham wants to settle here because we'll be cut off from the rest of the world until we accomplish a few things we've been sent to earth to accomplish. Brigham never does anything without a good reason. I'd go to hell if he told me to."

"Well, I wouldn't," Sam said flatly. "You and the others follow him like a herd of sheep. Lord A'mighty, Brown, you got brains and so have the others. Why don't you use them? The Lord give you brains to use. He didn't say, 'I'll give all the brains to Brigham Young and the rest of you do what he says.' He said, 'The Lord helps them that help themselves.' If I was you I wouldn't settle in this God-forsaken place. Why don't you follow me to the coast? I'll show you where you can settle and be rich inside of five years."

"I doubt that statement, Brannan. You're too much of a braggart for me to believe all you say. But even if what you say were true, I wouldn't do it. I think a lot more of my soul than I do of getting rich. And if you were as devout as you pretend to be, you would, too. You've got the scriptures on the tip of your tongue, but no religion in your heart."

"That's a lot of poppycock," Sam said. "You can stay here with religion in your heart and starve to death, if you want to. But me, I'm going back to the coast just as soon as I can and make myself a fortune. You can stay here and starve if you want to—" he repeated.

Brown wheeled his horse and went back to the others, and Sam rode on ahead, alone. The encamped people came out to meet them and made a rousing welcome. Sam noticed when he came to the camp that several acres of ground had already been flooded with water and plowed. As he dismounted Orson came to meet him.

"How do you like our new Zion?" he grinned.

"It's goddamned ugly," Sam said.

"You'll like it better when we get it growing. We've already planted potatoes and corn. We broke several plows the first day, the ground's so hard, but it's good soil when once you get it worked up."

Sam said nothing but turned to look over the little encampment. There were wagons drawn up in a circle to form an enclosure, in which fires were made and the meals cooked. Another enclosure of wagons surrounded the horses and cows. Already it was beginning to have a look of permanence unlike the previous camps.

"When did you get here?" Sam asked Orson at last.

"On the twenty-second of July—five days ago. I came down into the valley alone on foot. Brother Brigham stayed behind in the mountains because of fever, and our scout camp was well established, and had been for two days, before ever Brother Brigham and the main company arrived."

Half an hour after the arrival of the Brown company, Brigham Young climbed up into the Woodruff buggy and Orson seated himself beside him. Brigham was still weak from the effects of fever. Brown and Sam and Thomas Williams, together with half a dozen other horsemen, rode slowly behind the carriage. They were bound for a tour of inspection of the valley—their first wide view of the valley of the Great Salt Lake.

They drove straight west to the shore of the lake. Long before they reached it, they could smell it. They were forced at last to hold their noses, for the wide salt crust that covered the beach held the bodies of millions of insects, and also refuse, which smelled most vilely.

Someone suggested that they all go swimming, and soon the perspiring, dusty Mormons were walking, gingerly barefooted, over the salty rime to the green water. They found it unexpectedly buoyant, and even those who could not swim could float at will. When they had had enough of this strange kind of swimming they went back to the saleratus-covered ground and rubbed themselves dry.

"Gosh-all-fishhooks, but this salt is rough on your skin when it dries!" Sam exclaimed. "It feels like a body was rubbing himself with sand."

Afterward, when the party was once again dressed, they wound their way along the base of the Garfield mountains and entered a valley which they found pleasant and green. Here they made camp. Next morning the explorers went many miles south into the valley and found it full of little streams and good pasture land. Late in the afternoon they turned back, reaching the pioneer camp again on the following afternoon.

Samuel talked to anyone who would listen about the beauties of California, and urged several of the men, Orson in particular, to follow him to the coast. But none would heed. Although Brigham neither liked Sam much nor trusted him, he made full use of Brannan's abilities. First he had Sam show the company how adobe bricks were made, and then he had him describe the way in which the houses were put up. Thus Sam became the father of adobe building in a place one day to be known as the state of Utah.

On the night of the third of August, Brigham Young called three men to a conference in his tent. They were Samuel Brannan, Wesley Willis, and Jesse Little.[42] They sat on their heels while Brigham sat in his rocking-chair and addressed them. He held in his hands a copy of the *Journal of Explorations* written by Colonel John Frémont, who had explored this very same country in 1842. As Brigham spoke he tapped the cover with his finger.

"It says in this book that there is a valley south of here, and in that valley is the south end of the Great Salt Lake. We passed around the south end of the lake the other day, into a valley Frémont evidently never saw. Halfway out in this, our own valley, you remember, we waded through a river that flows from south to north. I think it empties into the Great Salt Lake, and I think it comes from another body of water south of here. But that we know is not the Great Salt Lake. I want to know more about it. I want you three men to ride out and explore this valley to the south. Find out if the soil is fertile, how much water it has, and whether there is a salt lake there too."

On August 4 the three men set out, carrying light packs. They rode straight south through miles of sagebrush and toward lower mountains than those to the east, yet seemingly impenetrable, even so. At last they came to a break in the range. An Indian trail led them high above a river, which tumbled and roared over rocks far below. When they came out on the benchland of the next valley, they saw a beautiful blue lake which began some ten miles from where they stood and seemed to stretch thirty or forty miles into the distance. At its widest point it was probably five miles across. The floor of the valley was covered with sage and greasewood, but the mountains which encircled it were even more majestic and beautiful than those they had left behind.

They followed the Indian trail down to the lake and found its waters clear, sparkling, and cold, and full of fish. There were trout, catfish and minnows. They caught several trout and fried them for lunch. Then they went farther into the valley. It was beautifully green along the many streams, and the soil was rich and loamy. Finally they returned to camp with glowing accounts of what we know as the

Utah Valley; and when they told Brigham that the fresh lake to the south emptied through the river into the Great Salt Lake, the leader smote his knee. "I thought it must be so. Now that I am sure, we will name the river 'Jordan,' after the river in the Bible which emptied into the Dead Sea."

Captain James Brown had secured powers-of-attorney from each man in his company and was making preparations to leave for the coast to secure their discharges and pay. A party of about twenty was finally organized to go with him to Monterey to report to Lieutenant Colonel Philip St. George Cooke, now in command of the Mormon battalion. More properly speaking, he had been in command when the battalion had been mustered out of service in the July just passed.

On the night of August 8, Brigham Young held counsel with the men bound for California on the coast; they were to start on the morrow.

"First," Brigham said to Brown, "I want you to deliver this epistle which I have written in the name of the Quorum of Twelve Apostles. It is to be read to any companies of battalion men you meet coming from the coast to this valley. They must be turned back to the coast until next season. As you know, our crops will not mature this year, and the supplies we brought with us are almost gone. We have nothing here to feed more emigrants. A small company and I will start back to winter quarters next week, and when we return again to this valley we will bring all we can haul of provisions. There is some doubt, however, that we will be able to get back this year before snow falls."

He was silent for a few moments as if pondering a problem. Then he turned to Sam Brannan.

"I have tried to teach you humbleness of spirit, but I have failed," he said. "You are a headstrong man. It has always been my belief that no man is fit to lead until he has first learned to follow. Therefore, I am going to test your fitness to be a leader of our people in the future by watching how well you follow in the next few weeks. I am hereby appointing Captain Brown as leader of the company which sets out on the morrow for the coast. You will take orders from him, Brother Brannan. You will show him the trail, because you know it well, having come over it. But you will not give him, nor any other man in

the company, orders. If you ever want to be a leader among our people in the future, you will prove on this trip that you can take commands."

Sam rose quickly from his heels and stood, tall and straight, be-
for Brigham. "I take orders from no man, Brigham Young, not even
from you. I had full charge of bringing a shipload of Saints from
New York to the coast, and I did a damned fine job of it if I do say
so myself. I've proved my ability, and no man is going to make me eat
crow to please his vanity. You may be the Lord High Mucky-Muck
here, but you're only one man among hundreds to me. William Smith
warned me that you were an ambitious man when his brother Joseph
was killed, and said that Joseph never wanted you to take his place;
that you would try to usurp power that did not belong to you, because you crave to be a dictator. I didn't believe him then. I do now.
I'm leaving for the coast in the morning, and I'm riding with Charles
Smith. If your goddamned company wants to follow me it can. But
I'll take orders from no man in it."

Brigham Young leaped to his feet, quivering with anger. "Take
heed, Sam Brannan, take heed. Do not try my patience too far lest
you be cut off from the Church."

"You won't cut me off the Church because I'll quit first. You'll
be in a hell of a fine fix trying to get these men to the coast if I refuse to show them the way. They might make it, but it would take
them twice as long as it will me. And they might get caught in the
snow like the Donner party did last year. It's getting late in the
season, and the Snowy Mountains are treacherous. I think you won't
cut me off the Church, not while you need me worse than I need
the Church."

Brigham stood looking at him for several moments, and then he
relaxed. "Let us not part in bitterness," he said at last.

"I don't give a goddamn how we part," Sam said, and turning,
strode from the tent.

The next morning Sam and Brigham avoided saying any words
of farewell. Sam and Charles rode out ahead, rounded up their horses
and mules, and set out before the others. An hour out, Brown and
his company caught up with them, and Brown pleaded for peace
between them. Sam's emotions were touched and he agreed to join

the company. He and Charles both turned their horses into the herd and rode on with Brown and his men.

There was little friction for the first week or two. Then Sam began to speak bitterly of Brigham, and this the other men resented. Finally their differences flared into open quarreling which Brown sought in vain to control. By the time they had reached the Sierras, Sam and Charles were again riding ahead of the company, having as little as possible to do with its members.

When they came into the Snowy Mountains they were harassed by Indians who lurked always under cover, shadowing them constantly. A horse disappeared. A mule was found in the morning with two arrows in its hide. Brown grew uneasy and felt that it would be wise to increase the sentry force and to change men every four hours during the night. One morning at breakfast he said abruptly to Sam, "You will stand the early watch, tonight, Brannan."

"If I feel like it I will. If I don't, I won't."

Brown frowned. "You are a member of this company. Your animals are herded with everyone else's. It's only fair that you should take your turn at guard duty."

Sam put down his dish and rose, towering over the other man. "I am not a member of this company. You followed me out of the camp in the Salt Lake Valley and begged me to lead the way. Unwillingly I consented, and with the understanding that I was showing you the way. I have never placed myself under your orders and I don't now. Remember, Brown, I crossed these mountains with my horses and mules and three men, and we had no trouble. I can go ahead now with no one but Charles Smith, and take my horses and mules and have no trouble. This company is dependent on me. I am not dependent on you. Brigham Young tried to make me knuckle to you and I told him where to get off. And I'm telling you again. You can go to hell!"

"If you're so damned brave," Brown shouted as he jumped to his feet, "take your animals and Smith and get out. If you're too big to take orders from the leader of this company, you're too big for the company."

"You're goddamned right I am!" Sam said and, turning, strode toward the animal enclosure, motioning Charles Smith to follow.

They sorted out their horses and mules, mounted their mares, and rode away. Since they rode alone they increased their speed, and were soon aware that the Indians had remained behind to shadow the main company, leaving the two men to their own devices. It was with a sense of relief that they moved on.

On September 6, 1847, Sam and Charles met a company of ex-battalion men but lately mustered out of the service at Los Angeles; they were thirty or so in number, on their way eastward, and had wagons and seeds and stock. The sun was high and their night's camp only an hour or so behind when Sam accosted them. The two men were soon surrounded by an excited, happy group, clamoring for news of the new Zion and their loved ones.

"What kind of a place is the new Zion?" asked Addison Pratt, a missionary just returned from the Society Islands.

Sam held up his hands in horror as he stood beside his horse. "Awful!" he exclaimed. "It's desert country filled with sagebrush and greasewood and little else, set in the very heart of the highest mountains. They tell you the lake is salty, and they mean *salty!* I'd say it's half salt, and the most desolate-looking body of water you could ever hope to find."

"You don't say!" Addison said in dismay.

"I do so. And I'll say more. I don't think our Mormon people are going to be content there. Brigham may keep them there at first, trying to grub a living from that barren soil, but in a year or so they'll begin to pull up stakes and come on out to the coast like I advised them to. It wouldn't surprise me none if Brigham didn't get discouraged himself in a month or so and head on out here to the coast."

It was suggested that Sam and Charles should travel with them back to their last night's camp to await the coming of Captain Brown, for Sam had told them that Brown carried an epistle for them from the Twelve Apostles.[43] For two hours Sam and Charles visited with their fellow Church members in camp while their horses grazed, and during those two hours Sam told them all he could of what had transpired in the Great Basin. When at last they rode away, Brown's detachment had not yet arrived. A Mr. White rode on with them to the fort.

SUTTER'S FORT, SACRAMENTO, 1847

The building on the far right bears a sign "S. Brannan." It was the
Magasin, which Sutter rented to Brannan for his store when the business
was moved from within the Fort.

SACRAMENTO, 1849

From the Sacramento River, with Sam's store and the
City Hotel which Sam built

SAN FRANCISCO IN 1849

San Francisco in pioneer days, showing the bay with shipping, Goat Island, and the
Contra Costa range of mountains

On the evening of September 8, Sam Brannan and Charles Smith entered Sutter's fort. The Captain came forward to greet them, and Sam swung down from his horse and shook heartily the hand of his German-Swiss friend. "Vell, haf you decided to open a store here?" he asked smiling.

"Yep, I have. Charles and me have talked it over. He's decided to stay and get a room ready, make a sign, and wait for me to get a load of merchandise up here."

"Dot is fine. I vill send mine launch down and you can haul your stuff back on her."

"We can settle all that later, after we decide on a room. Hope you got something good to eat—we're starved!"

"Ya, ya. You vill eat vit' me tonight."

Before the tired travelers went to their bunks that night, Sam, Charles, and Captain Johann Sutter had come to an agreement about the new store of "C. C. Smith & Company, Dealers in General Merchandise and Groceries." [44] The Captain agreed to rent them the vaquero house and let them use his launch for hauling merchandise from San Francisco up the Sacramento River to the landing two miles below the fort.

Mr. White was hired as a shoemaker by Captain Sutter.

In the morning Sam left his tired mount and his spare horses and mules to pasture under the care of the Captain, and borrowing a gray mule from Sutter he rode south, bound for New Hope. As he rode he thought over the situation which Brigham Young's stubbornness had created. The staying behind of the Saints in the valley of the Great Salt Lake had ruined Sam's dream of being a leader in a great California Mormon commonwealth. His only alternative was to build up a commonwealth which was not Mormon, and to be its leader from the start, so that no one could ever question his authority. He decided to spread the word to his own California charges that Brigham Young might lead the hosts of Zion to the coast in the spring, while in the meantime they were to be humble and obedient to himself. This would give him an opportunity to control them and benefit by their labors, since the common fund still existed. In fact, money from the common fund would pay for the first merchandise he would send up to the fort, on which only he and Charles Smith would make a profit. Later, if the Saints decided to desert the coast, as they had promised when they left New York, in order to rejoin the new Zion wherever it might be—why, he would fall heir to all the material things they had accumulated.

When he reached New Hope the colonists gathered around him in front of the community house and eagerly asked questions. Sam held up his hand. "Well, boys," he said, "I've brought you bad news. The Saints are not coming out to the coast this fall. They may not come until spring. They may not come at all. So we've got to give up this farm, sell the machinery, equipment, stock, and the harvest."

William Stout pushed forward. "Well, I ain't going to leave this farm. Nobody sells it without asking me first. Us boys have worked hard to establish it and by God we've got a right to decide what's to be done about it."

Alondus Buckland chimed in, "That's what I say. I'm staying here."

William Evans stepped forward and turned facing the others. "I say we ought to submit to authority. Our Church comes first. We've suffered a lot for it, and we'll probably suffer a lot more. What I want to know is, what did Brigham Young say we was to do?"

Sam spoke quickly. "He said we was to give up the farm, sell the things like I said, and send him the money. You're supposed to go to Zion next spring and take stock and seeds and things they need; but I guess you can do as you please about going or staying."

"Well, then, I'll consent to sell if it will help the whole Church," Evans said. "But like the others I am very much disappointed." [45]

"What do the rest of you say about it?" Sam asked.

Eventually all but Stout and Buckland agreed to sell, providing Sam would send what was left of the common fund, after the members had drawn what they needed from it, to the Church governing body.

"All right," Sam said. "You men pack up and come down to San Francisco as soon as you can. We'll appoint a committee there to sell the stuff and take care of the common fund."

"I'm staying," Stout stubbornly insisted.

"You can't stay if the rest of us decide to sell. This is a community farm and belongs to no one man," Sam pointed out.

"Then I'll buy it, but I'll be damned if I'll leave because somebody a thousand miles from here said I had to."

"You can settle that with the committee at the proper time," said Sam.

The next morning Sam mounted the gray mule and continued on toward San Francisco.

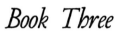

Book Three

Chapter XIII

SAM RETURNED to a San Francisco which had grown, during his absence, in leisurely fashion across the sand hills in every direction. His family was hungry for him, and Ann Eliza opened her arms wide to hug him to her bosom. Young Sammy stood to one side, afraid of this bearded stranger. Sam pretended not to know who his son was and made Fanny and Ann Eliza introduce him formally. But when he pulled the child close and kissed him on the cheek, and then tossed him high in the air to catch him expertly again, Sammy screamed—as usual, half in fear, half in delight—and begged for more. They were no longer strangers.

Fanny was bursting with news, when she could get Sam's attention. "William Glover built his house right next door to us and they just moved in. My, but we're glad to have them! We're always visiting back and forth, Sister Glover and me. And what do you think? William Glover has been elected to the town council."

"Bill Glover on the town council?" Sam chuckled. Then he turned to Ann Eliza. "How's the paper been getting along?"

"Just fine. Edward and Dr. Jones had a fight not long after you left, and Edward's been doing the editing. But he's a good boy. He's been agitating for a school house, like you told him to, ever since you went away."

"Good," Sam said.

While the women fixed supper Sam slipped out to the newspaper office across the yard. The boys greeted him with pleasure. They had seen him come home but had foreborne to intrude on the family reunion.

Sam fired questions at them, which they promptly answered, until his curiosity was satisfied. Then he sat down on a stool, leaned back, hooked his clasped hands around his knee, and asked, "What caused your ruckus with E. P.?"

Edward related the story. "You hadn't been gone long till Doc began to feel his oats. He took special delight in picking at Commodore Stockton in all his editorials. One time he said that Stockton was puffing and blowing around the country like a stranded grampus, cracking himself up as the greatest case out. Well, when that was published half a dozen citizens came in and got after us for speaking of the Navy with such disrespect. I reasoned with Jones and told him to go easy on such talk, but he wouldn't listen. Then I come right out and told him he would cease such intemperate language or I would take over his job. At that he went into a rage. He told me I was an officious upstart and that before he would take any more orders from me he would resign."

John Eager broke in to carry on the story. "Edward told him to go ahead—it would be better for the paper if he did. So Jones drew himself up and adjusted his green spectacles, and said he would take away with him the whole issue that had just come off the press inasmuch as it carried his name as editor."

Edward excitedly interrupted to complete the story. " 'You'll do no such thing,' I said to him—I was beginning to get hot under the collar—'John and me had more to do with printing this issue than you did, and we'll keep it,' I said. He started to gather it up from the floor, and John and me rushed him, making him drop what he had gathered back on the floor. Then he did get mad. My, what a rage he flew into!"

"Who got hurt?" Sam asked, laughing.

"Nobody," Kemble grinned. "But you'd have died laughing if you could have seen it. We practically threw him out into the yard, and when he got up he was sopping one of his eyes, and I gathered up what was left of his green spectacles and presented them to him. He took the rims and high-tailed it down the street, muttering under his breath. Wait a minute and I'll show you the editorial we printed in the April 17 issue, so as to let the public know we were through with Jones." Kemble went to a cupboard and abstracted the issue he wanted, and handed it to Sam, who read:

Dr. E. P. Jones having withdrawn from the Editorial Department of this paper, and Mr. Brannan, the Proprietor and Publisher of it being temporarily absent, during his absence, or until he can be heard from and some permanent arrangement made, the publication of the paper will be continued by the Subscribers, in whose charge the office was left by *Mr. Brannan.* They will give the readers of the "Star" the current news of the day and respectfully solicit contributions from those who feel interest in sustaining the Press in the town of San Francisco.

Edw. C. Kemble
John Eager

When Sam had finished reading he let the paper lie limp on his lap. "Well, Son, you've done a pretty good job. I guess from now on the paper can carry your name as editor."

Before he went back to the house for supper, Sam and the two boys sat down to compose an article about Sam's trip. It was to appear in the issue of September 18, 1847, and in its final revision it stated:

Mr. S. Brannan, publisher of this paper after an absence of nearly 6 months, arrived at this place on Friday morning last, 28 days from Fort Hall. Mr. Brannan said among other things that up to August 7, 1847—480 souls arrived at Great Salt Lake, mostly males and an additional caravan of four or five hundred wagons were expected. He said the Mormons had commenced a town, planted large crops and have at hand 18 months provisions. They contemplate opening an entire new road to this county, in connection with the present rendezvous, and which completed, they move en masse to the valleys of California.

Sam read it over with satisfaction. This should help him to start getting even with Brigham Young. At least it would keep all Saints on the coast under Sam's immediate supervision, since he was the only Mormon in the whole region endowed with authority to conduct Church business. Even though Brigham was angry at him, he had not as yet revoked any of Sam's powers.

As Sam was eating supper he casually mentioned to the two women his latest business venture. "I'm going to be a merchant from now on," he announced.

"Here in San Francisco?" Ann Eliza asked quickly, and Fanny stopped eating to listen.

"Nope. I've entered into a verbal contract with Captain Sutter to open a store at the fort. He is intending to build a flour mill a few miles above the fort on the river, and another—a sawmill—thirty miles up in the mountains. He's agreed to buy everything he needs from our store. Charley Smith is going to tend counter up at the fort, and I'm to buy merchandise down here and ship it up to him. We ought to make a pretty penny."

"Who are you going to buy from, and what are you going to use for money?" Ann Eliza inquired.

"I'm going to buy from Mellus and Howard. I'll see them first thing in the morning and sign a business contract with them. And I'm going to use what is left in the common fund to pay for it."

Fanny's back stiffened and she leaned forward. "You mean to sit there and tell us that you're going to use the Church money—money from the common fund—to finance your own private business affairs?"

"That's exactly what I mean," he said belligerently.

She gasped before she cried out, "Why, that's just plain stealing."

"It's not stealing, and your saying it is don't make it so. I'm just borrowing it for the time being."

She seemed a little mollified. "Well, if you intend to pay it back later it's not so bad."

"I may pay it back and I may not. Whether I do or not is my own business."

"It's my business too," she said grimly. "Some of the money that went in the common fund was mine."

Sam flung his answer angrily at her, "You'll get back what's yours. I've never treated you unfair." He went on passionately. "I've been a piker in Church affairs long enough. I put all I had into the common fund, and I worked like a slave to get a ship and to take care of our people on the way out. I never asked for a damned thing for myself, and what happened? As soon as we landed and they were safe, a bunch of them started abusing me and claiming I had been trying to cheat them. Of course, some of them stuck up for me, but a lot of them didn't. They got up in court and said I was crooked. That didn't used to be the truth, but now that I got the name I aim to play the game."

Fanny's chin trembled. "You don't sound like yourself, Sam Brannan. I think you've gone daft."

"No, you're wrong, Ma. I've just come to my senses after years of being daft. I not only done my best for our company, but I wasn't content to sit here and take things easy. No—I had to travel across the Snowy Mountains in winter to meet the pioneer company and try to show them the way out here. And what did I get for my pains? A kick in the backside. I hadn't much more than joined the company till Brigham Young was trying to belittle me in front of everyone. I told him where to get off and he didn't like it. But there's one thing I learned from him, and that is to rule things with an iron hand. He takes what he wants from the Church people and don't say 'please.' That's what I'm going to do from now on."

"It's a sin and a shame the way you carry on," she reproved him.

He laughed bitterly. "I want no more part of the Brighamite Church. From this day forward I intend to milk the Church people the same as he's doing, the way he'd do first if he had the chance."

"You mean you are going to apostatize?" she asked incredulously.

"No, not yet. I'm going to stay in the Church so I can keep control of our people. But I'll call no more meetings to order and I'll do damned little else as an elder. I'll let the others do the work and I'll take the pickings."

Fanny began to cry as she pushed back her chair from the table. "I never thought I'd live to see the day that the Devil would be speaking through your lips." She appealed to her daughter. "Talk to him, Ann Eliza. See if you can't talk some sense into his wicked head. You got to do something with him, or he'll go straight to perdition. There never was an apostate yet that didn't end up in destruction. Stop him before it's too late. He won't listen to me." She went to her room and closed the door.

Ann Eliza looked long at Sam, but he ignored her look and went on eating. At long last she sighed. "Poor Ma, she honestly believes that if you don't belong to the Church you'll go to perdition. She preaches to me sometimes till I could scream. If I was you I wouldn't talk against the Church when she's around. All you do is get her riled up."

"You've not said much. How do you feel about it?" he asked.

She pressed her lips tightly together. "I've never really believed it any time, and I've hated every person in the company since the day they tried to force me to do kitchen labor. I'm better than they are, and they can't understand it."

Sam stopped eating and looked at her long, a quizzical smile on his face. "Aw, come off your high horse," he said at last. "You're no different than the rest of us. I know you've never had any real interest in the Church, and I couldn't see why. Now I do. Still I'm not sorry

I joined. It's served its purpose." He stopped eating and looked directly into Ann Eliza's eyes. "Lizzie, when I was only fourteen I promised my Ma that I would grow up to amount to something. Well, I'm going to, and nobody or nothing is going to stand in my way. We're out here now in a new kind of world, and I aim to make my mark in it. You stick to me and I'll cover you with diamonds yet." He held out his hand to her across the table, and trustingly she put hers within it.

"If I hadn't thought you would, I'd never have married you," she smiled.

Chapter XIV

THE DAY AFTER his return Sam went down to talk with Henry Mellus and William Howard about furnishing him with goods for his store. Howard was a man of big build and at twenty-eight was already heavily fleshed. He was always good-natured and even-tempered, beloved by everyone and famous for his practical jokes. Henry Mellus was of a different type: tall, quiet, well-mannered, but already suffering from poor health although still a young man.

Sam told them of his plans and Howard made an instant decision. "I'll tell you what we'll do, Sam. We'll draw up partnership papers. You and Smith will be partners to Henry and me as far as business up New Helvetia way is concerned."

"It's a deal if Henry is agreeable," Sam said happily, looking at Mellus, who made no sign for several minutes as he stood seemingly lost in thought. At last he spoke. "I don't mind, providing Brannan has the money to put up as guarantee of good faith and to pay for the first two or three launch-loads of goods we sell him."

"I've got the money. I'll bring it over this afternoon," Sam replied.

The partnership deal was consummated and Sam sent up a launch-load of goods on the *Dice Mi Nana*, Sutter's little boat, which sailed back and forth on the Sacramento borne by the winds and current mostly, though when the air was quiet and they wanted to go upstream she had to be propelled by oars in the hands of passengers and the two-man crew.

After Sam had sized up public affairs so that he could boil down the facts for his paper, and when he had gathered up all the loose ends of his private and business affairs, he called a meeting at Barton Mowry's house so that he could acquaint the remnants of the *Brooklyn* company with the situation in the Great Salt Lake Valley, and how it would affect them as members of the Church. Sam stood straight and tall in the little second floor room with the men and women of the pioneer voyage on long rough benches before him. Most of the men had come down from New Hope, and they listened thoughtfully to Sam's words.

"The new Zion is in the top of the Rocky Mountains, in the Great Basin, and I'm free to own that it is desert country and about the most Godforsaken place I've ever seen. Brigham Young directed me to bring you word that you've got to pull up stakes here and move to Zion in the spring. You are commanded to bring seed and food and stock when you come to Zion, so that those there will have supplies. I said in the *Star* that they had provision for eighteen months. That was to fool the gentiles. The truth is that the people there are facing famine this winter. The long trek across the Great Plains used up practically all of the supplies they started with. And God knows there's nothing in that valley to eat."

"I said the Saints would build a road and come to the coast. That was to fool the gentiles. Brigham Young is bound and bent to stay in the Rockies."

He spoke at great length, telling them of the epistle directed to them and the ex-battalion men, urging them to stay in California for the rest of the year and come to Zion the next spring. When Sam had finished there was restless movement among the faithful. They were loath to leave the homes on which they had labored for more than a year. True, they had promised in New York to migrate to wherever the future Zion might be located. But now that the time had come they were reluctant to keep their promise. There were those among them, however, notably William Glover, who insisted that they must do whatever Brigham Young commanded.

This meeting was the last but one that Sam ever called for the Mormons.[46] He did not apostatize; he did not openly say that he was through with the Church. He simply dropped Church work, claiming that press of business prevented him from giving it his attention; and he left the services to be taken over by others. George Winner, Barton Mowry, and William Glover finally took it upon themselves to conduct worship and carry on the semblance of Church affairs. There was no elder in San Francisco who could properly officiate at weddings and funerals, at christenings or baptisms, except Sam Brannan. And although he refused to perform all other ceremonies, he could be prevailed upon to officiate at a wedding.

Later in September, Sam bought two more town lots at public sale and formed the nucleus of his future real estate business.

Now that fall had come, the Mormon families decided that their children must have schooling. For over a year they had run wild. J. D. Marston, a newcomer to San Francisco, came forward and offered to turn his little shack on Pacific Street, between Dupont and Kearny Street, into a schoolhouse, charging only a moderate tuition fee.[47] His offer was accepted. When Sam heard about it he was aghast, for he considered Marston an illiterate man. And after the Mormon children began to go regularly to Marston's house, carrying their slates and the schoolbooks the company had brought, Sam pushed his school project harder than ever in every issue of the *Star*, until at last a movement got under way to build a simple little structure on the plaza. This did not particularly please Sam, who had larger ideas, but at least it was a start.

In keeping with his plan to turn all *Brooklyn* company funds into cash as soon as possible, Sam appointed a committee consisting of William Glover, D. Stark, and John R. Robbins, to dispose of all community property. He allowed them to advertise free in the *Star*, inasmuch as they were only following his orders. Thus it was that in the issue of October 19, 1847, there appeared the following notice:

The subscribers offer for sale on reasonable terms the effects of the late firm of Sam Brannan & Co. as follows:

      A large quantity of wheat
      American cattle, horses, mule.
      Large quantity, good breed pigs.
      Valuable lot on the corner of Kearny and Pacific Streets. Lot and farm
          house on corner of Clay and Stockton.
      School books.
      Harper's family library, 168 volumes.
      Medium chest
      The launch *Comet*
      Wagons, chains, yokes
          also

2 drums, muskets, swords, powder, etc.

Linen, thread, wicking, 1 hat block, matches, sail needle and
twine. Castor oil, mustard, soap, 8 barrels salt, empty
hogsheads.

Agricultural implements.

> W. GLOVER
> D. STARK
> JOHN R. ROBBINS.

On October 23 the same subscribers advertised for sale a "Whole or
half of a large well-constructed Tanning establishment at Santa
Clara."

Meanwhile Sam was immersed in his activities at the Fort, and
on October 12, 1847, just a month after he had ridden away on the
old gray mule, he presided over the store in a little room of the fort
when it opened its doors for business. From this auspicious day the
Brannan store, administered by Charles Smith in the vaquero house,
became the leading emporium in the rich Sacramento Valley. People
brought in their hides and tallow and bartered them for produce.
Gradually the establishment came to be more than a store. Small
articles were accepted for delivery, so that they found themselves
carrying on a modest express business; little by little they became a
clearing-house for notes and a repository for money and valuables,
until the store had assumed nearly all the duties of a bank.

All through the month of September, 1847, Sutter kept hiring
Mormons as workmen. Most of those whom Sam had turned back
from the mountains entered the employ of the doughty Swiss, as well
as those who drifted in from Los Angeles after their release from the
Army. More than thirty of these Mormons [48] were sent to Brighton
to the site of Sutter's proposed flour mill, where they were to grade
and fill the land and begin the erection of a large building to handle
at harvest-time the miles of golden wheat that surrounded the fort.
Eventually seven other Mormons were sent up to the Indian lands at
Coloma, thirty miles up the American River in the mountains, to construct a sawmill under the direction of a strange, quiet man named
James Marshall.

Being in the store every now and then, Sam came in contact with
these Mormon workmen, many of whom he had known in the States.

He was interested in them, and they in him, for he was their acknowledged and appointed leader on the coast.

Sam especially liked the Willis Brothers, who were in and out of the store often during the first week after it opened. They were plain men, like himself, and fond of a good story.

When Sam returned to San Francisco he painted in glowing colors, to his wife and Fanny, the possibilities in his new business venture.

"You'd be richer in the things that are worth while if you'd concern yourself less with what you put in your pocket and more with what goes on in your soul," Fanny said acidly. "Meetings are no good any more since you quit taking charge. George Winner is doing his best, but George Winner is no Sam Brannan. And besides, he lacks the authority to do the things that ought to be done."

Sam shrugged. "Then they better send for someone with the proper authority, because I've no intention of wasting any more of my time for the glory of Brigham Young and the Brighamite Church."

"That's too bad," Fanny said with a knowing smile. "Thomas Kittleman and Angeline Lovett want to get married. No one can marry them but you. It seems a shame after all the years Angeline has been an old maid—"

Sam shouted with sudden laughter. "Don't tell me that prim old hen has decided at last to take the leap?"

Fanny nodded. "She has. I guess she'll have to undecide, though, things being what they are."

"No siree!" Sam bellowed. "I'll be glad to tie the knot for them. When do they want the wedding?"

"Sometime in December."

"Well, just tell them for me, I'll be happy to make them one."

In October of 1847 Kanaka Davis, who had been acting as supercargo for the vessel *Don Quixote*, came to rest for a time again at San Francisco, and when he came into the office of the *Star* he made an important announcement. "I'm going to get married next month at Mission Dolores," he said simply.

"Married?" Sam echoed. "Who in the world are you going to marry? I thought you were a confirmed bachelor."

William Heath Davis laughed embarrassedly. "No. I'm going to marry Miss Maria Estudillo. Her father owns the San Leandro rancho on the east shore of the bay. I've been wooing her for two years, whenever I've had time."

"You have? Well, I never suspected it! How does a feller go about wooing one of these California Spanish señoritas?"

"It's a little difficult," Davis admitted. "I've met her on ships twice when I was working as supercargo, and I fell in love with her the first time I ever saw her. Her folks sort of kept me away from the rancho, and it's only been lately that I have been able to meet her at her uncle's, Captain Richardson's over at Sausalito. It's all been very formal. I'll bet I haven't said more than a hundred words to her in all the times I've seen her. We're never allowed to see each other except when some member of the family is present, and she is not only very pretty but very shy." [49]

"Well, I'm afraid I'd have given up before now," Sam laughed.

In November, however, he hired two horses from Dan Sill, who ran the blacksmith shop, and took Ann Eliza with him out the sandy road to Mission Dolores to attend this very formal Catholic wedding. For a week they had been seeing twenty milch cows grazing on the hills above San Francisco, which Don Joaquin Estudillo had sent over for the marriage feast. Vaqueros rode herd on them all day long, so that the animals should not find their way home. When Sam and Ann Eliza saw only two or three cows left grazing they concluded that the feast must be ready.

The little settlement of Mission Dolores, dominated by the old mission, as its name implied, was an orderly place ruled by the firm but kindly hands of the old Spanish priest. Indians who had been captured and tamed by the priests tilled the fields and tended the herds of the beautiful pastoral spot, which had been built there on the creek because of the need for a good water supply. Sam and Ann Eliza found the open place in front of the church filled with a colorful representation of all the old families of the region. The men wore stiff blocked hats with brightly colored bands, silk blouses under embroidered bolero jackets, and tight knee breeches, trimmed at the knee with gold or silver lace. Their leggings were made mostly of soft deerskin, well-tanned, richly colored, and stamped with beautiful designs. These were tied with a silk cord wound several times around the leg, its gold or silver tassels hanging below the knee. They wore vests with filigree buttons of gold or silver, and over all, a richly ornamented poncho.

Their horses were no less handsomely garbed. The saddles were richly mounted with gold or silver, the bridles heavy with metal and fastened to the saddle; hanging down on either side of the horse was a beautifully ornamented *mochila* of leather, which looked like a blanket. Over the rump the horses were covered by the *anqueta*, which did not cover the tail and which was also richly decorated. The stirrups were solid blocks of wood covered with the *tapaderas* of leather which completely concealed the utilitarian foot-rest.

The ladies wore tight-bosomed and full-skirted dresses of heavy silk, also richly embroidered; their hats were ornamented with feathers or ribbons, and they always rode side-saddle. The wedding guests had been gathered since early morning, and it was now nearing noon. Finally the bride appeared, riding on a spirited, jet-black horse from the Rancho Pinole, owned by her uncle. She was led by Don José Martinez to the very steps of the Church, where she dismounted. The animal was caparisoned with gold- and silver-mounted saddle and bridle, while Don José would have put the sun to shame. The bride came dressed in richest white satin, with a lovely lace vein. Sam and Ann Eliza found the wedding ceremony inside the church very long and intricate, and could understand none of the priest's Latin chanting. Sam whispered to his wife, "Kanaka's got more guts than I have to go into this religion for a bride." Ann Eliza nodded and bowed her head, since everyone else was doing so.

At the ball in the evening, Don José was foremost in the activities. He danced the *jarabe*, an ancient country dance, with courtliness and grace; at certain points in the dance he and his lady partner would stop while one of them delivered a long verse in Spanish rhyme; then the dancing would resume. First the lady would go round and round her partner in ever smaller circles, her dainty feet always in view, and then he would respond. Later all the guests danced quadrilles, waltzes, country dances, and *la jota*. At intervals, luncheons of poultry, ham, cakes, coffee, champagne, and other wines were brought out.

The courtesy of these old-world families was surprising to these two Yankees, and they observed the alien customs with wide eyes.

Halfway through the evening several señoritas left the room and
came back with beautifully decorated baskets of eggs. Sam wondered
what they were for. When next he danced with Señorita Estudillo, the
bride's sister, he had his answer. She showed him an egg and laughed,
and he laughed, too, and wondered what was so amusing. Then in the
midst of the dance she held it above his head. He jerked to one side,
fearing an egg yolk on his raven locks, but with lightning rapidity she
broke it on his forehead, and he found his face wet with the daintiest
of cologne. He looked around. The women sitting around the edge of
the hall were laughing at him. At that moment he saw another beautiful young lady break an egg on her partner's shoulder; a cascade of
confetti fell over his clothes. Soon the free-flowing locks of the younger
señoritas were covered with the gaily colored confetti, and the room
was fragrant with the smell of many colognes. Sam secured some of
the eggs from a basket on the table and began to match his wits with
his various partners, to see if he could break an eggshell on their heads.
When he succeeded everyone laughed and applauded. He was flushed
and laughing when he went at dawn to get Ann Eliza from her
caballero partner, to go home.

As they rode away on the moonlit road they laughed over the
good time they had had. "I wish I'd been born a Californian," Ann
Eliza said. "They have such good manners and still have so much
fun." Sam agreed. Three days later the wedding festivities at Mission
Dolores finally came to an end, and stragglers passed through San
Francisco.

Thanksgiving dinner of 1847 was held in the evening at Brown's
Hotel for the leading citizens of the town. Sam Brannan was there
with the likable William Howard and genial Robert Parker, who was
soon to take over Brown's hostelry and rename it the *City Hotel;*
Colonel Stevenson, who had come to this new land to fight and had
stayed on; Edward Kemble, youthful editor of the *Star;* Kanaka
Davis, and half a dozen others were also there. A turkey had been
secured from some source, and along with the browned bird appeared
cranberries from Oregon and other Yankee dishes, that these exiles
had not tasted in many a month. A ship in the bay loaned the party
a cook and a steward, and sent canned lobster, sherry, champagne, and

port, to fill the gaps in the menu. The rain fell dismally without, but inside good fellowship reached its height, and these men, bound together by a common wish to make San Francisco a great city, pledged themselves to lasting friendship—a promise which they kept.

. And when they stood at midnight and lifted a glass to another promise—that they would make this an annual observance—they meant it. But that pledge was not destined to be carried out. History was marching toward them and they were soon to be engulfed in its forward surge. Sam and Colonel Stevenson weaved their way home up the hill, clinging to each other and singing happily in the early hours of the morning. Ann Eliza got up to help Sam into bed and wept tears of vexation when she saw the maudlin condition of her husband —and was glad that Fanny was asleep and could not see him.

The town was growing in its sleepy fashion, while the city fathers dreamed of a city which in fifty years might have a population of thousands instead of the few hundreds now living there. Sam saw a great future for San Francisco when the agricultural and grazing possibilities should be realized in the inland valleys; when trade routes should be established to all parts of the world; when the as yet scarcely touched mineral wealth should be uncovered. He often said that some day San Francisco would be the channel through which all the wealth of the interior would flow out to the world, and all the produce from foreign places pour in. To make the future certain, he was steadily building up business in his store and laying plans for buying more town lots at public auction. The lot upon which he had built his home had cost him fifteen dollars; the new lots had averaged about the same price, and those he intended to buy would not cost more. He felt that real estate was bound to increase in value as the town grew, and he could not lose money.

On the first of December the little redwood schoolhouse on the plaza, at the corner of Clay Street and Brenham Place, was finished. It was only a few feet removed from the jail. The next problem was to secure a capable teacher. Marston still taught the Mormon youngsters, but was not considered by Sam and other leading spirits of the city educationally fit to lead the youth of the growing metropolis. Sam urged in his paper that a teacher be secured forthwith, but, having built the schoolhouse, the city subsided once more into lethargy.

Sam grew apoplectic over this public attitude, saying that such lack of energy was plain laziness, and he kept prodding the city into action.

The school plan was not the only business Sam was trying to promote. November had seen the sale of the cattle, horses, and mule belonging to the company. The pigs had been snatched up by buyers; so had the lot on Kearny Street, and the lot and farmhouse on Clay. The wagons and yokes, the drums, muskets, and war-making implements, had been sold to newcomers, as well as the agricultural tools. And although the committee of three—Glover, Stark, and Robbins—had advertised the company goods, they were content to let Sam talk to the customers and consummate the sales in his newspaper office. As yet none of them had demanded an accounting of funds, and Sam had offered none. There was still the farm at New Hope to sell and various other items, including Harper's *Library* of 168 volumes. On December 11, 1847, the following notice appeared in the *Star*:

RANCHO FOR SALE

Very low for cash or short credit, one of the most valuable grazing Farms for Cattle in the Tulare Valley—green grass the year round, situated at the junction of the San Joaquin and Stonislau, with three log houses, and a Ferry boat for crossing the river. Terms of sale apply to D. Stark, J. R. Robbins, W. Glover or S. Brannan.

Fortunately for Sam, he was usually in the newspaper office when interested persons appeared to talk terms. The advertisement ran for several weeks, until a sale was consummated. The farm, its latest crops, and all its equipment were finally turned into cash. William Glover said in his memoirs that no one but Sam ever saw any of the money which the sale of company-owned lands and goods brought in. If an accounting was ever demanded, Sam put the committee off, and they, supposing that he would settle financially with Brigham Young, did not force the issue. William Stout insisted he would not leave the farm, but when the new owner took over, Stout and Buckland reluctantly moved out.

One of Sam's last official Mormon acts was to celebrate, as elder, the marriage of Angeline M. Lovett and Thomas Kittleman.

With the holiday season over, Sam settled himself to the task of getting the school started. He called a meeting of the city's leading men and urged them to appoint a committee to call upon the town council and ask that a permanent school council be appointed. A vote was taken to elect a committee to make this move, and Sam was one of the three committee-members who finally called upon the council.[50] After several meetings it was decided to appoint a five-man school council. The city agreed to pay $400 a year as wages to a teacher, the rest of his salary to come from tuition to be paid by the students. Much to Sam's disgust, his public school turned out to be only semi-public, for children whose parents could afford to pay tuition.

In January the rainy season began in earnest, but Sam did not mind. He was in the saddle now, riding toward the bright future which his mother had predicted for him and which he had promised to attain. Ann Eliza was riding high, too, as the wife of one of the town's leading citizens, and was taking herself very seriously. Her mother's admonitions to "get down off her high horse and keep her old friends" had no effect; the members of the *Brooklyn* company began to avoid her even more than before, though with Fanny they were still intimate.

Chapter XV

THE MOMENTOUS YEAR of 1848 was celebrated by San Franciscans
with a ball in the new City Hotel, which Robert Parker had bought
and renamed from Brown's old hostelry. Sam went dressed as Satan,
with a long tail which he switched back and forth.[51] Ann Eliza went
as Pocahontas, but spent most of the evening sitting sedately in a
chair. Robert Gordon came with a hat and umbrella with which he
clowned so cleverly that the company "was in stitches all evening,"
or so Kemble reported later. There were Army and Navy captains, mandarins, monks and Highland youths, Cavaliers and Indians.
The candle lighting was so poor that the costumes could not be seen
more than a few feet away, but refreshments on the other hand were
so lavish that the women retired early in dismay, while the men remained until a morning hour.

In January Sam took a flying trip up to New Helvetia with a fresh
stock of supplies. He was well pleased with the business the store was
doing. Sutter had closed up his own little store and was buying from
Sam all supplies for the men working at the flour mill and the sawmill. William Kountze had worked for a few weeks at the sawmill
site, but had quit and was now hanging around the fort much of the
time. Sam fell into conversation with him over the counter one day.

"How's the sawmill progressing?" Sam asked.

"All right, I guess," Kountze replied. "I was talking to the teamster that hauls the supplies up there, the other day. He says the mill
frame is up and the forebay dug, ready for the tailrace. They've hit
granite, though, in the tailrace, and it'll likely take them a little time
to blast it out so's they can get the old mill wheel to turning."

"Didn't you like it up there in the mountains?" Sam inquired.

Kountze shifted his wad of tobacco from one cheek to the other,
spat a stream on the dirt floor, and replied, "No, can't say as I do.
It gets too dang cold up there this time of year. I'd rather hang
around the fort here and do odd jobs."

"Can't say as I blame you. How many men has Marshall got up there working with him now?"

"Seven, besides the Wimmer family. By God, I hate that Wimmer woman! She's the naggingest bitch I ever run up against. She's the main reason I left up there."

Sam laughed. "I hear she's a shrew all right. But I ain't interested in her. Tell me about the mill. I'd like to put a little piece about that sawmill in my paper down in San Francisco. What made Marshall pick that place to put up a mill?"

Kountze chewed a moment before he answered slowly. "Well, I guess the main reason was because it's in the heart of good pine timber, and the American River can be used to float the logs down here to the fort. You see, his idee was to build the sawmill in the course of the regular yearly overflow, and then deepen the channel that it flows over and use it for a mill-race. At Coloma the river makes a wide sweep around a point of land. By digging a ditch through that narrow neck of land, the water flows through the ditch from above and joins the river again below. We built up a brush dam to force the water through the ditch the way we wanted it."

"Well, that sounds like a damned smart idea. But now they've hit base rock and will have to blast the channel deeper, eh?"

Kountze nodded. "That's right."

Sam was thoughtful for a time. "I guess if you fellers lived in tents up there in rainy weather like this, it must have been pretty miserable."

"We lived in a log house we built a hundred feet from the mill site. It was really two cabins with a porch between to join 'em. Marshall and us fellers lived in one, and Wimmer and his wife and younguns in the other. Mrs. Wimmer was supposed to do the cooking for all of us, but we got so doggoned tired of her chin-music with every meal that we finally moved off to ourselves in another cabin. Wimmer's all right. He's just hen-pecked."

"What's he do?" Sam asked.

"He has charge of the Indians that are helping dig the race. The white men are cutting timber and building the mill." ·

On February 21, 1848, Sam presided at the town meeting at which the first board of school trustees was elected. They were: Dr. J.

Townsend, Dr. F. Fourgeaud (a physician), C. L. Ross, J. Serrine, and W. H. Davis. Eight months before this meeting San Francisco had had a total population of 375, but now, Dr. Fourgeaud reported, there were 800 inhabitants in the town, including Indians. There were 473 men, 177 women, and 60 children of school age.

A short time later Thomas Douglass, graduate of Yale College and lately of the city of San Jose, was hired to teach the school, whose sessions were to begin on April 1, 1848. He was to receive a salary of $1,000 a year, the city to pay $400 of this amount and tuition to make up the balance.

But before this event took place Sam's main interest had flown to something else. He had engaged Dr. Victor Fourgeaud, brother to F. Fourgeaud, to act as special editor for an immense booster edition of the *California Star*. Leaving Dr. Fourgeaud with Edward Kemble (John Eager had left his employ to go with his mother to Monterey), Sam went up to the fort to carry supplies and discover Charles Smith's further needs. He had no sooner taken his place behind the counter than Jake Wittmer, Captain Sutter's teamster, strode into the store. Jake was a notorious spendthrift, and although Sam might trust him for clothes or food, brandy had to be paid for in cash by Wittmer and all other customers.

"Set me up a glass of brandy, Brannan," he said with an unusually positive manner.

"Not till I see the cash in your hand," Brannan laughed.

Wittmer looked at him with level eyes for a moment and then said quickly, "I got something better than cash."

"I'd have to be the judge of that," Sam countered.

"All right. Take a look, then," Jake replied, and poured a little pile of flakes from his purse into his hand. Sam leaned forward, breathless.

"Where'd you get it, Jake?"

"Up at Coloma. I got this sample from the Wimmers. The old Cap is going to send me to Governor Mason at Monterey to see if he won't give Sutter title to the land. It belongs to the Injuns now. Sutter's only renting it from them."

"God Almighty, that looks rich!" Sam whispered.

"It is, Brannan." Jake put his finger to his lips. "Don't tell a soul.

The Captain wants it kept quiet till he gets title to the land. Otherwise he'll lose out."

"I won't breathe a word of it," Sam said, and poured out the drink that Wittmer had demanded.

When Sam went back to San Francisco he kept his promise. No word of the gold discovery was spread abroad through him. But Jake got drunk at Benicia and let it out and through Robert Semple the word seeped into the city. Still, nobody paid much attention. Gold was always being found in little pockets somewhere or other. A few years back some had been found near Los Angeles, but the strike had not amounted to anything. Sam had little interest in the gold discovery anyway, for he was bound up in his booster edition of the *Star*, which was to come out on the first of April and was to be sent by special messenger over the mountains and the Great Plains to the Mississippi River region, where the first copies would be released and would then be mailed on to New York and the East. This was to bring a great wave of settlers to California. Already caravans were arriving weekly at the fort, bringing farmers and settlers, but Sam dreamed of the time when they would come every day or so, until the whole of California should be settled by an industrious people. This was not so much because he wanted to get rich from them, which indeed he hoped to do, but because he loved his new land and wanted it to be the greatest in the world.

The only concession he made to the gold discovery was to allow Dr. Fourgeaud to include a notice of it in the text of a long editorial he was writing for the booster edition, in which he extolled the beauties and possibilities of California. In the meantime the *Star* printed no word of the discovery locally.

In March, when Sam went up to New Helvetia, he talked with the ex-battalion boys who came to trade on the days they had off from the flour mill at Brighton. Ira and Sidney Willis came in late one afternoon. Sam was glad to see them and said so.

"How you boys doing?" he bellowed, and they grinned and said things couldn't be better.

"Want a little drink on me?" Sam queried. They looked at each other a moment and nodded to Sam. He reached under the counter and grasped the bottle, then jerked his head toward the table in the corner. "Come on over here, fellers, and set awhile. Got some questions I want to ask you."

The brothers looked knowingly at each other and followed Sam to the table, where they sat down and gulped the drinks he poured for them.

"Heard anything about this gold strike?" Sam asked, leaning forward and speaking in a low tone.

They laughed outright for several minutes, then Ira controlled himself and replied quietly, "You must of read our minds. We come down here on purpose to ask you to keep this dust in your safe for us." Both boys laid tobacco-sacks of gold before Sam, who pulled the strings of one and looked at the glittering particles within. He sighed as he closed it.

"Where'd you get these piles?"

"We've found a rich vein on an island in the American River a little ways above the flouring mill site."

"Jake Wittmer told me last month that gold had been found up Coloma way, but I didn't think it amounted to much," Sam said. "Now you tell me you've found it near the flouring mill. How did you happen to find it? There must be some connection between your find and the one up above. The story's what I want. Now begin at the start and tell me all about it."

Sidney shifted his position and began the story in his deliberate way.[52] "Well, it's kind of a long story but it all started with Harry Bigler, or Henry, as you know him. He was one of the seven ex-battalion men that went up to the sawmill to help Marshall. About the twentieth of Feb'uary he wrote down to Ezra Green, that's been working with us on the flouring mill, that they'd found particles of gold in the tailrace of the new mill. He said we wasn't to tell anyone, and we didn't. One Saturday night me and Wilf Hudson and Ira Fiefield made up our minds to walk up to the sawmill the next day and see if they'd found any more gold, and if so, how much. We told the fellers at Brighton that we was going deer-hunting, and we took a gun and they never thought nothing about it. When we got up to the sawmill it was just about dark and too late for us to see anything. But the boys was glad to see us and invited us into the house they was living in, for supper. Marshall was there and told us all about how he'd found the first gold. Said that he was walking along the tailrace one morning, looking at the water running through it and trying to figure out how he was going to deepen it, now it was down to bedrock. He seen something gleaming in the water, and he got down on his knees and looked and fished out some of it, and sure enough it looked like gold. He had the boys put some leaves and dirt in and dam it up some that night, and the next morning they all found gold, quite a bit of it. Marshall was awful excited then, but he wanted to make certain it was gold. He took some down to the fort and they tested it with aquafortis and sure enough it was the real stuff. He said that there was gold in the race every day.

"Then the boys said they'd examined up and down the river and found little pockets of it in the rocks in quite a few places. We asked Marshall if we could examine the tailrace next morning, and he said we could, and we could keep what we picked up providing we'd keep our mouths shut. He said he didn't want people coming up there and hunting for gold until Sutter had title to the land. It seemed more important to him to finish the mill. We talked till quite late and then turned in.

"The next morning, while the boys was cooking breakfast, me and Wilf and Fiefield went out and searched in the tailrace. We all found some flakes, but Wilf Hudson pried out a whopper with a butcher knife that must've been worth all of six dollars. We was so danged excited then that we couldn't eat when breakfast was ready.

"We stayed up there till Thursday, and every night after we was through helping the boys on the sawmill we'd all go upstream looking for gold—and finding it, too. I tied up a nice little pile of it in my shirttail. On Friday, when we started home, Bigler came with us to visit the boys below. Him and Fiefield follered the road down, but me and Wilf Hudson follered the river, stopping to hunt for gold at every likely spot. We didn't find none, though; not till we come to an island—a bar I guess it'll be when the water goes down some. There we found a few flakes, but there didn't seem to be much so we moseyed on down home. I guess I never would have thought about it again if it hadn't been for Iry here. He wouldn't give me no rest till I took him back and showed him where we'd found the last flakes. At last, tired of his nagging, I took him up there."

Ira, getting restive in his chair, broke in, "It's a good thing I made him take me, too, Brannan. 'Cause when we got there we found a lot of gold. We pried it out with our knives and picked it out with our fingers, and got as much as we could tie in our shirttails and our handkerchiefs, and then we decided to stake us a claim. And we done it. When we went back to the flouring mill we told all the boys and they went up there and all of them staked claims. There's plenty of room for all our boys. Any Mormon that shows up there can have himself a claim."

Sidney nodded and added, "I wisht we had a way of washing it or something. It's awful slow picking it up or digging it out. And we need food and supplies. It takes too much time to come down here to the fort every time we need tools, or clothes, or staples."

Sam sat back thoughtfully. Gold lay in front of him. There was a fortune within his grasp and his mind moved over the beautiful possibilities. Suddenly he leaned forward. "Tell you what I'll do, boys. You and Iry give me an interest in your claims, sign it over to me, and I'll grubstake you. You can stop working at the flouring mill right now and spend all your time digging for gold. I'll furnish you with tools, shelter, clothes, and whatever else you need. If a lot of you boys are going to be working up there I'll open a branch store there— it might even be a good idea to open up a boardinghouse."

Both men reacted with enthusiasm. "That's a smart idea," they agreed. "All our boys could quit the mill and go to work for theirselves. We can make more digging gold than we can working at twenty-five cents an hour," Willis exclaimed.

"Sure we can, and I like the idee of being grubstaked. That means we'll have nothing to worry about. Brannan feeds us and clothes us and gives us what supplies we need, and all we got to do is give him a third of what we dig up. I'm for it," Ira agreed.

"You can't lose anything by it," Sam urged. "The boys up at Coloma won't be as well off as you, either. Sutter wants title to that land and they're not free to help themselves to the gold like you fellers down here."

Willis nodded. Sam leaned forward. "There's another thing I want to remind you boys of. All you boys are Mormons. You say that you're only going to let Mormons stake out claims on your island. As members of the Church, you owe the Church a tenth part of all money you make. I am the only duly appointed representative of the Church out here, so it will be my duty to collect your tithing. Remind the rest of the boys of that, will you?"

They nodded. Sam's mind ran rapidly over the possibilities, and then he spoke again of the tithing. "We ought to build a church out here on the coast, and maybe later a temple. I think I'll collect more than ten per cent of your wages. The Church needs money now, and if you boys can have gold just for picking it up you ought to be willing to give more to the Church."

"I don't think none of us would argue with you about that," Ira said quickly.

Sam called to Charles Smith to bring them pen and paper, and the partnership papers were drawn up then and there. Sam felt well satisfied when he returned to San Francisco. He had no intention of making public the important news about the latest gold discovery, or any other gold discovery, at this time. First he wanted his own interest in the mines to start paying dividends, and he wanted to collect tithing before outsiders should come in and disturb the Mormons; for Sam had no intention of turning any tithing money over to the Church. Second, he wanted to get his store· and boardinghouse established before any outside rush started.

He disembarked from the *Dice Mi Nana* at the foot of Clay Street and walked up to the store of Mellus and Howard. Big Bill handed him the latest edition of Semple's *Californian* and pointed to a little article at the bottom of the third column on the second page, saying, "Know anything about this, Sam?"

"*Gold Mine Found,*" it said. Sam read on:

In the newly made raceway of the Saw Mill recently erected by Captain Sutter, on the American River, gold has been found in considerable quantities. One person brought thirty dollars worth to New Helvetia, gathered there in a short time. California, no doubt, is rich in mineral wealth; great chances here for scientific capitalists. Gold has been found in almost every part of the country.

Sam put the paper down and laughed. "I think he's talking through his hat. There's always rumors of gold strikes floating in here, but there's never anything to it. I don't think there is in this, either."

"Hmmm," Howard said thoughtfully. "I wouldn't mind getting in on the ground floor of a good gold strike."

"Me either," Sam replied. "But first I got business to tend to with you that's more important." They retired to the office to make up new lists of needs for New Helvetia.

When Sam went home that night he swore his womenfolk to secrecy and told them about the discovery of gold and how it was going to affect them. They listened, wide-eyed, and proved that women could keep a secret.

Back in San Francisco Sam once more forgot gold for the nonce. He joined Dr. Fourgeaud and Edward in working day and night to get out the great extra booster edition of the *Star*. Sam did not headline news of a gold strike. He was interested in attracting settlers who would work the soil and stay in California to build it up rather than fly-by-nighters who would come for gold, stay to create trouble, and leave when they had got what they came for. Therefore in the six pages of this edition of two thousand copies, California's advantages were extolled in expert fashion, with only passing mention of a silver mine near San Jose, a copper mine at Napa, and gold at Coloma.

In an article entitled "The Great Sacramento Valley" Sam told about gold at Coloma, not for home consumption but for Eastern readers. In the last paragraph, the story of the new discovery read as follows:

It has a mine of gold and a probable estimate of its magnitude cannot be derived from information we have received. It was discovered in December last, on the south branch of the American Fork, in a low range of low hills forming the base of the Sierra Nevada, distant thirty miles from New Helvetia. It is found at a depth of three feet below the surface, and in a strata of soft sand rock. Explorations made southward, the distance of twelve miles, and to the north five miles, report the continuance of this strata and the mineral equally abundant. The vein is from twelve to eighteen feet in thickness. Most advantageously to this new mine, a stream of water flows in its immediate neighborhood, and the washing will be attended with comparative ease.

To help defray the expense of the express carrier who would deliver the two thousand copies of this six-page paper, which had to be printed on a crude hand-press, Sam offered to carry letters to the

SAM BRANNAN

Photographed in Alpine climbing costume, in S. F.
about 1850

VIGILANCE COMMITTEE, 1851

The hanging of Jenkins on the south end of the old Mexican Customhouse on the Plaza

Missouri River region for fifty cents each, guaranteeing delivery within sixty days. Nathan Hawk, a former private in the Morman battalion, was hired to carry the papers and letters.

On the first of April the booster edition was ready. It was necessary only to await the arrival of the *Dice Mi Nana* from the fort to take the express carrier on the first leg of his journey. Meanwhile, one of Sam's dreams came to fruition. On the morning of the third of April, 1848, Thomas Douglass opened his first session in the little redwood schoolhouse on the plaza. Sam stood beside Douglass as ten children came to school. It was evident that Marston was keeping his school intact. When Douglass had followed his students inside and closed the door, Sam read the curriculum posted outside, in which the schoolmaster set forth his willingness to teach reading, writing, spelling and defining, and geography, for $5 per quarter. Adding mental and practical arithmetic, English grammar and composition, were $6. All the foregoing, together with mental and moral science, ancient and modern history, chemistry and natural philosophy, cost $8. Any or all of the foregoing, together with geometry, trigonometry, algebra, astronomy, surveying and navigation, $10. Any student who could not pay tuition might come for training free.

Sam walked thoughtfully down the hill. Marston was too ignorant a man to be a teacher. He must be displaced by the erudite Douglass. Sam met George Winner on Montgomery Street and buttonholed him at once. When they parted, George had promised to use his influence to get the Mormon children away from Marston and into the Douglass school. Eventually there came to be an enrollment of thirty-seven children in the new semipublic school—San Francisco's first real school. Marston's little school was forced to close for lack of pupils, and he had only his bride of a month, Selena Still, to comfort him.

On the afternoon of April 3, Sam and Nathan Hawk boarded the *Dice Mi Nana* for the trip up the Sacramento River. Both he and his carrier were elated. At the embarcadero two miles below the fort a pack train of mules waited to take on the two thousand copies of the booster edition, together with the teamsters who were accompanying Hawk on his hurried journey to the Missouri and Mississippi river regions. Sam always enjoyed these trips up the Sacramento, for he never tired of the infinite variety of scene it presented. Black cormorants swooped and gray and white gulls wheeled and screamed as the little boat sailed up San Francisco Bay. The smell of salt sea was mixed with the tangy odor of fish. The launch tacked past Alcatraz Island and sailed smoothly toward the San Pablo Bay, which lay at the mouth of the Sacramento. The hills all about were green after the winter rains.

It was dark when the boat had to buck the tide that swelled where the waters of the river met the tide from the bay. Under the expert fingers of her navigator she made it with only a few rough bumps. When morning came, the rolling hills had been left behind to make way for endless acres of wide flat lands. The river was hedged in by tall reeds, but occasionally there came open spaces through which Sam could see the hills on the northern horizon. The great sluggish stream turned and twisted slowly through this lowland, and at times the boat passed shallow little lakes where the mud-hens busied themselves. Ducks and geese nested among the clumps of grass in the marshes, and when night came on again a heavy fog rolled in to shut out all sight of land. Only the voices of thousands of birds disturbed the muffled air. With the fog came a cessation of wind. Sam took his place with the other male passengers at the emergency oars and the boat was kept moving. After two hours he was sore and weary. The boat was tied up for the night, and everyone bunked down as best he could on the deck.

It was the evening of the seventh when the launch pulled in toward shore at the little settlement on the fort embarcadero. All the inhabitants—half a dozen men—stood on Sutter's dock awaiting them. Sam's eye was caught again by the graceful beauty of the old oaks standing in a row a short distance from shore. When he had climbed ashore he stood for a few moments looking at the mountains, cool and gray-green, which loomed to the east. Then he threw off his coat and began to help unloading his papers and packing them on the mules. After a time Captain Sutter came riding down. He hailed Sam as he dismounted, and Sam stopped to talk to him.

"Vot haf you got dere?" the genial Swiss asked.

"My booster edition. I told you I'd have it ready by the first of April. And by the way, thank you for having the mules on the spot. Nathan here," he introduced Hawk, "will take good care of them and bring them back in good shape."

"Ya, ya," the Captain said, as if taking it for granted.

Sam grinned as he added, "They ought to have gold horseshoes, the price you're charging me for renting them."

At the mention of gold Sutter frowned. Quickly Sam asked after affairs at the fort.

"Dey are not goot. All dose Mormons haf left mine flouring mill to go digging after gold. Even de cook iss gone. I cannot hire v'ite men to harvest mine v'eat, and so I put de Indians to vork, and dey run off too, and I haf to leave more as two-t'irds of mine harvest in de fields. I tell you, I don't like de look of t'ings."

"How did you come out with Governor Mason? Has he give you title to the lands at Coloma?"

"Nein. He sends me vord dat de treaty between Mexico und de United States iss not signed, and nobody hass got title to dat land. I vill pe ruined if dis gold fever does not stop."

Sam laughed reassuringly. "No, you won't. Quit trying to harvest wheat and put on your digging clothes and go get you some gold. You know where it is."

The Captain waved the suggestion away. It was plain that he was not happy about the turn events had taken. Sam went back to his work.

The next day he worked behind the counter with Charles Smith. Mormon ex-battalion men came in an almost steady stream to buy goods, and each paid with gold from a little sack. When Henry Bigler came in, Sam stopped his work and led the man to the corner table. He poured brandy for both of them and invited Bigler to tell his story. Bigler loved to talk, and he told the story fully while Sam listened with shining eyes.

"We went up to Coloma with Marshall last fall late, and we worked hard. By New Year's Day the mill-frame was up and the forebay in the ditch dug for the tailrace. We found out then that the tailrace wasn't deep enough, and deepening it through granite base rock was a slow job. On the twenty-fourth of January I was at work with my drill, fixing to put in a blast. Marshall passed me on his way down to the lower end to see how Peter Wimmer was getting along with the Indian workmen. In a little while one of the Indians come running up and says to Jim Brown, 'Want tin plate for big boss.'

Jim stopped his whipsawing in the mill yard and went into the cabin
to get the plate, which he give to the Indian. He stood there looking
after the feller, wondering what Marshall wanted with a plate. But
he didn't say nothing about it to me and I guess he forgot it himself
after a few minutes.

"When we was about ready to quit for the day Marshall come
along and he says to us, 'Boys, I think we've found gold.' We all
laughed and said 'No sech luck.' Marshall let it go at that and went
on up to his own cabin that he'd had built on the side of the mountain.
We was jest getting ready for bed when Marshall come back down
to set and talk with us awhile. He's kind of a quiet feller and it takes
him a little while to get warmed up so's he can talk free-like. But after
talking around he finally says that he'd found gold near the lower end
of the race that morning, when he'd sent for the tin plate. We didn't
know what to think, whether to be excited or to wait and see if what
he'd found was gold or fool's gold. When he got up to go he says to
Brown and me, he says, 'Shut down the head gate early in the morning
and throw in some sawdust and dirt and old leaves, and make everything tight so's it will hold anything that might accumulate.'

"Well, we done like he said and the next morning after breakfast
we went to our regular work as usual. Marshall went down after
awhile, and when he come back he was carrying his old white hat in
the crook of his arm and his face was covered with a grin like I'd never
seen him have before. He usually looks glum, but by cracky, he sure
looked happy that day! Then 'Boys!' he yelled, 'Boys, I've found a
gold mine, by God!' He set his hat down on the workbench in the
mill yard, and all of us workmen came running to look. On top of the
knocked-in crown of his hat was a pile of gleaming flakes and dust.
About half an ounce, I'd say, and they ranged from the size of a
kernel of wheat to just dust. Most of it was in small flakes, but some
was round and others square-like. We went crazy then, all talking at
once, picking up little pieces and feeling it and yelling excitedly that
it sure was gold, all right. Azariah Smith pulled out a five-dollar gold
piece and held it down against the gold. It was the same color, except
that his coin looked brighter and was more whitish.

" 'Where'd you find this?' we asked Marshall, and he led us down
to the lower end of the race and showed us the spot. We went down on

our hands and knees like bears and begun crawling up and down the edge of the race looking for more, and sure enough, we found some— little particles caught in the seams and crevices of the base rock. We was so excited that we forgot work for the rest of that day, while we hunted high and low for gold.

"All we ever talked about, day and night from then on, was gold. Still, we was afraid it might be fool's gold, so Marshall concluded to strike out for the fort and have it tested. Four days he was gone, and we waited anxiously for him to get back. When he rode in he sung out, 'It's the ·pure stuff, all right, boys!' We couldn't hardly wait for him to get down off his horse. But when he did he started right off telling us what had happened. He said that when he got to New Helvetia, him and the old Cap went into Sutter's private quarters and locked the door. The old Cap got out his encyclopedia and looked up the description of gold. Their samples fitted the description. They applied aqua fortis, but it wouldn't mix with the gold. They weighed the stuff in water, using a scales with a silver coin in one end and the gold dust in the other. They let it down gradually over the water, and when the balances hit the water the gold went down and the silver up. That was enough for us. He said that Sutter was coming right up to see things for himself.

"About three days after Marshall got back he come hurrying into our cabin in the evening. 'Boys,' he says, 'the old Cap is up at my house. You know how he always carries his bottle in his hip pocket. If you want a swig from it I'll tell you how to get it. We'll all put our gold dust and flakes together and give it to Bigler.' He turned around and talked to me then. 'Henry,' he says, 'when you shut down the head gate, take the gold and sprinkle it on the base rock. When me and the old Cap come down in the morning and he sees it, he will be so excited he'll pull out his bottle and pass it all around. It's good whiskey, too.' We all laughed.

"The next morning we salted the gold like he said to,[53] and we was just finishing breakfast when we saw Marshall and the old Cap, with Wimmer hanging along, going down the trail. Sutter was dressed in his best suit and carried his silver-tipped cane. We hurried out and went down with them. Just then one of the Wimmer younguns came running by. He got down to the end of the tailrace first and jumped barefooted into the water and began picking up our salted gold. Then he came running back all out of breath, holding the gold in his dripping palm. 'Look what I found, Papa!' he bleated. The old Cap looked and his eyes popped out. Then he jabbed his cane into the ground and jumped with excitement. 'By Jo, it is rich!' he yelled. That danged nosey boy held about twenty dollars' worth of gold particles in his hand, and we couldn't say a word about our own gold. So we all hurried on down and the Captain got down on his knees and picked up half a dozen pieces of gold himself. When he got up he was so excited he could hardly talk. So he jest reached in his back pocket, got hold of the whiskey bottle, and handed it out. We all took good-sized swigs to even up for the gold it cost us."

Bigler fell silent and sat half-smiling at the recollection. Sam spoke: "And you couldn't keep a secret, and so you wrote down and told the news to Ezra Green."

Bigler laughed. "Yep, that's what 1 done, all right. I told Ezra not to tell no one. And everyone he told it to promised not to tell another soul."

"Well, in a way I guess it's not done any harm yet. If you hadn't let the boys know, they never would have made that rich find they got at Mormon Island."

On April 10 Sam boarded the *Dice Mi Nana* to return to San Francisco. Now that there was gold in circulation, the demands on his store had increased surprisingly, and it was necessary for him to make arrangements to get much larger stocks for the future. If Mellus and Howard did not have enough, he would have to buy what he could from the other merchants. As he rode down the current of the broad, sluggish, silt-laden Sacramento, he resolved to come back as soon as he could and examine the gold regions personally.

On April 22, 1848, he agreed for the first and last time with Robert Semple. He echoed Semple's words in penning his editorial for the *Star* for that date. In it he admitted that gold had been discovered:

We have been informed from unquestionable authority, that another still more extensive and valuable gold mine has been discovered towards the head of the American Fork, in the Sacramento Valley. We have seen several specimens taken from it, to the amount of 8 or 10 ounces of pure, virgin gold.

The readers of the *Star* read Sam's words but did not feel that eight or ten ounces of gold was enough to warrant any rush of citizens to the spot. They talked about it a little and forgot it.

Meanwhile Edward Kemble had taken the opportunity to go up to the Sacramento and look over the "gold fields." He arrived at the fort on April 17 on the launch *Rainbow*,[54] and the next day, accompanied by P. B. Reading and Captain Sutter, he rode up into the mountains to see where gold had been found. He remained four days prospecting, and returned to San Francisco filled with enthusiasm about the possibilities.

"Why, Sam, it lies in seams and crevices all up and down the river, above and below the mill. You can pry it out with your fingers or dig it out with a jackknife. I'm going to write an article and tell our readers that a fortune lies at their very doors," he bubbled over to Sam. But Sam shook his head warningly.

"You'll do no such thing, lad. I don't want no gold rush up there yet. I want to get a store up at Mormon Island and another at Coloma, so that I can really make money when men begin to pour into that territory. You realize that when a gold strike occurs the people come from far and near. We'll have not only men from San Francisco and Monterey, and other places near, but they'll come from the States. Who knows?—they may even come from Europe! If we play our cards right we can be in on the ground floor and make money from every man that flocks to the gold regions. And that's just what I'm fixing to do. You go ahead and write an article, but don't say too much about gold."

Edward obeyed. He wrote about the mighty timber in the mountains, praised the full-flowing streams, and extolled the beauties of nature. He spoke of the large crops in the Sacramento Valley, of the luxuriant clover and the beautiful flowers, and added, only as an afterthought, that he had seen also gold and silver while on his explorations.

About the time this editorial was in print, Sam was taking the *Dice Mi Nana* back to the fort. He arrived there on May 4 and made immediate plans to ride up to the gold fields. It was the fifth of May when he and his partner, Charles Smith, rode up to Mormon Island.[55] They passed the flour mill, which was destined never to be completed.

When they reached the settlement they saw some fifty or so men standing barefooted in the icy mountain stream, while the hot sun beat mercilessly on their heads. The stream was hemmed in on all sides by rounded hills, pine- and brush-covered, which ran into mountainous summits. From the spot where their two horses stood they could see the whole island. Sam nudged his mare down and urged her to wade the narrow stream which separated the hills from the island. "When the water gets low this island would become a bar," Sam said. When he drew up his mount, the men came running to surround and greet him. After he had spoken to each acquaintance, Sam told them that he had come to pick out sites for a store and boardinghouse. The men yelled with enthusiasm at the idea. Sidney Willis pointed up toward the eastern end of the closed-in little valley. "That's a good spot for it," he said. "Iry and me have 'looked the place over and we think that's the best location." Sam looked and nodded.

William Stout—who, with the exception of Alondus Buckland, had been the last to leave the farm at New Hope—pushed forward. "I been thinking ever since the Willis boys told me you was fixing to put a store up here, that you might need a partner to run it for you. I got a pretty good lumber business down in Santa Cruz. If I sell out and come up here will you let me buy in?"

"I sure will," Sam said heartily.

So business arrangements were settled then and there, and the miners drifted back to their work. Everything else being arranged, Sam made the rounds, and with variations said to each man, "Give me thirty per cent of all you've mined since you been here. I got authority to collect that large a tithe so that the Church can build a temple in San Francisco." Without much argument most of them paid. Those who wouldn't pay Sam did not argue with.

When they had finished at Mormon Island the two men set out for the sawmill site at Coloma. It was nearly dusk when they arrived and saw the freshly cut timber the sawmill had handled that day. They took supper with Marshall in his cabin on the side of the mountain, and discussed plans for a store, which Sam decided to locate on the road below the sawmill, about two hundred yards away. The next day they set their faces toward the fort.

It was Saturday when they reached the fort. On Sunday, in answer to an invitation from George McDougall and George McKinstry, Sam went down to Sutterville, where the two men had laid out a town-site which they intended to promote.

"Sam," they said. "We want to build a city here and we can't do it without stores, merchants, and money behind us. Close out your store at the fort and open one here. That will fetch people. We can make a fortune here and so can you, if you get in with us."

Sam scratched his chin and listened while they pictured the advantages of promoting this land, which was two miles west of the embarcadero on the river. "The ground is high here and won't get flooded like it does down there. This is the logical place to build a city that will be a gateway on the river to the mining country, once a gold rush starts."

At last Sam shook his head decisively and rode away. They had given him an idea which he intended to promote for his own profit. McKinstry had managed a little business for Sam before this, and Sam knew that George was not trustworthy if he could take advantage. Let the two Georges try to build up a city at Sutterville, as they called it; Sam would forestall them with a city at the embarcadero, which was the logical place for one. But he was content to leave the plan nebulous for the time; he had other fish to fry.

On the eighth of May, Sam boarded the *Dice Mi Nana* to return to San Francisco.[56] He carried in his pocket a quinine bottle full of gold flakes and dust, his first payment from his interest in the Willis brothers' claim. He stood alone on the deck that night, looking into the darkening sky. His hour had come. He had set the stage for the gold rush and was ready now to run up the curtain. While he waited, in that breathless moment, he remembered his mother's faith in him and his promise that he would leave his imprint upon history. He smiled to himself, satisfied that fate had treated him so well.

It was late on the afternoon of the eleventh of May when he left the launch at the foot of Clay Street. He stopped to speak to several acquaintances on Montgomery Street and to show them his bottle of gold. The news seemed to strike them like an electric shock and they clamored for more detailed news, but Sam smiled secretively and waved them behind him as he strode down Montgomery before turning up the hill toward the plaza. Like a snowball gaining momentum, his followers grew in number with every few steps. As he walked in long easy strides up the hill he could see the cluster of men on the plaza and could hardly wait to reach them with the exciting news. He lost sight of them as he passed in front of the custom house, then turned the corner and could see them again. He stopped dramatically, threw up the arm that held the bottle, and shouted, *"Gold! Gold from the American River!"*

Sam remained in San Francisco only long enough to buy out every store in town of all the stock they would let him have, and on the thirteenth he was again on his way to New Helvetia. He arrived there on the sixteenth and immediately took steps to move the store from the tiny room in the fort to a building outside. The fort *Diary* noted it thus: "Cleaned and whitewashed the Magasin and rented the whole to C. C. Smith and Co. for a store."

Sam and Charles Smith worked through the eighteenth and nineteenth with little help, getting their stock removed to the new location. This was about fifty yards east of the fort; a stone building which until this time had been used as a prison and was afterward turned into a hospital. Sutter's teamster spent the whole of the eighteenth of May in bringing up goods from the landing. On the nineteenth, in keeping with the agreement he had with Sam, Sutter sent three of his teamsters and three wagons down to the landing, where they loaded up with planks from Bodega which they hauled to Mormon Island. There William Stout supervised construction of the store and boarding-house, as he was Sam's partner in that business venture.

Sam, in his store at the fort, saw the onrush of the deluge of men he had himself unloosed. On foot, on horseback, in boats and in wagons, the long procession came, the first big caravan arriving at Sutter's fort on the nineteenth day of May. Sutter himself made his first despairing cry and the last wail of the old-time fort when he recorded in the *Diary* on the twentieth, "People continually arriving from below." And on the twenty-fifth the *Diary* was closed with the same prophetic words: "People continually arriving."

On the twentieth, Sam sent two more wagons to the mountains with lumber, this time for Coloma. The next day Sam mounted his horse and set out to inspect progress at Mormon Island; he ended up at Coloma, where he put a man in charge of the building. When he returned to the fort he found his store rushed to desperation by the steady demands upon its stocks. Every one of the hundreds of men wanted gold-digging implements: picks, shovels, pans, and then also heavy clothing. Sam's supply ran out the first day, and although he struggled valiantly to keep supplied, it was impossible.

As May ran into June he took in so much gold dust over his counter that he was hard put to find receptacles for it and finally hit upon a simple device: He set three chamber-pots under the counter, and as the dust came in, he and his clerks filled them up.

Day after day Sam saw faces he knew, and the story of the effect of the gold discovery upon the country was repeated to him. San Francisco was rapidly becoming a deserted town except for its women-folk. The carpenter dropped his plane in the middle of a plank, the shoemaker left the last. Business houses had put up signs "Gone to the mines," and their owners had bolted for the mountains.

Sam sent word to his partners in San Francisco to ship him everything they could get as fast as they could get it, and this they did. In order to have a place in which to store all this merchandise, he had a large warehouse constructed at the embarcadero on the Sacramento. Soon there was a steady stream of merchandise being poured into it from the docks, while a continuous line of wagons carried it out again to stock the fort, Mormon Island, and Coloma stores. While Sam worked like mad from morning until night, Johann Sutter sat be-fuddled in his rooms, overcome by the avalanche of humanity which filled every room in the fort and overran into tents and wagons out-side. The only peace he could gain out of all the confusion, he found in his bottle. Although he had beaten a way into the wilderness but nine short years before—subjugated the Indians and made them his willing helpers, so that the plain was golden for miles with the wheat he had planted—he was powerless now to direct the tide which swept upon him. A man of foresight, with a strong will and a healthy body, was needed to bring order out of chaos. Such a man was Sam Brannan. He knew exactly what he intended to do. First he would make all he could from his three stores—make it while the demand was great. Then he would promote a city at the embarcadero, for it was the logical stopping-place between San Francisco and the mountains. He gave unlimited credit, except for liquor, to any man who worked for Sutter; this for a purpose. He would collect eventually from the old Cap. He could always take real estate in payment.

Men came from near and then from far. From Monterey, from Santa Barbara, from Pueblo de los Angeles, and finally from San Diego. Weeks later they began to come from Mexico, from Peru and Chile. Ships sailing out to the far parts of the world carried tidings of the gold strike. Soldiers began to desert from the army which had been sent out to subdue Mexico. In two's and three's they came from Monterey at first, and later in larger numbers.

In the middle of June, Edward Kemble arrived. Sam looked at him in surprise. "I thought you'd stay with the paper," he said reproachfully. Edward broke out quickly, "I did stay as long as we had any readers. But on the fourteenth I had to give up the ghost. There's not more than eight men left in the whole town."

Sam sighed. "I can see your side of it," he agreed. "But don't start talking about gold. That's all I hear from morning till night. Go dig it if you want to, but don't talk about it to me!"

Chapter XVI

COLONEL RICHARD BARNES MASON, Military Governor, when all his servants and most of his army had deserted him, decided it was time to go up and look over the gold diggings. Escorted by his aide, Lieutenant William Tecumseh Sherman,[57] and also Captain Joseph L. Folsom, Army Quartermaster, and a military company, he arrived at the fort. Sam, the leading spirit there, rushed out to meet them and to conduct them into Sutter's presence. The weary old Swiss greeted them gladly. Perhaps they could enforce a little order in the fort. Certainly Sutter couldn't.

Preparations were being made for a Fourth of July celebration which would dwarf all others. The military guests were persuaded to stay over and enjoy it. As dawn broke on the national holiday, the fort's cannon roared a salute. At noon a great banquet was laid on long tables within the enclosure, and Alcalde Sinclair acted as master of ceremonies. Sam Brannan made a speech of welcome and toasts were drunk. The Governor gave a patriotic address, and then the toasts became more numerous. Finally the old Cap rolled under the table and had to be carried away to his bed, but Sam was still sitting and still drinking when many of the others had gone to sleep, their heads on the festive board.

By midafternoon the gubernatorial party was able to assemble itself and start out for the diggings. The sun was still hot when they arrived at Mormon Island. All along the river's edge men stood knee-deep in the water, washing gold in pans, filling crude rockers with sludge taken from the river, or rocking the devices to separate the sand from the golden harvest. And when night came and the men stopped working, they poured a steady stream of their day's earnings—which averaged about a hundred dollars—into Sam's store at the eastern end of the mushroom settlement; which consisted of thatched shelters, tents, a few shacks, and the building which held Sam's big store and boardinghouse.

Sam had accompanied the party up, and when, after a tour of inspection, the officials came into his store, he set up drinks for all of them and stood smiling behind the counter. W. S. Clark, a non-Mormon who had somehow secured a claim at the island, pushed forward and addressed the Governor.

"Has Brannan here got any authority to collect a tithe of 30 per cent from every miner on this island?" he asked.

"If you are fools enough to pay it, he has," the Governor answered, smiling.

Clark turned to Brannan. "You've collected the last cent you'll ever get from me," he said and went out. This man, a short time later, erected a wharf at the site of the all-tides landing, known thereafter as Clark's Point—in doing so, he was squatting on lands which rightfully belonged to Jacob Leese.

The Governor turned to Brannan. "This land belongs to the United States, Brannan. Nobody has a right to any gold from it without permission of the Government."

"Are you going to stop us digging?" several men asked, but the Governor shook his head. "Not so long as what you dig benefits all the people of the United States. But I'd advise none of you to pay tithing to Brannan or his Church. They have no right to any gold unless they dig it up with their own hands, or have an interest in a claim."

Sam laughed ruefully and shrugged. He knew that he would never be able to collect any more tithes from his miners. And this proved to be the case. But he consoled himself with the fact that he had already taken in something like tens of thousands of dollars, not counting what he was making from his claim and from his stores.

The Governor had not taken the long trip from Monterey just for pleasure. It had been made for the purpose of reporting officially to the Government which he represented as to the veracity of the report that gold had been discovered, and to what extent. His report, dated August 17, 1848, confirmed the news and predicted that there would be gold enough taken out of the country to pay more than a hundred times over for the war with Mexico. With the messenger who carried the report to Washington went also a small can of gold as proof.

While Governor Mason's report was just starting on its long journey to Washington, the news of the discovery of gold was being published in the *New York Herald*. Strangely enough, the wording was exactly the same as that of the article in Sam's *Star*, which had just reached the East. The *Herald's* article was supposedly a letter from a California correspondent; that correspondent, however, was the publisher of a newspaper in San Francisco, though the *Herald* did not give him credit for his words:

The gold mine discovered in December last, on the south branch of the American Fork, in a low range of hills forming the base of the Sierra Nevada, distant thirty miles from New Helvetia, is only three feet below the surface, in a strata of softsand rock. . . .

Thus it was that Sam was not only the announcer of the gold rush in San Francisco, in California, and all along the Coast, but over the entire world. From New York City the news spread in every direction, meeting its own likeness all along the Mississippi, where the *California Star* had already been distributed. And as if to verify the story Governor Mason's report now reached Washngton, together with the little can of gold which the Governor had purchased and sent along as proof. The sample and the report had traveled east in care of Lieutenant Lucien Loeser of the Third Artillery, by a roundabout route which had taken him first to Peru, then to Panama, thence to New Orleans by way of Jamaica, and at last to Washington. On December 5, 1848, President Polk turned the report over to Congress, and the United States officially recognized the gold strike which Sam had broadcast to an eager and waiting world. The emigration began.

Sam Brannan, at the fort, was entrenched and waiting for the horde which was soon on its way. Meanwhile he kept his stores supplied as best he might and laid his plans for the future. In the midst of the general chaos, in August, a strange young man appeared at the fort and introduced himself to the bewildered Swiss as John A. Sutter, Jr., grown to manhood during the years his father had been gone. The old man was overjoyed to have his son with him, and still more happy to learn that the rest of the family would follow in a few months. Immediately the Captain turned over the management of all his affairs to his son, so that he would be free to organize gold-searching parties, or set up rival stores to Sam's in the gold regions. He had not the shrewd head of Sam Brannan, and every business venture he entered made further inroads on his income. Young Sutter, on the other hand, was wise and deliberate and would have saved his father's fortune if the bewildered old man had allowed it. But such was the Captain's weakness and his love of the bottle that he was easily led into foolish situations from which his son found it difficult to extricate him. He did, however, prevail upon his father to deed all his property, land, and chattels, to himself, so that he could in some measure meet the debts which were beginning to mount. Chief among these was the yearly payment to Russia of $30,000 for Fort Ross, which old Sutter had purchased a year or so earlier.

Sam watched this family drama before his eyes and could not but feel a certain pity for his old friend. Yet he would not let pity prevent him from taking advantage of a good business deal when he saw one. Sam reasoned that if he did not profit by it, others would. In December, while a breathless world waited before starting its assault on this far outpost, Sam presented to young Sutter a bill of $16,000 owing to him for goods purchased by Captain Sutter and various men who worked for him. Young Sutter looked at the bill aghast.

"I have not the means of paying this bill," he said.

"I can help you out then," Sam replied briskly. "I've worked out a scheme that ought to interest you. In the first place, this fort has been a madhouse ever since the gold rush started. Nobody goes to the gold fields without coming here first. The embarcadero and the road here to the fort are the funnel that the gold rush pours through. Nobody will go near Sutterville because it's off the beaten track, and all the offers McKinstry and McDougall make will not take people there if we use our heads. All the land for miles and miles around this fort belongs to your old man. Why don't you and me put our heads together and promote a city that will lie nestled between the fort, here, and the embarcadero below. Lots will sell like wildfire."

"But I do not want to sell my father's land. It is all we have left. And what would you get out of it if I sell my father's land?"

"Plenty," Sam replied. "In the first place you owe me sixteen thousand dollars. You say you've not got the cash. Give me land enough to settle my claim. I'll promote that land so it will make you money as well as me, providing you'll do as I say."

"But it will cost money to promote this land. We will have to survey it and cut it up in lots."

"I'll pay for the survey and hire an engineer for a consideration," Sam countered.

"And what will the consideration be?"

"Enough land to pay my bill, in the location I choose."

Young Sutter shrugged. One part of the land was no more valuable to him than another.[58] Sam secured title to a good parcel of land in what he intended to be the heart of his new city. He even had the name ready; it should be called "Sacramento" after the river. The old Captain was snowbound in the mountains and had no voice in the arrangement Sam was making for his embarcadero lands.

Young Sutter hired a lawyer, Peter H. Burnett, who had just come from Oregon, to handle his business affairs. The survey was completed and Lieutenant William H. Warner was engaged as engineer to lay out lots and streets. The first lots were sold in January of 1849, at the fort end, by Peter Burnett for young Sutter. But within a short time the lots on the embarcadero, many of which Sam now owned, sold much faster, and soon a mushroom city of tents and shacks was sprouting on the banks of the river. Lots near the fort sold for $250 while those near the river cost $500. Buyers did not haggle, and the lots went quickly even though no one man was permitted to buy more than four.

Soon young Sutter was having no difficulty in meeting his father's debts. Gold poured into his hands as well as into Sam's.

Presently George McDougall began to feel it was time that he made money out of real estate. Sutterville was perched on the river to no advantage. He approached young Sutter and demanded the right to purchase the entire water front on the Sacramento River at Sutterville. Sutter refused.

"I demand that you sell to me," McDougall said.

"I do not care what you demand," young Sutter replied.

"You've not been in this country long. I think you will live to regret the day you crossed me, young feller."

"I think I will not. You cannot intimidate me. Go now, before I throw you out."

He advanced upon the bully and McDougall withdrew to stew up more devilment. He and George McKinstry rode straight to the mountains and had a conference with the bibulous Captain, who was entrenched at Coloma with a few of his boon companions. McDougall and McKinstry had bought Lansford Hastings' interest in Sutterville, giving them control of still more of that location. Now they pictured to old Sutter the destruction his son was making of all the old man had built up over nine years.

"Why John, you know that you always intended to build your city at Sutterville instead of at the embarcadero," McKinstry pointed out. "That's why you named the place after yourself. For a year now we've been trying to build up a city there, but everyone bucks us. Now your son wants to get rich for himself, and so he's building up this other place and letting Sam Brannan have his way. You sign over to us a square mile of land on the waterfront at Sutterville, and we'll outsmart them. We'll stop people before they get to Sacramento."

Sutter listened and wept in maudlin fashion into his cups, but would not sign.

At last they wearied of coaxing him and took him down to the fort so that he could see how his son was selling out his lands. Young Sutter tried to talk to his father, but the old man's heart was cold and he refused to see him. The conspirators then took the Captain down to San Francisco, where they kept him happily drunk for several days. At the end of the spree they had a bond, signed by Sutter, giving them the square mile of land at Sutterville which they had demanded.

It was not long before Sam decided that if the two Georges could get land so easily and cheaply, he would try their methods, too. He visited the Captain at the fort. Young Sutter had at last been accepted back into his father's good graces, but the old man would not listen to him in business matters, or to the new business manager who had taken Burnett's place. The old Cap was hard-headed and set on having his way.

"Captain Sutter," said Brannan, "I've got to do something about my store and warehouse. I can't accommodate all the trade that comes to this region with this little store outside of the fort here. I've got to make a move, and soon. McDougall and McKinstry have made me a fine offer to go to Sutterville. They argue that business will follow my store, and that if I come to Sutterville I can make the town boom. I've got to have a larger warehouse, and if I put it at Sutterville I'll be two miles further down the river, and naturally that will draw people from here."

The Captain sat up straighter in his chair. "Vell, vot do you vant I should do?"

"That's up to you. McDougall and McKinstry have offered to give me two hundred of the choicest lots in their town if I'll move my store and warehouse there."

Sutter bowed his head while he thought for a time. Then he raised his face. "I vill gif you two hunert lots if you vill stay in Sacramento. It used to be I vanted a town built up at Sutterville, but not any more. Not since dose fellers got most of it avay from me. I vant dat mine town should stay at de embarcadero so dat I can make enough money to keep paying mine debts. Mine creditors are driving me crazy."

"If you give me two hundred lots in the heart of Sacramento it will repay you in business and prosperity," Sam said.

At that moment young Sutter and Henry Schoolcraft, the clerk who had displaced Peter Burnett, entered the room. Sam explained his mission and taking out the letter from McDougall he showed it to young Sutter and said, "If I move my store and warehouse to Sutterville and anchor a storeship there, it will hurt business in Sacramento. I don't want to do it until I've given you folks a chance to match their offer."

Sutter turned to his father. "I will not do this," he said. "This man has already taken too much advantage of my ignorance and your good humor. Let him take his business to Sutterville. Other business houses will come to Sacramento. We do not need him."

"Your son is right, Captain Sutter," Henry Schoolcraft put in quickly. "Brannan and McDougall and McKinstry are all hand and glove together in trying to get the best of you. Don't listen to him! If he wants land, let him buy it like everyone else has to."

Sam smiled. "The Captain's got more sense in one minute than both of you fellers will have if you live to be ninety. He's not penny-wise and dollar-foolish. Why, don't you two nincompoops realize that I'm not the only one the two Georges have approached? They've invited Hensley, Priest Lee and Company, and Reading, to come there, too. We'll all go there unless you can better their offers."

Captain Sutter burst in excitedly, "Ve got to keep Mr. Brannan vit' us at Sacramento. I gif him two hunert lots to keep him, too. For a little land I should let mine city die right under my nose!"

And give the lots to Sam he did, over the violent protests of his son and Henry Schoolcraft.

Sam had been so busy in Sacramento that he had had little time to visit his family or watch the progress of affairs in San Francisco. He had taken a flying trip back to the bay city in September, when Edward Kemble had returned and was planning to start publication once more of the *California Star.* Sam told him frankly that he was no longer interested in publishing the paper and offered to sell to his young editor. Thus it was that for $800 Kemble became possessor of the press and all its appurtenances, and whatever good-will it might have. Semple had likewise lost interest in the newspaper business, and for a fair price Kemble secured the *Californian* also. When, in November of 1848, Sam went home to see the new baby Ann Eliza had borne him, the *Star and Californian* made its bow.[59] It continued thus for less than two months, however, and appeared on January 4, 1849, as the *Alta California,* a newspaper which was to mirror the history of California for many years to come. This was the parting of the ways for Edward and Sam.

But Sam hardly felt the parting, so interested was he in all the branches of his business. Even the new baby, Adelaide Brannan, only held his attention for a few days and then he was flying back to Sacramento to direct the tides of empire.

Sam's storeship, the *Eliza,* was a familiar sight, bobbing at the wharf at Sacramento. But Sam needed another storeship, for the one he had would not hold the overflow from the long wooden warehouse that stood on the corner of Front and J streets, just a stone's throw from the river. Sam bought for a song, on the San Francisco water front, the Chilean brig *Eliodora*, and soon she was busy moving his goods from the "Liverpool of the Pacific" to Sutter's embarcadero.[60] Sam would descend upon the bay city like a hurricane and go from one merchant to the other, buying their entire stocks and having them moved to his ship as fast as possible; then away he would sail up the river to fill his warehouse, storeship, and stores in a vain endeavor to supply the demands of the hundreds of people who daily poured through the Sacramento and fort settlements on their way to the mines. Many remained at the settlements to buy land, build canvas or clapboard shacks, and start small business ventures. These enriched Sam but little more than those who drifted through, stopping only long enough to buy supplies for prospecting trips. When Sam's own ship would not hold all the boxes and bales he had piled on the beach at San Francisco, the *Whiton* took the overflow, and his old friend George Winner piloted it up the long sluggish river.

Living at the fort along with many another eccentric individual was the terrible-tempered Charles E. Pickett,[61] who loved a quarrel better than food. Philosopher Pickett, regarded by many as a fool, one day late in 1848 picked a quarrel with a certain R. Alderman. Both men drew pistols, but Pickett fired first. Alcalde Bates was urged by the citizenry to arrest Pickett, but Bates was a peace-loving man; he resigned. The duty fell on the second alcalde, Fowler. Fowler resigned, too. Sam Brannan, who feared neither philosopher nor fool, decided that it was time for Justice to pay a visit to the fort. He called an election of the New Helvetia population, and found himself elected alcalde. A prosecuting attorney was now needed to punish Pickett. The crowd, fond of a joke, elected Brannan to this office, also. But there the fun ceased. A sheriff was named, the culprit arrested, a jury drawn, and the trial began.

Court was called to order in a room on the west side of the fort. When Pickett was brought in, glowering and angry, the sheriff pointed to the table before which sheriff, alcalde and prisoner were to sit. On it were a pitcher of water and a demijohn of brandy.

"Put your gun and your bowie knife there on the table in plain sight," he directed the prisoner.

Pickett did so and was waved to a chair at the end of the table.

He sat down. A member of the jury lighted a cheroot and the sheriff ordered him to put it out.

"Hold on there," Brannan shouted. "He can smoke if he wants to."

"Not in court," the sheriff said. "It don't show proper respect for the bench."

"To hell with respect for the bench," Sam said. "I'm sitting on it and I don't object. Besides, the California ladies all smoke at the bullfights at Mission Dolores. If it's proper to smoke at a bullfight, it's all right here. All in favor say 'Aye.' "

"Aye!" sang out the majority of the audience. Sam proceeded with the trial. He called witnesses and listened to Pickett plead his own case. Then Sam arose and began to present his plea for the prosecution of this archfiend. Pickett leaped to his feet.

"Hold on there, Brannan. You're the judge. You ain't supposed to take sides agin me."

"I am too," Sam responded. "I'm the prosecuting attorney as well as the judge. Now you sit down and keep quiet while I present my case." Then he went on addressing himself as judge and appealing to the jury.

As the trial progressed, any one who wished could come up to the table for a drink. None of them touched the pitcher of water.

When the prosecution had finished, Pickett, an able speaker in spite of his bad disposition, put up a brilliant defense. When he had done it was dark. The jury was tired and half drunk, and without asking permission got up and went to their beds. The sheriff looked at Sam and Sam looked at the sheriff. "What'll we do with the prisoner?" the sheriff asked.

"Put him in jail."

"We ain't got a jail, you know that."

"Well, then, put him in irons."

"We ain't got no irons."

Sam sighed and turned to the audience. "Shall we turn the Philosopher loose on bail? All in favor say 'Aye.' " The majority favored the idea. Pickett paid his bail, put his bowie knife and pistol back in their holster, and marched out.

The next day Sam polled the jury man by man as they drifted

into his store. They disagreed. A new trial was ordered and the prisoner acquitted. Such was justice at Sutter's fort in 1848.

Charles Smith decided now that he was rich enough to retire, and before the end of the year he sold out his entire interest to Sam and sailed away, back to the States. Sam worked harder than ever, when the store was exclusively his own. Kanaka Davis said of him that "no penniless stranger seeking provisions or goods ever left his store without being supplied." And it was true. Sam, who robbed with one hand his brothers in religion, his old friend Sutter, and others, helped with the other any needy stranger who presented himself.

Chapter XVII

"The California Year of 1849!
It stands out in the experiences of men,
unique and individual, each swift day
of it equal to many another year."

To Sam the merging of the year 1848 into 1849 was hardly noticeable. He was in San Francisco for the holidays, but had little time to watch the cunning yawnings of his baby daughter or to give his devotion to his little family, who sorely missed him. He spent most of his time attending to the many ramifications of his business. He was in conference with the likable Bill Howard in the Mellus and Howard store, one day in January, when Talbot H. Green came in. Sam had met Talbot several times before, when Green had been in town on business for Larkin, for whom he was a business agent. But what had endeared him most to Sam was that he had acted on Yerba Buena's first jury and had voted consistently to release Sam from any obligation to the errant Henry Harris.

Sam rose and shook Green's hand. "Bill has been telling me that you are coming into the firm, now that Mellus is sick."

Green nodded. "Yes, I'm thankful for the opportunity to buy into such a fine firm. I'm mighty sorry that Henry Mellus suffered that stroke a few months ago, but it certainly gave me a fine chance. Poor Henry! He'll be sailing for the States soon."

Sam nodded. "It's a dirty shame that Henry should have such poor health, and him still a young man. Why, I don't think he's forty years old yet."

Bill Howard nodded. "He is just forty. I hope that he'll be recovered when he comes back. He's been a mighty fine partner and I think a lot of him. His brother Francis is going to open up a branch for us at Los Angeles, so we'll still have a Mellus with us."

"Are you going to retain the firm name?" Sam asked.

Howard shook his head. "No. We'll change it to Howard and Green. When Henry comes back and can be active again we can put all three of our names in the title."

Sam bent his attention to the list of merchandise on the table, already immersed in his own business plans. "Good God, but you fellers are putting prices up! I see here that flour was fifteen dollars a barrel the middle of last month, and twenty-seven dollars it is now. And butter, ninety cents a pound!"

Bill laughed and patted him on the back. "What you kicking about? You're not paying those prices. You're buying at rock-bottom with us and selling up in the diggings for a damn sight more than we're getting. A feller has to be pretty hungry to pay seventy cents for a pound of cheese."

They all laughed and fell to making up lists of goods to be sent away with the next boat. Already the bay was dark with the hulks of vessels that had come in from Matzlan, Chile, Honolulu, San Blas, Callao, as well as Chinese and other Pacific ports. It was the custom of the day for Atlantic and European merchants to ship goods to all these Pacific seaports, where they were transshipped by local merchants to whatever region would prove a profitable market. And when the vessels laden with merchandise came into San Francisco Bay, and their crews learned of the discovery of gold, they were rapidly deserted. It was to be a month still before the first shipload of gold-seekers would arrive from the eastern States.

A few days later Sam was back up the Sacramento River, supervising the enlarging of his warehouse at Sacramento and preparing to open a branch store there at a time not too far distant. Since he owned two hundred of the choicest lots in the heart of the town—which was growing from an empty plain into a city with a population of thousands within a matter of a few short months—he was very civic-minded. He and Sutter and Schoolcraft had decided among themselves that they would be careful to whom they sold, picking always the best types of men. Squatters would absolutely not be tolerated. And even while they were making this determination, squatters were all about them. Sam and Schoolcraft sat on a bench back of the warehouse one evening and noticed that several shacks had appeared in the marshes beside the river within the last week.

"We got to stop this squatting," Schoolcraft said.

Sam arose. "Go get your horse and call a posse of our best business-men together, and come back here. I'll have my horse saddled and be waiting." Within an hour Schoolcraft was back with a dozen of the town's merchants, bankers, and businessmen. Sam sat his horse waiting for them. He had a Mexican *reata* looped over his saddle-horn and two revolvers in his holster. Sam took the lead and rode down to "I" Street. There he stopped and waited for the other riders to come up. He gave a few directions quietly, then rode up close to a shack in the marshland and slipped a loop of his reata over the pole which sup-ported the house. Then he rode back to the crowd and handed the end of the lariat to three other men. Together with Sam they put their might on the thong and pulled. There was no result. Sam jerked the reata end back and looped it around his saddle, then urged his mare. She put her weight against it, but still the house did not budge. Other men leaped down and began to pull on the leather rope, and in a few moments the shack fell with a crash.[62] They did not stop to see the result, but rode away. Opposite Sam's warehouse they approached the house of another squatter. The tenant came out with a shotgun in the crook of his arm.

"Keep on going, you fellers," he warned them.

Sam turned to the man behind him and called out, "Warbass, cover that bastard. If he raises his gun, shoot." Warbass drew a bead on the squatter. Sam waved the other horsemen to follow him. They edged the squatter away from his shack, set their horses against the frail affair, and pushed it over into the mud. As they rode away the victim shook his fist after them, "I'll git even with you sons-of-bitches!" he roared.

But Sam and his cohorts did not listen. They rode all along the water front, rousing out male squatters and urging them to get out before another sun if they didn't want the same treatment as had been meted out to the first two.

In January the citizens of Sacramento met together to organize some sort of civil government.[63] Although Peter Burnett, destined this year to become California's first Governor, was chairman of the meeting, this did not deter Sam Brannan from arising at the first opportunity to offer a motion that slavery in any form must never be permitted in California. Burnett laughed goodnaturedly.

"All right, Brannan, we all know how you feel about slavery. I come from Missouri and I'm not against slavery. What I want to be sure of is that no freed slaves are going to be allowed to come here, either. But just take your turn and we'll get around to those things later. First we want to elect officers."

Burnett was elected President. Frank Bates and M. D. Winship became vice-presidents, and Jeremiah Sherwood and George Mc-Kinstry secretaries. Then a motion was made that a committee of five be appointed by Burnett to draw up a preamble and resolutions to set forth the purpose of the meeting. Sam Brannan, John Fowler, John Sinclair, Pierson B. Reading, and Barton Lee were chosen. They decided that each city in Sacramento Valley should hold an election for delegates to a convention to be held in San Jose on March 5, 1849, at ten o'clock, for the purpose of drawing up a code of government for the region. Sam then made his motion about slavery and it was passed. He made three more resolutions, all of which were incorporated into the instructions given to the delegates to the San Jose convention. People listened to Sam. He was a rich and powerful man. Did he not own one-fourth of Sacramento, and was he not rapidly buying up San Francisco real estate so as to control eventually a fifth of the land in the bay city?

In February Sam officially opened the Sacramento store, which he had set up in the front half of his enlarged frame warehouse. Sam needed many clerks in his stores and there was a great labor turnover. A procession of young men marched through his employ; some of them were to become famous in other fields of endeavor.[64] Tallman H. Rolfe afterward became a Nevada editor. J. Harris Trowbridge, one of his clerks, was also well known in later years. There was George M. Robertson, who became a supreme court judge in the Hawaiian Islands. James B. Mitchell was to become public administrator of Sacramento County. Edward J. Stetson, W. R. Grimshaw, and James Queen, all worked for him at one time and left to become famous.

One evening John Fowler, who operated a trucking business and hired many teamsters, entered Sam's store. "I want a treat for my boys tonight. We're celebrating," he said to Grimshaw, the clerk. "How much are them oysters up there in cans?"

"Twelve dollars apiece."

"Twelve dollars an oyster, or twelve dollars a can?" Fowler asked, whistling in amazement.

"A can."

"How much for the lot, all twelve cans?"

"One hundred and forty-four dollars," Grimshaw said.

"You're a robber, and so is your boss. But wrap them up," Fowler replied, pouring out gold dust.

Sam would have made a special price for his friend had he been in town, but he was down in San Francisco, busy with another important venture. He sat in the little office of the Mellus & Green store. Gathered there were the leading men of the city, including the three who were considered San Francisco's first citizens: Sam Brannan, William Howard, and William Heath Davis. Also present were Talbott Green, James Ward, and James Folsom, formerly of the Army; DeWitt, Harrison, and the members of Gross, Hobson and Company. They were hatching an important scheme. Sam was speaking of the need for a new project.

"This town can grow no further until it builds a good big wharf. Why, the fiddling little landings we have to use now are no damned good at all!" [65]

Folsom—tall, thin, with nervous glance and piercing eyes—agreed. "There's not only the need of the city for a good wharf to make us do something about it, but the fact that there's money to be made out of the thing. We'll probably have to sink a hundred thousand or so in her to start with, but we'll take it out in the first year."

Howard interrupted, "I feel like Brannan does, that we've got to do something now. I own the land on the water between Sacramento and Clay streets, and I will gladly give it to any organization that will undertake to build a wharf."

He leaned forward. "I'm ready to put up fifteen thousand dollars right now. I move we form a joint stock company and put in our money to get this thing started."

The money was pledged there and then, and in several later meetings the financial arrangements were made of a project to build a long wharf from the foot of what became known as Leidesdorff Street, out into the bay. "Longwharf" it was one day to be called, and it was to cost over $200,000 before its two thousand feet of loading space stretched out into the water. On the day ground was broken for this wharf which Sam was so interested in having built, he stood on the very spot upon which he had first set foot in Yerba Buena, in 1846. Within another year a loading platform would stretch for two blocks on either side of him, to feed the wharf.

Sam went home from the first meeting of the wharf association to tell Ann Eliza of his doings. She wasn't much interested. It seemed to her that all Sam did any more was to flit from one business venture to another. "Now that you own a fourth of all the land in Sacramento and are buying land here in San Francisco to the point that you'll soon own a good part of it, you don't ever have time for your home or family."

"I'm busy now," he admitted, "but it'll only be for a year or two, and then we'll be rich and I can sit around the house all day."

She waved away his remark impatiently. "I don't want you around the house all the time. No woman could stand being cooped up with a man all day long, but I would like to see you for two or three hours all together once, just to see how it feels. You come flying down here from Sacramento, grab a mouthful of food, kiss us all, and run down town. Honestly, the children don't even know their own father."

"They'll git a chance to know me well enough in a few years," he would laugh, and dart off to another business meeting.

Ann Eliza had spoken truly when she said that Sam was trying to buy up all of San Francisco. Whenever town lots were put up for public sale, Sam was there to buy. First he had to petition Alcalde Leavenworth for the right to buy it; then when the petition was granted, he had only to pay the required fee and the land became his for a song.

In April, when Sam came up the Sacramento, he remembered that only six short months before, this plain which was a milling mass of humanity had been empty, with no sign of human habitation. And when he stepped off the boat he wished, in a way, that it were still so.

The water front, like every place which led to the gold fields, was
more like a madhouse than a frontier settlement. The screaming
frenzy of the stock market, with every man rushing madly about to
find his place in the chaos, was hardly so wild a place as this. Although
Sam was now selling lots for a thousand dollars that he had held at
fifty dollars in December, still he sometimes grew weary of the hubbub and looked forward to a day when he could live in peace.

He strode across the street to his store, and when he entered the
room there was a "Hello, Sam," on this side and "Hey, Brannan, I
want to see you," on the other; as he went the length of the long
low room he made slow progress against the tide of humanity that
awaited him. Suddenly he was glad to be a part of this hive of industry. It was good to have so many friends and to know that money
was pouring into his hands in a magical stream. He had started as a
youth in search of the Golden Fleece, and now he had certainly
found it.

That night he attended a mass meeting on the embarcadero, just a
little way from his store. Peter Burnett mounted an empty hogshead
to tell the assembled townspeople the result of the convention which
had just been held in San Jose.

"We decided at the convention to choose our leading men from
each community to go to a convention in Monterey, at a date which
will be set later, to draft a state constitution. Nominations are now
open for the men you want to represent you at this legislative convention."

"Sam Brannan," offered John Fowler.

Sam sang out quickly in reply. "No thanks, John. I got more than
I can do now to tend to my business. Send somebody else that's got
more time."

"John Sutter," another voice sang out.

A week later another mass meeting was held to elect a local legislature to enact laws and see to their enforcement for the city of Sacramento and the district which lay between the Sacramento, the Sierra
Nevada, and the Consumnes River, which included most of the gold
region. Eleven members were named to the local legislative body.
Sam accepted a position as member of this body, although he said in
accepting that he would have little time to devote to meetings.

In May Sam dashed back to San Francisco for the ground-breaking ceremonies for Central Wharf; or, as it became commonly known later, Longwharf. All the city officials were there, and San Francisco put on its gayest manner to celebrate this great civic achievement.

A few days later, with the *Eliodora* loaded down with cargo,[86] Sam was ready to return to Sacramento when William Davis approached him. "I hear the Mexican brig *Juven Guipizcoana* is for sale," he said. "She's a good boat."

"Just what I need for a storeship. My storeship *Eliza* can't hold all the goods we're shipping and my warehouse is running over. I'll pay a good price for that Mexican boat. You got an interest in her?"

"Not in the boat. But I did have an interest in a cargo she carried to Oregon last fall. She's been icebound up there in the river until last month. Aguirre, her master, is giving up the water."

So Sam called on Captain Aguirre and acquired another boat, which became a familiar sight in the months to come as she bobbed at anchor alongside the *Eliza* at Sacramento, while the *Eliodora* plied busily up and down the river, filled with Sam's goods on every up trip.

In Sacramento once more, Sam stopped at the water front store long enough to give instructions for the unloading and disposing of the merchandise he had brought, then ordered half a dozen wagons from Fowler and had them loaded to go up to Mormon Island. He went on ahead to talk business with Stout. He found William with a long face.

"I don't know how much longer I can hold out here," Stout greeted him. "A rowdy element is drifting in and pushing our boys out. In two months there won't be a Mormon left here. They're talking about pulling out now with their piles and striking for Deseret in the Great Salt Lake Valley. When those two companies pulled out last summer and headed for Zion, only the hardiest stayed here. But even they are getting afraid to risk it much longer. Why, it's getting so that neither your life nor your gold is safe any more. Many a feller that's too lazy to work'd just as lief cut your throat and take what you've worked for."

"Yeah, since the men been drifting in here from all the states, and all that foreign element from South America, gold mining is a risky business. And it's getting so these gold miners look on a store-keeper as his worst enemy," Sam agreed.

Stout nodded. "I'm almost afraid to tell a bunch of miners the price of goods any more. I know that prices are high—that they're getting outrageous—but I can't help it. You fellers set the price and it's up to me to get it; but I tell you sometimes I'd rather have a beating than try."

Sam laughed ruefully. "I see your point. It is a risky business. But we have to set the prices high. We got to make what we're going to get out of this business right now, because this gold will run out in a few months. Besides, we're having a hell of a time getting enough merchandise to supply the demand. The bay down at San Francisco is filled with ships. Their spars look like a forest in the water. As soon as any boat comes into port, the crew deserts and comes up here looking for gold. That means we have one hell of a time getting new merchandise. Masters of vessels aren't anxious to put in here and lose their crews, and that makes goods scarce—at least, the things that are in demand up here. We have to raise prices to make any margin of profit."

"Well, I'm getting out of here before much longer. If I don't you'll ride up here some day and find me with my throat cut."

"Don't stay any longer than you think you ought to," Sam said. "When things get that bad, we'll all get out and let some one else take the risk."

Sam rode from Mormon Island up to Coloma. He asked the store-keeper there if supplies were coming through regularly.

"Yes, but even so we ain't got half enough for the demand. Those two Chinks that opened stores down the street helped fill the demand for goods for a while, but the white men here got it in for them and are always picking on them. The Chinks are finding it as tough to please these bastards up here as we are, only more so."

At that moment the door opened and Pierson Reading and Henry Cheever entered. "We been waiting for you, Brannan," Reading said. "Got a proposition we want to talk over with you."

"Sure, men. Come on over here in the back of the store."

They sat down on three boxes and talked, while a steady stream of miners came in to purchase goods.

"Sutter's up here prospecting around. We been talking to him," Cheever explained. "We asked him about buying that two square miles of land that we've been talking about among ourselves now and then, down on the west bank of the Feather River, above Nicolaus Allgeier's farm. He wants two thousand dollars for that land." [67]

Sam was thoughtful for a time. "We could build up a good-sized city at that place," he said at last. "It's right on the way to the new gold fields that have been opened up above there. We can lay it out in city lots, make inducements to settlers, and promote the whole thing in such a way that we ought to make plenty of money out of it. Let's go up to the old Cap's cabin and pay him the money right now."

The three men arose. Reading said, "I would have closed the deal before, but Henry and me wanted to talk to you first. After all, it will take your push and foresight to put the thing over. Neither of us is much good at building cities."

They found the drink-sodden old Swiss in a happy frame of mind, and the deal was consummated. The land was to be deeded to them later when the Captain got around to it.

Sam stopped in Sacramento for a few days, and while there hired Joseph S. Ruth to go up to the newly acquired location, make a survey, and lay the land out in blocks, public squares, and streets. Sam followed a few days after, with Cheever and Reading, to look the proposed town over. The banks of the Feather River were at this point high and well adapted for vessel landing. Although no vessels had yet attempted to stem the current farther than the ferry landing at Allgeier's farm, Sam felt sure that a ship could also reach Yuba City, as the three had decided to name it. They found a group of Indian mounds which they had seen on their first trip of exploration to the spot, months earlier. The town would be grouped around these mounds, which would be levelled by workmen.

"Tallman Rolfe and me are going to come up here next month with a flatboat full of building material and goods, and open up a store," Cheever said. Then he proceeded to pick the spot upon which he intended to build. Ruth laughed and said, "That is the corner of Water and B streets, Mr. Cheever." They all laughed, then, for they stood on an empty plain.

It was not until August that Rolfe and Cheever actually did get up to found the city of Yuba. Marysville, across the river, had not yet even been dreamed of and was known simply as Nye's Ranch.

When Sam got back to Sacramento he went into conference with John Fowler, the teamster. They had bought from Sutter the frame of the old grist mill at Brighton, which had never been completed, and were setting it up in the center of the block, facing the river—a block away from Sam's Sacramento store. They were hard put to get material to finish this magnificent structure, which was to be known as the City Hotel and would eventually cost them eighty thousand dollars. Work did not progress rapidly, for men could not be persuaded to stay as carpenters when they could go off to the mines and very likely find a fortune. Lumber was hard to get because of the shortage of labor. Sam and Fowler did not plan to open the hotel before September, however.

It was early evening when Sam left Fowler's office and returned to his store.[98] The month was June. He went into the little room at the rear which was his office. A few minutes later one of his clerks opened the door and announced two men. Before Sam could arise they had entered. He recognized both of them at once; one an old acquaintance, the other familiar through descriptions Sam had been given of him. Amasa Lyman, a Mormon Apostle, was the first; he came forward and put out his hand. Sam shook it and motioned the two men to chairs on the opposite side of the table. Lyman introduced his associate.

"This is Brother Porter Rockwell, President Young's bodyguard," he said. Sam nodded to the other and shook his hand, and the giant with his hair in braids sat down beside Lyman. Sam remembered that Rockwell had once taken a shot at Governor Boggs of Missouri, when the Mormons were being hounded in that state and Boggs had been a party to their persecutions. As a result, he had been lodged in jail for many months, during which his hair and beard had grown long. Upon his return to Nauvoo, Joseph Smith (whose bodyguard Rockwell then was) did not recognize the hairy giant, but when he realized it was Rockwell he prophesied that as long as he wore his hair long like a woman's he would never be killed. Rockwell had never cut his hair since that day. He had cold blue eyes and a high-pitched, almost feminine, voice; he wore his hair in braids mostly, but sometimes left it floating loose. Though he seemed to be the friendliest of creatures, he was reputed to have killed several men.

As Sam sat facing them he knew immediately why they had come, but he was careful not to let them know that he was on the defensive. He reached for the brandy bottle and poured drinks for both of them. Lyman declined. Rockwell downed his full tumbler at a gulp. Sam decided that Lyman was a little stouter than he had been when last they met, and then sighed as he realized that the years were putting a little bulk on all of them. Lyman had a round face, kindly eyes, and a full beard but no moustache. Although he was very devout now, the time was not far off when, like Sam, he would become an apostate.

Rockwell approached the subject which had brought them. "I reckon you know why we're here, Brannan."

"No, I can't say that I do," Sam replied blandly.

Lyman watched the two men closely, for he knew both to be fearless and pugnacious. He seemed ill at ease.

"Brother Brigham sent us to fetch his money," Rockwell said coldly.

"His money? What do you mean, his money?"

"I mean all that tithing you collected from our Mormon miners. The two companies that come in last fall told us you had a lot of Church money. And on the way out here we passed some other companies. William Glover was heading one of them and he made quite a point of listing for us all the Church property you've disposed of, and kept the money, besides that tithing money. That money belongs to the Church, all of it, and I want it."

"You don't say!" Sam said sarcastically.

"Yes, I do say!" Rockwell shouted, and in a flash Sam found himself looking down the muzzle of a pistol. Sam smiled slowly, maddeningly.

"Put that gun away. It won't get you anything. I've looked down hundreds of them, but most of the men behind them are cowards like you." Sam arose slowly and leaned his weight on his hands, which were flat on the table-top; he went on speaking in a cold, ominous tone. "What I've got is mine. I take what I can get, and when I get it I keep it, just like Brigham does. Does he send me any tithing money? Does he give any of you a share of it? No. What he gets, he keeps, and so'll I. If you're fool enough to collect money and give it to him, that's your lookout. I could make a good guess that he's sent you and other men down here to dig for gold. And you suckers will dig for it, working and slaving all day long in icy water and hot sun. And when you get a nice little stake, you'll take it back to Zion for the Church. Who is the Church, and who will keep all you bring to the Church? I'll tell you: Brigham Young."

Rockwell replied coldly, "You're right handy with words, ain't you—but I ain't a-listening to you. Brigham has authority to handle Church funds, and you don't. That money belongs to the Lord, Sam Brannan, and I ain't leaving here till you give it to me."

"Have you got a receipt from the Lord?" Brannan taunted him.

"No, I ain't. I ain't even got a receipt from Brigham Young, but I aim to collect it just the same."

"You'll play hell! I'll give you that money on the day you bring me a receipt from the Lord, marked 'Paid in full'; until then, get out!"

Sam strode to the door and threw it open. Then he stood waiting for the two men to leave. The noise and hubbub out in the main store filled their ears. Curious eyes looked at Sam, standing belligerently in the door of his little office and pointing to someone inside to get out.

Amasa Lyman got up, shaking his head sadly. "You're a wicked man, Sam Brannan. The Lord will punish you for your actions this day." He went slowly past Sam, through the door, and into the store, and stood waiting for his companion. Rockwell, still holding his weapon, got up and walked toward Sam.

"Better get that gun out of sight before those miners out there see it," Sam suggested. "If I should tell them that you are a Mormon they might tear you apart. They don't like Mormons."

Porter stopped in front of Sam and looked calmly into his eyes. "Oh, I don't think they hate the Mormons so bad. They think you are one and they let you go on living, you dirty skunk."

Sam tensed in fury but Rockwell stood his ground.

"You wouldn't dast act like this if you was back in Deseret," he said tauntingly.

Sam's lips curled back from his teeth. "So I've heard tell. I hear you got several notches on your gun."

Rockwell smiled coldly. "I wouldn't say that," he said deliberately, "but if I was as bad as I been painted I'd have one on it right now, and take considerable pleasure in putting it there."

"Get out!" Sam bellowed. Rockwell put his gun back in the holster and moved deliberately out into the room.

Sam watched the two men leave the store, then he slammed his office door and went back to his accounts. Sam was never to know what Brigham said when Porter returned to Zion in November, but he learned presently that in the months that intervened Rockwell had headed a group of miners who dug in the gold fields for the Church.

Shortly thereafter Sam left for San Francisco. As he walked along Montgomery Street he was surprised again at the rapid changes taking place in his city. The sidewalks were a moving series of kaleidoscopic scenes with rarely a familiar face. There were men in every type of clothing, but he seldom saw a woman. These men who flocked to San Francisco came without their women, and the few women who already lived there remained modestly in their homes, afraid of this Wild West boom-town. The only women who ventured onto the streets were prostitutes from the ends of the earth, come to sell their charms for some of the yellow gold so freshly dug from it. Men did not come to stay in San Francisco; it was only a stopping-place on the way to the mines. The bay was a forest of spars of abandoned ships, and sailors could not be hired at any price to sail them out again.

Sam stopped in to talk with William Howard and to settle a little business. It was soon arranged that he could have the greater share of all stock on hand; but as this was not sufficient Sam said, "I'll have to do like I usually do, I guess, and make the rounds. I'll clean out every store in town before I sail back up the river or my name is mud." The two men drifted to the door and watched the ceaseless travel up and down the street. Howard shook his head sadly.

"San Francisco is not the same town it used to be. When all the men deserted last year and went away, leaving just a handful of us, we was lonesome. But, my God, when they come back, and others begun to pour in, we wished we could be lonesome again. And since the gold rush has really got under way the town ain't fit to live in.

No more do we get up on Sunday morning and think about going over to the little schoolhouse to listen to the Reverend Hunt preach. No, my poor sick wife don't dare show her head out of the door." He paused thoughtfully and added, "I'm going to send her over to Honolulu for her health, the first boat I can get that will sail out of the harbor."

Sam said a few words of sympathy about Mrs. Howard—who was to die within a few weeks—and they retraced their conversational steps back to the gold rush.

"Digging in the mines and gambling and chasing prostitutes is the main job of most of the men in California now," Sam said wrathfully, and pointing to a ragged miner he added, "Take that feller there. He thinks it's smart to go around the streets in a dirty, smelly red flannel shirt, with his pants tucked down in his boots and his hat ragged and caked with dust. He thinks it makes a man of him to roll up his sleeves and show his hairy arms and chest. If his shirt wasn't red, it wouldn't be no good. There's a million just like him, and they make me sick. I hope I never get so far down that I don't want to dress clean and look like a gentleman."

Howard nodded in agreement and pointed out a Mexican in silver-buttoned trousers with leather leggings and a bright-colored *serape* draped over his shoulder, and a hat alive with color. "Yeh, the miners look down on furriners, but notice how much better that Mexican looks than most of these dirt-covered miners."

It became a game to the two men to pick out the various kinds of dress. They saw Irishmen in corduroys; New Englanders in severe black. There were men with sharp beards who could be nothing but Parisians. There were men in soft, wide-brimmed hats who spoke with a Southern drawl. And lastly, there were the leading businessmen of San Francisco, dressed, like Sam, in neat frock coats with fancy vests and top hats, and wearing neatly trimmed beards. Sam was one of the most dandified men in this city which prided itself upon dress. He would have felt undressed if he had appeared on the street in anything but formal clothes. His Vandyke was a trade-mark which cartoonists used and would use for many years to come.

"I don't know what most of these fellers are going to do for fresh linen," Howard said at last. "There's no one but a few Chinks to wash their dirty clothes, and it's pretty hard to buy new ones. I hear that some of them sent their laundry to China or to the Sandwich Islands, but it took too long to get back and cost so much that they didn't try it again."

Sam laughed. "Yep, there's barely enough water for drinking without doing any washing. My old mother-in-law looks after mine, bless her heart. She stores rain water in winter and manages somehow to get enough spring water in summer to keep us clean."

"Fanny's a good-hearted old soul, for all she's so bent on staying a Mormon," Howard laughed.

"Yes, she is. She's as thick with the thirty or so Mormon families that still live here as she can be. They're a pretty good outfit, though; stay to theirselves and mind their own business."

"Yes, that they do. The menfolks are hard-working and decent, and the women modest and industrious," Howard agreed, and added, "That reminds me of something I saw the other day. I was going past young Mowry's house, and his two younguns was playing in the yard inside that picket fence. A whole bunch of men was gathered around watching them. Some of them poor lonesome fellers was jest standing there bawling, with the tears running down their leathery cheeks, they was so lonesome. When Mowry's wife come out to call the younguns in, those men ate her up with their eyes. And let me tell you that whenever one of those Mormon women comes down the street with one of their menfolks, every man they meet steps off the sidewalk and holds his hat in his hand to show his respect."

Sam nodded. "Yep, I've seen that. They do it for Lizzie whenever I bring her down town." He sighed in weariness. "At least it shows there's still some decency left in the most of them, even if they do spend their nights in bawdy houses."

Howard poked him in the ribs and winked his left eye. "That's right, Brannan, you speak with righteous indignation. You, being a former elder, would never be found in such a place, would you?"

Sam flushed and then laughed. "Well—hell's bells, Bill! A man has to have some fun once in a while. And I'm no worse than you and a few others I could name."

"Well, at least I don't pretend to be no Saint," Bill said and laughed his great rolling, hearty laugh.

"I got to get on home," Sam said. "See if my family's grown any more since I left. It's getting so I'm almost afraid to go home for fear I'll have a new youngun." He spoke lightly, but there was a note of pride in his voice, and Howard knew that he meant it to be funny and laughed accordingly.

When Sam approached his house he noticed a man loitering a short distance up the hill. There was something familiar about the figure and he stood waiting for the man, who was now hurrying toward him. "Sam! Is it you?" It was the beloved voice of his brother-in-law, Alexander Badlam.

Sam took the hard hand into his and pumped it with joy. "You old son-of-a-gun!" he roared. "When did you get in town?"

"Just a little while ago. I been up here waiting for you to come. Didn't want to go in, not knowing your second wife."

Sam motioned him to silence. "Go slow on that second wife talk, Alex. Lizzie don't know she's a second wife. Whatever you do, don't mention Hattie's or the youngun's name in this house, or I'll be in a hornets' nest."

Alexander grinned knowingly. "All right, I won't."

While going up the walk and across the porch Sam learned that Alexander had come out hoping to make a gold strike; if he were successful he intended to send for his family. "I'll take you up to the gold fields my very next trip," Sam promised. "I can sure show you the ropes."

When Sam threw open the front door Ann Eliza was waiting. She lifted her lips for his kiss. "I saw you coming up the hill. My, but I was glad to see you! We wasn't expecting you today."

Sam introduced Alexander to her. She acknowledged the introduction and then turned her attention back to her husband. "Come see Addie smile. My, she's getting to be smart!"

Sam took Alexander into the bedroom to see the baby girl in her cradle. Both men chucked her under the chin, and she smiled a toothless smile and cooed up at them. Fanny came in from the kitchen wiping her hands on her apron.

"Well, hello, stranger," she greeted Sam. "Wasn't there no place else to go?"

Sam grinned and kissed her on the cheek. "This here is my brother-in-law, Alex Badlam. You've often heard me speak of him," Sam presented his relative.

"Yes, 1 have," she smiled warmly. "I'm mighty glad to meet you." She held out her hand and shook his big one warmly.

After supper Sam rose from the table. "I got to go down town on business, Alex. Want to come along?"

"Sure do," Alex agreed. Ann Eliza looked up unhappily.

"Oh, Sam, do you have to go out tonight?"

"Yep. Got to sign some papers with J. W. Osborn. We got a lawyer meeting with us tonight to draw up partnership papers."

"Partnership in what?" she asked.

"A store. I'm going to sell out my stores up at the mines and go in business down here."

Her eyes shone suddenly with happiness. "Oh, Sam do you really mean it?" He nodded. "How wonderful! Then we'll be able to see you every day."

"You sure will, if you can stand it," he teased.

"I'm glad," she said simply, but then asked quickly, "Why sell out up there if you're making money?"

"Don't want to be bothered with it any more. Too many rowdies and criminals drifting into the gold fields. They make it tough for us storekeepers. They act like they think we're gouging them—and we are."

Alexander laughed. "Stop cheating them and they'll be all right," he suggested.

Sam laughed grimly. "You don't know them. Uh-*uh*! I've made enough up there. Now I'll let someone else take the risks. I can make all I want here in San Francisco and be safe at the same time. I've cleared over a hundred thousand dollars up there, and after I sell out I can average over a hundred thousand a year on my rents alone, here and in Sacramento. That'll satisfy me."

"Well, I should hope so!" Alexander said, looking startled.

The two went down the hill, Sam pointing out the sights as they went. They turned in at Osborn's office in a crude lumber building. An hour later the papers were ready to sign. The lawyer gathered up his documents and made ready to go. Alexander arose and suggested that he would walk around for a few minutes and then return for Sam. Osborn and Sam remained to discuss details.

"You'll have to run the business down here until I can sell out my three stores up the river. After that, I can help here," Sam explained.

Osborn nodded. "So I understand. By the way, Brannan, I've signed several contracts to fetch us shiploads of China merchandise."

"Good!" Sam exclaimed. "That's the kind of get-up-and-go—the kind of business foresight—I like to see in a man. We'll go far together. I've leased a good piece of land on Montgomery Street, between Sacramento and California, from the clerk of E. Mickle and Company—that bunch that struck out for South America. I'm having some fellers put up a shack on it. We can use that for our first store, like I told this lawyer tonight. Why, do you realize that ships from Peru, from Chile, from Honolulu, from China, and from all other parts of the world will unload practically in our back door?"

Osborn nodded enthusiastically. "That's right, and now that Central Wharf is making such good headway we can go down there and buy whatever we want at the auctions, and have it whisked up to our store with very little effort."

"Yep, we can have it carried over by hand and not have to bother with hauling any but the heaviest stuff. For a while, though, I'll be taking most of the stuff up the river; until I get rid of my stores."

"Well, we won't be ready for it for a little while yet." Osborn rubbed his chin reflectively. "Trouble now is that although the ships are coming in regular, there ain't none going out."

"That'll soon be changed," Sam said positively. "Already men are drifting down from the mines without gold. There'll be more. Pretty soon they'll be glad to sail the ships out."

The final partnership papers were signed the next day. Then Sam called again on the clerk of the firm of E. Mickle and Company. He paid the clerk $9,000 in gold dust for the purchase of the land, but he neglected to do one thing—he neglected to make sure that the clerk had the authority to sell. When that person left town a few days afterward, Sam thought nothing of it. Ten years later he was to pay

$50,000 to the firm of Pratt and Campbell, attorneys, to clear title to the land which had cost him only $9,000.

July 4, 1849 was the rowdiest day San Francisco had ever seen.

On the next sailing of the *Eliodora* for Sacramento, Alex was aboard.

Getting the new store building put up, and buying merchandise for it and the other stores, took a great deal of Sam's time. Gillespie was the chief auctioneer in San Francisco at this time, and Sam was always at auctions whenever he was in town. At Sacramento Sam himself had long been the main auctioneer, and he was soon to overshadow Gillespie in San Francisco; for the moment, however, he was content to be chief buyer, while Gillespie did the work. Sam was never so happy as when perched on a high box, smoking a long cheroot, while he sank the small blade of his pocket-knife in the soft pine.[69] On one particular day, Gillespie ran the price of tea up to sixty-one cents a pound. He tried to run it higher, but no one would bid. He looked at Sam. "Well, Brannan, you get first choice. I suppose you'll take fifty out of these five hundred cases of tea?"

Sam stopped stabbing the pine box, folded his knife, put it in his pocket, and said quickly, "With tea selling from $1.25 to $5.00 a pound, you think I'll only take fifty cases? Give me the whole damned shebang."

Gillespie's mouth dropped open. Talbot Green protested, "Hold on there, Brannan, our store wants some of that tea."

Sam grinned down at him. "Every merchant here wants some, but that consignment is now mine. If you want any tea you can buy from me. You'll have to pay my price."

Talbot laughed ruefully. "You drive a sharp bargain, Sam. We'll be sorry when you pull out of our San Francisco business."

"You ought to be," Sam teased and jumped down from his box to pay over the money to Gillespie.

Sam saw many things in San Francisco which displeased him. Chief among these was the big tent at the southeast corner of Clay and Kearny streets which served as headquarters for the San Francisco

"Regulators," commonly called the "Hounds." The tent bore a sign saying "TAMMANY HALL," and within it gathered the scum of New York's Bowery, which had come to California on Stevenson's four ships to fight in the Mexican War. At first, many of the disbanded members of Stevenson's regiment of New York volunteers had drifted from community to community, trying to find ways of living without working. Then they had gone up into the mines and engaged in criminal activities. Many were still there. Others had drifted back because the miners had run them out. They were banded together now under the leadership of Samuel Roberts, a villain of considerable ability. It was their habit to go about the streets in groups, dressed in odds and ends of their Army uniforms, and indulge in petty thievery. Sam had wanted his city to build up, and he deplored the fact that so many criminals roamed the streets at will with no attempt made by legal authorities to curb them. As a matter of fact, Sam discovered that the duly constituted officers of the law even hired these ruffians to collect bills, or to make arrests of those unfortunate enough to be unorganized.

A few days after the new store of Osborn and Brannan opened for business, Sam and his partner were standing in the doorway talking. Two customers were inside being waited on by the clerk. There was a high pile of blankets beside the two men on the sidewalk—as was customary—and in front of the store were picks, shovels, pans, and other gold-digging equipment. The customer picked what he wanted and came into the store to consummate the deal. A half dozen Hounds came around the corner, and when they reached the new store they stopped to look. Suddenly one grabbed half a dozen blankets, while the others all secured various articles from the outside display and started away. Sam ran after the fellow with the blankets and caught him. The ruffian turned and struck him between the eyes. Sam staggered back, blinded for a moment, involuntarily releasing his hold on the man's coat because of the pain. When he could see again the culprits had gone. In a fury, Sam strode down to the sheriff's office and demanded that the thieves be arrested at once. The sheriff looked at him as if he thought Sam were mad.

"Arrest some of the Hounds? Not me. Why that bunch of men has got more power than all the officers in this city put together. You go down and try to tame them, if you want to, but I've got more sense than to tackle them."

Sam looked at him with disgust. "You're yellow enough, God knows, but that's not why you won't arrest them. I'll tell you why. It's because you're hand in glove with them. I know, and so does everyone else in town know, that you send those dirty dogs out to collect bills or make arrests, because you're afraid to go yourself. Are we going to have law and order in this town or are we going to clean out you filthy politicians?"

"Aw, go blow off steam somewheres else, Brannan! I ain't got time to listen to you," the sheriff said, and walked out of the room. Sam went after the man, grabbed him, and turned him around. Then he shook the officer like a terrier. "You ain't got time to do anything you ought to be doing, but you're going to start pretty goddamned quick or you won't have a job to tend to. I'm going to do something about law and order, and when I do you better high-tail it out of town." He released the sheriff abruptly and strode out of the office.

As he walked along the street his brain whirled with angry thoughts. There must be some way to bring order out of this crazy pattern of life which was the gold rush boom-town of San Francisco.

He thought long into the night after he had gone to bed and at last, out of sheer weariness, fell into a troubled sleep. Along toward morning he was awakened by distant screams. He ran out on the porch in his underwear and saw that the little valley which lay between the rolling hills north of Jackson and west of Stockton was aflame. He went back into the house and slipped on his trousers. A few minutes later he heard a knock on the door, and when he opened it there cowered before him three women, half-hysterical, with coats thrown over their nightgowns. They said that they came from the *Chileno* village; that the Hounds were burning their tents and shacks, and that their menfolk were away, gone to the mines. Ann Eliza came running in to listen to their story. She roused Fanny, who made coffee for them, and while the refugees wept they told the story of their unhappy plight; how the drunken Hounds, many of them on horseback, had come down into the little village, which was used as a temporary stopping-place by nearly all foreigners bound for the mines, and had beaten several of the men, injured children, and attacked a mother and daughter. They had stolen everything of value in all the habitations, which were mostly tents, and set fire to what was left so that the inhabitants had to flee for their lives.

"What started it all?" Sam asked one of the ladies—who was well educated and beautiful—in her distress.

"They say that these men came to collect money from Pedro Cueto, that he was owing to a merchant. This Pedro claims he does not owe it, so the sheriff he send these Hounds to collect it. They collect from all of us. This is a bad night," she moaned.[70]

Sam began to walk back and forth, his lips grim. At last he strode out into the kitchen where Fanny was working over the fire. "That dirty son-of-a-bitchin' sheriff must've gone right down to see the Hounds right after I left. I told him I'd fix him and them, and by God, I'll do it or die!"

"Sam, watch your language," she admonished, but he made no reply.

At daylight Sam left for town. He stopped to talk to Kanaka Davis and found the Davis home sheltering four hysterical women. Then on down to Howard's, to find several more, together with their children. Mrs. Howard had sailed for Honolulu the day before and the hired girl was helping William to soothe the frightened creatures. Sam called his genial friend onto the porch.

"Bill, something's got to be done. We've either got to regulate the 'Regulators' or let them regulate us. Which is it going to be?"

Howard shrugged his shoulders. "I'm for backing anything you can do, Sam; but honestly, I don't see what can be done. I'm sick and tired of having my store robbed and being pushed off the sidewalk by rowdies, but they're organized and the officers won't touch them."

"Hell's bells, Bill! It's time we got some new officers, then."

Howard turned a haggard face toward him and put his hand on Sam's shoulder. "You go ahead and work out a plan, old man. I'll back it to the limit. But I've been up night after night with my sick wife, and now she's gone and I've not got the mind nor the energy left to do anything."

"I'm sorry, Bill," Sam said, suddenly grieved for his friend. "I'll do something all right and let you know about it later." By ten o'clock he had talked to every businessman of importance in the city,

and all had agreed to follow his lead in whatever attempt he made
to bring order out of chaos. Shortly after ten, Sam mounted a barrel
on the corner of Clay and Montgomery streets. The men who had
come with him gathered around as he began to address them, and
loiterers came closer to listen.

"How long are you people of San Francisco going to stand for
the dastardly kind of thing that happened in our city last night? A
whole village of men, women, and children was burned out last night
by a bunch of drunken hoodlums. Every man in this city today ought
to be filled with indignation. Why are these criminals allowed to go
where they please, and do what they please, never arrested nor even
chided by the officers of the law—officers elected, if you please, by you
people standing out here in front of me? Do you want to know why?
I'll tell you! It's because Alcalde Leavenworth and the sheriff are
hand in glove with those thieves. I've talked to Leavenworth this
morning, trying to get him to issue warrants for the arrest of every
Hound that was on that raid last night. And all he says is that he
can't prove anything. He don't want to prove anything. Do you know
why the Hounds went down there last night, and burned people out
of their homes and attacked women and injured men? They went
because the sheriff had sent them down to collect a bill he was too
goddamned yellow to go and collect himself. He told me yesterday
afternoon that he was afraid to arrest a Hound. Well, I'm not. If
you men will give me the authority to do it I'll arrest every goddamned cur among them!"

His audience stirred and there were cries of assent, but Sam could
see that they were not yet properly aroused. He whipped himself into
a frenzy of words that lashed the crowd.

"You stand there like sticks. What are you going to do—just
stand around and let these men steal your houses out from under
you, and rape your women and cut our throats? I ask you, what are
you going to do about it?"

"Stop them!" a hoarse voice bellowed.

"How?" Sam demanded.

"You tell us," several voices answered. The crowd in front of him
had quickly grown to such proportions that all traffic was stopped, and
still more men came from all directions to listen.

"Come on, everyone, let's go up to the plaza where everyone can hear," Sam shouted, and getting down from the barrel he led the vast crowd up the hill. The roof of Alcalde Leavenworth's office on Clay Street, at the rear of the City Hotel, faced the plaza. Sam climbed upon it, his legs spread wide, while he waited for the crowd to gather itself and make ready to listen.

"What's going to stop the Hounds from killing all of us when they begin to feel like we need killing? What's to prevent them from destroying all legitimate business and setting up a government of criminals here? We've practically got that kind of government now. In a few months there'll be none of us left to demand justice; there'll be nothing here but a huge robbers' roost. I tell you, men, we need action and we need it now. We've *got* to make this city safe for legitimate business—and for our women, and for children. A lot of you men have not got your families with you, but some of you will be bringing them out someday, and when you do you'll want a decent, law-abiding city for them to live in. I'm more fortunate than most of you. My wife and children live here. It's our home and we want it to be a good one. I swear that I will see these Hounds extirpated or die in the attempt. How many of you are willing to back me?"

There was a monster roar of enthusiasm from hundreds of throats. Sam, as he paused, noticed here and there little groups of dissenters, apparently men who belonged to the Hounds. Sunlight flashed on the barrels of pistols suddenly drawn from holsters. Sam's fury rose and he lashed out at the Hounds, calling them yellow-livered curs, vermin, cowards, and lice. Presently Talbot Green climbed up beside him and whispered in his ear. Sam motioned him to get down, and when Talbot had done so Sam turned back to his audience.

"I see that the Hounds have spies placed throughout this crowd, and these spies are threatening to shoot me if I don't shut up."

He ripped open his vest and his shirt, baring his hairy chest. "Go on, shoot!" he bellowed and stood waiting dramatically. There was a breathless pause. No movement was made in the crowd as men eyed their neighbors out of the corners of their eyes. Then suddenly Sam pulled his clothes together and fastened the top button of his shirt. "My friend was telling me that they've threatened to shoot me, and if they miss they're going to go after my family, or failing that, burn up my house some night."

Sam leaned forward. "Why, you dirty, cowardly lice, there ain't a man among you that dares to attack me. I invited you to shoot, and you didn't have the guts to do it. No, and you've not got the guts to bother my family or burn my house, because if you do, by the Gods, you'll live to regret it, every goddamned last one of you. 1 was the first to welcome you to these shores when you arrived with Stevenson's regiment to fight in the Mexican War; but I'll live to beat hell out of you with a cat-o'-nine tails on the beach, before I shake my fist at your boat in farewell, if you don't behave yourselves— and right now! Come on, aim up your guns. Just one of you fire a shot and this crowd will tear you limb from limb. Hey you, George down there, grab that skulking cur next to you and throw him out of the crowd."

The man addressed turned and saw one of the Hounds slipping his gun into his holster. Instantly the near-by crowd man-handled and hustled him away. Half a dozen other men were kicked out in the same ruthless manner and then the crowd came to attention again.

For many minutes Sam talked, telling them of the hopes of the pioneer settlers in San Francisco for a great future commercial city; and showing how the existing criminality was strangling this future. When he brought his speech to an end he said, "You men come back here this afternoon at three o'clock, and we'll get an organization started that will show the sheriff how to regulate the 'Regulators.' "

At three, the greatest crowd ever to assemble in San Francisco met on the plaza. Lovable big Bill Howard was elected chairman of the meeting. Dr. Victor Fourgeaud was chosen secretary. Then the crowd began to roar for Brannan. Sam arose and began his speech. He began by listing the depredations which the Hounds had committed, and ended with a vivid description of the raid of the night before. Then he paused dramatically and called out, "I want every man here to dig down in his jeans and bring up gold. Then I want you to hand it to Dr. Fourgeaud. File up to his table and give him the money. He will see that it is given to those poor destitute Chilenos who were burned out of their homes last night. Come on, one by one. Start now."

He waited while the collection was taken; it took the better part of half an hour. Then when the crowd was orderly again, Sam said, "Now I will give you the suggestion that brought all of us here this afternoon. It is time that the citizens of this town organized their own police force. We want volunteers who will give a few hours of every day or every night to patrol the streets. You are to go armed, and if you catch criminals in the act of stealing or other crimes, you are to arrest them. Then you will see that they are lodged in the jail. As soon as Alcalde Leavenworth calls court together each week-day morning, these men will be tried. Leavenworth is afraid of these curs, but maybe with us behind him he will have a little courage. You folks are going to be given the chance right now to pick two able men to help him administer justice. Nominations are in order."

Dr. William M. Gwin and James C. Ward were finally chosen.

"Now we want a district attorney and an assistant for him," Sam said.

Horace Hawes was elected, and Hall McAllister, a newcomer, chosen to be his assistant.

"Now," Sam said, "to finish our business we want all you men who are going to volunteer to act as police to come forward and give your names."

Two hundred and thirty men were soon enlisted. They were named to act as special constables under the command of W. E. Spofford. The meeting adjourned with a feeling of satisfaction all around. Sam and the volunteers remained, and Sam outlined their duties. Each man was to arm himself with a musket, and they were to go out—always in groups—on certain shifts each day; the shifts to be set by the leader. Criminals caught were to be lodged on the U.S.S. *Warren*, lying in the harbor—the only jail San Francisco now had.

Sam went down next morning to Alcalde Leavenworth's office to attend the first hearing. Twenty rioters from the Chileno village tragedy had been rounded up, after violent fights with the patrol, and were now being tried by Leavenworth. A grand jury of twenty-four citizens was impaneled and sat listening to the evidence. The trial lasted throughout the day and into the next, but ended in true bills against Sam Roberts and his fellow-criminals for riot, robbery, and assault with intent to kill. Roberts was found guilty on all counts and sentenced to ten years at hard labor. Others drew lesser sentences. However, for lack of a jail the penalties were never exacted. The prisoners were deported instead, and Sam kept his promise; he stood on the shore and shook his fist in farewell.

The volunteer police force did a thorough job of cleaning up the city of crime and criminals, and after ten days of patrol duty the men gathered on the plaza on July 27, 1849, to organize themselves into a permanent guard unit. The First California Light Guard was born that day and was destined to survive for many years, to unite eventually with the National Guard of California. The organization was financed by private individuals. Sam's name headed the list. Afterward he was to serve in the guard as a captain.

But on the day when the California Light Guard organized, Sam was in Sacramento. He was in conference with Captain Sutter, who presented him with the title to the land which was to become famous as Yuba City.[71]

Sam was trying to find buyers for his three stores, but as yet had found no offer acceptable. He was, however, much engrossed in the construction of the new City Hotel which he and Fowler were building, on Front Street, in Sacramento. It was taking shape now; three stories in height, with iron balconies on all the street windows. And Sam was having the best of furniture shipped from Boston.

On August 11, 1849, the *Placer Times* carried advertisements for Sam's stores as follows:

> S. Brannan and Co. Wholesale, Retail. Forwarding storage and commission merchants. Corner Front and J Streets and at Sutter's Fort.
> S. Brannan and Co. Auction and Commission Merchants
> S. Brannan—Auctioneer—Sacramento City.

Another said:

> Daily expected in the schooner *Petrel* from Hong Kong, four wooden houses, 12 x 24 feet. Two rooms each. Also window glass, four couches, six tables, one dozen chairs, 10,000 pounds rice, 7,500 pounds sugar, 3 cwt. paint. Apply to S. Brannan & Co.

All eastern merchants sent goods to California on consignment. Some of these consignment goods were absolutely unsalable. Virginia tobacco and kegs of New England nails were a drug on the market. But Sam made an attempt to get rid of everything, and for this purpose he held auctions on the Sacramento water front for every cargo which he could not handle in his own stores. It was well that he had had practice as an auctioneer, for when he returned to San Francisco again he soon became the leading auctioneer of the bay city water front.

A new honor came to him in San Francisco. He was elected to the City Council and served, as well as his busy enterprises would allow him, for the next year.

On one of his rare evenings at home he talked to Ann Eliza, who sat sewing tiny stitches into a dress for Addie—the baby now crawled around the floor playing peek-a-boo with Sammy. Fanny, still engrossed in church work, was away for the evening, and Sam said how nice it seemed for them to be alone for a change. Ann Eliza lifted her face to smile fondly at him. He lighted up a cigar, and leaning back in his rocking-chair crossed one leg over the other.

"Gosh-all-hemlock, but this year has been a hectic one!" he soliloquized. "Seems like I've lived three lifetimes since it started. Just think, I'm only thirty years old and close to being a millionaire. I guess poor old Ma would turn over in her grave if she knew how famous my name is around these parts. She wanted me to make a name for myself, and by gum, I have!"

Ann Eliza nodded. "I always knew you could if you wanted to. I guess that's why I fell in love with you."

"You're not sorry you married me, then?" he teased, but she answered his question seriously.

"No. Even though I've not seen much of you the last year, I wouldn't do any different if I had it to do over again. I get to thinking sometimes about all the things we can do when once you get time for a breather." There was a glow of excitement in her eyes. "Can we go to Europe sometime, Sam? I've always dreamed of going there."

Sam removed his cigar. "Why, yes, Lizzie, I guess we can one of these days." He leaned forward and looked out of the open door; for the evening was warm. "Look at the lights down there. It don't seem possible that six thousand people are milling and churning up the dust of our streets, does it?"

"It sure don't," she agreed, and laughed. "Why, only a year ago we thought we had a big city because we had eight hundred people here." She got up and went to the door to pick up the baby to prevent her from crawling out onto the porch. Before she came back to her chair Ann Eliza stood looking for a long time into the city that twinkled at her feet. "Tents and shacks and shanties," she sighed. "There must be hundreds of them around the plaza."

Sam came to stand beside her. "Yep. A lot of those shacks are built out of packing boxes, and those lumber houses with canvas tops run all up and down the hills. Tinder-boxes, that's what they are. We'll have an awful fire down there some night if folks don't be careful with their candles."

The next morning when he went down to his store, Sam stood on the high side of the plaza and looked over the dusty, rutted square, which stood unfenced and uncared-for, draped crazily on the side of the hill. All around it were places of business. The *Eldorado*, the most famous gambling house, stood on the corner of Kearny and Washington streets, in a ramshackle half-tent structure. The games inside ran from poker to monte. Gamblers were in their paradise in the various houses of luck and occupied the best rooms in the City Hotel, the Bella Union, and other ramshackle lodging-houses.

Places of business had no storage houses, and goods were piled in the street. As Sam stood watching, half a dozen Chinamen with big bags of laundry on their backs, wended their way down toward the lagoon, near Mission Street, where they would do washing at exorbitant prices. But even they did not attempt to meet the demand for laundry, and many a fine shirt could be picked up any day under a hotel window, cast off because it was dirty.

In September Sam returned to Sacramento to be present when the new hotel opened its doors.[72] He hoped to be able to close a deal for his stores, too, while he was there.

Arrived in the river city, he went straight to the new structure, in front of which he found John Fowler rocking on his heels, his hands deep in his pockets as he viewed it with pride.

"Pretty nifty, ain't she?" he said when Sam came up.

"Sure is," Sam agreed. The building, which had a thirty-foot frontage decorated by its many iron balconies, was certainly the most striking in this city of shacks and shanties, now spreading far on the plain beyond the river. Sam dreaded the coming of winter rains, when the plain would be flooded with waters from the mountain streams. He knew that the city fathers would have to put in dykes or even fill in the city proper. But he did not know how often. Many years later, when the city had been filled in year after year, builders excavating for basements would find pots and pans from these first settlers' camps, six feet down.

"Think we'll lose the eighty thousand dollars this hotel is costing?" Sam asked playfully. Fowler laughed.

"Not you. The way you do business we ought to get rich in a hurry. I ain't forgot that I paid your clerk $144 for a dozen cans of oysters a while back."

Sam guffawed and slapped Fowler on the back. "That's what you get for buying from my store when I'm not there. If I'd been there you could have had them for half the price."

It was an old joke between them and they never failed to play it out. "Half?" Fowler said sceptically, raising his eyebrows. "Why, you old skinflint, you'd have charged me double!"

Sam chuckled and turned back to look at the building.

"Is she all ready, so that we can open up on Friday like we've advertised?"

"Yep. Got the placards all nailed up around town yesterday, and the notice in the paper. Yes siree, this town is going to see an opening as is an opening!"

Early on the morning of the opening, men began to pour into town from the mines. Boats arrived on special excursion trips, bringing the wealthy citizens of San Francisco and ladies of questionable virtue. Rich men's wives knew better than to come to the opening of a hotel in a frontier town. Sam Brannan and John Fowler, expansive hosts, stood just inside the ornate lobby—brilliant with red plush and cherry-wood—to shake hands with each guest. The Axminster rug upon which they stood was crimson, with pink roses running riot on its surface. On a raised dais at the far end of the lobby a band played foot-tickling melodies of the day. Now and then the musicians stopped for a rest, and then the assistant bartender would carry drinks to them to revive their flagging spirits. The two hosts shook hands all day, until they lost sight of faces and seemed to be seeing only hands. Each guest was waved toward the bar, which sparkled with its expanse of mirrors, the dark mahogany beaming under crystal glasses. The patrons drank free whiskey, free wine, free brandy, and to the choicest guests were given baskets of champagne to be carried up to private rooms where special friends of the hosts were entertaining their feminine companions. To show their appreciation, these respectable citizens and their guests went out onto the balconies and threw bottles of the sparkling liquor on the wooden sidewalks, so that they might have the pleasure of watching it foam. By nightfall there was scarcely a sober citizen in Sacramento, but the celebration had only just begun. A magnificent display of fireworks was set off from a barge in the river, making the night brilliant with light. Every room in the hostelry was alive with hundreds of candles, and men sang barber-shop ditties and drank the night away. Most of the two thousand inhabitants of Sacramento stayed up all night. In another year there would be seven thousand of them.

The City Hotel had been open only a few weeks when Sam and John found that they would average about thirty thousand dollars a year by way of profit on it. Early in October Sam told one of the guests, Franklin Buck, that his income from rents alone would in this year run close to a hundred and forty thousand dollars, not counting his profits as a merchant and real estate dealer.[73]

As a result of the move made months before by Sam, Peter Burnett, and other interested citizens, a constitutional convention was held in Monterey on October 10, 1849. California was not yet a state; neither was it a territory. It was only a conglomerate mass of land and people, waiting for Congress to vote it into statehood, and while waiting it set up its own constitution. Sam had been named as a delegate to this convention, but the press of business had forced him to let the honor go by and another was appointed in his place. He was to regret in later years that he had not been present at this history-making event. While the convention was in session in Colton Hall in Monterey, Sam was in San Francisco buying goods for his store and auctioning off whole cargoes of consigned merchandise which lay on the still only partially finished Central Wharf. The wharf had started from the middle of the block between Sacramento and Clay streets, but was now running across blocks as far as Drumm Street. Here there was a sufficient depth of water to allow the Pacific Mail steamers to lie alongside. At the shore end of the wharf the office of the Pacific Mail Steamship Company was being built, and already, along the land end, small stores were being hastily put up on stilts, bordering the thirty-eight-foot width of the wharf. These would eventually become commission houses, grocery stores, saloons, mock auctions, "cheap-John" shops, and every kind of miscellaneous little business. The loading platform stretched for two blocks now in either direction, at right angles to the wharf, and was always covered with bales and boxes. The platform and wharf were to become the favorite promenade of the townspeople, and every prominent citizen arriving in the future would walk their length. Later, when it was completed, drays and carriages would drive out to deliver loads to the ships or to receive them. Not even Sam, standing on its unfinished boards while he hoarsely called out the auction bids, could dream that one day this very wharf would become known as Commercial Street. But one thing he did know: that it was costing him and his associates almost $200,000 to build it. Similar enterprises were being undertaken all along the water front from California Street to Broadway, but none would ever be so successful as Central Wharf.

In October Sam was able finally to close a deal for his four stores. William Stout breathed a grateful sigh of relief when his partnership with Brannan came to an end and he was able to leave Mormon Island alive and well. The Coloma and fort enterprises went to a small merchant; the Sacramento store to a large business concern, which bought out the three ships, the *Eliodora*, the *Eliza* and the *Juven Guipizcoana*, as well as the warehouse and whatever good-will Sam may have commanded.

Although Sam sold the three faithful old vessels because they were no longer useful to him, he immediately entered into a plan with William Howard, Bezar Simmons, and Kanaka Davis to buy a steamer which had just dropped anchor in San Francisco Bay. This was the *Senator*. Lafayette Maynard—formerly a lieutenant in the U. S. Navy—and his associates had purchased the vessel in New

York and sailed her through the Strait of Magellan to the California coast. They intended to use her on a regular run between San Francisco and Sacramento. However, as soon as these leading citizens of San Francisco saw the trim lines of the self-powered boat they yearned to own her. They rowed out to the *Senator*, and Sam made the proposition to Maynard.

"We've come to make you an offer for your boat," he began. "We're prepared to go as high as two hundred thousand dollars for her."

"The *Senator* is not for sale," Maynard replied.

"We'll make it two hundred and fifty thousand," Sam tempted.

Maynard smiled. "I said, the *Senator* is not for sale. I'm going to put her on the run to Sacramento and give the fastest boat service on the line. I'll make as much as you are offering in the first year. But that's not important to me. I'd keep her if she didn't make a cent. This boat is the fulfillment of a life's dream. I've always wanted to own a ship, and this is the kind I'd have picked. Now that I've got her I'm going to keep her. I'll be doing the one thing in life I'd rather do than anything else."

Sam looked at him and said no more. Disappointed, the four men returned to shore and stood enviously watching the *Senator* bob at anchor.

In November the rains began; the worst rains that California had seen in years. This did not deter Sam from buying twelve more business lots at town sale by permission of Alcalde Geary. He intended to concentrate more fully on real estate from now on; that was where the money lay, when one could put up a shack on a lot which cost fifteen dollars and rent it for six hundred or a thousand dollars a month.

By the early part of December all of California was a mudhole and San Francisco had begun to bog down in its slime. Mules sometimes stumbled in the mud and drowned before their riders could pull them out. Drunks fell off the sidewalks and never rose to the surface. Montgomery Street was the main business thoroughfare and had to be used; for sidewalks the merchants made stepping-stones out of boxes of consigned goods for which there was no market. Virginia tobacco, kegs of New England nails, a piano or so, were sunk in the mud so that people might walk. And still the mud continued to rise, and more cases of tea or flour and other merchandise were put down to make a walk. Time and again the streets were filled in the middle with brush, but it sank out of sight, and ultimately mules' legs got caught in it and many of them drowned as a result. Here and there, as the rains continued, barrel staves were nailed to planks and these laid down, but there were not enough of them. One wag put up this crude sign on the corner of Kearny and Montgomery: "This street not passable, not even jackassable."

As Christmas neared, Sam spent more time at home than he had in months. It was hard to get about to business in a town which had few sidewalks, and he left a great deal to his business associates and his clerks. Ann Eliza and Fanny were busy seeing to the making up of pies and puddings for Christmas, and Sam romped on the floor with the children. At six o'clock in the morning on the day before Christmas, Sam was awakened from a sound sleep by the fire bell. He ran to the window and saw leaping flames down on the plaza. He dressed rapidly and ran in great strides down the hill. Dennison's Exchange and the Parker House were both blazing. Sam found many of his friends there, and they all joined together in trying to fight the fire, but what with mud and lack of water they could make no headway. At last Sam gave up and went up the hill to the house of a man who did a great deal of hauling for him.

"Get your wagon hitched up and go on up to my house. If the fire veers that way, start putting our stuff in it and take my family out. I'll be up in a little while."

Sam went back again to help, but there was nothing to be done. He went on home. The teamster was there and the wagon, almost hub-deep in mud, stood at the sidewalk. Ann Eliza and Fanny ran back and forth through the rooms, madly trying to gather up what they would need if they had to get out in a hurry. Sam stood on the porch with the teamster, and they watched the flames leap and crackle below. First they blew north, then spread southward, and finally started up the hill. "Why, of all nights, don't it rain?" Sam moaned. "It has every night for forty days until now." In a frenzy the two men began to carry things out to the wagon. The night had gone, and daylight was upon the raging inferno which had been a city only a few hours before. Slowly the flames crawled up the hill, until the destruction of the Brannan household seemed inevitable. Sam swore softly as he carried furniture, clothes, and children out to the waiting wagon. Suddenly the wind veered, and the flames were blown back in the direction from which they had come. Within an hour the wind died down. Sam left his house and dashed back down the hill to aid the fire-fighters. The city was free of fire again before nine o'clock that morning.

The next day Sam held solemn conclave with William Howard and Talbot Green. "I think it's about time us fellers got these ready-made houses put up, that you had shipped around the Horn from New York."

Howard nodded. "Yes, I guess so. I been sort of holding back, waiting for the rains to stop. But I guess we can get at them pretty soon now. Agnes sort of wants to have a new house to ourselves, where there's not so many memories." Howard's wife had died in Honolulu, and he had a new bride.

Sam nodded. "Yes, I guess it is hard on a bride to have to live in a house another woman furnished." He paused. "Let's get our houses set up over on Mission Road in Happy Valley, out of the fire region. It's going to be nice over there where there's not so much fog, and no hills. My younguns will like it."

"We all will," said Green. "My wife is anxious to get over there, too. She thinks there'll be more freedom for the womenfolk when they can visit back and forth with each other and not be cooped up to keep out of the way of a lot of strange men."

Howard said, "Well, leave it to me, Sam. As soon as it looks like we can get those houses out of the warehouse and set up, I'll do it. But there's no sense in trying to put them up in knee-deep mud. I didn't have them brought all the way around the Horn, ready to be assembled, just to sink them in mudholes. By the way, Folsom is buying one of them. He'll be a neighbor of ours, too."

On the last day of the year 1849, Sam stood on his porch and looked out over a city which was already rebuilding with tents and packing-boxes and whatever lumber could be had. He thought back through the momentous days the year had seen. It had been ushered in by the first of the gold rush horde from the States, and was going out in the blackening embers left by fire.

Chapter XVIII

CAPTAIN SUTTER had established his son in the real estate business together with three men: Dr. Brandes and the Wetzlar brothers.[14] Sam bought an interest in the firm, but did not take an active part in it at this time. However, he did use the office, when in Sacramento, as headquarters for a rather extensive loan business to which he found himself inadvertently a party. It had started when the Federal Government began to claim title to all lands in this newly acquired territory. Landowners who had paid high prices for lots in the swiftly growing city suddenly found themselves forced to defend their title to the land, and those who had little or no money went to Brannan to borrow. Sam, having more than enough, was willing provided the borrower would pay interest. Since loans were secured by mortgages against the borrower's land, Sam charged very high rates; he felt this was only fair because he was taking the risk of losing the land to the Government. If the borrower fought a long court case to secure his title, and lost, Sam lost too. Many landowners sold out their interest to Sam altogether, for a mere pittance, leaving it to him to fight for title against the Government. Until January of 1852 these land suits were to be conducted in a haphazard, demoralizing way, and only men with money stood to benefit. Sam had money. When in 1852 the U. S. Land Commission investigated the titles, men like Brannan, the Wetzlar brothers, and Bruce Graham were in a position to reap all the advantage. Sam was never known to lose an advantage.

In January of 1850, while the rains continued to deluge San Francisco, Sam attended a sale of town lots which had been advertised three months previously. Four hundred and thirty-four water front lots were offered by Alcalde Geary. All the council members were in a position to secure the choicest lots, and Sam, being a member, was able to take nineteen in his own name while the firm of Osborn and Brannan bought thirteen. By the end of the month Sam owned

Being a councilman had given Sam advantages which he did not deplore, but when in April the State Legislature passed a charter for the City of San Francisco, the old Mexican form of government was automatically discarded and Sam found himself out of office. A Board of Aldermen was elected immediately, and within a few months Sam, much to his dissatisfaction, as well as the rest of San Francisco, discovered that they had once more elected to public office a group of men who were bent upon one purpose only: to mulct the public of as much as possible in the shortest time.

However, Sam watched political progress with only half his attention, for he was engrossed in settling his family in the little new home in Happy Valley, on the old Mission Road between Fourth and Fifth streets.[75] He had for neighbors William Howard and his bride, the former Agnes Poett; Joseph Folsom, and Talbot Green, who had married the widow Montgomery. Now that the rains had ceased, the children could play on the grassy meadows which stretched level for a mile or so in either direction. The women were soon visiting back and forth, walking the narrow dirt path between their homes. Rarely did bearded miners or strangers come over to this residential section of the city, where there was little fog, no wind, and a great deal of sunshine.

Going diagonally through the plaza one sunny morning, Sam met Barton Mowry and George Winner. He inquired after their families and learned that all was well.

"How are the Ladds and the Kittlemans and the Glovers getting along in Deseret?" he asked.

"Just fine," Winner replied. "One or another of our colony hears from some of them once in a while, and they all seem to like it there in the Great Salt Lake Valley, though they do say that they have to work awful hard to make a crop."

Sam laughed shortly. "I told them they'd have to before they went there." His eye was caught by the sight of Robert Parker going into his hostelry across the plaza. Sam waved to him and Parker waved in response. "Well, he's got a wooden building up instead of half-tent and half-lumber, like he had last year," Sam said. "In fact, he's got about the only wooden building in town of any size. We all got to begin building more solid."

"What for?" Mowry asked. "We ain't got no fire protection, and solid buildings burn as easy as canvas ones."

Sam nodded. "Yeh, you're right. We got to get some fire companies organized around here pretty soon."

"Well, I'm going down to the Bella Union to see a feller. Want to come along?" Barton asked. They assented and fell into step. Sam's eyes again took in the sight of the great canvas houses that faced the plaza—now properly named Portsmouth Square—on the Washington, Kearny, and (in part) Clay Street sides. Even this early in the day miners and gamblers, bums and gentlemen were going in and out of the numerous gambling tents. The old Brown Hotel, now called the City Hotel, still stood on the corner of Clay and Kearny, and was still doing a rush business. Inside, its bunk beds were mere wooden layers built one above the other, where a traveler might rent space and a blanket at an exorbitant price.

Sam and his friends stopped to look into the door of the *El Dorado*. Tables were covered with stacks of Mexican dollars and doubloons, which made coin ramparts around the lacquered boxes into which the gold dust of the losers was being poured in a steady stream. Eager men surrounded each table. "Come on in for a few minutes and I'll buy you a drink," Sam suggested, and they went in. It was the largest gambling hall in town and even this early in the morning a band was playing at one end. The three men ordered drinks and sipped them slowly while they listened to the music and watched the ceaseless milling of the customers.

"Who ever would have thought, four years ago when we landed here, that we'd ever live to see a place like this in Yerba Buena?" Sam said at last.

"Things sure have changed," Winner agreed.

"Changed is no name for it," Barton said quickly. "Why, there was less than two hundred people in this town when we landed, and now there's ten thousand. If we can get ten thousand in four years, chances are we'll have a hundred thousand people here before we're through."

Sam grinned. "Remember nearly three years back, when I wrote an editorial and said this would be the Liverpool of the West, and you fellers made fun of me?"

They both grinned sheepishly. "Well, come on. I got to get over to the Bella Union. I'm late," Barton urged them.

As they crossed the street they saw Captain Sutter going into a store half a block away.

"Wonder what he's doing in town," Sam said. "I see he hasn't got his missus with him."

"His missus?" Barton said. "She's back in Switzerland, ain't she?"

"No, his family come out here two or three months ago," Winner replied quickly.

"Yep," Sam explained. "It was the last week in January, and Captain Sutter and a feller named Lienhard was in my City Hotel up in Sacramento, talking over a real estate deal. Part of the city was lying under water and you couldn't get around some parts of it unless you swam. A feller got off the San Francisco boat and come over and told the old Cap that his wife and family had just landed safe in San Francisco. The old man was so happy he got roaring drunk. Him and Lienhard had to spend the night in the hotel warehouse, 'cause they couldn't get back to the fort on account of the flood, and all our beds was full."

When they entered the rococo lounge of the Bella Union Hotel, which was a ramshackle frame structure, they could hear the band playing in the bar. The men went straight to that mirror-bedecked retreat, which was elegant with red plush and brilliant with crystal. A Negro minstrel band played on a raised dais, but the hubbub of men's voices almost drowned the very good music. Barton excused himself while he went to keep his appointment. When he returned, the three men made their way toward the door. In the lobby an elaborately dressed woman stopped Sam. The other two men went ahead to wait for him outside.

"You haven't been up for quite a spell, Mr. Brannan," she said. "Is anything wrong?"

"Hell's bells, no!" Sam said in exasperation. "You know better than to speak to me in public."

"I'm sorry," she said, flushing. "What I really stopped you for was to ask your advice on a business deal."

"I attend to all my business in my office," he said coldly. "Send your representative there, but don't ever stop me on the street or anywhere else again."

He strode out then. Barton was on the point of leaving. He said good-by, and then Winner looked at Sam curiously for a moment and then said, "Yep, you sure have changed, Sam. Time was when you was decent through and through."

"Oh, mind your business, George. I don't need any of your advice I live the way I please."

"Well, it's a way that us who are faithful in our religion deplore," George replied, and walked away in turn.

At five o'clock on the morning of May 4, 1850, the dread cry of "Fire!" again echoed through the streets. Sam, like other citizens, ran down to the plaza to assist in the fire-fighting. The block bounded by Clay, Washington, Kearny, and Montgomery streets was almost consumed when they arrived. Bucket brigades were formed and after several hours the fire was conquered. The city had lost property estimated at four million dollars. The *El Dorado* was a smoldering ruin, and so was the Stephen Smith house, which had been Sam's first home in Yerba Buena.

A week after the fire the Light Guard went on its annual picnic to Calistoga, a small settlement in the Napa Valley where there were many warm springs and geysers.[76] Sam had secured a piece of land there which contained natural warm springs; he had bought it because it was an ideal spot for picnicking, and he had also been instrumental in naming the town. He had been telling his associates that he intended some day to make of it the Saratoga of California, but in saying the words rapidly his tongue slipped and he said "Calistoga," and thus the town received a name to replace its old one of Agua Caliente.

Ever since its formation, the California Light Guard had been Sam's pet project, and so liberal were his contributions that it was known more often as Brannan's Guard than by its rightful name. His brother-in-law, now that his wife and family had come out, was taking a prominent part in developing the Guard and was already a captain. He marched proudly at the head of his company as it paraded down to Central Wharf from the plaza. People lined the streets and clapped as the military unit passed with such precision and grace, in time to the martial music of its band. At the wharf the companies broke ranks and embarked on the boat Sam had chartered for the day. It took them to Vallejo, where they changed to a line of stagecoaches which flew up curving roads and over low hills into one of the most beautiful valleys in all California. High mountains crowned by the peak of Mount St. Helena hemmed in the valley to the north.

Sam and his own family were accompanied by the Badlams, who now lived but a short distance from them in Happy Valley. Young Aleck at fifteen was a handsome lad, tall and gangling, with a very endearing smile. Sam was particularly fond of Aleck. The younger Mary Ann was a pretty, shy girl of seventeen, and her uncle never tired of teasing her about beaux just to watch her flush; but Mary Ann was still too much of a home body to think a great deal about boys. Sarah, at thirteen, was just budding into the beauty which would soon be her trade-mark in San Francisco. Ezra was only ten, but young Sammy Brannan at five looked up to him as a man of authority, and Ezra tried to live up to the small boy's opinion. They were a merry, laughing crowd that day, with Sam driving the coach and the women alternately watching the scenery and scolding the children. Ann Eliza grew weary of holding the squirming Addie, and Mary Ann, her sister-in-law, offered to hold the child awhile. Fanny's attention was taken by the two boys, who had a mania for leaning out of the coach window; she was afraid that a bounce would throw them out and kept pulling them back and admonishing them to sit quiet like good boys.

There was a beef-barbecue and plenty of beer for the men at the picnic ground. In the afternoon there took place contests of marching, of sharpshooting, and various other forms of skill. At target practice, Company B won. The first prize was a horse and buggy, presented by Samuel Brannan to the winner, Colonel John Hanna.

When, at dusk, the party disembarked in San Francisco and the Guard started to march back to the plaza, an altercation developed between the members of two companies. Edward Kemble reported it thus in the *Daily Alta California*: "On their return from the day's excursion, however, they succeeded in getting into a row among themselves which at one time seemed to threaten serious consequences and at all events was disgraceful in the extreme."

As soon as the ashes had been cleaned up from the last fire, Sam began the construction of two large, substantial office-buildings on Montgomery Street, as evidence of his belief in the future greatness of his city. To his exasperation, the city began to be harassed by a series of fires, large and small. He and other merchants were at their wit's end trying to cope with the situation, while city officials were filled with such apathy that nothing was done to prevent the obvious sabotage.

It was in June, just one month after the last big fire, that another, more devastating, blaze struck the city. By midnight, all the land lying between Clay and California streets, from Kearny to the water, was a smouldering ruin. The Osborn and Brannan store showed but smoking embers when the partners finally stood in front of it at dawn next morning.

Osborn stood looking at the ruins for several minutes, then he rubbed his head and said, "Well, this finishes me. I sunk nearly all I had in that store. Now I'm ready to call it quits and go back to the States where a body can make a living without so much trouble, and live peaceable-like."

"Don't be a fool," Sam said violently. "I'll help you get started again if you want to stay. This is new, wild country. You got to be prepared to fight if you want to get ahead here."

Osborn sighed. "There's no fight left in me, Sam. I'll sell you my interest in our land. I'm taking the next boat out of here."

"Well, there's plenty of fight left in me," Sam bit out the words. "I've not even begun yet, but I'm going to. I'll clean the nits out of this city if I have to do it single-handed."

Osborn looked at Sam, standing there young and handsome and full of vitality, his dark eyes flashing with determination, his skirted coat unbuttoned, revealing the silken waistcoat and high winged collar. His flat-brimmed beaver was pushed back, and as he spoke his fingers unconsciously sought the handle of his gun, which was sheathed in a fine Spanish hand-tooled leather holster. A bowie knife protruded from the other side. Osborn's tired face lighted with a smile.

"I believe you could do it, Sam. You got more push and go than any other two men in this town. San Francisco wouldn't be San Francisco without you. I'm going to miss you."

Sam started out soon after daylight that morning, talking to all his friends and urging them to get together with him once more to start a citizens' guard to patrol the street. But most of them were too interested in their rebuilding plans and their efforts to recoup to give willing ear to him. "We got an American form of government with a board of aldermen. We can't afford to interfere with the courts now," several of them objected. Sam grew angry and argued hotly, but could find no backers.

Although he fretted at the lethargy of businessmen in the rapidly growing city, he forgot his scheme when the National Theatre opened its doors and professional actors and actresses made their debut on the boards of San Francisco. In October the famous Jenny Lind was to make her appearance, and meanwhile several companies took their turns on the stage of the new theatre, among them Robinson and Everard's Dramatic Museum.

In July Sam had a letter from Joseph Ruth about the settlement at Yuba City which had been started the year before. Ruth had taken land at Yuba City in partial payment for his surveying and planning of the town, and he was much upset now at the turn affairs had taken there. He wrote from Sacramento:

I don't know how long it's been since you were up to Yuba City but right across from her some fellers have started up a rival town they've named Marysville. When the steamer *Lawrence* felt its way up the River this far those fellers got first whack at the officers of the craft and persuaded them to make Marysville the terminus for their shipping. This was in January. By now all the travelers for the mines get off there and as a result Yuba, being on the wrong side of the River, is losing out.

This spring a man named George M. Hanson bought lots at Yuba and started a ferry across the River. This is the only reason we've got any settlers left in Yuba. Better go up there first chance you get and see if you can't figure out some way to boost Yuba before everyone moves away. I understand that besides Cheever and Tallman Rolfe and Reading there is a son of Sutter's living up there and Henry Schoolcraft and W. S. Webb. There's been a stampede to move across the River to Marysville and if something is not done in a hurry Yuba City will die a natural death.

Sam, now no longer a merchant in San Francisco, left for Sacramento to attend to business there before going up the Feather River to Yuba City. It was July when he reached Sacramento, and he found Captain Sutter drinking at the bar at the City Hotel. Sam mentioned that he was going on up to Yuba City in a day or so.

"Ya, mine Emil, he is up dere already," Sutter said. "But my Johann he iss got trouble in de head. He vorries all de time. So he is going to de States to see if de healt' comes back." Sutter turned and looked at Sam. "Dis means dat you vill now haf to take his blace in de firm vit' Brandes and de Vetzlar brudders. Dey vill skin me vitout some von to look oud for my interests."

The poor old Swiss had completely lost his grip, and the neurosis from which his son suffered was the final blow that conquered the old man. Sam did take the place of Sutter's son in the firm, but Sam was looking out for his own interests, and the large grants of land which Sutter had deeded to his son all eventually came into Brannan's hands. The old man spoke prophetically to Sam that day when he wept into his beer glass and blubbered, "Mine sun she is setting, Brannan. I am losing everyt'ing. Yours now, it is yust rising."

In Yuba City Sam went straight to the store of his former clerk, Tallman Rolfe—a store whose first stock had been furnished by Sam Brannan.

"What's the trouble up here, Tallman?" Sam asked.

"It's those damned steamboats. We tried to talk the captain into making his landing-place on this side, Henry and me, but those Marysville fellers had talked to him first. Now, Marysville is on the beaten trail, and all the settlers we lured up here with cheap land and inducements have moved over there."

"Is that so?" Sam said grimly. "Well, I'll go back down to Sacramento and make real inducements to settlers. We'll show Marysville a thing or two."

Sam did go back to Sacramento to make inducements, and Yuba City did slowly grow, so that a year later there was a population of 150 people and several business houses, including two saloons; but the city was destined never to show up Marysville to any appreciable extent.

Sacramento Sam found seething with strife between the business-men and squatters, of whom there were hundreds—well-organized too, by now. Sam met with the civic leaders and urged them to fight it out in drawn battle-lines, with guns if necessary. Then he left a clerk to handle his business affairs in the office of Brandes and Wetzlar, and returned to San Francisco.

The first thing Sam did there was to have a rough lumber building erected on the northeast corner of Bush and Sansome streets, to house his own and two other stores, when he should be ready to go into the mercantile business again. The building was soon finished, with three entrances on Bush Street. Sam used the little office in the center section. This was at the head of a narrow, steep stairway, partitioned from the loft at the Bush Street end. Pending the completion of one of his two large office-buildings on Montgomery Street, still under construction, Sam found the location convenient. Here he transacted his real estate business and his banking activities. He had found it profitable to borrow money from New York banks at 4 per cent and loan it out in San Francisco and Sacramento at from 10 to 12 per cent. Most of the details of renting lots, buildings, or office space he left to his clerk, Mr. Wardwell.

It was in August that Sam called his friends William Howard and Talbot Green into his office and suggested that they three be the nucleus of a Pioneer Society, to which only men who had come to California before January 1, 1850, would be admitted. A few days later, in his store building on Bush Street, the organization meeting of the Pioneer Society was called. Howard was elected first president. Sam Brannan, G. Frank Lemon, and Jacob B. Snyder became vice-presidents, while Talbot Green was treasurer. Eighteen directors were named and the society formally launched, although no regular meetings were destined to take place for many months.

Central Wharf was now completed and it was the center of commercial San Francisco. It was crowded at all hours with drays and wagons moving up and down. Sailors, businessmen, miners, men from all parts of the world, speaking many tongues, paraded its length or stood chatting in groups. Boats were always arriving or leaving— stately clipper ships or the new steam vessels. Some went only as far as Sacramento, others around the world. What appeared to be only noise and confusion was really the orderly building of a great commercial center.

The wharf was the dominating feature of San Francisco. Sam

stood on the hill above the plaza one day and looked down upon the city. A mass of men moved up and down the narrow streets, all headed ultimately, it seemed, for the wharf, which appeared more like the edge of a forest than of an ocean; there were so many masts of ships standing upright behind it. Sam drew a deep breath. This was his city. He had built it almost single-handed, it seemed to him.

He was well content. Was he not the richest man in San Francisco—perhaps the richest in all of California? Yes, it was so: he was rich in money and rich in friends. He had everything in life to make it worth while: a fortune, a lovely family, and a position in the community which any man could envy.

He went slowly down the hill and homeward. As he opened the front door Sammy came rushing breathlessly to meet him. "Come in the bedroom, Papa, and look! The doctor brought us a little new baby sister. Grandma has been looking all over for you this afternoon to tell you."

Sam hurried in to see his little new daughter, who slept peacefully in a clothesbasket. They decided eventually to name her Fanny Kemble in honor of the famous actress, and Fanny proved to be like her namesake, even-tempered and beautiful.

On October 18, 1850, the steamer *Oregon* berthed alongside Central Wharf, ignoring completely all the lesser wharves that ranged from Market Street to Broadway. The *Oregon's* flags were flying gaily as she came to rest. Soon Sam was running down the length of the wharf with other excited citizens to hear the glad news. "California's been admitted to the Union," the captain bellowed.

California's first Admission Day celebration was late, but it was nevertheless the greatest display the region had ever seen. On October 29, the city turned out en masse to throng the streets and gather in long lines to watch the parade, in which every prominent man had a place. San Francisco did not as yet boast many carriages, but those available were all pressed into service. Men who could not ride in vehicles or procure a horse walked, carrying tiny flags. The Chinese were represented by a great dragon with fiery eyes and hundreds of legs, which breathed smoke as it went. Native Chinese dancers, resplendent in their brilliant silk costumes, accompanied the writhing beast and set off firecrackers all along the line of march.

Shortly after noon the California Guard band leading the parade came to a halt in front of the reviewing stand. The townspeople gathered to hear the patriotic speeches. Sam was one of the main speakers and he said to his listeners:

"A pro-slavery Congress has for many months defeated the wishes of us who live here in California to belong to the Union. And I guess I have been as much to blame as any one man in the territory for this condition. Ever since the day in 1846 when I first set foot on this soil, I have spoken out against slavery. I have used every ounce of my influence to keep this vile institution from our free shores."

There were a few jeers, which were drowned out in a tumult of applause.

When night came bonfires blazed on all the seven hills of the city, and fireworks leaped and sizzled from the crests of Rincon Hill and Telegraph, and even a few from Goat Island in the bay. At ten o'clock that night Sam Brannan and his wife Ann Eliza led the grand ball, at which five hundred representative businessmen of the growing city, and three hundred ladies, bowed and curtsied.

Chapter XIX

IN FEBRUARY of 1851, two robbers were caught by a merchant named Janssen in the act of stealing merchandise. He attempted to stop them. They struck him repeatedly over the head and left him for dead. Within a few hours two suspects were captured and Janssen from his hospital bed identified them both as his assailants.

On the date of their hearing, Sam Brannan and Colonel Jonathan Stevenson met to talk in heated tones in front of the jail.[77] A crowd collected. Sam was furious when he mounted the porch steps of the city hall and shouted, "Men, we've had over a hundred murders committed in this city. How many murderers have we executed?" He paused, and a hundred throats gave the reply: "None!"

"That's right," he prompted. "It's about time we hung a few. Come on, men, let's go in and get these murderers and hang them right now."

The crowd surged forward to follow him. William Coleman, a young merchant and a newcomer to the town, leaped up on the balcony ahead of Brannan and stood with his arms spread wide.

"No, no—stop!" he yelled. "Listen to me! Let these men have a fair trial—they may be innocent."

"Janssen identified them as the men that attacked him," Sam roared. "That's proof enough for me."

"You're a known hothead, Brannan," Coleman countered in a loud voice. "Janssen is a sick man, near to death. He could be mistaken. Let's wait and be sure before we take human lives. Killing is a serious business. Let's here and now organize a people's court and consult with the authorities. We can see that they administer justice. What do you say, men?"

The crowd faltered and fell back. Sam turned and bellowed at them. "I am very much surprised to hear anyone talk about justice where our authorities are concerned. I'm tired of such talk. These men are murderers as well as thieves. I know this and you know it. I will die or see them hung by the neck. I'm tired of this farce we call law and order. We had enough of that eighteen months ago, when we had to organize the citizens into patrols to rid the town of the Hounds. At that time we allowed ourselves to be the tools of judges who sentenced convicted men to be sent to the States instead of killing them like they deserved. We are the mayors and the recorders, the hangmen and the laws. The law courts in California have never yet hung a man. Every morning when you pick up your paper there is a new account of murder and robbery, sometimes two or three. I'm damned sick and tired of living in this kind of a town. I want to hear no more talk about technicalities. Such things are to shield the guilty. Come on, I say! Let's go hang them!"

Again the crowd surged forward. The sheriff and his deputies came out with drawn guns. "Disperse, you sons-of-bitches or we'll shoot you down like dogs!" the sheriff bawled, and moved straight across the porch until he faced Brannan. "Get back down those steps, Brannan. You're too smart for your pants."

Sam backed down the steps, and when he had reached the bottom he spoke. "When I get through with you this town will be too hot for you," he said. He made a way through the crowd, and soon it had followed him away.

What Sam feared most came upon the city again. On May 4, 1851, just one year to a day since the largest blaze of 1850, fire struck once more. Only a few weeks earlier the first fire company in San Francisco had been organized by Howard; it was known as the Howard Company. Forty members had been accepted, all rich men, and their headquarters were an iron building which had been shipped from England and set up on the west side of Montgomery, just south of California Street. Sam reached the enginehouse just as Ferdinand Vassault, Charles Warner, George H. Howard, and Thomas Haynes pulled the silver-decorated engine—newly arrived after a long voyage around the Horn—through the door.

Two less aristocratic companies of later origin were already at the scene of the fire when the Howard Company arrived. The California and Monumental boys were pumping frantically. The fire set up an awful roar as it swept through the tunnels made by the planked streets which had been built solidly throughout the main business district. From block to block the flames spread by way of these tunnels. Sam saw the *Niantic* burn to the ground, a ship which had formerly belonged to Kanaka Davis and had for some time been beached and used as a hotel at the corner of Clay and Sansome.

When Sam could get away, he ran down to the water front to see how Central Wharf had fared. A good part of the loading-platform on shore was a charred mass, but men had chopped holes in the main wharf, separating it from the land, so that most of it was safe. Other wharves fared less fortunately.

For ten hours the flames fed on the city. By noon of May 5 two thousand buildings, including the newest *El Dorado*, were gone. Eighteen city blocks lay in smoking ruins, as did portions of many others.

The firm of Howard and Green was burned out. Sam found the two men in front of the smoldering remains of their store.

"This is just about my ruin," Howard said sadly. "All I've got left of value in the whole blessed town is my land."

"I can help you, Bill," Sam offered quickly, but Howard waved it away. "No one can help me but myself. Thanks just the same, though."

"It's the Sydney 'Coves' that are setting these fires," Talbot Green said positively. "They've got into the way of setting fires so's the excitement that follows will cover up their pilfering. And when they are through with their depredations they congregate down at their hideout on Broadway and Pacific. There's not an officer in this town, nor anyone else for that matter, that dares to go down there after dark."

"No, nor before dark either," Sam said. "That's just what I've been telling you fellers for months, begging you to get behind me to get a citizens' patrol started again. But all you'll do is sit back and say you can't do anything. Maybe now you'll be willing to try to do something."

"There's little we can do even now. The biggest mistake we ever made was when we let the city officials have their way about landing that boatload of convicts from Australia. You remember how we talked about it among ourselves and then went down to the Mayor and demanded that they be sent on to some other port. He said he would take it under advisement."

"He did," Sam said sarcastically. "He thought about it all night and then went down the next day and let them pay him a nice bunch of hush money, and then he opened wide the gates of the city and said: 'Come on in, boys. The pickings are fine.' He was right, too. Those Sydney ducks have lived off the fat of the land ever since they got here, and not one of them has ever done a stroke of honest labor. We thought the Hounds were bad; they were innocent babies compared to the Coves."

"You're right," Howard said quickly. "One of those Coves will come out of his hideout at Clark's Point and kill a man for a dollar."

"It wouldn't be so bad if they just came out to kill a few unfortunates. That's bad enough, but it's not as bad as when they come out and set the city on fire in order to steal a few dollars. So far they've been able to do all these things without any interference from the sheriff or his men because they've always been willing to give back a part of their pickings to the authorities."

"Well, I begin to feel like you do, Sam," Howard said. "I say it's about time the citizens took things into their own hands."

"Will you back me in whatever action I take?" Sam asked. Green and Howard both assured him that they would.

"All right, then. I'll go to work on a plan that will solve this whole problem. Just tend to your knitting and sit tight till I call on you."

Three weeks later, on a Sunday morning in June, Sam and Ann Eliza were on their way to services conducted by the Reverend Hunt when the fire bell on the Monumental house clanged a sharp warning. "Run back home, Lizzie, and take my frock coat and high hat with you. I've got to get down in harness," he barked sharply, thrusting the articles into her hand. He was gone before she could reply. This time an entire block of buildings was destroyed before the fire was conquered. Sam and Colonel Stevenson stopped outside of the Howard Engine House afterward to discuss the cause of the fire.

"It started in one of the shacks I own," Stevenson was explaining.

"Benjamin Lewis has a room there, and they tell me he come home early this morning, dead drunk, and knocked a candle over. I'll have his hide for this. He's cost me a pretty penny."

Before the day was over the drunken Lewis was in custody. On the day of his hearing, Sam Brannan and Talbot Green arrived early outside the city hall, around which three tiers of balconies ran on three sides of the building. When the testy Colonel arrived he joined the two men at once.

"I suspect the authorities will whitewash that scoundrel," he said. "I want you men to stand with me to demand that he be punished."

Sam laughed shortly. "We'll see that he gets his just deserts. That fire was no accident, Colonel. Lewis is a Sydney duck and he deliberately set that fire so that his comrades could steal. I intend to see that the wretch gets what's coming to him. If the officials don't punish him, we will."

"I'm for going in after the fire-raising fiend and giving him a public hearing," Green suggested.

"Better yet, let's go get him and bring him out and hang him, as a warning to other arsonists of what they'll get if fires keep raging in San Francisco," Sam said.

"Aye," the Colonel agreed. "Let's hang the fire-raising wretch!"

Sam mounted the bottom steps of the stairs and faced the crowd. "Let's have no more law's delays. Let's go get Lewis and hang him as an example to others of his ilk," he shouted.

"Aye, hang him!" Stevenson echoed, and then mounting the steps he began to harangue the crowd, urging them to follow him in. As his excitement grew he waved his fists and grew red in the face and his white hair streamed in the wind. Minute after minute he spoke, and the crowd began to tug at the reins. Suddenly there was an electric movement in the mass; someone at the rear shouted "Fire!" and the gathered men stampeded in every direction. It was several minutes before the tumult ceased. Sam had remained on the steps of the city hall, waiting for the sound of the fire bell. It did not come. He shouted then at the top of his powerful lungs, "Come back, you idiots! That fire scare was only raised to get you away from here."

With an angry glint in their eyes, men returned to the bottom of the city hall steps. Stevenson finished the indignant speech he had been making. Then he motioned the crowd up the steps and strode up onto the porch with Brannan right behind. The main door opened and Charles J. Brenham, the new mayor, emerged.[78] He closed the door behind him and stood with his back against it. "Wait," he said. "I want to be heard by you men before you do anything you will regret."

The crowd halted, impatiently waiting for him to say what he had in mind.

"Don't take the law into your own hands! Let justice take its course! This man Lewis will have a fair and impartial hearing and be sentenced according to the evidence found against him. Put your faith in our courts and we will not fail you."

Sam stepped out of the crowd, walked up to the Mayor, and then turned to address the mob. "He tells us to have faith in the courts. Has any court in San Francisco ever given its citizens justice except when we've forced them to?"

"No!" the crowd roared.

"Come on, then. What are you waiting for? Let's go get this fire-fiend, Lewis. We can turn him over to the California Guard, my guard, and we will see that he really has a fair trial and is given his just deserts."

"That's the stuff, Brannan," a dozen men replied from various places in the mob.

Green stepped forward. "I move that we appoint a committee of ten right here and now, to go in and get the prisoner and bring him out to the Brannan Guard." There were a dozen seconds to the motion.

"You pick the committee," Stevenson suggested to Sam.

"What say the rest of you?" Sam sang out. The mob made it plain that Stevenson's suggestion was agreeable to them all. Quickly Sam named the men he wanted, picking out faces in the crowd before him. When the committee had come to join Sam, it discovered that the Mayor had disappeared inside. Straight to the new chief of police the committee went. Sam acted as spokesman.

"We want Benjamin Lewis," he said.

"You'll have to find him first. I don't know where he is," Benjamin Ray, chief of police, said blandly. "I lost track of him during that fire scare a few minutes ago."

"You mean you deliberately hid him away," Sam returned angrily. "You had one of your men go outside and yell, 'Fire!'" Sam measured the official with a cold glance. "You think you've pulled a smart trick, but you'll find out that it was not smart at all. That little scheme will cost you your job." He turned back to his committee. "Come on, men, let's get out of here. I've got business to tend to."

The chief of police came to attention at once. "What you going to do, Brannan?" he asked quickly.

"You'll find out soon enough," Sam replied and herded his men out ahead of him. As they came out of the main door and crossed the wide porch, Sam stopped at the head of the steps and held up his hands for attention. The men in the crowd stopped chatting among themselves and waited for him to speak.

"Citizens of San Francisco, the duly constituted authorities of the law that you voted into office have seen fit this day to flout your desires. One of his men was sent out by Benjamin Ray to start that fire scare in order to cover up the fact that the chief of police was having Lewis taken away from here and put into hiding."

The crowd howled with rage, and after a few moments Sam spoke again. "It serves you right. For months I have talked to the men in this city, trying to get them to organize a citizens' patrol to stop this arson and robbery and murder. But you've every one been so damned busy trying to get rich, each in your own measly way, that you wouldn't listen to me. Are you ready to listen to me now?"

"Aye," the many voices replied.

"All right, then. Go on home now and think about the public officials you've elected, and make up your minds what you're going to do about them on election day. But keep yourselves in readiness. I have a plan which I will put into action when the time is ripe. I will call on you then for help. I hope every man-jack of you will back me up when I call."

"We will," voices called. The crowd melted away and Sam, together with Talbot Green and Colonel Stevenson, went down the street. There was no longer a proud store in San Francisco bearing the name of Howard and Green. Both men had been almost ruined in the May fire and they now kept only a small office in a shack on Montgomery Street, from which they rented their vast properties. Since the city was still in its growing stages they were making nice profits, as were all real estate men of the day. The three men stopped in the office to talk, and after a time William Howard came in.

"I want all you fellers to come over to my office on Bush Street," Sam invited. "I've got a plan for bringing law and order to this city. I'm ready to set it in motion, if you men and a few others I got in mind will back me."

When at last they were seated around the table in Brannan's empty storeroom there were present not only Howard, Green, and Stevenson, but also Selim Woodworth, who had led the rescue of the suffering remnants of the Donner party in '46; Julius W. Salmon, a businessman; and a goodly assortment of other leading figures in the town. Mr. Wardwell, Sam's clerk, placed bottles and glasses on the table, then the men bent their heads over it and began to map a plan of action based upon Sam's idea for bringing order into San Francisco and ridding it of its preponderant criminal element.

Hours passed and the men still talked in an endeavor to work out details. At last Sam leaned back and passed a hand wearily over his eyes. "Julius, you got a head for this kind of stuff. You take all the suggestions that we've outlined today and whip them into shape. We'll all meet here again tomorrow and Julius can read us the constitution, which he should have in shape by then."

Salmon gathered up the notes. "I'll have it ready by noon tomorrow to read to you gentlemen," he said.

On the next day, June 8, the same group of men [79] sat back expectantly while Salmon began to read the preamble to a constitution for a citizens' organization:

> The citizens whose names are hereunto attached . . . do bind ourselves each unto the other to do and perform every lawful act for the maintenance of law and order and to sustain the laws when faithfully and properly administered but we are determined that no thief, burglar, incendiary, or assassin shall escape punishment, either by the quibbles of the law or a laxity of those who pretend to administer justice. . . .

After a short session, this nucleus group felt ready to present the plan to their fellow citizens. It was decided to call the organization meeting the next day. Thus it was that at twelve o'clock on June 9, 1851, at the California Engine House, Sam mounted a chair and called the milling crowd before him to order.

"I'm mighty glad to see that there are so many men of fine caliber in this town," he began. "When those of us who have been planning this organization parted yesterday, with the promise to bring in as many men as we each could reach and could trust, I never expected to see so many today. Now you men all know by now what we've called you here for. Whoever directed you to come to this meeting told you what our purpose is. Our first order of business, therefore, is to find an appropriate name.

"Committee of Vigilance," a voice called out. Every man in the hall began to clap his hands. "All in favor say 'Aye,'" Sam requested. The name was spontaneously accepted.

"All right. Now begin to name the officers you want elected," Sam invited.

Selim E. Woodworth was named president to head the general committee. Eugene Delessert, the banker, became treasurer. Isaac Bluxome was elected secretary. Many a criminal in San Francisco was to quail in terror within the next few months when the mystic "67," Bluxome's signature, appeared on a summons to appear before the committee. Samuel Brannan became president of the executive committee. According to the plans worked out by the men in session, the executive committee would formulate all plans and conduct all trials, while the general committee would carry them out.

Elections out of the way, Sam began to outline all the plans conceived by the formulating committee. After this was finished there were many other things to decide; at dark, the organization meeting had still not completed all details. The meeting was adjourned by weary men who agreed to gather next day in Sam's store building on Bush Street to complete the organization of the new Vigilance Committee.

After the close of the meeting Sam stopped to talk for a few moments with Julius Salmon. Julius was very enthusiastic about the new organization. "I tell you, Brannan, it was a stroke of genius when you thought up this idea. Why, the Sydney Coves are so entrenched in the grog-shop area down around the old embarcadero at Clark's Point, it will take a citizens' army to dislodge them."

"From the looks of things, that's what we'll have by tomorrow night," Sam replied. Neither of the men could know that the Sydney Coves, or Ducks, had laid the foundation of San Francisco's toughest quarter, which would within the century become famous all over the world as the "Barbary Coast."

Seven hundred men appeared at Sam Brannan's store building the next day, June 10, 1851. As men continued to arrive Sam realized that the center room, with a frontage of twenty feet on the street and a depth of about fifty feet, was not large enough to accommodate them all. With his pocket-knife he cut the canvas partitions that separated the three sections at the sides and bottom, between the studdings, and the three rooms were suddenly thrust into one. The apertures thus made were curtained by the tattered canvas. A table, boxes, stools, chairs, and benches were brought to the rooms, but still most of the applicants were forced to stand.

Each man, as he sought entrance, was asked to swear. to utter secrecy, and if he did so was admitted by the sergeant-at-arms. When the meeting was finally called to order, Sam addressed the men within the hall:

"Fellow members of the Committee of Vigilance, we are gathered here today to rid the city of crime and criminals. Our job is to ferret out the criminals and, catching them in crime, see that they are punished and driven from the city. Each man here has promised secrecy. We are going to ask you further to sign a pledge of secrecy, and you must promise on your honor to protect the lives and property of the citizens of San Francisco, and to purge the city of ruffians. Come forward one at a time and sign your pledges." After this was done, Sam continued.

"We have rented rooms on Battery Street between Pine and California streets, which will be our permanent headquarters. No one will ever be admitted to those rooms except those who know the watchword. A guard will be on duty twenty-four hours a day. We will assign members to patrol the streets. They will go in armed groups, and when they find men in the act of committing depredations they will arrest the culprits, bring them to our committee rooms, and hold them for trial. Whenever criminals are found guilty as charged by our judges, the judges will there and then set the punishment to be meted out.

"Now, for the information of every man here let me say that when you are wanted quickly—whenever an emergency session must be called—you will be summoned by a tocsin of two strokes of the bell on top of the Monumental Fire House, on the plaza. This tocsin will be rung and repeated at intervals until all you members have gathered at headquarters. You might be interested to know that our first guard unit has already been appointed and is even now patrolling the streets of San Francisco.

"Again let me warn you that no man in this hall is to speak outside of these walls of what he sees and hears here tonight. If he does, let him beware."

Sam then set forth the rules of the committee and had one of the men read the by-laws. It was almost ten when the meeting finally adjourned. But men did not go home; they remained to gather in groups of three and four to discuss the shape of future events, many still within the hall, others on the street outside. A fog had begun to roll in and men pulled their coat collars up. A little after ten, those outside saw the members of the committee guard emerge from the fog pushing a big, burly man in front of them. The new vigilantes fell back to let them pass and recognized the prisoner at once as a vicious character named Jenkins, one of the Sydney Ducks. A guard knocked on the Bush Street door. The sergeant-at-arms opened it a crack and held conference with the guard. A moment later the door swung wide and the patrol pushed Jenkins into the room and closed the door behind them. Shortly thereafter a man emerged and ran down the street. The tocsin on the Monumental House began to toll its dismal news. Soon the eighty men who were to have an active part in trying John Jenkins were admitted to the rooms. They found Sam Brannan and the other members of the executive committee sitting at the table, while across from them stood the defiant Englishman. Sam ordered the members allowed within the hall to take seats. Then he nodded to the guard who had headed the patrol. "Go ahead," he said.

"Well, we started out like we was told, going up one street and then down another. When we got down to Central Wharf a bunch of men was talking together all excited. We went up to them and asked them what was wrong. A Mr. Virgin told us that he'd stepped out a while before we got there, leaving his office door on the wharf open. This Jenkins had walked in while Virgin was gone, and, bold as you please, picked up Mr. Virgin's safe and walked out with it. Then he put it in a boat and started to row over toward the east shore. A bunch of fellers was hanging around and they saw what he was doing, but he was so calm about it they thought he was supposed to move the safe. A few minutes after that Virgin came back and, missing his safe, he set up a holler. That was what they told us when we got there. Well, we all piled in a longboat and took out after the Cove. When he saw that we was following him he begun to row hell-for-leather. But the safe was heavy, and there was only one of him and a dozen of us. We gained on him right along. Then he got scared and threw the safe overboard so he could go faster. But that didn't help him much, either. A few minutes later we caught up with him and nabbed him. He put up a fight, but it didn't do him much good. Here he is. I hope you hang him."

Sam pointed up the stairs toward the little office off the loft. "Lock him up in that office until we're ready for him."

The guards hustled the protesting Jenkins up the stairs. Halfway up he stopped. The guards allowed him to speak. "I'll be out of here in the morning," he bragged. "Get me a lawyer and call my friends and I'll be out of here by daylight."

Sam looked up at the man, who was barely visible in the dim light. "A lawyer won't do you any good in this court, and if you don't think up a good reason for the crime you've just committed you won't be alive by daylight. You might give us the name of your friends, though, if you have any. We'd like to talk to them."

"And why would I be giving you the names of any of my friends?" he asked belligerently.

"To give you a good character, if possible," Sam replied. "If someone don't give you a good character you won't need any friends by daylight."

"My friends will tell you I'm all right," Jenkins said, a little quieter. He named two to be called as witnesses. Then the guards hustled him into the little room and locked the door.

The rooms were cleared of all except the officers of the Vigilance Committee, which included general and executive committees, guards, and all who would weigh evidence. This left about fifty men in the room. They conferred among themselves for a long time before Jenkins was brought down to answer their questions. The guard who had him in charge forcibly pushed the man to his place in front of the table. "We asked him if he wanted a preacher to talk to him while he was waiting, to give him comfort. We explained that he might not live till morning. All he did was curse and tell us to leave him alone."

"All right," Sam said. "Stand back and leave him there. We'll soften him up a little before this night's over." Jenkins glared at him defiantly. He was tall, powerful, of fine physique, with a typically English face and dressed in clothes of an English cut, and he looked into the faces around him in the dim candlelight without the slightest show of fear.

"What have you got to say for yourself?" Sam asked.

"Not a goddamned word," Jenkins spat out the reply. "You bloody fools won't hurt me. You don't dare. If you do, you'll all hang for it. I got friends."

"So you said before," Sam reminded him. "We've sent for the two friends you named to come and say something good about you, if such a thing is possible. They ought to be here by now. Well—suppose you explain why you were stealing Virgin's safe."

"I didn't steal nothing and you can't prove I did," Jenkins snarled.

Sam laughed shortly. "You forget where you are, Jenkins. This is not a court of law. This is a court of justice. We don't have to prove you did anything. All we have to do is prove that you are a criminal, and I don't think it's going to be hard to do. You'd better talk and talk fast, for if you don't others will talk for you, and what they say here tonight will decide whether you walk out a free man in the next few hours or get carried out feet first."

"You ain't scaring me," Jenkins sneered. Sam turned to Gerrit Ryckman. "Gerrit, you were telling some of us a little about this man's record. Suppose you repeat it for Jenkins. He might like to explain it as you go."

Ryckman arose and began to recite a long list of crimes at which Jenkins had been caught at various times. He had been allowed to go each time after a night in jail. Others added to the story. As the list of evidence piled up against Jenkins he merely drew his lips tighter and stood with his legs wide apart, breathing defiance in his very attitude. It was plain that he considered the candlelight trial a farce and believed that with morning would come another release.

The sergeant-at-arms came and whispered in Sam's ear. Sam spoke to John Jenkins. "One of the friends you have been bragging about is outside. We'll soon find out how much he thinks of you." Sam arose and went to the door. None but committee members might enter and witnesses must be questioned outside. After a few minutes he returned to his seat. "He says he don't know any John Jenkins. If he did, he wouldn't admit it," Sam said, and added, "If he does know you he don't want anybody to know it now. He's scared out of his wits and he's smart to be that way." He waved his hand. "Come on, let's get on with this trial."

At eleven o'clock the vote of the executive committee lay in front of Sam. Sam looked through all the slips of paper, lifted his eyes to Jenkins's face, and said, "Guilty!" Jenkins merely stood and glared.

"Take him back upstairs," Sam directed the guards, "while we decide upon the punishment." As they took hold of Jenkins's arms Sam stopped them with a gesture and spoke to the man. "Better let someone call a preacher for you. You'll likely want to make your peace with God, for you'll not live to see daylight."

"I'll have no sniveling preacher bothering me!" Jenkins roared. "I'll break my way out of this shack with my bare hands!"

Sam gestured him away and his captors hustled him up the stairs while he fought and swore. When the noise of his going had subsided, Sam spoke of the criminal's punishment. "I say we've got to make an example of this man. The sooner we serve notice on criminals and city officials that we mean business, the sooner our work here will be done. I say let's hang the man and warn those of his ilk that if they don't reform, or get out of town, they will be served the same treatment."

William Coleman, the young merchant, spoke quickly. "You are too impetuous, Brannan. Hanging is a pretty serious cure. If we hang this man we will all be murderers and subject to the civil authorities for trial. Take heed that we don't all put our heads in the noose."

"If we are going to be cowards and start worrying about what will happen to us, we had better give up hope of ever accomplishing anything," Sam replied heatedly. "We all know now, and have known from the start, that what we are doing is illegal. You were told when you came here that if you were afraid you'd better go on home. Now is the time for strength, for action. We can have no half-measures at such a critical time. I say, hang this man or give up trying to bring law and order to San Francisco!"

Selim Woodworth, the former naval officer, spoke. "I agree wholeheartedly with Brannan. Let us here and now serve warning on our so-called civil servants that we will no longer put up with their half-hearted measures and their harboring of criminals in this city. We have organized to bring order. We must take drastic steps. I vote to back Brannan."

There was immediate pandemonium as the more cautious tried to yell down those who wanted to follow Brannan. Sam allowed the men to argue for several minutes, then he pounded the table for order and when he got it, asked for the vote. It was greatly in the majority for hanging.

A committee of three was named by the executive committee to go out and arrange a suitable gibbet which could be put into immediate use. William Coleman, the peace-maker, was placed in charge of the committee. After the three had gone from the room, Sam rose and motioned to Gerrit Ryckman, one of the ablest lawyers of the day. "Come on outside with me, Ryckman. We're going to notify our members outside, and whatever townspeople are hanging around, what we have decided to do this night."

Ryckman rose. "Better consider well before you go out there, Brannan. If you publish abroad what our purpose is, we may be stopped by Chief of Police Ben Ray before we can accomplish it."

Sam laughed wickedly. "I'd like to see Ben Ray ever try to stop me again with you men behind me. I promised him I'd run him out of office and I will. Besides, he's too yellow to do anything. It's the right of the citizens of this town to know that this committee is going to give them justice, and law and order. If we don't tell them so, they'll never know it."

Sam turned and strode to the door, Ryckman following him. They made their way through the men who thronged the street just outside the door, crossed the street, and mounted a sand hill opposite the old Rassette House. The crowd followed them and stood waiting.

"Men," Sam began, "this is a historic night in San Francisco. This is the night when you citizens are going to show the denizens of darkness that their rule of San Francisco has come to an end. We have had a rough-and-tumble sort of existence in this town ever since the gold rush started, and we've all been so busy getting rich that we've not had time to think about building homes and looking after our loved ones; at least those of us who have our loved ones here. A lot of you men live alone; your families are back in the States. You're not so concerned with making this town safe for women and children as we are, who've got them to think about. I've got three small children, a wife, and a mother-in-law living here. The way things are now it's not safe for them to walk along the street in broad daylight. Criminals walk our streets boldly and could strike a woman down and rob or attack her, and no civil servant would lift a finger. Daily, men are attacked in our streets; some are left dead, many are only stunnned by assailants who rob them. Our stores are ransacked, our merchants injured by common thieves, our buildings are fired, and many a man has been murdered. Yet our civil authorities claim they can do nothing to prevent these crimes or put a stop to them. When you go into their offices and arouse them from a daytime siesta and demand that justice be meted out, they say there is nothing they can do. If you do succeed in getting one of these ruffians arrested, what happens? A lawyer is sent for. The criminal pays him a large part of the money he has stolen from the victim. The lawyer splits with the officers of the law, and the criminal walks the streets again, ready to commit other crimes. Our law courts are a farce. Never yet have they convicted any man for murder. Our judges are as guilty as the criminals they try. There is no such thing as justice in all the length and breadth of our city. Now, are we going to sit idle while our city becomes a robbers' roost—or are we going to rid ourselves of these vermin and build a great commercial center here?"

His audience stirred, but made no audible response. Sam pointed a finger at the crowd. "You men are as guilty as our graft-ridden public officials. You elect them to office and then let them go on—year in, year out—protecting the guilty. Once in a while some of you grumble and complain, but that's as far as any action goes. For over a year I've appealed to many of you to get behind me and help me clean up the city. Most of you agree that conditions are terrible but say there is nothing you can do about it. Some of you told me that it was a scourge of God which had to be endured. Time after time the city has been set ablaze by fire-bugs. You have wept and wailed and gnashed your teeth, and when the ashes were cold your righteous indignation was cold also. You have prayed to God to protect you from further fires. God helps them that help themselves.

"Now, men, we are helping ourselves, and we want you to be one with us. Many of our most influential citizens, men who have the courage of their convictions, have now banded together to form a Committee of Vigilance for the purpose of putting the fear of God into the criminals who infest this city, and of warning public officials that our patience is at an end. We will have peace and harmony in San Francisco, or die in the attempt. We are tonight taking the administration of the law into our own hands, and we will continue to do so until such time as the city officials are prepared to do it the way we want it done.

"Today a Sydney Cove was caught red-handed in crime. He stole a safe from the office of Mr. Virgin down on Central Wharf. This thief is now lodged in our committee rooms. He has been found guilty by a jury of his peers and condemned to death. We will, this night, hang him. Thus do we serve notice to you, and all the citizens of this town, that justice has come to stay. How many of you approve of our action? Those in favor say 'Aye.' "

There was a giant swell of ayes, followed by a mildly echoing "no."

"The ayes have it," Sam bellowed joyfully, and added, "I want to warn you men that this is no rowdy organization. We are substantial citizens, acting as officers of the law. When Jenkins is brought forth we want no boisterousness. We will escort him to his place of execution, and those who follow must act in an orderly way. When the commission of this court is executed, we expect you to act with the solemnity such an occasion demands of all men."

Sam descended the little hill, followed by Ryckman. They re-entered the committee rooms.

Shortly after midnight, in a fog which drifted steadily in from the bay, Coleman and his two assistants returned. Standing in front of the committee table, Coleman reported, "We've looked all over town, and the most likely spot we could find is the custom house on the plaza. We threw a rope up over a high beam on the end of the south veranda, fastened it to a pulley, and fashioned a noose. On the other end of the rope we've tied knots for the hangmen to hold."

"That's fine!" Sam said quickly. Turning to Woodworth he added, "You take over now."

Woodworth gave orders to tie the prisoner's hands behind him and bring him down. Minutes passed while the last-minute preparations were made. Sam went outside and assisted Woodworth in giving orders to the men who were to conduct Jenkins to the hanging. When at last the guards brought the burly man out into the fog-draped streets, two long lines of pickets, holding two stout ropes, opened to receive him. The ends of the rope enclosure were drawn together, and the group as a whole moved slowly towards the plaza accompanied by the steady toll of the California Company's bell, which made a solemn death-knell for the condemned man in those early morning fog-bound hours of June 11.

Arrived at the plaza—that dusty square which had witnessed every major drama that had thus far unrolled in San Francisco— Sam and Woodworth were intercepted by Benjamin Ray, the chief of police.

"In the name of the law, I command you to halt," he said melo-dramatically, and to humor him the two men halted while he asked them, "What are you men doing here tonight?"

"You just stay where you are for a few minutes and you'll find out," Sam retorted.

Ray nodded towards the prisoner who was still being led toward the veranda of the old adobe building. "I hear you aim to hang that man. I demand, in the name of the law, that you turn him over to me."

Sam's color rose. "Demand and be damned," he said hotly. He turned and motioned toward the lantern-bespeckled crowd which was filing slowly past them. "There's a good many men there that say you can't have the prisoner. If we did give him to you, you'd yell 'Fire!' and see how fast you could lose him. No siree, Ray, you're not fooling with us any more. We mean business. This man hangs tonight. If I was you, I'd get away from here before some of us decide that a few public officials who are traitors to their constituents need hanging, too. Go on, git."

Ray stood uncertainly for a moment, then turned and went away. Sam hurried up to the porch of the custom house and watched Woodworth and his men test the rope. Sam himself adjusted the noose on Jenkins's neck.

"You'd better pray right now if you ever intend to," he said grimly to the prisoner.

"Go to hell!" Jenkins growled.

Suddenly Sam felt a little sick at his stomach. He had never helped kill a man before, and the prospect of the next few minutes was a little unnerving. He stepped back and looked at the fearless giant who faced them all defiantly. To steady his nerves, Sam lighted up a cigar. Jenkins sniffed its fragrant aroma. Sam felt a sudden pity for the man and he took the lighted cigar from his mouth and placed it between Jenkins's lips. The man half smiled as he hungrily drew in great draughts of smoke.

Woodworth gave the signal that all was in readiness. Sam moved swiftly to the end of the rope and lifted it calculatingly. Then he pulled it taut to test it. "Grab hold!" he shouted. "Every lover of liberty and good order, lay hold!" Fifty hands jerked the rope, and Jenkins was lifted by a mighty tug high into the air. His teeth clamped down on the cigar and it fell to earth as his head rolled crazily to one side. A faint curl of smoke came from his grimacing lips. The rope was fastened to the porch rail. Sam let go and looked up at the body, which swayed spectrally in the moving fog.

"Leave him hanging there until daylight," Sam told the men who were being placed on guard by Woodworth. "After that you can give him to whoever wants him."

Sam stood waiting until Woodworth joined him. The former Navy man was filled with excitement. "This has been a good night's work," he exclaimed.

"I guess it has," Sam said. "At least we accomplished what we set out to do," he sighed. "Come on, let's go home and get some sleep; there'll be hell to pay tomorrow."

Sam spoke prophetically, for a few days later he and several of the ringleaders of the committee were called to a hearing at which guilt was to be determined for the murder of Jenkins. Sam was questioned. Knowing that he had the confidence of at least three-quarters of the city's population, Sam voluntarily made a statement when he took the witness stand.

"John Jenkins was tried by our committee, before from sixty to eighty men. He had a fair and impartial trial and was found guilty unanimously and sentenced unanimously."

Then he sat down and the city attorney began asking him questions. "How was this jury of sixty to eighty men impaneled?"

"I don't know," Sam replied blandly. "They probably impaneled themselves. They are all businessmen and citizens of this town, as are all members of our committee."

"What is the object of your committee?" the attorney asked.

"To protect the lives and property of our fellow citizens; to see that they are not troubled by burglars, arsonists, or murderers; and to arrest and punish men caught in any of those crimes."

"Was not what you did wanton and cold-blooded murder?"

Sam forced himself to speak calmly. "No. The man was executed in accordance with the finding of the Committee. I believe that a record was kept of the evidence presented at the trial. The prisoner had the privilege of bringing in evidence in his behalf. He said that he had friends, witnesses. One came, but when I questioned him he said that he did not know Jenkins."

"But you gave the prisoner no counselor?"

"None."

"Were your witnesses put under oath?"

"Not that I know of."

"And when your committee found the man guilty, did none of you make a motion for a new trial, just in case an error might have been made?" the attorney persisted, in an endeavor to put Sam and the other committee members in an unfavorable light.

"No."

"Were any men present at the hearing other than members of your infamous gang of murderers?"

"I'd take a less sarcastic tone, if I were you," Sam said firmly. "As a matter of fact, I don't know whether any persons other than those of the committee were in the room or not."

"Is it not a fact that any reprobate can join the Committee of Vigilance if he will promise to do what the rest of you ruffians demand, and is he not bound by secrecy to prevent him from appealing to the law?"

Sam grinned suddenly at the barrister. "You're a pretty one to be calling the kettle black. We have no reprobates or ruffians in our committee. The law already has enlisted them all on its side. A man who is admitted to the committee has to be a man of standing and good character. His character has to be vouched for by a member, and he has to promise to devote a part of his time to watching for burglars and other scoundrels. I don't know of any secrecy that binds him other than that of any honest man. There is no oath used. Our object is to assist the law and administer justice."

"Then if you are assisting the administration of justice, you will not mind giving me the names of the members of the committee," the lawyer said.

"I'll give no names," Sam said flatly. "My own is sufficient."

"You realize that you belong to a group of murderers, and that if you are found guilty of murder you may hang," the lawyer insisted.

Sam laughed shortly. "Your threats do not scare me. I've been threatened before. I have been told that my house will be burned if I do not get out of the committee; some of the prisoners in the county prison predict that I will not live ninety days. None of you scare me. Neither I nor any other member of the Vigilance Committee has done anything which we would conceal from the officers of the law under proper circumstances. Now, you can do your damnedest, but you will not break up this organization until we have run the last criminal out of this city—yes, and the last crooked politician too. You can put that in your pipe and smoke it!" he bellowed, and got down from the witness stand. The lawyer wiped his brow and called the next witness; with the same kind of success.

When the hearing was completed, the police authorities were afraid to arrest Sam or any of the other nine men named in the coroner's verdict as implicated in the death of Jenkins. The public was too solidly behind them.

The next issue of the *Alta California* published a list of 180 members of the committee, with the statement that all were equally involved in the death of Jenkins; if Sam and the other nine were guilty, so were these leading citizens. The authorities decided that the investigation was at that moment too hot to press, and forthwith dropped it.

The committee, after getting settled in its permanent quarters, appointed thirty men to meet each arriving vessel. A list had been obtained of ships sailing from England which had at one time or another carried convicts from the mother country to Australia, and passengers freshly arrived in San Francisco were questioned, if they came from Australia, and particularly as to the vessel which carried them from England to the colony. If the ship named was on the convict list, the man was immediately deported. Steamers from Sacramento and Stockton were boarded by the Vigilance Committee patrol and any man who could not give proof of good character was sent back. Riffraff fleeing from the mines were caught in the net. This clean-up campaign of the Vigilance Committee suddenly cut off the bulk of their income from lawyers who had flocked to the city, and the city authorities found their takings by graft practically nil. As a result they raised a great cry of illegality, but to no effect. The committee went even further, and took upon itself the right to enter and search any premises which might yield up evidence against a criminal.

The instant the tocsin sounded, committee members were on the run to headquarters. On arriving, they would find a new prisoner. Immediately the executive committee, or inner council, sat to hear evidence. It had all power, knew all secrets, assigned all tasks, and issued all orders through Number 67, its secretary, a designation which cloaked the identity of Isaac Bluxome. If the prisoner did not tell the truth about his life and crimes, others did it for him. No one was convicted upon less evidence than a court of law would demand.

At the meeting held on June 16, 1851, Sam in his capacity as president suggested that the executive committee appoint a member to call upon the district attorney to investigate a certain criminal case then pending. This was done.

The brandy bottle which sat at all times at the elbow of the president was referred to. Then Sam arose to suggest that a committee of three be sent to visit the Mayor and the chief of police to find out whether they were willing yet to co-operate with the Vigilance Committee, or whether they still intended to obstruct them privately. This committee was also named. Sam took two more drinks and waxed very loquacious. He suggested to the three members of the newly appointed committee that they investigate the condition of prisoners in the city jail, and the jail itself, to make sure that things were as they should be. The men agreed to do this.

William Coleman had watched Sam ever since the meeting began. He had little patience with a man who was so emotional and headstrong, and less with those who were over-fond of spirits. At last he arose and put a motion.

"I move that henceforth all spirituous liquors be barred from the committee rooms. After all, this is a place of business and not a grogshop. We have important things to attend to here and no one can deny that it is necessary for our leaders to have clear heads at such times."

Sam was on his feet instantly. "I'll vote no on that," he bellowed. "Coleman is aiming his shaft directly at me. If I want to drink, by God, I'll do it. I've got a better head on me when I'm half drunk than he's got sober."

"I resent your remarks, Brannan," Coleman shouted.

Gerrit Ryckman arose. "Gentlemen, gentlemen, watch your tongues. We must have no brawling here. A motion has been put. And I hear a second to it. Let us vote on this in the regular manner." He pushed Sam back into his chair, fuming. When the vote was counted Coleman had won, and the brandy bottle was removed.

On Sunday, June 22, Sam came out of his house at ten in the morning to see flames shooting skyward, up on Pacific Street near Powell. A high wind was carrying the sparks before it. He ran madly for his firehouse. When the fire companies reached the scene with their apparatus it was discovered that the newly erected cisterns on the plaza and in three other locations had carelessly been allowed to remain empty. The engine companies stood helpless while the flames swept the district between Clay and Broadway, from Powell to Sansome. The many-galleried city hall was burned, which did not pain Sam overmuch; but when he saw the old custom house crumble in ashes he felt grieved. This was the last old landmark but one in the city. Only the Casa Grande, which had housed his family on their first night ashore, remained, and it was soon to be torn down to make way for a new building.

On Monday morning the Vigilance Committee met in solemn session. "I tell you men that somebody has got to pay dear for yesterday's fire," Sam said between grim lips. "The executive committee has picked a list of men that we want to go as a patrol down into Sydney Town. This patrol will round up the men they find most likely to have had a part in that fire." He named the list of men for the patrol, and when they stood in front of him he added, "Don't come back until you've caught the real criminals. The police made a pretense yesterday of searching the low grog-shops, the dancing halls, the gambling dens and lodging houses over there, and came back to their headquarters last night to report they could prove nothing. They arrested half a dozen insignificant down-and-outers, and today those fellers will be out on bail. It's up to us to clean things up. See that you make a good job of it. Now start out."

By that night there were over a dozen "Sydney Ducks" in jail at the Vigilance Committee headquarters. As soon as they had been tried and found guilty, they were taken out one by one, stripped to the waist, and flogged in public with a cat-o'-nine-tails. Then with fifty or more of their fellows they were placed on an Australian-bound vessel and sent away. With their departure, arson combined with pilfering came to an end in San Francisco.

Since the old prison bark, the *Euphemia*, had been burned, and the prison in the city hall also, there was great need for a public house of detention. The county had started to build one, but work had stopped for lack of funds. The Vigilance Committee now raised the money for the purpose of completing the jail and saw to it that it was finished within a month.

Sam, as head of the executive committee, sat in conference with his fellow members. He became so interested in the business at hand one day that he forgot himself and drew out the bottle which he carried in his pocket and placed it on the table in front of him. Immediately Jackson McDuffee, the sergeant-at-arms, spied it and came forward. Without a word he took the bottle and started from the room. Sam arose quickly.

"Bring me back my bottle," he ordered. McDuffee made no reply but went on out with the bottle. Sam followed. There was a physical encounter between the two men, and after a time Sam came raging back into the room.

"I resign," he roared. "I've been president of this executive committee for some time and I think I've got a few rights. If I have to be told when I can take a drink it's time I hired myself a keeper." He went back to the table, picked up his hat, and started from the room. Ryckman jumped up and intercepted him before he reached the door.

"Come on back, Brannan! Don't go away in a huff. After all, McDuffee was only carrying out his orders. Remember, we voted in a body to bring no more spirituous liquors into these rooms."

"I didn't vote for it. If I want to drink, by God, I'll do it, here or anywhere else. No son-of-a-bitch is going to treat me like a pukin' baby. McDuffee will bring that bottle back to me and apologize or I'll walk out of here and never come back."

"No, no," Ryckman protested, and Woodworth came also and tried to talk to Sam. But he would not listen. In high dudgeon he finally slapped his high hat on and stalked out of the room, slamming the door behind him. When he had gone the remaining members looked at each other with stricken eyes. At last Coleman said, "I have no love for Brannan as a man. But our cause owes everything to him. Let us appoint several members to call on him tomorrow, when his anger has cooled, and ask him to come back. He's a stubborn man once his ire is aroused, and he won't come back unless we ask him to. He must not be sacrificed to his own irascibility."

"No. We need Sam and he needs us," Woodworth agreed.

So a committee was appointed, and it did call upon Samuel. By the next day he was over his anger and feeling rather sheepish, and the feud was healed. Never again did he take his bottle with him into the committee rooms.

When the merchant Janssen had identified his two assailants almost a year earlier he had made a grave mistake, for he had identified a man named Burdue when the real culprit was a notorious criminal by the name of Stuart. Burdue had lain in jail for months. It was almost a year since he had been arrested, due to the unfortunate fact that he was in looks a duplicate of Stuart. If Sam had had his way with the mob, the innocent Burdue would have been hanged shortly after his arrest. By the efforts of the Vigilance Committee, Stuart was apprehended red-handed in crime, and on July 11 was sentenced to death by its members. When he realized that his life was forfeit, Stuart confessed that he and not Burdue had attacked Janssen and went on to give a history of his many crimes, which included numerous assaults and robberies.

At half past two on the day he was sentenced, Stuart was marched in solemn procession down to Battery Street and over to the Market Street wharf. There the men in charge of the hanging stopped beside a huge derrick. The ropes were thrown over its arms at sunset. Shortly thereafter Stuart's form dangled high in the air as a warning to all on land and sea that men of this sort would not be tolerated. A few days later Burdue was released and presented with a sum of money collected from the citizens, as partial repayment for all that he had endured. Central Wharf became the scene of his next activities, for he was seen there daily thereafter presiding over a three-card monte.

The hanging of Stuart was only a preliminary to that of two of his confederates, Samuel Whittaker and Robert McKenzie. These two men had been condemned to death by the committee, and announcement was made that they would be hanged on August 21. David Broderick, Whig leader and boss of the political machine which controlled all of northern California, felt that it was time to check the power of the Vigilance Committee. It was certainly a drawback to him and his political activities. He appealed to Governor McDougal to interfere with this self-appointed body—which he, Broderick, termed "hoodlums"—and remove from its possession the persons of Whittaker and McKenzie. The Governor ordered Sheriff Jack Hayes to take a posse and secure the captives, and it was done.

The following Sunday, August 24, Sam Brannan and Stephen Payran gave hurried instructions for the day to the Vigilance Committee police force, which had been augmented considerably for the occasion. Shortly thereafter the force entered the jail. Most of the guards were off duty for the day. Without confusion the committee police forced an entrance into the cells of Whittaker and McKenzie, took the two men, and returned them to the committee. Seventeen minutes later their bodies hung from gibbets suspended from the second-story windows of the committee rooms. While they slowly turned in the wind, Sam Brannan from another window addressed the crowd of six thousand people which thronged the street below. He outlined the events that had led up to this public execution, and in closing asked, "How many of you citizens of San Francisco approve of what we are doing?" A thunderous tumult of approval roared from thousands of throats.

Sam went back to the table and gave instructions to the guards to turn the bodies of the two dead men over to the civil authorities whenever they should present themselves and demand them. When the crowd had dispersed and everything was quiet, Sam and Gerrit W. Ryckman went to the nearest saloon. Sam was weary and he seated himself at one of the tables, while Ryckman drifted over to the bar. A little later he came back to Sam filled with mirth.

"What's so funny?" Sam demanded, turning his attention from several men who had drifted, one at a time, to his table.

"You see those men just going out the door?" Ryckman asked, motioning to three men who were almost running in their endeavor to make a hurried exit. Sam nodded. Ryckman continued, "Well, when I went up to the bar those fellows were talking together about the hanging this afternoon, and they were using some pretty strong language about the members of the Vigilance Committee. I tapped the biggest fellow on the shoulder, and when he turned around I showed him my committee emblem. When he saw the eye on it he looked sort of sick and asked me if I wouldn't have a drink with them.

"I recognized the three of them right off as henchmen of Broderick. 'I don't drink with Broderick's thieves,' I answered. 'You must have us mixed up with someone else,' one of the others said quickly.

" 'No, I know who you are and I just heard what you said about the Vigilance Committee,' I said, 'and I don't like it.' They looked scared and the big one said, 'You must have misunderstood us. We have the highest respect for the Committee.'

"I just stood and glared at him with a sarcastic look in my eye, and then I said, 'I didn't misunderstand. I heard you say Sam Brannan is a crook. I heard you say that he ought to be run out of town on a rail. I heard a good deal more. Gentlemen, I shall take great pleasure in repeating your remarks to the Vigilance Committee.'

"Well, they were fit to be tied for a few minutes. They damned near got down on the floor and crawled. One of them asked me to have a drink. 'I don't drink with Broderick's scum,' I said. They begged me with tears in their eyes to forget what they'd said. At last I said I wouldn't report them if they'd mend their ways and remember to speak of the committee with respect in the future. They will, too. They fell all over themselves trying to get out of here in a hurry."

Sam grinned appreciatively.

On the night of September 2 Sam came home late to find Fanny knitting by lamplight. Ann Eliza and the children were in bed asleep. Fanny dropped her knitting in her lap.

"I been waiting for you," she said simply. "I got news."

Sam threw himself full length on the sofa. "What?" he asked.

"Us Mormons met up at Barton Mowry's tonight," she paused.

"Well, what happened?"

"Parley Pratt presided. He's leaving with his wife Phoebe for a mission to South America in a few days."

Sam yawned. "Very interesting, I'm sure. Did you wait up till this hour just to tell me that?"

"No, I didn't. I waited up to tell you that tonight you were disfellowshipped from the Mormon Church."

Sam sat up quickly. "You don't say! What for?"

"For a general course of unchristianlike conduct, neglect of duty, and for being at the head of a lawless assembly that commits murder and other crimes.[80] They might have added stealing but they didn't."

Sam put his feet on the floor. "You mean that you Mormons call the Vigilance Committee a lawless assembly?"

She nodded vigorously. "It is lawless. You hang men and flog them and deport them, don't you?"

"Sure, we do, but only because the civil authorities won't do it for us. We had no choice, you know that. We have to hang criminals or run them out of town, so that we can make this place a decent place for women like you and for children to live in. You know what this town was like before the Vigilance Committee was started, and you know what it is now."

"I don't care," she said doggedly. "Parley Pratt said that you men are wicked for taking the law into your own hands. He says that no man has got a right to sit in judgment on his fellow-men."

"Then he's a fool," Sam burst out, and getting up he began to pace the floor. "He's been listening to Broderick spout off at his mass meetings. Broderick don't like us because we're interfering with his political machine and stopping his graft."

"No one has a right to commit murder," Fanny insisted.

Sam whirled and faced her quickly. "You're wrong, Ma—dead wrong. If a murderer is left to roam the world, everyone's life is in danger. It is better to murder one man for the common good, if in murdering him you are saving hundreds of lives. You go tell that to Parley Pratt. Tell him what this city was like and what it has become."

Fanny faced him uncertainly for a long moment and then her glance fell. "Sometimes I don't know what to think," she admitted.

"You ought to stay away from them Mormons and listen to me."

"I'll never listen to you, Sam Brannan," she said bitterly. "You've got the Devil in you, and with that Irish tongue of yours you could make a person believe anything. But when I get by myself I pray, and God tells me how wrong you are. I'm glad they put you out of the Church tonight. I'm glad! I voted with them to do it." She began to cry softly. "I'll never know a happy day again until some way I've brought you back into the path of righteousness."

Sam turned abruptly on his heel. "I'm glad, too," he said. "I'm glad they disfellowshipped me. I'm sick and tired of being called a Mormon elder when it's not true. Maybe from now on people will believe me when I tell them that I'm not a Mormon."

On September 23 the Vigilance Committee held an election. Stephen Payran became president of the executive committee in Sam's place. For the next twelve months Sam was to function only as a member of the executive committee.

Although the Vigilance Committee was not to be dissolved for some months, on October 3 it ceased to function actively and announced publicly: "We hold ourselves ready for action should the community be again situated as at the time of the organization of said Committee."

Sam was well content now that his city was rid of criminals, and the civil authorities seemed willing to take over law enforcement.

Chapter XX

PARLEY P. PRATT, Sam's former associate on the New York *Prophet* and still an Apostle of the Mormon Church, had arrived in San Francisco while Sam was deeply engrossed in the work of the Vigilance Committee. Pratt had come for the purpose of gathering up the reins of Church affairs which Sam had so unceremoniously dropped after his return from the Great Salt Lake Valley. Sam did not see Parley, but he was kept informed of that individual's activities by Fanny Corwin, who grew more devout in the gospel as the years rolled on.

Twice each Sunday Parley preached to crowds in the new Adelphi Theatre, which stood on the site of the old Casa Grande which had offered shelter to the Brannan family on their first night in Yerba Buena. When the Vigilance Committee activities grew less strenuous, Fanny attempted to get Samuel to go to Pratt and beg forgiveness for his sins, and ask to be reinstated in the Church. Sam refused.

Fanny persisted. "It's too bad about you! Ten years ago you was not too busy to go to church, nor to give a little of your time to those who were spreading the gospel. Ten years ago you were a penniless missionary yourself. You traveled without purse or scrip and you know what a hard life a missionary has. But now that a true disciple of God has come to town, a man who hasn't a selfish bone in his whole body, you won't even go to listen to him preach. You ought to go, Sam. You need the message he is teaching."

"What message?" Sam asked.

"Humbleness. Parley Pratt has humbleness and godliness. You have arrogance and the spirit of the Devil in you. A body has only to look at the two of you to see the difference. Ten years ago you were both fine-looking, spiritual men with the Spirit of the Lord shining from your eyes. He's still that way—but look at you. You've turned your back on everything good and spiritual. You drink and carouse around and you've even committed murder." She began to cry. "All the clean youth has gone out of you. You're a good-for-nothing apostate! Please come back into the Church! You could be a good man again if you only wanted to."

Sam's nerves were frayed and his head big, for he had come home drunk at an early hour that morning. He had no patience with the old lady's preaching. "Stop your infernal nagging at me!" he bellowed. "I suit myself all right. I'm good enough to support you and all the thanks I ever get is your eternal nagging, nagging, nagging!"

"That's right, get mad when I try to show you your faults and beg you to mend your ways. It's your good I'm thinking of and not my own. Well, go on and get a little madder, because I've not said my piece yet. It may be true that you support me now, but there was a time when I supported you and it gives me a right to speak when I feel like it. And it might be a good thing for you to remember that you couldn't support yourself in such fine style right now if you hadn't stole your nest egg from the Church in the first place. The money you took from the common fund, the money you got from the sale of land and houses and machinery at New Hope, the tithing you collected from the Mormons, all belonged to the Church. The least you could do now, out of all decency, even if you won't go to church, is to give that money back to them that it belongs to. Parley and his two wives are living in a little shack over on Pacific Street and they go hungry sometimes. Give them the money you owe the Church and he'll be able to live decent and perform his mission and return to the Great Salt Lake with plenty left over. You can spare it now without hurting you."

"No!" Sam shouted. "I've told you a thousand times that I've got no money that belongs to the Church. What I got I keep. If Parley's not smart enough to make enough money to get along on, let him come to me and ask for help. If he don't need it bad enough to come and ask for it he don't need it very bad."

"Parley Pratt would never come begging to you, and you know it," she shouted back at him.

"He'll beg or he won't get it," Sam retorted.

Seeing that Sam was furious Ann Eliza interfered.

"Now Ma, you've had your say. Leave Sam alone. Go to church

if you want to but quit nagging at us. We don't believe in the Church and we want no part of it."

"You're as bad as he is," Fanny lashed out at her. "That I should live to see my daughter act the way you do!"

"That's enough, Ma," Ann Eliza said.

Fanny went weeping to her room. Later she came out and without speaking went away to church. She came back in time to sit down at the dinner table. She said nothing until the meal was finished.

"I told Parley what you said about asking for money if he needed it," she said to Sam. "He looked at me for a long time and then he said kind of soft-like, 'Sister Corwin, I don't need to ask Sam Brannan for money. The Lord is my Shepherd, I shall not want.' I could just feel a thrill start in at my head and run clear to my toes. And then he said something that gave me cold chills. He said, 'Tell Sam Brannan that he may be a Midas now but he will live to see the day when he will want for a dime to buy a loaf of bread.' "

Sam laughed shortly. "He couldn't prophecy a hard rain," he said and left the room. A few minutes later, while Fanny still sat at the table, he came through with his hat on.

"Where are you going?" Ann Eliza asked.

"To a meeting. A few of us fellers are going to organize a branch of the Odd Fellows Lodge."

"Don't meet at a bar," she said quickly, "and please don't stay out all night."

"Now, don't you start nagging!" he replied petulantly and flung himself out of the house, banging the door behind him.

Ann Eliza looked at her mother with tears in her eyes. Fanny got up and looked down at her daughter. "I'm not sorry for you, Ann Eliza. If you'd stayed in the Church and used your influence to get him back, you could have straightened him out. Now it's too late and you'll both have to suffer for it."

"Stop preaching!" Ann Eliza screamed and fled into the kitchen. The children, subdued, got down from the table and went outside to play.

While Sam was busy with the organization of the Odd Fellows Lodge, Fanny came home to announce that Amasa Lyman and C. C. Rich, Apostles of the Mormon Church, had arrived in San Francisco to help Parley stage a religious revival, and also to raise funds to help buy the land belonging to the Lugo brothers. "Our Church has sent a wagon-train of families down there to settle," she explained. "They're going to build a city and name it San Bernardino. You remember John M. Horner, of the *Brooklyn* company? He subscribed two thousand dollars toward buying that land. He's got rich off farm lands across the bay on the east shore."

"How much did you give toward building a new Mormon city?" Sam grinned.

"None of your business."

"Well, whatever it was, you had a right to," he said. "I'll make it up to you."

Fanny burst into tears. "Sam Brannan, I declare you are the aggravatingest man on earth. One minute you're so mean and cussed a person could beat you, and the next minute you're so good and kind a body could kiss you."

"Well, you might try a little of that," Sam suggested. "It's been a long time since you felt like that."

"You big tease," she said drying her tears.

"You give away whatever you feel like giving," he said. "We can afford it. We've got our Odd Fellows charter now and I'm giving what I feel like to them. We pick up men that came out here to get rich and ended up in the street. We send the able ones home. The sick ones we take care of. We help everyone that asks for help." He was thoughtful for a time. "Sometimes they ask too late and they die. At first we didn't know what to do with them, but today I've fixed that up too. I deeded them a good-sized lot up on Mission Road to be used as a cemetery. It only cost me one hundred and fifty dollars but it's worth more than that now."

A century later this same cemetery lot would be paying rents to its owner which would run into six figures.

Into Sam's office one day came an acquaintance from Napa Valley, James M. Estill. Sam waved him to a chair and, throwing his leg over the arm of his own chair, turned to face his visitor. They discussed the weather and the condition of the country in general, and then Estill leaned forward.

"Brannan, my associates and me have been working over a scheme that we think will make us a lot of money. We're about ready to make a move, and we'd like you to come in on it with us. We need a man of your brains and ability and courage."

"What is it?" Sam asked bluntly.

"We've studied the possibilities of making money in the Sandwich Islands, especially around Honolulu."

Sam nodded. "You mean in land?" The other nodded.

Sam removed his leg from the arm of the chair and turned the chair around so that he could face Estill. "H'mm, there might be possibilities there. I visited the Islands on my way here to the Coast in '46, and I'm free to own I never saw such a paradise. What you got in mind?"

"Well, our idea is that if a picked group of us went over there and .bought up a lot of land, we could come back here and sell at a profit to settlers. Then we would haul them over there and put them on the land, and when we got enough Americans there we could claim the islands in the name of the United States. We'd be in at the start and in a position to formulate policies and such. Then as American citizens, we could confiscate the rich sugar plantations there, and ship sugar here to the Coast and make fortunes for ourselves, and run the foreigners out of the place."

Sam thought it over for several minutes, and then nodded his head. "It's a damned smart idea. I'll go in on it with you. We can't lose. Even if the Government won't take it over, we'd own rich farming lands. I'd like to retire there someday and live out my days."

"We're planning on sailing for Honolulu sometime within the next few weeks."

"Fine!" Sam exclaimed. "I'll take a rest and make myself some money all at the same time."

Sam went home filled with enthusiasm for the idea of annexing the Sandwich Islands to the United States. He outlined the plan to his wife.

"My, but it's pretty over there. I wouldn't mind going to the Islands on a visit," she said.

"I'll take you sometime," he offered, "but not on this trip. We're going strictly on business."

"I wouldn't want to tag along with a lot of men," she agreed. "Anyway, I'm having a good time here. We're getting *real* society here in San Francisco now and it keeps me busy, what with our teas and dinners. I wish you'd take more interest and go with me sometimes."

"No thanks. Ever since the custom house has been importing those Southern dandies here to work, the saloons and public places are not fit to go into. I see enough of them in business without going around to parties where you have to put up with their folderol."

Ann Eliza's chin went up. "Folderol is it, to act like a gentleman? Then I wish you'd get some such airs. You come over to Howard's house tomorrow afternoon to the charity tea we are giving, and see if you can't learn to handle a teacup and escort a lady to her carriage. A few graces wouldn't hurt you. Most of the time you just open the door and bolt through it and let me get through any way I can. That's not the way for a gentleman to act. Yes, I think you'd better come to our tea tomorrow, and learn how a gentleman treats a lady."

Sam guffawed and slapped his leg. "So you want me to learn how to dandle a teacup on my knee and maybe make love to my neighbor's wife while his back is turned? No thanks. I got more important things to do than play with teacups and if I got to make love to ladies I'll pick unattached ones. You can have all the dude Southerners you want. I like men with hair on their chests."

"Hair on their chests?" she cried. "Is that any way for a refined man to talk to his wife?"

"I'm not refined," he shouted back at her. "I never pretended to be, nor do I ever want to be. I'm a man and proud of it. If you can't stand to hear a spade called a spade, then you don't want to keep on living with me. I'm no prude and I never will be."

Ann Eliza was getting angry. "So I've heard," she retorted. "And that reminds me. This afternoon two ladies called on me and one of them said that she had heard that some of the town's most prominent businessmen made a practice of going to some of the high-priced brothels in this town, and she looked at me in an awful funny way. I want the truth, Sam Brannan. Did she mean you?"

Sam looked her in the eye and lied like a gentleman. "No. With a wife I like and such a nice family, is it likely I'd be running after whores?"

She looked at him piercingly for a moment and then put her arms around his waist and gave him a quick hug. "I didn't hardly believe it," she admitted. When she released him he quickly changed the subject. "Has Ma got dinner ready yet? I'm awful hungry."

"I'll go see," she replied. "I can hear the children coming in the kitchen, anyway." She hurried out, and Sam sank into his favorite rocking-chair, lighted his cigar, and began to look over the paper. He felt guilty. If Ann Eliza knew that he and Howard and Green spent many a night in a luxurious brothel when they were supposedly at Vigilance Committee meetings, there would be hell to pay.

Sam and Estill and the group of businessmen who were going to take over Honolulu sailed in October. They had bought their tickets on Central Wharf with newly minted gold pieces which had been made in private assay offices in the city, instead of the foreign coin or gold dust which had been in use until now. Sam stood at the rail as the ship moved out into the bay and waved to his wife and mother-in-law and the children. Sammy was excited about his father's trip, three-year-old Adelaide waved cheerily, and the baby only waved because they told her to. Baby Fanny was still too small to understand such things.

When the *Brooklyn* had stopped at Honolulu in 1846 the whaling industry had already begun to wane. On this occasion Sam had only been in the town a few hours when he learned that it was entirely at an end so far as Honolulu was concerned. Only a very few vessels put into port, to take on supplies or to leave disabled American seamen at the still functioning Government hospital.

Samuel and Estill started out immediately to look over land on the various islands. The other members of this "gamecock" expedition traveled in other directions. Sam bought several choice pieces of land on Oahu. Then he visited the sugar plantation of a Scotchman who was anxious to sell out and return to his native land. He had bought, thinking that he could make money on sugar, but the United States tariff was so high that he barely made a living out of his crops. Sam found the island of Kauai, upon which the plantation was located, the most beautiful place he had ever seen. Miles of tasseling cane rippled in the breeze, and Sam sat on the wide veranda of the ranch-house and looked up at sheer cliffs which punctured the clouds so that little silver streams of water cascaded mistily down the precipices. He bought the plantation without haggling over the price. That night he drank toast after toast with his host.

The native workers on the place learned that the land was to have a new owner, and they drifted up to surround the house. The Scotchman went out on the veranda to address them, and told them in simple words that Sam Brannan, an American, was the new master there. They wanted to hear words from the new head of the plantation, but Sam was much the worse for drink when he came out to grant their wish.

"You can all keep your jobs," he assured them. "But things are going to be different from now on. It won't be long before you won't have to answer to your drunken king who swings in his hammock in his palace all day. I'm going to tip him out of his hammock and out of his kingdom. You're going to all be citizens of the United States and you'll have me to thank."

The natives in their picturesque native dress looked at each other with frightened eyes. They wanted no change in their paradise, and certainly they did not want to lose their beloved king. As things were, they had only to work enough to provide a few necessities and then could rest for days at a time attending to their native customs, wearing flower leis, and singing their native songs. This Yankee was full of vigor and profanity, they discovered as he continued to address them, and he made it plain that he did not like their customs nor their king. They wanted none of him, especially when he told them that he had brought a party of men to buy up most of the land and see that the Americans took control. A messenger was sent straightway to tell the king about this obstreperous individual.

The next day Sam departed for other islands. Later he returned to Honolulu, where he bought many city lots, some with houses upon them. He and the other members of the "gamecock" expedition sat on the wide veranda of the hotel in Honolulu one evening much satisfied with themselves, for they had bought several plantations, much good farming and grazing land, and a great deal of property in Honolulu.

Sam laughed. "Our next move now is to go home and send one or two of us to Washington and put pressure on our Senators to start war against these islands. It won't take much effort to win that kind of a war. We won from Mexico without much fighting. This little group of islands will be a cinch to capture."

Estill agreed with him. "It's sure been easy so far."

A messenger arrived and approached the group. He was a carrier from the king, he said. Asking for Samuel Brannan, he handed Sam a document bearing the king's official seal. Sam opened it up and read it by the light of a candle. Then he snorted and read it to the others.

"The king has ordered us to leave for the Coast on the next ship, according to this," he said. The others sat forward excitedly. They chattered like a flock of angry birds for many minutes.

"Tell him we'll go," Sam said at last to the messenger. "Our business is done here anyway." When the messenger had gone, Sam winked at the others. "We'll show that old greaseball a thing or two when we get home," he laughed.

When their ship rode into San Francisco harbor, Sam looked with pride on his city. No more tents huddled over bleak hills. Substantial buildings were making a metropolis out of this frontier town. The semaphore on top of Telegraph Hill wagged a notice to the city that a vessel was coming in. When the steamship docked at Central Wharf a large crowd awaited the voyagers. Sam could see the planked streets of the city. As he turned his gaze up the water front, he saw that every street now had a wharf of some kind. Montgomery Street was no longer the water front, but was two blocks uptown; busy little cars flew back and forth all day long on their tiny tracks, hauling the sand hills from the center of town into the bay under the wharves, which were thus constantly forced to extend themselves farther and farther out into the water to accommodate ships.

When Sam came down the gangplank, Ann Eliza was waiting for him. She was dressed in a full-skirted green taffeta with bell sleeves and she carried a tiny parasol over her quilted poke bonnet. She kissed Sam dutifully and told him that Fanny was not feeling well and had stayed at home with the children.

"Come on over here. I drove the buggy down to meet you," she informed him.

She got into the one-seated vehicle and Sam untied the horse from the rail and climbed up beside her. As they drove up the planked thoroughfare Ann Eliza told him all the news.

"The new Jenny Lind theater is done. It opened last month. My, but it's pretty! Holds about two thousand people they say, and it's got the biggest stage in town."

"You don't say! We'll have to go, first chance we get."

"And Talbot Green," she said quickly. "You'll never guess what's happened to him."

"He's not dead?"

"No, worse. His name ain't Talbot Green at all. His real name is Paul Geddes. He was carrying a lot of money in a bag on the train from his employer's place to a bank in another city, years ago in the States, and he just run away with it and come out here to California. They say he deserted a wife and several children."

"I don't believe it!" Sam exclaimed. "Why, Talbot wouldn't do that. He just married the widow Montgomery a year or so ago. He wouldn't marry her if he already had a wife."

"Oh, wouldn't he? Well, they say he did."

"What does he say?"

"He says it's all a mistake—that he just looks like this Geddes."

"Then I believe him," Sam said firmly.

A few days later a farewell dinner was given to Talbot Green at the Rassette House.[81] He was taking a business trip east.

"I wouldn't have gone so soon," he told his friends over the dinner table, "if this ridiculous story hadn't been started. But now I'm anxious to go back to the States and hunt down this Geddes, and prove that I am the victim of a horrible mistake. I'll get my proof and come back. This Geddes must be the spitting image of me."

Sam and the others drank toast after toast to him, and affirmed again and again their implicit belief in his innocence. They saw him off on the boat the next day. Just before Green walked up the gangplank he said to Sam, "Look after my wife. See that these ugly lies don't hurt her."

"I sure will," Sam assured him.

Talbot sailed away. Before many months it became evident that he was not innocent at all. Mrs. Green, hurt by the facts which came gradually to light, withdrew from society and would have nothing to do with any of her former friends. William Howard sent her a check each month as a part of her husband's profit in the business. It was to be two years before Talbot wrote to any of them, and then it was to Howard, asking for money.

Meanwhile Sam and the others of the "gamecock" expedition had sent representatives to Washington to get a war started with the Sandwich Islands. Eventually the men returned, much chagrined. They presented letters to Sam and Estill addressed to them by the Government of the United States. The expedition was warned that the United States had the friendliest feeling towards the Islands and would tolerate no meddling of private individuals. Every man of the party was ordered to sell whatever lands he owned there and to stay away from the Islands in the future. Sam learned from Washington newspapers what had happened to scotch their plan. While Sam and the other members of the expedition were on their way back to the Coast, the king of the Islands had made a speech to his parliament in which he warned them that they must suppress immediately any idea of American invasion. Then he had written to the United States Commissioner asking that steps be taken to protect the Islands from American buccaneers. When representatives of the "gamecock" expedition reached Washington, the Government was waiting for them.

Sam was much chagrined at the backfiring of their scheme. But he had no choice but to advertise his Honolulu and other Hawaiian real estate for sale. Inasmuch as his business was now largely that of dealer in real estate, he did not have great difficulty in disposing of his Island holdings; but he sold at a loss—to be exact, a loss of $45,000. Nor was he destined ever to occupy the beautiful plantation house—the newspapers called it a palace—on the island of Kauai.

Chapter XXI

SAM OPENED HIS MAIL one morning to find a richly embossed invitation. Madame Blank was opening her elaborate new house formally the following week end, and desired his presence. Sam read it through and then whistled in amazement. At last he tossed it over to Wardwell's desk.

"What do you think of that for being brazen?" he laughed. "San Francisco can take its place with the hoity-toity cities of the world. Where else do the madams send out embossed invitations when they open a new whore-house?"

Wardwell read the invitation and his face revealed the shock to his sensibilities, but he made no comment. At noon William Howard stopped by to invite Sam to lunch with him. It was winter, and rain and fog made the days wet and dreary. As they walked down toward the restaurant Howard inquired, "Wet your whistle yet today, Sam?"

"No. Let's go over to the Oriental bar and have a drink. Then we can eat later in the dining room."

"All right. I guess we can get a better meal there than at the greasy United States restaurant."

Sam noticed that Howard was limping a little. "Hurt yourself?" he asked.

"No, just a touch of rheumatiz in my knee. I like it here in San Francisco, but sometimes I get awful sick of the wind and the fog. It seems to strike clear to the bone. I been thinking a lot about going back home to Boston for a while. I've got a pretty good income from my properties now, and no store to keep me busy, and Agnes and me've been talking about how much we'd enjoy getting back to civilization, where people live quieter and more genteel. Now that I've got the rheumatiz I've just about decided to go right away and get out of this dampness."

"You won't stay there to live, will you?"

"No, just go for a nice long visit. I'm still a young man, only thirty-four, and I want a vacation and a rest while I'm still young enough to enjoy it. Besides, we want to show the baby to my folks."

"You won't find much warmth in Boston this time of year. As I remember it, there was plenty of snow and frost the last time I was there. It makes me think of the days when I was a boy back on the farm in Maine, with snow waist-deep."

"We grew up in the same country and not so far apart," Howard pointed out, "and yet we had to come half way around the world to get acquainted." He was silent as they made their way over the wet planks of the sidewalk to the most ornate hotel in town. "Why don't you and Ann Eliza come with us when we go? We'd all enjoy ourselves more that way."

Sam shook his head. "No, Lizzie can't go now. She's in the family way again. I'd kind of like to go back home again and see all my folks, now that I'm rich and could show off to them. They was all so sure I was never going to amount to anything—that is, all of them except my Ma. She always believed in me. I wish she was alive so I could go back and show her that she was right."

"Better plan on coming along, then," Howard said. They turned in at the door of the Oriental Hotel to enter a lobby filled with potted plants, French gilt chairs, and brocaded sofas. Ladies in trailing gowns moved across the wide expanse of Axminster rugs. The two men made straight for the bar, which was behind massive swinging doors to the right of the lobby. There they met Hall McAllister, Gerrit Ryckman, two city aldermen, and Mayor Benham. They found these worthies laughing over invitations which were duplicates of the one Sam had received that morning. "Don't tell me that Madame Blank had the nerve to send invitations to all of you fellers," Sam exclaimed.

"Yep, every one of us got invited to this fancy affair," one of the aldermen said. "And I'm going to be there, too," he added.

On the night designated, Sam and Howard walked up the hill together and stopped in front of the elegant white house which Madame had had built in the most exclusive residential district of the city. Dainty white curtains framed the windows. The two men laughed as they looked at the disapproving front doors of neighboring houses and commented on the probable feelings of their feminine inmates. They walked up the steps and Sam pulled the bell-cord. They could hear a band playing inside, and after a moment the door was opened by a big Negro dressed in blue satin. He bowed them in and turned them over to a colored woman who bore away their hats and coats. From where they stood they could see into the wide door-way of the parlor, where judges, aldermen, members of the legislature, prominent businessmen were whirling beauties in décolleté over the Turkish carpet to the strains of the music. Madame herself came bustling up.

"Welcome, gentlemen," she beamed. "How do you like my lovely house?"

They looked, by her request, at the crimson damask hangings at the doors and dutifully felt the deep pile on the Brussels carpet in the entrance hall, and agreed that the house had everything to be desired. At last two lovely girls were summoned to play hostess to these two guests. Behaving very modestly, the girls led the men into the ballroom to join the dancing.

Sam had consistently refused to attend any of the society affairs his wife gloried in, giving in to her only so far as to escort her to the door and call for her afterward. She would have been surprised to see how much he was enjoying this "affair." He talked as he pleased, told rough jokes, and slapped a pretty bare back if he felt inclined, and no one chided him for being vulgar or whispered about his manners. He had a wonderful time.

At supper caviar was served. Sam refused to taste it. "I tried it once," he told Yvonne, his partner, "and it's filthy stuff, salty and oily. I never will understand what those damned Russians see in it."

"If you won't eat caviar, then drink some champagne," she urged him. "The Madame is only charging ten dollars a bottle for it."

"Ten dollars?" he demanded. "I thought this party was on the house."

"It is, everything except the liquor. That you have to pay for yourself. You see, she knows what guzzlers the politicians in this town are."

Sam guffawed and slapped his knee, "Trust a Frenchwoman to get the best of you some way. They're the sharpest bitches on earth. But it's all right with me. Go ahead and order half a dozen bottles.

I'm having a good time and no expense is too good for you, is it, Yvonne?"

She dimpled at him and then called to the waiter and ordered the champagne. Over the third glass she smiled into his eyes invitingly, "Remember, you must come back and see me often. The Madame didn't give this ball for charity; she gave it so that you men would get acquainted with us and come back regular."

"I'll be back," he promised and poked her playfully in the ribs.

It was late in the year '52 when little Don Francisco Brannan was born. Sam's new brick house on Bush Street was almost completed, and the Brannans planned to move into it as soon as Ann Eliza was up and around again after her confinement. The little ready-made house in Happy Valley was entirely too small for a family with four children in it.

The day Sam's second son was born he was so proud and happy that he knelt beside his wife's bed and made a solemn promise. "I'll stay home more, Lizzie. I'll try to be a better husband and father from now on. I know I've neglected all of you quite a bit, but I've not done it on purpose. It's just that I've been so busy."

"I know," she murmured. "I get awful cross with you sometimes, but it's like Ma often tells me. You belong more to San Francisco than you do to us, at least right now you do."

"Yes, I guess it is something like that."

She stirred restlessly and made a grimace of pain. "I don't hold it against you, your being away from home so much of the time, as much as I do the way you been drinking lately. Why, there's hardly a day any more that you don't get three sheets in the wind."

"I don't hardly ever get drunk," he defended himself.

"Often enough," she insisted. "But even if you never got drunk, still, if you keep drinking steady every day you'll end up a drunkard. Try to settle down and stop your wild ways. You're not setting the right example for our family." Her eyes filled with tears. "We could be a lot happier if you'd be more of a family man and spend more time taking us out among nice people instead of running around by yourself with the wildest men in the city."

Sam smiled sheepishly. "I guess you're right. Well, I'll try. It's like you say, I ought to start setting a better example to our boys."

As soon as Ann Eliza was up and around they moved into the new red-brick house on Bush Street. Sam kept his promise for several weeks and came home religiously to an early dinner every evening. As proof that he was going to be a more substantial businessman he spent weeks with architects and builders in the preparations for two magnificent office buildings which were to be erected at 400 and 420 Montgomery Street. One was eventually to become famous as the Express Building because it housed the offices of Wells, Fargo. Sam was destined to spend $180,000 on it. The second building was being put up with the Light Guard in mind; the upper floor had been designed for use as an armory, and the whole building came to be known as the Armory for this reason. This building cost Sam $205,-000, and as soon as it was completed the city was to pay him $500 a month as rent for the armory floor. William Howard suggested that he might be a little foolhardy to invest so much money in business buildings when the fortunes of the city were diminishing as a result of the backwash of the gold strike, which had ceased to attract new-comers.

"I don't think so," Sam replied. "Those buildings are my testimonial to a greater San Francisco. At a time when the rest of you are retrenching and being scared for the future, I feel it is best to put out money and prove to the world that this is a great commercial center with a future."

"Well, every man to his own ideas," Howard admitted, "but now that I don't feel the pinch of poverty any more I'm going to use my money for my own pleasure. We're leaving on the Pacific Mail steamship next week for Boston."

"So soon?" Sam asked surprised.

When the Howards boarded the steamer Sam was on it. Ann Eliza had refused to take a trip east while the children were so small. And as she explained to Sam, she couldn't leave now because she was giving a grand ball in the Oriental Hotel the following week. She wanted to establish herself as a social leader.

Sam parted from the Howards at New York, since they were bound for New England, and went immediately to the bank with which he did all his business. The president of the bank came out to greet him. He admired a man who could borrow money from his institution at 3 and 4 per cent and lend it out at 10 and 12. There was much they could discuss. At the end of an hour's conference the banker suggested that Sam stay at his house during his sojourn in the city.

"I will, providing you and me can go out alone and see the sights," Sam suggested, winking his eye and nudging the richly dressed man in the ribs. The banker laughed and winked back. "It's always a pleasure to show a client around," he laughed.

Sam had never been in such a beautiful house as the New York businessman had on Sixteenth Street, just beyond Greenwich Village. As they went up the steps Sam admired all the iron grillwork and the marble stairs. "This used to be way out in the country when I lived here," Sam said. "New York sure does grow fast."

After a few days in the elaborate home which was so well staffed with servants, Sam began to wish he could have such a place. "You're rich enough to keep up an establishment here in New York," his business friend told him. "Why don't you take a year's lease on the house down the block? I could put a caretaker in it, and whenever you are coming you could let me know and I could staff it with help and have things ready. I'd be glad to."

So Sam became the possessor of an establishment on Sixteenth Street in New York. When he signed the lease he said, "This will sure make Ann Eliza happy. She can come here with me next year and bring the younguns, and even have parties of her own, if she wants to."

One morning he wandered, as of old, down to the water front. It made him think of the time when he had lived in the city, and as he walked along he remembered little incidents that had occurred then. Busy with his thoughts, he turned into a side street and bumped into a hurrying stranger.[82] Sam apologized and then noticed that the man wore a captain's uniform. The seafaring man looked long into Sam's face.

"Excuse me," he said, "would you mind telling me your name."

"Yes, I would mind. What the hell business is it of yours?"

The man, dark and tall, smiled suddenly. "Take it easy, mate, I don't mean to give offense. I was just hoping it might be Brannan."

Sam studied the face before him; it reminded him of someone. "My name is Brannan," he said slowly, in a wondering tone.

"So's mine!" the other shouted with gladness. "John Brannan."

"Well, you old son-of-a-bitch," Sam yelled, and flinging his arms around his brother he pounded him with joy. "How did you ever recognize me?"

"I don't know," John was bellowing, "but somehow I'd know that monkey face of yours anywhere."

They automatically found their way to a restaurant and sat talking for hours, unaware of anything but their joy in the reunion. At last John took Sam home to a modest little house on a side street and introduced him to Mary, his wife. There were two children, a boy of a year or so and a baby girl named Sophie.

"This is my long-lost brother, Sam," John told his wife. "I've explained to him that I got to take ship bound for China tomorrow. He wants us to come out to San Francisco and live. He's rich, Mary —a millionaire—and he says he can help us get rich if we'll go out there. I can give up the sea and live at home with you and the younguns."

Mary's eyes grew big with happiness. "Tell him we'll go," she laughed.

"I have already, girl. He'll be back in a few months on business, and then he'll get you and the younguns and take you to San Francisco with him. I'll sell my cargo and pick up another of China merchandise, and put back into San Francisco and sell my ship—and I'll be through with the sea forever!"

"You'll never regret it. I'll help you make a fortune," Sam promised.

"Oh, it's wonderful," Mary exclaimed, "just wonderful!"

Before he left New York, Sam ordered sent to San Francisco the most beautiful carriage he could buy. He was curious about Hattie, the wife he had deserted, and his daughter, and journeyed to Painesville to make inquiries about them. There he learned that Hattie's father had moved to Kirtland years before and had died there. They said that Hattie lived alone with her daughter in the house her father had left her. Sam went over to Kirtland. He found the house they said belonged to Hattie, and when he knocked at the door it was opened by a plump, placid-looking woman of middle age. Sam hardly knew her, yet there was something familiar about the face. He wondered how he could ever have imagined himself in love with her.

"Do you know me?" he asked.

She looked at him closely and then nodded. "Yes, you're Sam," she said simply and added, "I never expected to see you again."

"I guess you are surprised," he admitted. Then he said, "Ain't you going to ask me in?"

"Yes, come in," she said, and stood back so that he could pass her. She ushered him into a dark little musty-smelling parlor.[82] Then she went to the door and called sharply, "Almiry, come here." A moment later a dark little girl of nine came in. She was awkward and homely, with all of her father's darkness and none of her mother's prettiness. Sam felt dismayed. This child was not the little beauty he had always pictured his daughter to be.

"This is your Pa," Hattie said. "Go over and shake hands." The child gave him a frightened look and advanced shyly and held out her hand. Sam shook it and smiled into her face. "Wouldn't you like to give me a kiss, too?" he asked, but she shook her head dumbly, and when he let her go she bolted from the room.

"She's awful bashful," Hattie explained. "Queer, too, in lots of ways. She's more Brannan than Hatch."

Sam felt a sudden pity for this child who must be something of a stranger to her own mother. He was sorry that he had never done anything for her, had never known her. The Irish emotionalism of him flooded to the fore. "I'm sorry for the way I've treated you two," he said to Hattie. "I'd sort of like to make it up to you, if you'll let me."

"We don't need you no more," Hattie replied and motioned him to a chair. She sat down stiffly on the edge of the sofa opposite. "I take in sewing and earn enough to keep us in food."

"But I'm rich," Sam expostulated. "You must have read about me in the newspapers. I went out to California and got rich when the gold rush came along."

"You did!" she exclaimed. "I did read about a Sam Brannan

but I never thought it was you, Brannan being such a common Irish name." She beamed at the thought of his good fortune and then asked suddenly, "Why didn't you never write to me or let me know what you was doing?"

Sam flushed uncomfortably. "I just as well be honest, Hattie. I didn't love you no more and I just thought I'd go out of your life and let you fall in love with somebody else."

"You know I wouldn't do that. And if I did, what good would it do me? I couldn't marry no other man while you're alive. I wouldn't get one of them horrible divorces."

"I married again," Sam announced. She sighed. "A man can do things like that. A woman can't." They sat silent for several moments and then Hattie asked, "Is she alive yet?"

"Lizzie? Sure. We got four children."

"Then if she's alive what did you come hunting me up for?"

"To see if I couldn't help you."

"How?"

"With money."

"I don't need your money. I need a father for my girl and a home for her like other girls her age have."

Sam spun his hat in his fingers before he answered, self-consciously. "I couldn't do that. I married polygamously, but I wouldn't want to live with two women at once."

"Then go back where you came from."

"I intend to," he said quickly. "But I'd like to make arrangements to do something for you and her."

Hattie was thoughtful for a time; then she asked, "Would you take us out to California to live, if I wanted that?"

Sam thought. Then he replied, "I might. But if you did you'd have to go as a friend."

"You mean you don't want me as your wife ever again?"

He shook his head. "No, Hattie. I don't feel that way about you any more."

She sighed again. "I was afraid of that. Still and all, I'd sure like to go out to California to live. They say it's just grand out there."

"It is," Sam agreed and began to tell her of the advantages

of San Francisco, and at last, noticing how downcast she was, hit upon a bright idea.

"I'll tell you what I'll do: I'll take you and Almiry out there, providing you don't ever let Lizzie know about you. She wants to be society in San Francisco and if she ever heard about you she'd never get over it. I'll take you out and I'll support you, but you'll have to pretend you're just a relative."

"I don't think I'd like that," she said quickly. "After all, I am your first wife, your only legal wife. Why should I play second fiddle to her?"

"Because I can't take you there any other way. It's that way or no way," he said flatly.

She considered this for a long time and then made her decision. "All right, I'll go on those terms. I'll tell people I'm just a relation if they ask me."

"Give me your word of honor," he said. She did so. Then he arose. "I'll be back later in the year on business. When I return to San Francisco I'm going to take my brother's wife and children out with me. I'll let you know in plenty of time, and you and Almiry can come along. In the meantime, here's a bank draft I had fixed for you. It will be enough to live on till I see you again." Her eyes grew big when she saw the check in four figures.

Sam boarded a river boat for the trip down to New Orleans. Arrived there, he made connections with the Atlantic steamship for Panama. He had not been long aboard before he learned that the notorious European dancer, Lola Montez, former mistress of the now exiled King of Bavaria, was a passenger. He first saw her walking along the promenade deck with her black poodle in her arms and a French maid hovering in attendance. There were four hundred and sixty other passengers, so that Sam found himself but one of hundreds of men who gathered to watch her royal progress.

If Lola was notorious, Sam was at least famous. And it soon became apparent that she had read about him in the papers, for she picked him out to smile upon as she passed on her morning constitutional. He was not particularly surprised, because everywhere he went the papers published stories of his wealth and he was accus-

tomed to the adulation of those who hoped to benefit by his acquaintance. But when one day Sam saw the handsome young Irishman,
Patrick Hull—who had a job on the San Francisco *Whig*—walking
with Lola and carrying Flora, her poodle, as he smiled down into
the fascinating woman's face, Sam decided that it was time to answer
Lola's smiles himself. Within a few days he was walking with
her and sitting with her over drinks in the salon, but he refused to
carry her poodle or to have anything to do with the pampered
animal.

When the boat reached the Isthmus of Panama they were faced
with the long journey by mule and boat to the Pacific Ocean. Sam
did what he could to make the journey easy for Lola, but he soon
discovered that she was independent and willing to take care of herself. She rode her mule like a man and made none of the tiresome
complaints that other females did. On the Pacific side the voyagers
boarded the Pacific Mail steamship, the *Northerner*.[83]

During the following weeks as the *Northerner* plied her way up
the coast of California, Sam spent his most enjoyable hours with
Lola Montez, otherwise known as the Comtesse de Lansfeld and
Baronne de Rosenthal. Sam had read that she was a woman of many
loves and had been married several times. He remembered all the
lurid stories the newspapers had printed about her affair with
Ludwig, the aging Bavarian monarch. And all this made her the
more attractive in his eyes. She was a dangerous woman, and yet
she had the appearance of being the most naïve of creatures. Sam
never tired of looking into her enormous blue eyes, and he was
fascinated by the play of sunlight in her dark hair with its bronze
highlights. She usually wore black or dark blue velvet dresses, cut
tight in the bodice and full in the skirts, with simple lace collars.
She seemed more a beautiful child than a woman of thirty-five.

Many evenings she walked the moonlit deck holding hands with
the lovesick Patrick Hull, while Sam smoked impatiently in the
lounge. But Patrick's devotion did not prevent her from opening her
stateroom door to Sam when he knocked late at night. Many nights
she lay close against him until daylight began to show through the
portholes. Nor did Patrick's fevered pursuit of her or Sam's atten-
tions prevent her from conferring her charms on other wealthy

patrons. She who had once been divorced for adultery drew no line between her loves if she could gain financially by them. Sam spent a small fortune on her before the *Northerner* arrived in San Francisco. But this was but a drop in the bucket to what he was to spend. He thirsted for much more of her charms.

At thirty-five, Sam was a realist. He knew Lola Montez for exactly what she was, yet her worldly sophistication, her wit, her personality, her temper, combined with her independence of spirit, enthralled him. He was completely infatuated.

When he went home to his family he discovered that he was happy to see the children, but Ann Eliza seemed somehow distasteful. Perhaps it was because she seemed a little strange—perhaps after he had been home a few days he would feel the old rush of affection. He made an excuse to get back to town as soon as possible. He inquired at the warehouse about the carriage he had bought in New York. It was there. He had it uncrated and sent over to the livery stable. Then he ordered the stable manager to keep his finest team apart for his use.

"The first thing I want you to do is to hitch your best team to my carriage and send it with a good reliable coachman over to the Oriental Hotel. The coachman is to report to Lola Montez and tell her that I sent him. That carriage is to be at her disposal every day from two o'clock until midnight."

"All right, Mr. Brannan, you're the boss. What if your wife wants to use it, though?"

"My wife don't know I own it, and I hope she never finds out. I bought it for her but she'll have to wait awhile to use it." He laughed and winked.

Sometimes Sam stopped at the livery stable and got the carriage and drove it to the hotel for Lola. Then they would drive out the new plank road to the Mission Dolores settlement, where the bullfights took place every Sunday; or to the beach, or out into the country. Sam asked her if she'd like to attend a bullfight, but she shuddered and said no. When they drove out to the seal rocks they loved to listen to the roar of the sea lions. Sam was usually rollicking good company and had a fund of off-color stories at which Lola howled with enjoyment.

The papers of San Francisco had heralded the arrival of the famous beauty, and after her coming they were filled with constant stories about her. On Monday, May 23, the *Alta California* carried this news item:

The public of San Francisco will have an opportunity to gratify its long awakened curiosity, on Thursday night next by visiting the American Theatre where Lola Montez makes her debut before a California audience.

On Thursday night Sam and Ann Eliza sat in a box waiting for the curtain to rise on *The School for Scandal*. This was their first glimpse of the new American Theatre, and they looked with admiration upon the paintings on the ceiling and the rich red draperies on all the boxes and the stage. Every now and then Ann Eliza bowed to an acquaintance in a very formal manner, while Sam was waving broadly to dozens of friends. His boisterous spirits annoyed her and finally she spoke sharply, "Sam, stop waving to everyone that comes in. Try to be a little genteel. After all, you're the richest man in San Francisco and you have a certain position to uphold. Try to act like you are someone instead of being as common as dirt."

Sam looked at her, dressed in pale blue satin with a very full skirt and a deep lace bertha. She seemed overdressed to him and a little sickening with her airs. "Go to hell," he said gruffly. "I'll act as I please. I don't like the way you act either, but I'm trying to keep my mouth shut. You think you don't stink the way you act, but you do."

She flushed and spoke rapidly under her breath. "Sam Brannan, don't you dare talk to me that way. I won't put up with it. I don't know what's come over you lately; you certainly don't act like yourself."

"Neither do you," he replied.

"Oh, shut up!" she said petulantly and moved as far away from him as she could.

At eight-thirty a man came out from behind the curtain and turned the oil lamps in the main part of the house low and the row of lamps in the footlights high. Then the curtain parted and Lola as Lady Teazle was presented to view in the midst of a gay scene, dressed in a pale yellow gown. Sam watched every move and clapped loudly and whistled for curtain calls between the acts, which Ann Eliza deplored. When it was all over, Ann Eliza got up with an uncompromising air and announced that she thought very little of the notorious Lola's acting and less of her looks.

Outside they were caught up in a crowd of friends who were arguing about Lola's talents. The women agreed that she was a vulgar hussy whom they would never come to see again. The men thought she was charming.

The next day Sam sent Lola jewels and a note saying that he would visit her in the afternoon. That night he sat alone in a box and watched her performance in *Yelva*, after which she danced her famous spider dance. Ladies of San Francisco who had been unable to get tickets the night before sat watching this bold woman who dared to have a career of her own and a life apart from the dictates of any man. And they were shocked. They made no secret of their dislike, some of them even going so far as to hiss her encores. In fact, it was the encores that outraged their sensibilities. For the first, Lola appeared in a filmy dress made to resemble a spider web. Large imitation spiders clung to it. Her hair curled back in a childishly simple style from her girlish face and dainty ears, and a glistening bead skullcap kept her hair in place. She began to undulate and then to whirl, and wound up with a mad dance in which her dress flew high and the beads reflected the light in a thousand joyous movements. When she had finished the men shouted and stamped and cried for more. The women sat grim-faced. After the last act, Lola appeared in a sailor's suit with her hair caught up in a cap, and her legs encased in breeches. She danced the sailor's hornpipe with childish simplicity. To Sam, in this boy's dress she was more irresistible than ever.

Lola played night after night, appearing as Charlotte Corday, Yelva, the Maid of Sargossa, Lady Teazle in *The School for Scandal*, and as Olla in the dance. Lastly, she gave a grand performance of a play she had written herself, dealing with her life with Ludwig, King of Bavaria. After a week of seeing Lola, the newspapers changed their tone from belief in her perfection as an actress and dancer to slight criticism. They admitted that her dancing was not excellent and that as an actress she left something to be desired, but still clung to the views that as a personality she was unexcelled.

Lola took a week's rest before repeating her repertoire, and it was then that Sam gave a theatrical supper in her honor in the ballroom of the Oriental Hotel. Every man of wealth and standing in the city attended; but none of their wives. The only ladies present, other than Lola, were those playing in her own company. Such impecunious young men as Patrick Hull had no place at this resplendent celebration, where imported crystalware sparkled on snowy linens. Squab, duck, fish, choice dishes served up by a chef but lately arrived from France, went almost unnoticed in the general hilarity. Toasts to Lola were drunk in gallons of champagne, and as soon as dessert was served the steward brought to Lola's plate Sam's gift for the evening. She squealed with delight as she saw its expensive wrapping. As she removed the ribbons and tissues everyone seated at the long table watched her. She lifted a plush box from the papers and opened the lid. A diamond tiara flashed back the light from the crystal chandelier over her head. There was a gasp from the guests. Wordlessly she lifted it from the box and set it on her dark tresses, while exclamations of admiration rippled down the crowd. At last Lola turned to Sam at her right, with tears in her eyes.

"It is quite the most beautiful present I have ever received," she said.

"Better than the King of Bavaria ever gave you?" he teased, but there was deadly earnestness behind his words.

"More beautiful, yes. He gave me a country estate and many jewels, but nothing so beautiful as this."

Sam seemed satisfied then. Already he had showered her with gifts of every description; bolts of silk from China, rare laces from Europe, jewels which had cost him a small fortune. But his one desire had been to give her something better than even a king had been able to afford. And now he saw it accomplished.

Lola was accustomed to being sought after by the stage-door Johnnies of her day, but San Francisco was a new and exhilarating experience for her. Many men waited for her at the stage door each evening, and more than once they removed the team from Sam's carriage and pulled the actress to her hotel themselves. There were many of these same men waiting outside the hotel early in the morning, and they would remain throughout the hours hoping for a glimpse of her. Lola rarely emerged before two o'clock, and when she did she was besieged by these admirers. She would wave her little parasol to them gaily as she came out the door, would trip across to her carriage, followed by the maid and the poodle (the latter helped in by a score of willing hands), and then would throw kisses to the dozens of men, young and old, who had waited to see her. Then she would tell Sam's driver to start, and carefully the coachman would guide the horses through the crowd until they were free.

Sam was not unaware of the fact that a wife is usually the last to hear of her husband's indiscretions.

One afternoon, when he had come to ride with Lola, after they left the usual crowd behind and were moving over the road toward the seal rocks, she pointed her parasol at a heap of refuse at the side of the street, where several rats were feeding.

"San Francisco is the most exhilarating city in the world," she exclaimed, "but why do you citizens not do something to clean up such piles of filth? Those awful rats would frighten me to death if I had to walk on your streets. Besides, the smell is terrible when the sun is warm."

"Why do we leave it lying around? I'll tell you why. Because our board of aldermen is a sight more interested in figuring out how to steal from the pork-barrel than in making a good city here. I've argued with them, pleaded with them, offered to put up money to start a dump clean-up, and written them open letters in the newspapers. But I can't get any results. Now, if you go talk to them or write, I think they might listen to you."

She laughed her tinkling little laugh. "Oh, no, Sam, I wouldn't do that. I've made a mint of money since I came here, and I intend to make a lot more. If I start criticizing the city or its officials I might kill the goose that's laying the golden eggs."

"You see," Sam pointed out, "you're just like them, you want the money."

"Seriously though, Sam, the citizens ought to do something about improving the looks of the city. You yourself own much property on Montgomery Street, and yet it is a dusty, uneven street, higher on one side than the other. It ought to be leveled and cobbled."

"I know it. We had it planked once but tore it up to put in water mains, and it's been left just the way the ditch-diggers left it. I can't pay to have a whole street made level, and it's a cinch the board of aldermen won't cooperate. Why, I've been trying to get the biggest obstacles to the city's growth moved out of the way, those sand hills. We need level space all over the central part of town for our buildings, and up there at Third there's a big one we have to go around all the time. I thought I could remedy the situation, and I had a great big locomotive built at the Globe Locomotive Works in Boston and had it shipped all the way around the Horn last year. I figgered we could set up tracks and haul the sand away and dump it into the bay in trainload lots, and give the city a chance to spread out. And what happened? The board of aldermen went down in a body to look at my beautiful engine. It was so big it scared them, and they went back and passed an ordinance making it unlawful to run a big engine on city streets."

They were moving out now on the old presidio road through the sand dunes. "What did you do with it, then?" she asked.

"Had a big barn built and put her away."

"What a shame! It is a pity that all little officials have little minds. But it is true of every place; Europe, America. Give a little man a big job and he will always act little."

Sam nodded. "My engine will come in handy someday, though, in spite of our aldermen. It won't be long now before California will be needing railroads, and then I'll have a use for the 'Elephant' as they call her."

When they came out to the edge of the last sand hill, Sam and Lola could see the far reaches of the Pacific stretching to far horizons; in a dim blue haze even the Farallones were visible. Lola sat up and stretched her arms wide. "I love the restless sea today. It fits my mood."

"You are a restless body," Sam commented, "—almost as bad as me."

"Always I have been restless. I do not stay long in any one place.

As entrancing as San Francisco is, I could not stay in it the years you have."

"I never have stayed any one place so long before, except when I was a little boy. But San Francisco is a city of changes. A feller can stay right here and still be seeing different things every day. I hope I never have to leave it."

When the coachman had driven down onto the hard-beaten sand of the beach he turned and looked enquiringly at Sam. "Shall we have a run today, Lola?" Sam asked, and she nodded, her eyes sparkling with anticipation. The coachman gave the horses their heads and away they went, dashing madly down the beach while Lola and Sam held on and laughed into the wind and spray that splashed against their faces. At the end of two miles the coachman slowed the horses and then turned them for the run back. When they stopped again it was at the top of the cliffs opposite the seal rocks, where hundreds of brown seals could be seen lying in the late after-noon sun after feeding.

"This is a magnificent spot," Lola said, her cheeks pink with the excitement of the run. "I could just imagine I am queen of the world, sitting up here calmly surveying the universe."

"As far as I'm concerned, you are," he said, and the banter was gone from his voice. His brown eyes were filled with the infatuation he felt for her.

She laughed trippingly. "You do say such nice things," she chuckled.

"My wife don't think so."

Lola smiled. "Most women are dull, and few of them under-stand their husbands. That's why their husbands run after women like me."

"Yeh, I guess so," he admitted. He sat silent for a time and they both watched the seals. At last Sam said, "I'm going to build a big resort sometime, right on this spot where we are sitting now."

"How lovely! You will, of course, have a gay European kind of restaurant, with an orchestra and dancing and the very best of food that can be obtained."

Sam nodded excitedly and added, "And a bar and a game room, and everything people could want to have a good time."

"Interesting people, you mean."

Again he nodded. "Why, sure. I certainly don't want to do anything to attract that so-called society crowd that my wife is trying to run. I want the kind of people at my place that want to have fun and don't give a tinker's damn about impressing other folks with their importance."

"Yes," Lola put in. "That kind are such bores. I have noticed these would-be society ladies in San Francisco. Most of them look as if they had been maids or washerwomen."

Sam roared with laughter and slapped his knee. "Most of them have come from pretty common origins. You take my wife; her Ma was running a boardinghouse when we got married, but now she's talking about going to Europe to meet the Queen of England."

Lola made a grimace of distaste. "Victoria is a very dowdy woman. You would not like her. Dull, too."

"Well, you're not." There was a look of complete admiration in his eyes. He looked at her for a long moment. "And by the way, I see that Patrick Hull is still following at your heels most of the time when I'm not around. You're not in love with that penniless Irish scamp, are you?"

"That is none of your affair," she said quickly. "I have never yet let any man tell me how I should spend my time, or with whom. But I might say, for your information, that I find Patrick an excellent story-teller. If I ever should decide to marry him, it will be because I find him so amusing."

"If you ever do marry him you will be a damned fool," Sam replied and motioned to the coachman to turn back to the city.

One morning Sam picked up the new issue of the *Golden Era,* a weekly paper, to read:

There is no end to Lola Montez' pranks. Her agent recently left her, and at the time she heard of his determination to do so, some conversation in regard to his character then ensued, in which the "fair countess" reflected severely upon some of his conduct. Just at this time the gentleman stepped in and a "scene" followed. Mlle. Lola bestowed upon the astonished gentleman divers unmentionable epithets, and finally pitched into him, knocked him down with her pretty little fist. One of the bystanders held the "gentle lady" and endeavored to pacify her; but before her fury subsided, she destroyed checks to the amount of $200, to show that filthy lucre was no object to her.

On the fifteenth of June, Lola made her last appearance on a San Francisco stage. Five days later the *Alta California* reported that she had been seen rolling tenpins in a Commercial Street saloon. Sam couldn't get away from his office early that afternoon, and when he did go around the clerk told him that Lola had gone out early in the day with Patrick Hull. Sam was furious that she should use his carriage to ride with Hull. Next morning a reporter wrote that he had seen her lately, riding in her carriage and puffing on a cigar with as much gusto as a Broadway dandy.

Sam went around with the carriage early the next day and found Lola just ready to leave the hotel. She stopped uncertainly when she saw him. Then she crossed the planked sidewalk and spoke to him. "I wanted to use the carriage today, Sam. I have an appointment."

"I'll take you," he said.

"No, I want to go alone."

"Get in," Sam said gruffly. "I want to talk to you. It's been nearly a week since I've seen you."

She stepped into the carriage and Sam motioned the coachman to drive slowly. "What do you want?" she asked petulantly.

"The first thing I want is a little of your time. I've spent enough money on you so that I'm entitled to some of it."

"You are entitled to nothing except what I wish to give you."

"Now, don't get your feathers all ruffled!"

"I'll do anything I damn please," she retorted.

Sam felt his wrath rising. "You certainly do. Every time I pick up a paper I see where you've been doing what you damn please. First you were pitching into your manager with your fists, then you were rolling tenpins in a saloon, and the last thing, you are seen smoking big black cigars. What do you think the people in this town must think of you by now?"

"About the same as they think of you: that I am a bad one through and through. And a lot I care what they think! I live my life to please me, not you nor any one else."

Sam was so furious that he took notice of nothing but Lola, who sat beside him, her face hateful in its anger. "So I've heard. I guess that's why one feller divorced you for adultery and another left you because you are a bigamist."

"Look who's calling me names!" she ridiculed him. "I might be all of those things. In fact I may commit bigamy again. I'm on my way now to meet Patrick Hull, and I may end by marrying him. At least he has the sense to mind his own business."

Sam shouted to the coachman to halt. When the carriage had rolled to a stop, Sam took Lola firmly by the arm and helped her quite urgently to the ground. "Go meet the poor bastard if you want to, but you'll not ride in my carriage again, not with him or alone." Without waiting to hear what she shrieked at him in rage, he urged the driver to speed away. He had the carriage driven back to the livery stable and there he got out; he walked for two hours until his anger cooled and then he went home. Ann Eliza was waiting for him in the parlor. He could hear Grandma Corwin in the kitchen, talking to the Chinese cook, and the children were playing noisily outside.

"I thought you were never coming," she said accusingly. Her color was high and her eyes angry.

"What's the matter?" Sam asked.

"Sit down and I'll tell you," she said tersely. He let himself down in a rocker, and she sat on the edge of her chair. "I saw you with that notorious hussy today," she said, and began to cry.

Sam heaved a great sigh and slumped in his chair, waiting for her to go on. At last she controlled her weeping and went on, "I've taken everything from you, Sam Brannan. I've stayed home night after night, tending your children and being alone while you was out carousing around and coming home early in the morning too drunk to stand up straight. I guess there's nothing bad for a man to do that you haven't done." He started to protest, but she waved aside his words.

"Oh yes, you have. I've been told a lot of things over the last two or three years, but I wouldn't believe them. I thought the women that told me were just jealous and trying to break up our home. But I saw you today riding in your buggy with that Montez woman. And I could see the way you were quarreling that she was not just a friend, but a woman you'd been intimate with. A man don't talk to a woman the way you was talking to her unless he knows her pretty well. You didn't even see me."

"It's not my carriage," he said quickly.

"Oh yes, it is. You bought it the last time you were in New York. I heard about that too and I didn't believe it, but I inquired around today after I saw you two and I learned quite a lot. It seems like that carriage has been setting out in front of the Oriental Hotel every day since Lola Montez came, and that she can use it all she wants. I walk wherever I have to go, while your mistress has the best of everything. It's things like that that hurt." Again she dissolved in tears. When she could stop her crying she went on.

"While I carry your child you go running around after that horrible whore, who goes in and out of saloons and acts like the worst kind of a man—and from what I hear she'll go to bed with any man that can pay her price."

"Not any man," Sam said quickly. "I'm not saying she is too particular, but she won't go to bed with any man."

Ann Eliza spoke bitterly. "I guess if she'll go to bed with you, she'll go with anyone."

"Oh, I don't know. I'm not such a bad bargain," he said angrily.

"As far as I'm concerned, you are," she retorted. "And I just as well tell you, you'll never sleep in *my* bed again."

"What are you going to do?"

"Leave you. I've thought it all out and talked it over with Ma. You own the Larkin House down in Monterey since you took it in on that business deal a while back. You said I could use it for a summer house. I want it now. I'm going to take the younguns and go down there and live. I don't want anyone here in San Francisco to know that I'm going to have a baby, not while they're laughing behind my back at the fool you've been making of yourself over this notorious Montez woman. After the baby is born, I don't know what I'll do. Get a divorce, I guess."

"A divorce," he gasped.

"Yes, a divorce. Nobody knows better than me what a scandal a divorce will cause, but before I'll put up with any more of the things I've been putting up with the last few years, I'll go through a scandal."

"What do you want me to do?" he asked, humbled at last.

She looked at him with a great weariness in her face; she lifted her hands as if to plead with him, and then let them drop. "Nothing. It's too late. All I want is to get away from you. Right now I feel like I never want to see or hear of you again."

Sam looked at her. Once he had been very much in love with her, but of late years his love had died into a passive affection. It had been a long time since she had stirred his senses. Certainly he was fond of her, but he would welcome a vacation from her; a vacation during which he could come and go as he pleased and not have to account to her for every hour he had spent away. Perhaps after the baby was born she would regain her sense of equilibrium, and they could re-establish their home on a more solid foundation. Meanwhile he could have his little fling. He did not try to persuade her to change her mind about going to Monterey.

"I'll have the papers made out in the morning for the house to be put in your name."

"Thank you," she said coldly. "Your bags are all packed. I've told the younguns that you are going away on a trip."

"You're not going to throw me out of my own house," he said passionately. "After all, it's my money that keeps it going. When I leave it'll be because I want to and not because you're throwing me out."

She sighed. "All right, then, Ma and me and the younguns will go. I thought I was offering you the easiest way, the way that would cause the least talk."

Sam threw up his hands angrily. "You win. I'll go. But mark my words, I'll never come back to any house you live in till you get down on your knees and beg me."

"Then you'll never live in any house with me again. I wouldn't even let you come back if you got down on your knees and begged."

"To hell with you and all women!" he shouted, and without saying good-by to anyone he turned on his heel and went back to town.

William Howard and his wife, just recently returned from their long sojourn in Boston, were living in quarters at the Oriental Hotel and there Sam also took a suite. Howard was unwell and looked years older than his actual age. Sam was still very angry at Lola and avoided her. But Lola was already regretting that she had driven away the "golden goose," and sent him several little notes, which he ignored. He suddenly found himself cured of his infatuation. Moreover, his business took so much of his attention that he had no time for women. Squatters were everywhere, menacing the rights of every man who owned property in San Francisco. The lot he had given to the Odd Fellows for a cemetery was covered with tents and shacks; the grave mounds were being used as tables and chairs. The trouble was not recent; it had gone on over a period of many months, but seemed at this particular time to have reached a frenzy. Penniless newcomers were determined to have land, and since in court possession was a substantial part of the law, they squatted. Folsom hired gunmen to patrol his property, and poachers were run off at the pistol's point. Sam took a tip from Folsom and also hired men to guard his lots, but in many cases squatters were entrenched before the guards made an appearance. His only recourse was to take the claims to court. Eventually he would win, of course, but for the time being this squatter trouble was a constant nettle in his flesh. An edition of the *Golden Era* carried a warlike poem dedicated to Sam, and when he read it he was furious that any newspaper should take the part of the have-nots.

> Thus far into the bowels of the land
>   I'll set my stakes; here will I pitch my tent
> Even on Brannan's lot;
>   And while my "Colt" is loaded, and my nerves are firm
> The ground I'll hold, or bathe its face in blood.

He smiled grimly to himself and charged his guards to be more bloodthirsty.

At noon on July first, Sam left his office and went over to the Oriental dining room for lunch. He recognized several prominent businessmen lunching with overdressed women. No wives appeared at these luncheons, for respectable women did not dine at the Oriental Hotel; only those who had no care for their reputations were so daring. Shortly after Sam sat down, Lola came tripping in. When she saw him she came straight to his table and with her most engaging little-girl mannerism smiled down on him. "Are you still mad at Lola?"

"No."

"Then ask me to sit down and have luncheon with you."

"You can if you want to. I don't own the table."

She sat down, settled back in her chair, and heaved a delicious sigh. "It's good to make up again," she trilled.

He looked at her coldly for a moment or so; then she tilted her head, bird-like, and looked up at him through her long lashes, and he had to smile in spite of himself. "That's better," she laughed and patted the hand that lay on the cloth. When they had finished luncheon she took his arm possessively and fairly danced along beside him to keep up with his great stride.

"I've missed my carriage," she said plaintively. "Let's take a nice drive before you go back to the office."

"You'll have to walk to the livery stable with me."

"Oh, I don't mind."

Lola was at her sparkling best as they drove around the edge of the city. When they came back to the hotel it was midafternoon. Sam helped Lola from the carriage and was escorting her to the door when Patrick Hull fairly hurtled from the lobby and stood glaring at them.

"Do you realize you've kept me waiting two hours?" he demanded of Lola.

She looked at him with stricken eyes. "I forgot all about you," she gasped.

Hull turned his angry glance upon Sam. "It's all your fault. What right have you got hanging around after her, and you a married man?"

A crowd of curious onlookers began to collect. Lola observed them and said quickly, "Patrick, do not make a scene!"

"I certainly will," he said harshly. "It's time he and everyone else knows that we are engaged."

Sam looked at Lola with a question in his eyes. She looked away quickly and said, "I will not have two men stand in the street and fight over me as if I were a bone and they were dogs. I am going to my room and I don't want to be followed, either." In a flash she was gone. Sam made as if to follow her, but Patrick barred his way.

"You've made a fool of yourself over her long enough. It's time you stopped. Everyone in town knows that your wife has left you because of the way you've been carrying on."

Sam laughed a short, hard laugh. "My wife has not left me. She is away on a little vacation. And you might like to know that I've not been chasing Lola. It's been the other way around."

Patrick swung at Samuel, but Sam ducked and the blow did not land. "You'll not speak so of my future wife," Hull panted.

"I don't know how she can marry you. She's still married to several other men," Sam taunted him.

"I'll kill you for that," Hull said and swung again. Sam stepped back and waited a moment. When he struck, Hull went down in a heap. Sam stood over him and spoke.

"Go on and marry her, you stupid idiot; marry her if she'll have you, but if you had any sense you'd know that she is using you the same as she's used every man she ever knew. And that's a lot of men. When you get up from there, better run home and ask your Ma to wipe your nose." As Patrick struggled groggily to his feet, Sam turned and walked away.

Two days later Sam read an interesting item in the *Golden Era*.

Married yesterday morning at Holy Church of Mission Dolores, by Rev. Father Flavel Fontaine, Lola Montez and Patrick Hull. We wish the happy couple many years of uninterrupted happiness and conjugal felicity. The question of "Who's got the Countess?" we presume, is thus forever put at rest.

When Sam read the last sentence he realized that this was a dig at him. He felt like seeking out the editor and giving him a whipping, but instead he went to the livery stable, took out the carriage, and drove to the cliffs. He sat for a long time, watching the seals on the rocks. When he came back to the hotel he was weary and out of sorts. He never mentioned Lola's name again.

Sam soon blossomed out as a broker, with offices in one of his new buildings, at 120 Montgomery Street. To his office, one day in July, he summoned all the original members of the Society of

California Pioneers so that they might reorganize. This time no Vigilance Committee interfered with their activities by absorbing their attention; from this time forward they were to hold regular meetings, and the day was to come when they would, as an organization, exert a powerful influence in the community. In the new organization Sam was named president. Wiry, small, red-haired William Tecumseh Sherman, now working in a local bank, was elected treasurer. His famous march through Georgia was still some years in the future.

A month passed, during which Sam became so immersed in business that he had no time to ponder upon the vagaries of women. Fanny wrote now and then to give him news of the children, but he received no direct word from Ann Eliza.

In this year the general elections aroused great excitement in San Francisco. Campaigning was loud and colorful, with Broderick working always behind the scenes to maneuver his henchmen into power. But the solid citizens of San Francisco wanted none of Broderick's machine, and to circumvent him they nominated a man who was fearless and had great foresight; the only man in the city they felt could beat Broderick's nominee—Sam Brannan. Sam, however, had no desire to be a senator in the California Legislature, and would wage no campaign. In spite of his inertia he won the seat by a large majority. At other times in his life he would have been pleased and flattered by the honor, but now he was not interested. Life had somehow gone flat, and he had an aching desire to get away from San Francisco for a time. He wrote a letter to the proper authorities declining the office, giving as his excuse that he had to go to the States on business.

And to the States Sam did go. Several months later he returned with his brother John's family, his own wife Hattie, and his daughter, Almira. He rented a house for Mary Brannan and her two children and they settled down to await the coming of John, who was momentarily expected from his China voyage. Hattie and Almira were given the little ready-made house on Mission Street which Ann Eliza had outgrown, and which had been rented in the interim. No one outside of John's family and the Badlams ever knew that Hattie Brannan bore any close relationship to Sam. If Ann Eliza heard of her, the news came at a time when it made no difference, being just one more injury to her pride.

On the first day Sam spent in his office after his return, he was waited upon by a delegation of men.

"Mr. Brannan," the spokesman began self-consciously, "we've come to inform you that we've organized the Brannan Protective Association in your honor."

Sam tipped back in his chair, caught his thumbs on the armholes of his vest, and smiled. "Well, that's mighty fine of you boys. To show you my appreciation I'll buy you the best fire engine that's ever been made. Of course, it will take a little time to get it because I'll have to have it made to order. But I'll tend to it right away."

He sent his order to Boston within the week, with detailed specifications. It was to be two years before it could be finished and delivered. Meanwhile the enginehouse on Halleck Street, near Sansome, had to make shift with a second-hand engine—not nearly fine enough for the Brannan Company.

Armory Hall, on Sacramento and Montgomery streets, was finished at last, and the California Guard moved in. Within the same week the Express Building was completed, and the new tenants moved in there, too. It was a busy week for Sam, who had innumerable details to settle. When it was all over he sat alone in his hotel room one evening, half-undressed for the night, with one shoe off and the other in his hand. "It's nice to be rich and famous and courted by everyone that wants an advantage," he said musingly to himself, "but somehow there comes times when a feller gets sick of it and would give it all up for a good romp with his younguns on the floor, of an evening." He sighed and finished his preparations for bed

Chapter XXII

SAM, now in his prime, was an affectionate man, and having no family of his own to turn to, often went to the home John had established in Pleasant Valley, a little beyond Happy Valley. John had arrived in San Francisco a few days after his wife and had immediately bought a home to celebrate his retirement from the seafaring life. One evening when Sam was down on the floor playing with young Jackie Brannan, Hattie and Almira arrived. Sam tried to coax Almira to join their game but she hid back of her mother and would not play. Sam gave up trying. Almira was decidedly an unfriendly child and somehow different from other children, not quite so intelligent as Sam thought a normal girl of eleven should be.

When Sam tired of playing he threw himself into a rocker near Hattie. She smelled liquor on his breath and drew in her lips. He recognized her old look of disapproval and asked, "What's eating you, Hattie? You look just like you used to."

"Oh, I know it's none of my business," she said, "but every time I've seen you since I came to California, you've had liquor on your breath. You ought to stop it, Sam. You'll end up being a drunken sot. Then sober men will steal the fortune you're always bragging about."

"Like hell they will!" he boasted. "I can drink with the best of them and never get drunk. I know how to hold my liquor. Besides, it never gets the best of me. I can take it or leave it alone."

"Then I'd say you better start leaving it alone," John said suddenly from his seat on the sofa. John was an abstemious man. He abhorred liquor after years of watching its effect on the men who had worked for him on his ship. "You talk like a fool. The man don't live that can drink like you and then leave it alone. Oh, no! There's nary a day passes that you stay sober all day. I've been watching you and hoping that you would check yourself, but you don't seem ever to be going to."

"That's just what I was trying to tell him," Hattie said mildly.

"Sam's his own worst enemy. He always was. It's the wild Brannan blood in him that's no good. It makes him wild and reckless. He never seems to have any judgment."

"Judgment!" Sam exploded. "I got more in my little finger that you two got in both your bodies put together. I'm the one that's rich and famous. And I got that way from using good judgment. When either of you can show better results than I can, then I'll listen to you."

"There's none so blind as them that don't want to see," John said quietly and let the subject drop.

When the new baby Lisa arrived—always later referred to as Lizzie by her father—Fanny wrote to tell Sam. He was pleased and happy and wrote back to ask whether he should come down. Fanny wrote saying that Ann Eliza would not consent to see him.

In the spring of 1854, however, she returned to the Bush Street house so that the children could have proper schooling. Fanny was waiting for Sam one morning when he arrived at the new Express Building. He kissed her on her withered cheek, helped her up the stairs, and ushered her into his office. She looked at the roll-top desk and the leather chairs.

"Got things pretty fancy, ain't you?" she said nervously.

Sam hung up his hat and motioned her to a chair. He sat down and waited for her to speak. She fumbled for words and then plunged into her message.

"Sam, ever since you and Ann Eliza busted up I been trying to reason with her. I tell her she's not acting right, but she won't listen. Of course, you ain't acted right either. I know how you've carried on; drinking, carousing around and running after those kind of women, but I tell her that all men act that way. At least, nearly all men. My husband didn't, thank God, but there's not many like him. Ann Eliza remembers him and thinks you ought to be the same, but I tell her you're different. Most men are polygamous, and that's the way you are. But no matter what you do, you're her husband, and I think she ought to cleave to you till death do you part, just like she promised the day she married you."

Sam shook his head gloomily. "Lizzie is a strong-willed woman.

When she makes up her mind to do a thing there ain't much that can change her."

"That's right. She won't give in to me an inch. The only place she's give in at all is where the younguns are concerned. She's consented to let me come and tell you that you can come home and see the younguns, if you want to. They keep asking for you and begging to see you. She says you can come up a couple of evenings a week, Wednesdays and Fridays. She's willing to have it that way in order to stop the gossip that is going around. People know there's trouble between you two, but she don't want them to know just how much."

Sam nodded. "Yes, I think she's right, for once. I've been doing a lot of thinking, and it's not exactly comfortable to me either for people to think we've separated. I've missed the younguns and I'll be mighty glad to romp with them again. As far as I'm concerned the arrangement is agreeable."

Fanny leaned forward. "Sam, there's something I want to know. Are you still in love with Ann Eliza?"

"I guess so," he said uneasily, but Fanny persisted.

"If you are, there's no guesswork about it. I want to know if you still love my daughter."

"Do you want the truth?" he asked. Fanny nodded.

"I like Lizzie, but I'm not in love with her the way I was when I married her. I respect her and I'd be content to live with her till she died, providing she'd take me on my own terms; but if I had to put up with her determination to make me over to suit her society notions, I'd soon quit even liking her. She's a fine woman in a lot of ways—too damned fine for me. If I could have my choice in the matter I'd pick a woman with less ideas and more love and affection. Still and all, as I said, I respect her and I'd live out my days with her if she was willing and would leave me be to live my life in my own way."

"The trouble with you, Sam Brannan, is that you never was in love in your whole life with anybody except yourself."

"What makes you talk like that?" he asked reproachfully.

"'Cause it's true. There's only one person in the world you're absolutely crazy about, and that's yourself. I don't think that anybody else could every really hurt you. You're all wrapped up in your own ideas, your own plans, and you don't have time for anything else. I believe you could lose Ann Eliza and the children and everything, and it wouldn't make any great difference to you so long as you could go along your own way, doing the things you want to do. Now would it?"

Sam pondered her words and then he shook his head. "I don't know, Fanny. I honestly can't answer that question."

"I think you'll know the answer to it someday," she said grimly.

"I don't think so," he said easily. "Lizzie will come to her senses one of these days, and we'll go back together just like we was before."

Fanny sat back in her chair. "You might. I ain't saying you won't, but my daughter is a determined woman. That's what's worrying me. She's still in love with you and she's eating out her heart over you. I'd feel a good deal encouraged if I knew that you felt the same way. I know now that you don't and never will."

"Well, then, if she's still in love with me there's every chance we can patch things up," Sam said smiling.

Fanny shook her head. "I don't think so. I don't think she'll ever forgive you."

"She'll have to wait a long time before I ever ask her to," he retorted.

The first time Sam went up to the house to see the children he took toys for all of them. Sammy, nine, was a handsome lad with his father's dark eyes and Celtic beauty. He took the Chinese junk his father offered—a handsome toy model—with delight in his eyes. Adelaide, at five, was quiet and selfish. She took the doll her father brought as if it was to be expected and did not even thank him. "Wait a minute, Addie," her father said sharply. "Stop and say 'thank you.' " She looked at him out of the corner of her eye and sullenly said "Thank you," and went away. Sam was not drawn to her as he was to the chattering, engaging baby Fanny, who, nearing her fourth year, was loved by everyone. When Sam gave her the Chinese doll he had brought, she climbed up on his knee to kiss him wetly on the mouth and hug him until he groaned in pretended exhaustion.

But Don, at two, was still his father's favorite. He was an exceptionally intelligent child, with wide eyes and questioning mind. He doted on his father and would not go to play with the other children so long as his father remained. Sam saw Lisa, his new daughter, with mixed feelings. She was an adorable baby, but he wished unconsciously that she had been another son. At the end of an hour Sam explained to the children that he must go back to town, and when they begged him to come live at home again, he said that his business kept him away for the time. Later, perhaps, he would be able to come home to stay. As he was leaving, Ann Eliza came into the front hall. She inquired about his health as a stranger might, and Sam looked at her with bewildered eyes. They were exceedingly polite to each other as he made his departure. Only Fanny was cordial and said that they would be happy to have him again on Friday.

In May came warm days, with no prevailing westerly wind. The city had made a poor disposition of its sewage, dumping it into the cove. The washing of the waves carried it up under the piles of the numerous wharves which ran out into the bay from every street that ended on the water front. On windless days San Francisco was an evil-smelling place. Cholera began to break out. The new hospital was soon filled to overflowing. Sam went his merry way unworried about the mild epidemic—there had been such small epidemics every year.

Shortly after their marriage, Lola Montez and her new husband had gone to Grass Valley to live. Now the papers said that Lola was back in town preparing to make a tour of Australia; her marriage to Patrick Hull had ended in disaster. Sam's clerk came in at ten one morning to announce Miss Montez. "Tell her I'm not in," Sam said. He took every precaution to make sure that he would not encounter her.

He was aroused in his hotel room one morning in mid-June by a violent knocking. "Who's there?" he growled sleepily.

"It's me, Sam. Fanny!"

Sam pulled on his pants and ran to open the door. "Come quick," she panted. "Little Don's awful sick and he keeps crying for you."

Sam threw on his clothes and hurried up the hill with Fanny. They were met at the door by Dr. Fitzpatrick. He took Sam into the bedroom where the tiny boy seemed lost in the immense rosewood bed. When Don saw his father he smiled happily. "You got to go to sleep and rest," Sam said as he knelt beside the bed and took his son's chubby hand in his own great paw. Sam was alarmed at the heat in the baby's flesh and looked questioningly across at Ann Eliza, who sat anxiously watching her baby son and occasionally pushing back the damp hair from his fevered forehead. She did not look up at Sam.

Sam remained in the house for the next twenty-four hours, watching beside Don's bed and walking distractedly up and down the parlor. But there was never any hope. When Sam stood and looked down at the dead face of his most beloved child, the hot tears ran down his cheeks and he felt that he could bear no more. He went around the bed and put his hands on Ann Eliza's shoulders as if to pull her to him that he might comfort her and in some measure be comforted. But she resisted him. He stumbled from the room into the parlor, and there Fanny came to him a few moments later. They clung to each other, Sam and this elderly second mother of his, and wept their grief away. After a long time he went back to town.

The next afternoon he rode in the carriage beside a wooden-faced Ann Eliza, who neither wept nor spoke. Fanny and the two older children sat opposite them as they drove to Yerba Buena cemetery, a desolate burying-ground in the sand dunes east of the city. In his wildest dreams Sam could not have imagined that a majestic City Hall would one day cover the very earth in which his dearly beloved son was put to rest.

The death of Don left a profound impression upon Sam. The first thing he did after the funeral was to get drunk. He stayed numbed by liquor for a week. At the end of that time he found that he still had his sorrow to conquer. To his brother John he expressed his feelings:

"I'll miss that baby more than I would have missed any other one of them, except maybe Fanny, my little girl. Don and Fanny were the only ones that really seem to care a damn for me. Their Ma is sort of turning the others against me. I don't think she'll have much luck with Fanny, and she wouldn't have had with Don either. I don't believe I'll ever get over losing him."

Sam put all his business affairs into the hands of his brother and sailed up the Sacramento River. He visited in Sacramento for a day or so, looking over the scenes of his old triumphs and recalling the time when he had had vast business interests there. These had all been liquidated and the money invested in San Francisco. Then he took a boat up the Feather River and looked over the huge ranch he had secured from Johann Sutter several years earlier. It was on the river a few miles below Yuba City. He decided that he would improve this land and perhaps devote himself entirely to ranching. He scoured the valley hunting for stock to place upon the choice bottom pasture lands of his ranch, and bought several cows and a few blooded horses, but they were not of as good a breed as he desired. One day, he determined, he would go to the States and to Europe and import the kind of stock he wanted. He remained for a week supervising the construction of a fence around his eighteen hundred acres of land. Then he became bored and restless. He took his buggy and one of the best mares and rode farther inland.

He found Placer County to be beautiful country. Ten thousand acres of the Keseberg ranch, comprising country which ran from the present Roseville to the tule lands of the Sacramento River, were his within a few days. Leet's Grove, an old landmark and a favorite picnicking spot, also came into his possession. In the years to come, Sam played host here to picnics sponsored by the Masonic Lodge and the Odd Fellows Lodge—historic picnics, remembered by old-timers for half a century.

When Sam tired of the quiet life of the country he returned to San Francisco and threw himself into another venture which he had dreamed about for years. Hearing that a ship carrying lumber had been wrecked off Point Lobos, he sought out its master and purchased the cargo. This he had hauled to the cliffs opposite the seal rocks, and there a long rambling structure was soon taking shape. The Seal Rocks House [84] had a spacious dance-hall and a dining room destined to become famous for its fine cuisine and for the sporting crowd that could always be found there. Staid, respectable people did not drive out to the Seal Rocks House on moonlit nights for their fun.

During the first three years of its existence Sam made a great deal of money from the venture, then its popularity began to wane in favor of other, newer places of entertainment; for six years, however, it was patronized by those of the younger set who wanted to break away and go where they could have entertainment without restraint.

At the end of six years a new palace of amusement was built south of Sam's Seal Rocks House; being much more ornate, and the newest thing, it took the last of Sam's patrons. Then Sam's old wooden building became a house of mystery, and young couples who came out to the new Cliff House would stop to peer into its blank-looking, cobwebbed windows, and go away to tell stories of ghosts that haunted the musty old building.

Late in 1854 Sam set out once more for New York City. He finished his business with his bankers and then took the ferry over to Brooklyn. He liked the look of the little city, for it had houses which were homes rather than mere buildings, and many of them had attractive lawns and gardens. He had not renewed the lease on the Sixteenth Street house, and decided accordingly to lease a house in Brooklyn. It took him only a day's search to find just what he wanted.

He was living in this house when, in December of 1854, he wrote to Ebenezer Childs in Washington, D. C., in answer to a letter Childs had written. Childs, acting as intermediary for Talbot Green, rightfully known as Paul Geddes, had written to Sam asking him to help Green re-establish himself in society.[81] Sam wrote to say that he would do all he could to help his former friend, whom he had not seen in three years. Then Sam had a letter from Howard in San Francisco saying that Green was writing to him constantly for money. Now he was pressing Howard to buy out his share in the partnership, so that Green could pay back the money he had embezzled and thus find himself free to return to San Francisco and to an active business life. Green had been hiding in Tennessee ever since he had run away from the Coast. But Howard explained to Sam that he was in no financial position to give Green any large sum of money. For three years the man had contributed nothing to the partnership, and Howard had been turning over monthly checks to the deserted widow Montgomery, Green's bigamous wife. Meanwhile Henry Mellus had sued Howard for a larger settlement than he had originally obtained, claiming that he had signed an agreement while not in his right mind. Although Mellus had lost the suit, fighting it had cost Howard a good deal of money, and now that his own health was failing, so was his fortune. Sam sent an appeal to Thomas Larkin, former employer of Green at Monterey, to send money to Green. Larkin and Howard evidently made some arrangement in San Francisco, for Green eventually received six hundred dollars from Howard, forwarded to him through Childs.

In February of 1855 Sam wrote to Childs that he had not lost confidence in Green, and that if he would send Talbot to Brooklyn he, Sam, would do everything he could to help him clear up his early mistake. "Green has many friends still left in San Francisco and he could walk through Montgomery Street with a head as erect as any man there, and meet with none but friends," Sam's letter said.

On March 3, 1855, Talbot Green arrived at the Brooklyn house. On the sixteenth he wrote: "Friend Larkin: Mr. Brannan has done all he promised. He has settled up all and everything. T. H. Green."

Sam urged Talbot Green to return with him to San Francisco and start over again. The newspapers said that Sam was going to take the errant businessman into his own firm in order to re-establish him. They took boat and sailed south. At the Isthmus of Panama they rode across the miles of jungle on the new railroad and found it much less enervating than the old mule and boat trip. Their ship left Panama in September. The two men spent many of their hours in the salon playing cards and drinking with other businessmen.

Arrived in San Francisco, Sam did his best to effect a reconciliation between Talbot and the widow Montgomery, but she would have none of her former partner. Instead she secured an annulment of her bigamous marriage and left the city. Talbot could not overcome his past. He went about with a hangdog look, his old push and vigor gone. He looked and acted like a man whom life had thoroughly beaten. He did not go into business with Sam, but simply hung around the streets for a few months and then disappeared. Sam never heard from him again and supposed that he had returned to his wife in Tennessee, where there were now several grown children.

Sam still lived in his room at the Oriental Hotel and went daily to his office in the Express Building. There he found Harriet awaiting him one morning. He ushered her into his private office and waited for her to speak.

"I want a divorce," she said abruptly. Sam pondered her words for a time.

"If you get a divorce here, the cat will be out of the bag. Everyone will know that Lizzie is a bigamous wife. None of us could ever live the scandal down."

"But I got to have a divorce," she protested. "I'm in love with someone else and I want to marry him and have a family by him. I'm still young enough to have the kind of life I'm entitled to."

Sam got up and began to walk back and forth so that he could think more clearly. At last he turned to her. "All right, Hattie. We'll work it out some way. You've had a dog's life so far, and you're entitled to better treatment. I hope this man will give it to you. What's his name?"

"Whitney."

"What does he do?"

"Nothing right now. I was hoping you could give me some kind of a money settlement so that we could start up a ranch or something of our own."

"H'mmm. That don't sound so good. However, I'll see that you get enough to buy a ranch. You realize, don't you, that a divorce is going to cause scandal for you? Decent people will never speak to you again."

She looked worried and fumbled with her handkerchief. "I can't help it," she said at last. "As it is I'm neither wife nor maid. I'm sick of it."

Sam paced back and forth. At last he stopped with an "I've got it" look. "Tell you what, Hattie. You take the boat down to Los Angeles. It's just a dinky little place, but it's got courts and lawyers. You get your divorce there and no one up here will ever know about it. When you come back I'll have your settlement all ready for you."

Hattie eventually did as he planned. When she returned, she married Whitney and went to live in Petaluma. Almira went with her and adopted the name of Whitney. She was to see little of her father; eventually she was to marry a man named Hudson and have two sons. Both died young.

The San Francisco of 1856 was a city which was rapidly reaching maturity. Many large brick buildings lined the main streets and business rushed hurriedly through their doors. The cove was filled in, so that many blocks of buildings stood between Montgomery Street—

its first water front street—and the bay. Stately clipper ships moored alongside the numerous wharves, which were still being extended out into the bay as the filling-in process continued. The trend of improvement was toward the south and west. Russian Hill had several very fine homes upon it, competing with Rincon Hill as an elaborate residential district. However, many of the older citizens clung to their beautiful houses on First and Second streets and all the cross-streets between.

The year of '56 saw the formation of a second and larger Vigilance Committee, in which Sam took only a minor part because of the fact that he was away from the city when it came into being. He was immersed in a history-making project: a railroad for California.

Theodore D. Judah, the brilliant civil engineer, had surveyed the land and had talked to Sam and other wealthy men about building a railroad in California. It was to run from Sacramento to Folsom and was to tap the rich Placer regions. At last they had agreed to finance his plan. All through 1855 construction had been going on, and the grading crew had often uncovered gold on the roadbed. Even now the old rails still rest on "pay dirt." William Sherman, now in charge of the bank which employed him, was financially involved along with Sam.

On Washington's Birthday in 1856 the first leg of the railroad was complete and the initial run was to be made.[85] The engine which was to pull the train was Sam's old "Elephant," which he had had shipped around the Horn in 1849. She had been taken from her barn and hauled up the Sacramento River on a boat.

A great crowd had collected at the new depot in Sacramento on Washington's natal day, and when Sam arrived with Sherman, Judah and his wife were up on the platform with the mayor waiting to break a bottle of champagne on the nose of the "C. K. Garrison." Sam was as proud of this engine as if he were its father. It was a woodburner equipped with a large funnel-shaped smokestack. It had a hook motion with a half stroke cut-off, of the 4–4–0 type with inside cylinders 15 by 20 inches, and a driving wheel 71 inches in diameter. This miracle of power was trimmed now with red, white, and blue bunting and flags. Mrs. Judah broke the bottle of champagne; the engine was officially named. Then the Governor mounted the platform and gave a long, pompous address upon the importance of this new enterprise. When he had finished, the crowd applauded dutifully. The dignitaries descended from the platform; those who were to ride on the train got into the three cars and took their seats. The engineer tooted the whistle. Sam and Tecumseh Sherman sat facing each other as the train slowly began to move.

"Well, Mr. Sherman, we're making history today," Sam said.

"Not enough to suit me," Sherman said grumpily. "We'd have made more history if we could have built this road through to Marysville, like Judah planned we could. Then we could have tapped the mining region and been sure of a return on our investment. As it is, I think we're only pouring money in a hole."

Sam laughed ruefully. "Well, let's hope not. Judah didn't tell us before we started that it was going to cost us $60,000 a mile."

"No, I don't think he'd have started the project in the first place if he'd ever dreamed it would cost that much. I know I wouldn't have put my money in if *I'd* known it."

"Me neither," Sam agreed. "But anyway we've got it as far as Folsom. We can sit back and let the road pay us something for a while, and then maybe when it's self-supporting we can extend it. If we can ever get it up as far as Marysville and then north into the Sacramento Valley, where the rich farm lands are, and south through Stockton to the bay, we'll have a real money-maker on our hands."

Sherman laughed shortly. "You got too much imagination, Brannan. We'll never do it."

"We might," Sam said optimistically. "Why, we'll make money on it, short as it is. When you stop to realize that a lot of folks have come here from hundreds of miles to see this train—the first most of them have ever seen—and that they'll all want to ride on it sooner or later, you can see that we'll probably make money hand over fist."

"Not enough to make it pay us to build it farther at the rate of sixty thousand dollars a mile," Sherman said skeptically. And he proved to be right.

When Sam returned to San Francisco he found the newly formed Vigilance Committee functioning under the presidency of William Coleman. Five thousand members were enrolled. Sam rushed to the rooms of Truett and Truett, on Sacramento Street, to register his own name. On the Sunday following its formation, the committee sent thirty thousand armed men to fetch the gambler Cora and the crooked politician Casey from the jail to the committee for trial. A few hours later the men hung from gibbets erected outside the second story windows of the committee rooms. Casey had murdered Sam's former associate on the executive committee of the first Vigilance Committee, James King of William. After a few short weeks of this second Vigilance, law and order returned to San Francisco, this time permanently.

Sam met Thomas Larkin, one evening, just as he was leaving his office. They shook hands, heartily glad to see each other. "What brings you down to San Francisco?" Sam inquired.

"I've got some business with Bill Howard."

"Well, then you're going my way. The Howards live in my hotel. We can all have a drink together." The two men went swinging along the street, talking of a dozen mutually interesting subjects. As they neared the hotel Sam said, "Bill is a mighty sick man. He's changed; lost all his fat. He began to feel bad before he struck out for Boston, a year or so ago, and when he come back I could see that he was getting worse. He keeps moving around tending to his business, but he's not much longer for this world."

"I'd heard that," Larkin admitted, "but I hoped it wasn't so. He's a fine man and I'd sure grieve to see him go."

"We all would," Sam agreed moodily. When they entered the lobby of the Oriental Hotel Sam stopped to speak to an acquaintance and Larkin went on in search of Howard. He asked the clerk at the desk if Howard was in his room, and the clerk replied, "No, he's sitting somewhere here in the lobby. Do you know him by sight?"

"Yes, I'll find him," Larkin responded. He wandered across to a group of chairs, letting his eyes wander over the faces in them. A thin, haggard-looking man directly in front of him cried out, "Larkin, don't you intend to speak to me? Don't you know me?" Larkin looked into the man's face and uttered an exclamation of surprise. "Bill! I didn't recognize you!"

"My God, have I changed that much?" Howard cried. Larkin

could see that Howard was shaken by the revelation, but after a moment he smiled uncertainly and motioned Larkin to the chair next to him. A moment later Sam joined them. "Come on in the bar and we'll have a drink," he invited, but Howard gestured wearily with his hand. "Not tonight, Brannan. I'm not up to it."

Sam talked to them for a few moments and then started to go to his room. At the foot of the stairs he was intercepted by his son, Sammy, now a gentlemanly lad of eleven. He was too quiet for Sam's taste; Sam liked boisterous, rough boys. He still regularly visited his children.

"Grandma's had a heart attack. The doctor says she won't live long, and she wants to see you," Sammy explained.

Without a word Sam went with his son. When they arrived, Ann Eliza met them at the door. Her eyes were swollen with weeping. She took Sam to her mother's bed. He drew up a chair and sat down beside the old lady. When he spoke her name she opened her eyes.

"Oh, it's you, Sam," she said quietly. "Bring Ann Eliza. I want to talk to both of you." Ann Eliza came within range of her mother's sight and stood waiting.

"I can't die happy until I know you two are going to make up," she said, and her words came hard.

"I'm willing if Lizzie is," Sam said quickly.

"I'll try," Ann Eliza said.

Fanny shook her head back and forth petulantly. "That ain't enough," she moaned. "It does seem like you could do one last little thing for me."

"It may seem little to you but it's not to me," Ann Eliza answered sharply. The doctor stepped forward and touched her arm. "Don't excite her," he whispered. "She only has minutes."

Fanny was looking at her with wide eyes. Ann Eliza leaned forward and patted her mother's cheek gently. "I'll do it, Ma."

"Promise?" Fanny asked and tried to sit up.

"I promise!" Ann Eliza cried out. "You must keep quiet, Ma. You've got to."

"I will," Fanny said dutifully and relaxed. "I can rest now, anyway, knowing that I've got that settled."

Half an hour later Fanny died, smiling peacefully. As soon as she knew that her mother was gone, Ann Eliza burst into hysterical weeping. Sam took her in his arms, and some emotion that she had kept dammed up for years broke down and she clung to him like an unhappy child.

Sam did not go back to the hotel. He had his things moved into Fanny's old room and waited patiently for Ann Eliza to accept him back as a husband. But this Ann Eliza did not do. She seemed overcome by the shock of her mother's death and spent so much time weeping that Sam cast about for something which would divert her. At last he fell upon a happy suggestion.

"Let's take the younguns and go to Europe for a nice trip," he suggested one evening [86] at dinner, which was served by the Chinese cook who had been with Ann Eliza for more than a year. For the first time in weeks Ann Eliza showed an interest.

"Europe," she said musingly. "I'd like that. I've always dreamed about going there. I wish I could have the children educated there, where they could learn to talk French and be real cultured. I don't want them to grow up to have ideas like most of the people that live here in San Francisco. I want them to be real ladies and gentlemen."

"All anybody needs to make them a real lady or a real gentleman is a little consideration for the other feller," Sam reproved her, looking around at the children so that they would pay heed to his words. "It don't matter how little education a man has got; if he considers other people's feelings and tries to make them feel at ease, he's a gentleman."

"That's true," Ann Eliza agreed, "but I've got big hopes for our family. I want them to have all the advantages that money can buy. A good education will help them socially and financially and every other way. I want them to have some schooling in Europe."

"Well, I don't know about any schooling in Europe, but I do know that a trip will do us all good."

Sam read the paper in the parlor while Ann Eliza herded the children off to bed. When she came in to say good night Sam motioned her to a chair.

"We may just as well have an understanding now, Lizzie. When are we going to be man and wife again?"

Ann Eliza sat stiffly in the chair, her eyes on the nervous fingers in her lap. At last she faced him determinedly.

"Never, Sam. For the sake of the children I'm willing to live in the same house with you and let people think that we are a united family, but that's as far as I'll go. I told you once, after you'd made yourself a laughing-stock by chasing that notorious hussy, that I'd never share a bed with you again. For a long time after I left you, I still loved you and grieved over you. But that's gone now. I'm dependent on you for a living, and for that reason I feel that I owe it to you to make as good a home as I can for you. I'll do it, too, but I'll not share you with half the women in San Francisco. Go and stay in brothels all night if you want to, or stay out until dawn at noisy parties for stage hussies and stagger home blind drunk. I'll not care. Because I won't be sharing you with any one. You said once that you belonged to San Francisco more than to your family. It was true then and it's true now. Belong to it. I don't care."

Sam was angry. It wasn't that he particularly wanted Ann Eliza to resume a marital relationship with him. He simply hated to be frustrated in anything he desired, and right now he wanted to resume his marriage.

"Then I'll not support you, nor will I take you to Europe or any place else. I've got a few rights as a husband, you know."

Ann Eliza arose. "I won't fight or argue with you, Sam Brannan. You don't have to take me to Europe if you don't want to. But you'll support me all right. If you don't do it willingly I'll go to court and have a legal settlement made."

He said violent words to her then, and she retorted with even more violence and soon they were yelling at each other. Finally, exhausted at last, Ann Eliza fell into hysterical weeping and ran from the room. The next morning Sam begged for forgiveness and promised that he would not quarrel with her again. The plan for a trip to Europe was broached once more and this time they found harmony in their mutual planning.

It was summer when they sailed south on the Pacific Mail steamship for Panama. The children were enchanted with everything: the vastness of the Pacific, the new railroad across the Isthmus, and all the monkeys and birds of brilliant plumage in the tropical forest through which the train passed. Arrived at New York, the family took up its abode in the Brooklyn house so that Ann Eliza could shop for clothes for herself and the children before they set sail for Europe. At the end of two weeks the Brannans went aboard the palatial ocean steamer which would take them to Liverpool. New York papers had carried several articles about Sam Brannan and his great wealth, and there were those on board who had read the articles and who paid homage to him because of his money. Among them were two or three Englishmen who privately laughed at his blatancy and crude manners, but who pretended friendship because they hoped to benefit financially through knowing him. Sam accepted them at face value, as cultured continentals who accepted him as an equal.

The found the London hotel damp and uncomfortable even in July, and Sam grew furious every morning when he could not get water hot enough for comfortable shaving. When one of their shipboard friends invited them down to his country house for a week, Sam accepted with alacrity. There were other house guests and it was their custom to go out early in the morning, dressed in red coats which they called pink, with a pack of hounds, to chase a fox over adjacent farms. Sam declined such sport.

"Naw," he said, "I wouldn't have fun doing that kind of hunting. Out in California when we want to hunt we go up in the mountains and hunt bears. That's real sport. A slap of his paw and one of those bears can lay a man's insides open. You don't take dogs to corner him, nor sit safe on a horse. You get within reaching distance and shoot, and hope you'll kill him with the first bullet."

"That must be delightful," one of the ladies said with a *moue* of disgust. Sam caught the sarcasm and turned away cursing under his breath. He could not understand these people, and they could not understand him. Ann Eliza chided him later, in the privacy of their own suite. "Don't keep talking about California and how much better everything is there. These people look down on us both because you brag so much."

"Now you look here," Sam said heatedly. "Don't you start using the spurs on me. I've had about enough." Ann Eliza flung out of the room.

He watched a group of men playing a silly game they called "golf," in which they walked over well-trimmed lawns to hit a little ball with sticks. He was bored after half an hour and tramped back to the house alone. He went into the library, picked up a London paper, and sat down in a high-backed chair by the fire to read. He was gratified to find an article about himself, telling how wealthy he was and how he had gained his wealth. The article said that he was planning to go to Scotland to purchase sheep to stock his California ranches and added that he might stay for the shooting. "Shooting!" Sam thought to himself. "These fellers don't know anything about shooting. They're too damned ladylike to get out and indulge in he-man sports." No sir! He didn't want any of their shooting, nor any other of their damned folderol. Two women drifted into the room, and when his name was mentioned their conversation caught his attention. One of them was his hostess.

"He's just like something out of a book," the young woman was saying. "He wears such extreme clothes and gets himself up in wide ties and flashy diamonds until he looks like a typical American in a music-hall comedy."

"Well, I don't suppose we should criticize," the hostess replied. "After all, he doesn't know any better. I don't suppose he ever went to school and he hasn't the slightest conception of manners or culture; but he is rich, my dear! After all, that excuses a lot of bragging and a lot of vulgarity."

"It certainly does," the other agreed. "I could forgive his loud clothes and his bragging too, if only he didn't have that harsh, American twang when he speaks. It sounds as if he were talking through his nose and trying to make every consonant hurt your ears."

"Americans are dreadful people," the hostess sighed. "His wife is even worse than he is with her pretensions. Her mother probably took in washing, but she pretends to be a society woman. She doesn't fool anyone but herself. At least her husband is just himself and doesn't pretend to be something he isn't. And those children! Such lack of breeding and such English as they use! This San Francisco must be a horrible place to send children to school. I'll be heartily glad when their visit is over and we can be rid of them."

Sam was furiously angry. He arose and confronted the astounded gossipers. "Not half as glad as I will to get out of here," he roared.

"Talk about bad manners! You people could teach any American a lesson in how not to be ladies. At least when we invite people to our houses we give them the best we got and don't talk about them every time we think they're out of earshot. If you two are ladies, God save me from any more."

He stalked out of the room, climbed the stairs, and waited for his family to gather. Then he bundled them all into a carriage from the village and headed for the station and the train for London.

When Sam purchased longhair Merino sheep in Scotland, the Edinburgh papers were filled with fabulous stories of the American millionaire. Sam and his family saw the beauties of the country and then traveled to Ireland and visited Waterford, the home town of the Brannan clan.

From Ireland they went back to London and took the boat across to France. While Ann Eliza and the children saw the sights of Paris, Sam went into the French countryside to buy grape cuttings and sheep, and to study farming methods.

To Spain and Germany and Italy they went, stopping at all the famous watering places. Sam bought blooded Arabian horses in Spain. In Italy he bought more grape cuttings and more sheep. Whenever he saw a tree or a shrub or an extra fine animal, he bought it. All these purchases he directed home to San Francisco by way of the Horn. And wherever the rich Americans traveled they were met with a deluge of newspaper publicity about their wealth. Many silly fabulous stories were told about Sam, and he had them all translated for him, and grinned, denying not even the most far-fetched. He loved all this adulation.

They wound up their tour in Switzerland in a hotel in Geneva, on the beautiful lake. Sam was tired. He arose late one morning and walked out onto the verandah of their suite, where he stood watching the boats moving on the surface of the lake. Then he turned back to Ann Eliza, who sat knitting in the drawing-room. Down below Sam could see the children playing on the lawn and laughing happily. Sam went inside and drew up a chair so that he could talk to Ann Eliza.

"Don't you think it's about time we began to think of going home, old girl?"

She looked up startled. "No," she said. "I thought you understood that me and the younguns are going to stay here for a year or two."

"A year or two? What for?"

"I'm going to put the children in school here. I thought you understood. I told you before ever we left San Francisco that that was the main reason I wanted to come to Europe. It's almost time for school to open and I've made arrangements for all of them but Lisa to start next week."

Sam flew into a rage. He swore that he would not give in to her; that he would refuse to give her money. He resorted to all sorts of threats, but she would not yield. He had known before he started the argument that she would have her way; but Samuel Brannan had never learned to give in graciously. He sailed for home alone a few days later.

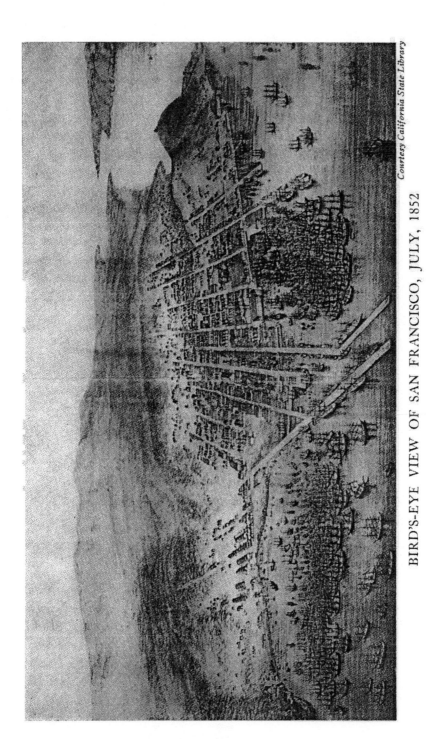

BIRD'S-EYE VIEW OF SAN FRANCISCO, JULY, 1852

Drawn from Merriam's model and nature

FIRST CALIFORNIA RAILROAD

Chapter XXIII

AFTER 142 DAYS on the water, the new Brannan fire engine arrived on the clipper *Bostonian*. This was on January 13, 1857, just a few weeks after Sam himself reached home.

The fire engine had been building since 1853, and when Sam and John went down to the warehouse after it was uncrated, they felt that the wait had been worth while. This was certainly the most beautiful piece of fire-fighting equipment the world had ever seen. Every portion of its metal frame was overlaid with pure silver. Painters of ability had pictured a lake on the left side of the box; a lake which contained a boating party and had a background of trees and houses. On the right side was a view of Niagara Falls from the Canadian side. Upon one face of the bulbous air-chamber, three females and a swan played, in brilliant colors, in a pool. On the other side a group of Englishmen in pink coats rode forth to the hunt. Sam's nose wrinkled when he saw this painting, but he forgot his distaste for the English in his enthusiasm for the beauty of the whole. It was a symphony of green, gold, silver, and the richest red. Surmounting the whole unit were gleaming cut-glass lanterns and buckets of red and gold. Sam pointed out the twenty-foot pumping levers to his brother. "We can use forty-four men on those pumps."

"Yes, sir," John said admiringly, "she is certainly a beauty! She ought to be though, costing you ten thousand dollars."

A few minutes later the members of the Brannan Protective Association began to drift into the warehouse to see their pride and joy. Sam went around and around the engine with each newcomer, exclaiming over this and pointing out that. At last he felt he would not be satisfied until every one in San Francisco had seen it. "I'm going to give a reception party for our company," he told the president of the fire company, "a reception for our new fire engine. We'll have a big banquet and ask every important man in town to it. And the next morning we'll have a parade, and you men will all wear your new uniforms and pull the engine down the street."

A few days later the *Alta California* wrote: "Those who have not secured tickets for the Brannan Reception Ball at Musical Hall tonight, should not fail to do so as it will, undoubtedly, be the grandest affair of the season."

Sam led the grand march on the night of the ball. Dancing lasted until ten o'clock. Then the doors were thrown open into the banquet hall, where long tables were laden with fish, squab, roast fowl, champagne, and wine of rare vintages. Proceeds from the ticket sale went into the fire company's treasury. Sam paid the bill for the expenses.

Next day's papers were filled with detailed stories of the night's events, and with effusive praise for the rich and generous first citizen, Samuel Brannan, Esq. But there was more to come. The Brannan Association, in red uniforms, every brass button gleaming, hauled their prize beauty at the head of a giant parade in which every fire company of the city took part. City officials rode horses or sat in flag-bedecked carriages between battalions of fire companies. At noon the marchers came to a halt in front of the Rassette House at Bush and Sansome streets. Sam came out to usher his guests into the famous hostelry for lunch at his own expense. He sat at the head of the long table and beamed upon all and sundry; he was in an expansive mood. This was one of his dreams come true, this reality wherein a whole city paid tribute to his wealth and power.

Sam had been laying plans for a long time, to open a bank. Since all his property was community property he could not pledge it in trust to cover deposits unless Ann Eliza signed over a power of attorney to him to act for her portion. Sam had sent her the proper papers to fill out immediately upon his return from Europe, and had written her setting forth his plans. He waited impatiently for the papers to return. Meanwhile the cattle, the horses, the sheep, the grape cuttings, the trees and shrubs that he had bought in Europe, began to trickle into San Francisco as freight boats arrived after their long voyages around the Horn.

Sam traveled up to his farm at Nicholaus to supervise the construction of a large ranch house on the property, and the placing of his blooded stock on the land as it arrived on river boats from the bay. Sam was a lover of beauty and all his dreams of beauty went into his ranch house, which he planned to name the "White House." When completed it would have eight rooms, with a fireplace in each, and would be a story and a half high, with a beautiful winding stairway going up from the front hall. The trees and shrubs he had imported from Europe were arranged by his gardeners to landscape the spacious grounds. Singing fountains and shady pools graced wide lawns. Here, in years to come, he would give royal entertainment to all the wit and beauty of San Francisco; gay river-boat parties were soon traveling up to Brannan's farm with their quota of celebrities, rich men, and famous beauties on every trip.

But Sam's feverish activities were halted by an occurrence which shook him to the core. News was brought to him that William Howard was dead. Sam went back to the city and joined a funeral procession which was truly representative of the spirit of San Francisco. The city was shocked and grieved by the death of one of its favorite sons, and Sam felt no shame when he wept openly for the loss of a dear and very great friend.

In September he was back inland. He traveled up the San Joaquin to buy more rich marshlands, and he thought of the time when, as a pioneer, he had been the one to open this very land to cultivation. It was in the San Joaquin Valley, on lands which he drained and reclaimed for pasture, that he eventually placed most of his sheep from Scotland, Italy, and Switzerland.

When he returned to San Francisco he found the letter from Ann Eliza that he had been waiting for so long. The power of attorney had been signed by her in the name of Ann Lisa Brannan on February 20, 1857. It had been witnessed by Nathaniel Bolton, U. S. Consul at Geneva, and his wife, Sarah T. Bolton.

On October 21, 1857, the Brannan Bank opened its doors to the public. The building was on the northeast corner of Montgomery and California streets. A circular announced that deposits were secured by a pledge in trust of ten parcels of real estate, most of which were productive; after listing the properties, which included Armory Hall, the Express Building, and the California Building, it stated that the value of the holdings totaled four hundred and fifty thousand dollars.

It was as a banker that Sam came into his own. He had reached the pinnacle of all his dreams. He had money, power, was the acknowledged financial leader of the city and the titan to whom all other businessmen deferred; and now he sat on the throne labelled "king." As president of the bank that bore his name he had the robes and crown which proclaimed him what he had long been.

John Brannan, hard-working, conscientious, sober, took the full responsibility of managing all the many ramifications which went to make up Sam's business activities. Sam let him do the work and basked in the glory. He came to his office a little before ten in the morning and went slowly down the length of the marble floor, calling bright "good mornings" to all his employees, swinging his gold-headed cane and carrying his high hat. When he entered his own private sanctum he let his eyes dwell lovingly on the deep leather chairs, the brass trimmings (which must always be polished until they looked like burnished gold), and the rich oak desk and tables. He would hang his hat and cane on the many-armed hatrack and sit down in his swivel chair before the roll-top desk. Then his clerk entered to lay papers before him to sign. If they had John's signature initialled in the corner, Sam signed without investigation. If they had not been thus approved, Sam instructed the clerk to take them to John in the next room.

Every morning there were people waiting to see Sam: a man who wanted a loan for which he could give no security, a woman left widowed and asking for charity, a man who wanted a favor, and sometimes just a beggar. Sam had left orders that any person who wanted to see him must be given access to him. He had an immense curiosity about people and a deep sympathy with the unfortunate. He would listen to their stories, ask questions, ferret out what might seem unimportant details, and if he felt they were deserving of help, he gave it. If he felt that they were trying to impose on him, he told them so in blunt words and had them put out without ceremony. But no one ever found him an easy mark. If he helped a man once, and that man returned again with a woeful tale, Sam would scourge him with bitter words.

Sam had initiated a plan of deposit insurance which made his clients' investments secure. As there was a shortage of currency in the city's business life, and coin was still being issued by private assay offices, Sam took it upon himself to help in solving the problem these two conditions had brought about. He began issuing his own currency. The editor of the *Evening Bulletin* took umbrage at this. In the issue of November 16, 1857, he attacked the bank's policies. The *Bulletin's* editor was amazed and indignant when he went into a local restaurant and offered one of Sam's bills as payment for his meal and the manager of the restaurant accepted it without question. He referred to Sam's notes as "shin-plaster currency," and described them as having pictures of Washington and Franklin on the face, and on the back a view of Mormon Island with Mormons digging gold while an iron horse stood waiting to carry it away. The editor knew full well when he wrote "Mormon" that he would make Sam wince, for the very word fell hard on his ears of late. How the editor could tell that the miners were Mormons and the location Mormon Island, he did not reveal. But to Sam the pictures had a deeper meaning. The pictures of Washington and Franklin embodied his love for the country which he had once accused of betrayal; the "diggings" were the basis of his wealth, and the train was the symbol of the hope he held for California's future, in which he had already sunk a small fortune to bring it to partial fruition.

The *Bulletin's* editor was not the only person who objected to the new currency. The *Alta California*, which had grown out of Sam's initial newspaper venture, published a story on January 13, 1858, about one man's effort to have Sam indicted by the Grand Jury for circulating paper money. The attempt came to nothing. The Brannan Bank was a safe institution and a prosperous one. For the next five years it held its position as one of the city's soundest financial establishments.

While Sam was riding the crest of the wave, Lola Montez returned to San Francisco from her Australian tour. The papers were filled with stories of her latest love affair, which had ended on shipboard, a few days previously, when her young lover jumped overboard. As a result, the newspapers intimated, Lola had become mentally affected. Sam read the articles and wondered if a sight of this woman would arouse the old quickening of the pulse which she had once set up in him.

Lola settled down in a small iron building not far from the plaza. Sam passed it one day and noted that gorgeously plumaged birds hung in all the windows in lacquered cages. Lola was definitely still Lola—eccentric in every way. He strode on past and turned up toward the plaza. When he reached the lower corner he started to cut across diagonally. A small, lithe feminine figure appeared on the slope, walking down toward him from the opposite side. He recognized the sway of the hips and paused. She was dressed all in black and would have presented a somber picture but for the magnificent white cockatoo perched on her shoulder. Half a dozen dogs trotted contentedly at her heels. The bird screamed and talked as it rocked on the frail shoulder of the swiftly moving figure. Sam determined to see the encounter through and moved directly toward the little cavalcade. When they were within a few feet of each other, Lola's eyes lighted suddenly with recognition and she started to smile. It was only a promise of a smile which died quickly, and she looked at him coldly and passed by. Sam went swiftly past her; for a moment he was caught by an elusive perfume which called up a thousand conflicting emotions. Then she was gone. When he reached the high corner he turned and looked back, but there was no sign of Lola. Sam shook his head sadly. Truly, Montez had changed in looks as well as in actions. The old beauty, the old allure was gone. She was a little "cracked," the papers had hinted. Sam was content to let sleeping dogs lie.

Chapter XXIV

IF SAM HAD LOVED extremes in style when he was a coming industrialist, now that he had arrived there was no limit to his vagaries in taste. Each day saw him emerge in a new outfit, different in every small detail. He invariably wore a silk top hat; but not the same one. His goatee he wore trimmed to a fine point. His snowy linen was always set off with a wide silk black tie, fastened with a great diamond pin. His waistcoats were of brocaded or embossed satin, usually white, with lapels and diamond studs. His watch-chain of heavy gold was looped across his vest and attached to a Swiss watch of finest workmanship. It struck the hours. Sam's favorite costume was the latest cut of dark coat, short in front and running to a long tail at the back. Wide revers finished the front. Buff nankeen trousers, skin-tight and fastened under polished boots, showed off his clean-cut limbs to perfection. Some of his suits were in shades of dark blue, some in brown and tan; for business meetings he wore black broadcloth.

Sam always thought of himself as a Lord Bountiful; he was not only interested in helping unfortunate individuals, but could not refuse organizations which came begging for support. Eventually he found himself playing patron saint to libraries, churches, military companies (mainly the California Guard), hospitals (including those set up by the Odd Fellows and the Masons); and finally, struggling painters, authors, and even singers.

The days of the gold rush were so recent that no one was interested in putting them into literature; no one, that is, except Sam Brannan. He advertised that he would finance anyone who would write an epic about the gold rush. His enemies said that he wanted an epic written because he hoped to be the hero of it. One paper suggested that the great poem be patterned after the *Argonauts*, with Sam as Jason, Michael Reese as Theseus, and the editor of the *Union* as Orpheus. Nettled by this sarcasm, Sam announced that he would pay for the publication of any genuine collection of Western poetry.

California writers laughed publicly in the prints at this announcement. "What does Sam Brannan, that gold-lined Philistine, know about the arts?" one of them asked. Sam showed them. Eventually he financed the publication of *Poetry of the Pacific*, edited by May Wentworth and published by H. H. Bancroft in 1866. There were those who said that Sam might pay to advance the arts, but it was their belief that he would not go so far as to read the books he "angeled."

It was true that great artists came to San Francisco and that Sam gave fabulous entertainments for some of them; but it was true also that he never suffered through their performances. When Gottschalk, the great pianist, came to San Francisco to give a concert, he called upon banker Brannan in his office to discuss a benefit performance, and found him sitting before his desk with his boot off. As the clerk announced Gottschalk, Sam was solicitously rubbing the big toe of his right foot. Sam was a man of importance in San Francisco; he could see no good reason for rising for some itinerant musician. He waved towards a chair with his free hand as he continued to massage his aching toe, and the great musician sat down.

"Gottschalk, Gottschalk?" Sam muttered, trying to place the name. Then his eyes lighted up. "Oh, you're the feller that's come to town to give a concert. What do you sing, tenor or bass?"

"I play the piano," Gottschalk said with dignity, a look of disdain on his face.

Sam stretched out and placed his tired foot on another chair. "Piano," he said conversationally. "Can't say as I care much about listening to a feller play a piano for a whole evening. Gets too tiresome."

Suddenly Gottschalk arose from his chair. He looked at Sam as if he thought the westerner were out of his mind. "If you will excuse me," he bleated, and bolted from the room. Sam sat looking after him with surprise in his eyes and thought he heard the muttered word "barbarian" as the door closed.[87]

Ultimately the story of Gottschalk's interview with Sam reached the newspapers, and Charles Henry Webb in referring to Sam called him "a thing of booty and a bore forever." Sam never lived that title down and it never ceased to irk him.

In 1859 Sam secured title, through the bank, to a square mile of land in Napa Valley adjacent to the small farm he already owned there. The location had once been known as Agua Caliente because of the natural hot springs found upon it, but Sam had changed its name to Calistoga. When he stood upon the newly purchased ground and surveyed the surrounding valley, he felt that this was a good investment. It would make an ideal place for a health resort, where hot sulphur baths could be made available. He purchased more and more land, until his estate exceeded two thousand acres. A few miles away were many geysers which would prove an attraction to tourists. Sam had seen all the famous watering places of Europe, and he felt that he could make his Calistoga estate into one that would put them all to shame. During the next ten years he was to pour half a million dollars into this estate.

At first he sold a lot or so at a time to settlers who wished to move to Calistoga; then, as he continued to buy more land, he began to promote the part of it that he wished to convert into a settlement. He made every inducement to get people to come to the little valley, which was entirely surrounded by the mountains of the Coast Range —an ideal pleasure spot which knew sunshine the year round and would grow any kind of fruit from the northern apple to the semitropical fig. He wanted a little town to grow up near his resort, so that when it should be put into operation there would be stores and shops to take care of the wants of health-seekers who would come there to live for a part of each year.

In 1860 Sam began the erection of a mammoth resort-hotel in his Calistoga grounds.[88] Avenues were laid out by engineers, and gardeners planted long rows of palms beside them. Along the avenues Sam had thirty cabins built for his future guests; small cabins for those who did not want to stay in the hotel proper. This wonderful pleasure resort, built in a remote valleyhead accessible at the time only to the lumbering stagecoach and its six sweating horses, was to be the greatest California would ever know. While workmen made slow progress on the hotel and cottages, others were building a roller-skating rink, sixty by ninety feet, on the top of a low hill directly above the outlet of the sulphur springs, beneath which the great swimming pool would be built. On a higher hill he was having a great reservoir constructed, so that fresh mountain water would be available in every room of the hotel and cottages. At the north end of the grounds he had engineers lay out half a mile of stables and a great race track for his blooded horses to compete on.

Eventually he had workmen lay six-inch pipes from the reservoir to the grounds, and from these pipes came the water to fill the numerous fountains he planned on the wide lawns. He had roads laid out to the geysers, several miles to the north, and a mountain road to the forest of fallen petrified trees to the west. Even while all these plans were still nebulous dreams, Sam thought and talked of little else beside his grandiose venture. He described it thus to John one evening in San Francisco:

"I'll build a tepid swimming bath of sulphur water right underneath the hill, at least forty feet square, and I'll have it covered over by a fine building so that people can swim winter or summer. And right in front of that my hotel is already being built. From the hotel to the front gate there is a long straight driveway, lined on both sides by palm trees. And down just inside the gates I'll have a little mud-bath house built. I've got three winding avenues in the grounds, and along them I'm putting up little white cottages. Rich people will come not only from San Francisco, but from all over the world, to swim in our baths and drink our healthful sulphur water. They can stay for months and have a good time every day. If they don't want to loll in our mud-baths they can go roller-skating upon the hill, or watch the horse races, or mosey around the museum I'll have built; or they can hire a horse and go over to the geysers, or ride up in the hills to the petrified forest; or they can go trout fishing in the nearby mountain streams. I tell you, any spa in Europe would turn green with envy if they could see what we've got here."

"Maybe so," John agreed, "but I'll turn over in my grave if you don't stop spending money up there. Do you realize that it will take the best part of a million dollars to do all the things you want to do? And do you realize that you can never hope to take out in revenues what you'll sink in your original investment?"

"I don't care," Sam said heatedly. "What good is money if you can't do the things you want to with it?"

"But you're spending it too fast, Sam. Good heavens, man, you can spend a lot of money and have fun, and still put it into something that will pay you dividends! From what you tell me about this resort you'll have more of a sporting house than a health resort."

"Maybe so," Sam grudgingly admitted, "but I'd rather people would go there to have a good time than have a bunch of old blue-noses sit around there and bellyache about their aches and pains, and make it miserable for everyone around them."

"Why build a health resort then? Why not just build a race track and gambling casino, and let it go at that?"

"Because I want what I'm building," Sam retorted. "It's my money, and I can have what I want." John shrugged and dropped the subject.

The more time Sam spent watching his dreams take form in the Napa Valley, the more grandiose the scheme seemed to become. Soon men were planting acres and acres of vineyards with choice cuttings from Italy, Spain, and France. Eventually Sam would construct a great distillery to make brandy from his finest grapes. Then he was struck by another brilliant idea. He had silkworms and mulberry trees sent from Japan, with the idea that he might start a silk industry in this lush valley. Sam was only forty-one now, and he began to build feverishly for the future. "By the time I'm sixty, I can retire to this hemmed-in valley and live like a feudal lord for the rest of my days. My vineyards, my distillery, my resort hotel, and my stock-raising will keep me rich when I don't feel like working any more," he told his cronies. Some of his finest Merino sheep he had sent to the valley, and soon herders were watching them on the slopes near Mount Helena, which towered over the whole scene. Sam pictured the time when Ann Eliza would be tired of Europe and would bring the children home. They would be marrying in a few years, and he would give them land so that they could build homes around him and he could live in the midst of his children and grandchildren.

Whatever time Sam could spare from San Francisco, he spent at Calistoga. And when he wasn't at Calistoga he was talking about it. One evening he was drinking at the Oriental bar with half a dozen associates, when John came looking for him. John ordered a sarsa-parilla and remained to talk for a time. Sam was drinking champagne. Whenever a bottle was finished Sam scratched his initials on the cork, knowing that the bartender would present it to John the next morning at the bank, for payment.

"You ought to stop such shiftless business methods," John said sharply, after Sam had signed three corks. "You know as well as I do that these bartenders present twice or three times as many corks for payment as you ever actually drink or allow your friends to drink."

"What the hell!" Sam said. "I got plenty of money. If some of them scrooge up on me here and there, let 'em do it. They need it worse than I do."

"They won't always need it worse than you do, if you don't trim your pace," John said grimly.

Sam looked at him angrily for a moment and then turned back to his easy-going friends. "As I was saying, I named Calistoga in the first place. It was right after I bought my first little piece of ground up there. I was trying to tell some fellers that I liked the look of the sulphur springs up there, and that it would be a good place for a resort. 'Someday I'll make this place the Saratoga of California,' I started to say, but my tongue slipped and what I said was, 'I'll make this place the Calistoga of Sarafornia.'"

"Yeh, we know," Hastings broke in. "I've heard that story about five million times already."

"You might hear it five million more if I feel like telling it," Sam said truculently, "and you may hear this a lot of times, too, but I'm going to keep on saying it. I'll have the best damned watering place in the whole world when I get Calistoga finished."

It was while Calistoga was still in its nebulous state that Sam was called to Sacramento to a reorganization meeting for the Sacramento Railroad. The road had proved financially unsuccessful, and it was decided now to invite new stockholders to invest so that the line could be extended. The plans went through. New funds supplied by the new investors, augmented by further support from the original investors, made it possible to extend the road to Lincoln. The name of the road was changed to the "California Central."

Sam remained a day or so in Sacramento after his railroad affairs were satisfactorily settled, to visit with his sister, Mary Ann Badlam, and her family. Alexander had started a small mercantile business of his own, and young Aleck, a handsome youth of twenty-three, was helping his father. The younger Mary Ann was already married to Dr. William Carpenter, a famous physician who thought nothing of charging fifteen dollars for an office consultation. Mary Ann had grown into a handsome, buxom woman. But Sarah was the beauty of the family. At twenty-one she was being courted by the most eligible men in Sacramento, though one Joseph W. Winans had the edge on them all; or so it seemed to Sam, who had met the man several times before.

"We hope she will marry Joseph," Sam's sister told him. "But she is such a flirt and so spoiled, she don't know what she wants. The more Pa and me encourage her to marry Mr. Winans, the more set she seems on marrying someone else. If she does do what we want her to it will be because Mr. Winans has money."

"Yes, Joseph Winans is a fine man," Sam agreed. "He seems a mite too old for her, though. He's not more than a year or two younger than me, and Sarah is only twenty-one."

Mary Ann nodded her head. "Yes, he's going on forty, but that's all to the good. He'll be a good steady husband for her and that's what she needs, being so flighty and all. She's got the, wild Brannan blood, and it's no good. Thank goodness Ezra is quiet and plodding. I never have to worry about him."   ·

"Joseph Winans is slow and plodding, too," Sam commented. "I remember the first time I ever saw him. It was in '49, and he sailed up the Sacramento on his ship the *Strafford*, and stopped in at my store. Him and some other fellers had bought the boat and fitted her out for a hotel. They planted her right next to my storeship and made a fortune renting out rooms. Joseph had a good head. He graduated from Columbia University and practiced before the Supreme Court of New York before he threw it all up to come chasing out here for gold. He never did mine enough to stick in your eye, but he made plenty of money just the same. He's won many a land suit for me in the courts and got well paid for it, too. He's got a good education. He's the kind of a man Lizzie would have liked me to be."

Not many months later Sarah did marry Joseph Winans, and Sam read the details in the *Alta*. Joseph was characterized as a man "of lofty integrity, of scrupulous regard for the rights of others, and of a most gracious and charming personality."

In two years the swimming-baths at Calistoga were completed, and Sam brought parties up occasionally for a picnic and a swim. His two lodges—the Odd Fellows and the Masons—held their annual picnics on the far-flung estates. The vineyards were beginning to bear and the distillery was almost finished. Sam took time out to go once more to Sacramento, this time to attend the wedding of his nephew, Alexander Badlam, to beautiful Mary Burgess, only recently arrived from Scotland. After the ceremony Sam kissed the bride and she shyly told him that she never had hoped to meet the rich Mr. Brannan—and here she was married to his nephew.

"Why, child, how did you ever hear of me way over in Scotland?"

"Our papers were filled with stories of you in '57, when you came over to buy sheep. Don't you remember?"

Sam laughed and pinched her cheek appreciatively. He would never get old enough to lose interest in beautiful young women, as staid folk in Calistoga well knew. For Sam's parties were talked of behind respectable doors, and the womenfolk said it was scandalous, the way he carried on with women.

When young Aleck approached him in a corner at the wedding, Sam put a fond arm about the lad's shoulders. "I want to get into business down in San Francisco, Uncle Sam. Have you got a place for me in the bank?"

"Why, yes, I think John could work you in. You go down to see him when you're ready. I know he'll be right glad to have our nephew working with him."

And it proved to be so. John was a good and wise teacher, and young Aleck learned the intricacies of business well.

Sam remained in Sacramento to attend a second reorganization meeting of the California Central. The bondholders took in still other stockholders, and plans were formulated to push the road through to the Yuba River. The road was again renamed. This time it became the Yuba Railroad, and Sam was elected president. But all these attempts to make the railroad venture live were destined to failure, for three years later the Central Pacific—one day to become known as the

Southern Pacific—bought out the little road at auction. All that the original investors (except for Sam) were ever destined to get out of the venture was a very little glory.

As soon as this business was satisfactorily settled, Sam returned to San Francisco and took boat for New York City. He found the East a tinder-box waiting to be touched off, for war clouds threatened. New York was itself mostly pro-slavery; most of the big business there was on the side of the slaveholders. Sam found himself in perpetual argument, and being fanatically against slavery he was bound to have fights. The *Alta California* for October 16, 1860, told the story to the home folks:

Sam Brannan of San Francisco, came near having a serious encounter in the barroom of the St. Nicholas Hotel, in New York City on the night of the 26th of September, with Captain Farnham of the slaver WANDERER notoriety, who was a few months ago forcibly taken from a Savannah Jail and liberated by his friends. The exact origin of the trouble could not be ascertained, but from brandy punches and politics, the belligerents came to blows. Pistols were quickly drawn, and a general melee seemed inevitable, when policeman Mingary rushed into the saloon and put a stop to the difficulty. Brannan was locked up for the night and released under bond of $500 to keep the peace for six months. Farnham got away when he heard the police coming.

The pony express had been inaugurated in this year of 1860, and thus it was that Sam's escapade was printed in San Francisco just twenty-one days after it happened. Truly, the world had moved fast in the fourteen years since he had left New York for an unknown town on San Francisco Bay.

Chapter XXV

LINCOLN, IN MANY of his campaign speeches, spoke of the need of a transcontinental railroad to open up the rich possibilities of the country. There were men in various sections of the country who took Lincoln at his word when he said that, if elected, he would throw the resources of the Government behind such an undertaking. In California, those most interested were four mediocre businessmen of Sacramento. Sam was not present at the organization meeting of the Central Pacific, which was held in Sacramento on June 27, 1861, but he was to have a vital part in the railroad scheme before it went far.

It was in 1862 that John Brannan took ship for China, bound on business of his own. He contracted what was known as "galloping consumption," [89] and before the ship reached the Orient he was dead. Because of Sam's kindness and foresight, John's widow was left with a comfortable income and property which made her independently wealthy. It was fortunate for Sam that young Alexander had been well taught by his Uncle John, for he was able now to take over John's activities as Sam's business manager.

Sam was unwilling to buckle down to the day-by-day labor involved in the desk work of a bank and the many other ramifications of his numerous business enterprises. He found it more pleasurable to travel often to Calistoga to watch construction, or to take a boatload of actresses or professional beauties with their escorts, who were wealthy businessmen of the city, up to the "White House" near Nicholaus for a gay house party, which might last a night or a week. His men friends often told him how fortunate he was to be so footloose and woman-free. And how many of them envied him his bachelorhood. He looked forward to the day when the Calistoga resort would be ready and he could entertain on a still grander scale.

In 1862 Joseph Winans brought his beautiful wife, the former Sarah Badlam, to San Francisco to live. He opened up a law office and became immediately one of the most substantial men of the city—

one who frowned upon Sam's excesses and yet trusted him in business. Sarah was soon a familiar sight on the streets, being driven in a shiny carriage with two white horses and a Negro coachman. She was a wilful woman, soon famous for her beauty and notorious for her erratic temper. She had never been taught to curb it and had grown up selfish and lazy. Now that she had servants to do her housework she was free to come and go as she wished, and her husband was rich enough to indulge every reasonable desire. But Sarah was not, nor would she ever be, a reasonable woman. She had a passion for gambling, which she shared with her older sister, Mary Ann Carpenter. They were often to be seen together, sitting in Sarah's carriage outside of brokers' offices, while messengers ran to and fro placing speculations for them. Sam, seeing the way they were going, tried to reason them out of this gambling mania, but they would not listen. He shook his head sadly, knowing that they were bound for disaster.

On a brilliant day in the summer of 1862, while the States were embroiled in civil war; when the Napa Valley was dressed in its brightest green, the great hotel and pleasure grounds at Calistoga were thrown open to the public. Sam had chartered a ship to carry everyone from San Francisco to the gala opening celebration. A train of stagecoaches and carriages met the thousands who trooped off the ship at Vallejo. They were whisked over curving roads and beautiful mountain highways into the lovely sheltered valley. Sam was on hand standing in the wide, graceful portico of the hotel to greet them as they rode up the palm-fringed drive, descending then before the wide steps of the Mansion House. When the last guest had stepped from his carriage, Sam made a little speech of welcome and invited them to come and go as they wished. "We've planned some games and amusement for you which will start after our big barbecue lunch. In the meantime you can wander all over and see all our sights. Inside we got the greatest museum you ever saw, and I want every one of you to take a peek at it. I've gathered objects of art and curios from all over the world for it."

Sam's guests took him at his word and scattered far and wide over the wide lawns, exclaiming at the gold-fish in the many fountains.

They gazed up at the high peak of Mount Helena to the north, and at the ragged cliffs and crags of the rocky range of mountains which hemmed in the valley to the north and east. A lower range of hills held it in loving embrace on the west and south, and the slopes were covered with scrub oak, chaparral, and small pines. When they had seen the stables and race track, the distillery, the mud baths, the swimming pool, the skating rink, when a few had even climbed the hill to see the great reservoir, they finally drifted inside to inspect the large, airy sleeping rooms, richly furnished parlors, and the vast dining room, equipped with fans which could be manipulated from a long distance—no small wonder in the era before electric power. An orchestra.played in the ballroom for all who cared to dance.

Sam's specially invited guests dined in the great dining hall, sipping champagne and partaking of roast fowl, fish, and meat from the great barbecue pits outside, where the masses were being fed by Sam's chefs. At two o'clock everyone went to the race track and saw Sam's Arabian horses compete in half a dozen races. Afterward, there were potato races, one-legged races, and peanut derbies, for the guests themselves. At night the valley was brilliant with the fireworks set off from the top of the skating-rink hill.

In the days that followed, until the hotel was closed at the end of the season in September, a fun-loving crowd could always be found at Calistoga, and usually they found their host at Calistoga, too. Many notables were entertained there: actresses, actors, rich men from New York and other cities. The "Four Hundred" of San Francisco stayed stubbornly away from this notorious spa, looking down their blue noses, and the *Alta* spoke for them: "The hotel is the abode of a spendthrift, sporting crowd. It is less a health resort than a house of pleasure," [90]—which was just what Sam had planned it should be. The citizens Sam had enticed to the settlement near the resort, by offering them good land cheap, stayed strictly away from the hotel and whispered about the amours they watched from a distance. Many a lovely lady came to spend a few days with Sam, then would disappear back to San Francisco to be replaced another week by another pretty face.

Although the townsmen deplored Sam's morals, they did not hesitate to do business with him. They hauled their grapes to his great distillery and accepted twenty-five dollars a ton. Sam took all they would bring, for he could use all they had as well as the yield from his own vineyards; he made a choice grade of brandy, which was shipped by wagon to Vallejo and thence to New York City and a select clientele. There were those, however, who said that Sam was becoming his own best customer, and their claims were not without merit.

There was a lumber mill down in the town, on the beautiful little creek which meandered through it. The owner, a man named Buck, found himself pressed for funds and came to Sam to borrow money. Sam loaned it to him and took a mortage on the mill, a minor business venture which in the future was to cost him dear.

In 1863 the Brannan Bank was the worse for the lack of a strong guiding hand. Young Alexander was still too inexperienced to make wise decisions, and Sam was unwilling to give his time to it. It became necessary, therefore, to reorganize the bank and take in a man who could take the position which Sam now had and which he had so woefully neglected. The stockholders presented Sam with an ultimatum. He either would settle down to managing the bank, or would resign as its president. Sam, in a temper, resigned. Peter Burnett, the man who had been California's first governor, was persuaded to take over the presidency.[91] Other subscribers were invited in, Joseph Winans chief among them. Sam wanted his bank to survive and to continue as sound as it had been. When other stockholders refused to increase their subscriptions, he increased his own by a great deal. The bank was newly named the "Pacific Accumulation and Loan Society," and was known during Peter Burnett's presidency as one of the soundest banks in the state. Sam's money remained in it for several years more and then he withdrew.

All through Lincoln's first troubled administration and the Civil War, Sam Brannan was one of his staunchest adherents, and when the time drew near to nominate a new Republican candidate, Sam and William Ralston, a newcomer to San Francisco and head of a rival bank, took charge of the Republican Convention, which met in Platt's Hall on June 9, 1864. Sam was the main speaker of the day, and he rose to poetic heights when he put forth the name of Abraham

Lincoln as the people's choice. The hall went wild with joy. Ladies in the gallery waved small flags and tiny handkerchiefs, and the men whistled and shouted and clapped until it seemed as if the place would explode of its own noise. Sam seated himself at last and looked up and down the large hall at the flags and bunting which covered all the gallery, and he tapped his feet as the band played "We Are Coming, Father Abraham." When the tumult and the shouting had died down, Sam's name headed the list of five presidential electors for Abraham Lincoln, on a strong Union ticket.

He was deep in plans for a whirlwind speaking campaign for Lincoln, when two gentlemen were ushered into his office in his newest building, the Masonic Building. They were Mexican officers, as he could see at a glance by their uniforms.[92] Sam motioned them to chairs while he looked them over. The elder man ignored the chair and bowed stiffly from the hips.

"I am General Gasper Sanches Ochore. This is Placido Vaga." He stretched out his hand toward his associate. The younger man bowed quickly.

"Sit down," Sam said, and they did so. "Now, what do you want?" Sam asked bluntly.

"We have come from Mehico City to this place to raise money to fight Maximilian. He has been sent by the villain, Napoleon III, to gain a foothold on this continent for one purpose only. Your country is engaged in a bitter Civil War. Napoleon thinks that if he can conquer Mexico he will be in a position to march right into this country if the South wins the war. For the sake of the future safety of your own country, as well as for our people, who are being slaughtered by European soldiers who have no right here, you should use your immense wealth to help us get rid of them."

Sam rubbed his chin. "Well, I don't know much about international politics, but it's plain to see that Napoleon has picked this time to invade Mexico because he hopes to profit by our Civil War, all right. And I say, to hell with him!" He got up and began to walk back and forth. Finally he stopped in front of General Ochore. "How do you want me to help you?"

"I have an American, a good soldier named George Green, and a friend of his, named Harry Lake, who can organize a company of

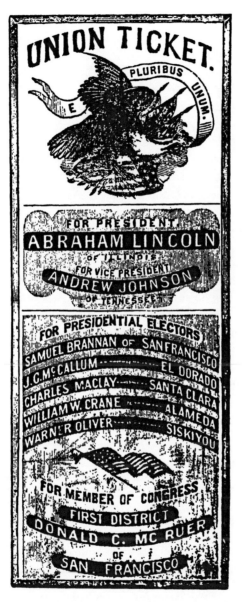

THE UNION TICKET SHOWING SAMUEL BRANNON AS A
PRESIDENTIAL ELECTOR IN 1864.

Americans and will lead them to Mexico to help us fight this European interloper. All they need is money to equip and feed their men through a campaign."

"Where are these two? I want to talk to them."

"Outside. They wait for us."

"Well, bring them in. I want to size them up and listen to them before I give them any of my money."

Sam was impressed by George Green and Harry Lake, and when the five men had conferred for several hours, a plan of campaign was complete. Sam would finance the outfitting of one hundred men, would pay their transportation by boat to Mexico, and would bear all expenses until the "American Legion," as they termed it, or "Brannan's contingent," as the men later named it, were disbanded again in San Francisco.

Sam went to the boat to see his contingent embark and waved them farewell as they sailed out toward the Golden Gate. He was not to see them for three years—not until 1867, when they returned victorious after the death of Maximilian; but he was to hear from them often and was to spend almost seventeen thousand dollars on this gesture for freedom.

Before the campaign for Lincoln's re-election officially opened, Sam took a flying trip up to his own "White House" at Nicholaus. When he stopped at the general store in the town, the local newspaper reporter saw him and talked to him, and later wrote his impressions thus:

He [Sam] is affable, kind, and without the least show of arrogance, although very wealthy. Smokes a fragrant Havana and takes in everything with his calm, all-seeing eyes. It was Sam Brannan who established a telegraph between San Francisco and Calistoga and has this year contributed money to the building of a railroad from Vallejo to Napa. Mr. Brannan is desirous of extending the road from Napa to his resort in Calistoga.

He passes through Nicholaus in a buggy with a highland bonnet on his head, on his way to his splendid ranch on the Feather River; in an hour or two he can be seen listlessly smoking in Yuba City, ten miles above his ranch. The premium for the finest wool was awarded to Mr. Brannan at the Marysville fair. Then up he goes to Stockton to look at his reclaimed tule land, then to Lincoln, Sacramento and on to Petaluma. He can dodge a streak of lightning. He is just 45 years and yet the same Sam Brannan he has always been, with pale face and beautiful dark eyes.

Early in August, Sam set forth on his tour of small towns speaking everywhere to enthusiastic crowds in favor of the re-election of Abraham Lincoln. On September 25, 1864, he wound up at Weaverville with a rousing Union lecture. The miners gave him a rough but hearty welcome.

Sam's old friend and former associate, Theodore D. Judah, had interested four small merchants in his plan to start a transcontinental railroad from the bay over the mountains. They were Leland Stanford, C. P. Huntington, Mark Hopkins, and Charles Crocker. They claimed that they invested sixty thousand dollars in cash of their own money upon the day of organization, but Sam doubted this and said so in court at a later date. Sam claimed that between the four of them they had never paid into the venture more than six thousand dollars of their own money. They were using money, but not their own, when they bought the defunct Yuba Railroad at auction. Sam said that when they bought anything they used the money that other stockholders had invested. However, on the first day of November, 1864, he entered into an agreement with the "Big Four" whereby they were to take over the rolling stock of the old Yuba road, which Sam owned; in return for this, Sam received two hundred shares of stock in the Central Pacific Railroad—all he was ever to get back after an original investment of many thousands of dollars. The rolling stock included the "Elephant," which Sam had had brought around the Horn in '49.

After securing his stock, Sam put it away and sat back to watch the four men roll up a fortune, which amounted within a few years to $156,000,000 by Sam's estimate. Like Bancroft, he wondered how four men of meager resources were going to build a transcontinental railroad with a professed capital of $8,000,000 and an actual starting capital of a few hundred thousand. Huntington went to Washington. It was soon evident that he was using the original capital for one purpose only: to lobby whatever bills he wanted through the United States Senate. He bought Senators at cheap prices, it seemed to Sam, considering the amount of public funds and public domain they were thus giving away. Stanford remained on the coast and spent thousands of dollars getting himself elected Governor of California. Once elected, he proceeded to apportion out to the State of California the cost of building whatever part of the railroad the "Big Four," as they became known, felt the State should build. The Federal Government was donating the land upon which the road was to lie and furnishing most of the funds, but wherever the company ran short Stanford saw to it that the State or the counties or the cities took up the burden. Sacramento County ultimately advanced $400,000, Placer County advanced $550,000, and the State of California put up $2,000,000, not to speak of the amounts advanced by San Francisco City and County, to build a railroad which would never pay a penny in dividends to its stockholders but would eventually pour fortunes into the hands of the four men who controlled its destinies and used them for personal advantage.

Before Sam became involved with the company, in 1862, Congress had given the Central Pacific $250,000,000 in cash and 4,500,000 acres of public domain—which was four times as much land as the road actually needed for a right of way. The additional land was sold by the Big Four at a high profit after the railroad was completed. And in 1864, when Sam came into the picture, an act of Congress was passed to relegate the first act to a second mortgage; if the road failed, the Government would thus be the last to get any return on its investment.

Sam was amazed at the way these robbers of high finance worked. They controlled the California Legislature as well as most of the Senators in the National Government. They paid graft in the right places. They manipulated stocks and bonds on the market so that the little stockholder would quickly be frozen out. They tried to freeze Sam out, eventually, and failed. And therein lay sorrow for the Big Four. Sam was destined to make them cry "uncle" before he finished with them.

The year of 1865 started auspiciously. In January the members of the Musical Fund Society, escorted by the Howard Engine Company—San Francisco's first and most exclusive fire company, of which Sam was a charter member—marched up to the Russ House, where Mr. Brannan was having lunch. The parade stopped outside and serenaded Sam. Having been warned, he was prepared; he stepped out on the balcony and looked down upon the Howard boys,

CALISTOGA SPRINGS, 1871

CALISTOGA SWIMMING BATH WHEN NEW

SAM'S WINERY

Still in use on the Calistoga estate

resplendent in red hats and capes. A spokesman stepped forward and thus addressed him: "Mr. Brannan, we have come here today to give you official notice that you are hereby appointed an honorary member of our organization. We do this as a token of our appreciation for the new silver-trimmed engine which you have just presented to us."

"That's mighty nice of you boys." Sam smiled and waved his cigar in an expansive gesture. "I'm glad that I was able to be of such assistance to you, and I want to thank you for bringing the Musical Fund Society up here to entertain me. But when all is said and done, there is nothing else I could have done but buy you a new engine when the old one couldn't be used any more. Your company was named the Howard Company after one of the most beloved men that ever came to San Francisco. Now that he is gone there is no one who has your interests more at heart than me. I was a charter member of your company, and although another one bears my name and is entitled to a certain part of my loyalty, no fire company will ever replace the old Howard Company in my affections."

The Howard boys clapped and the Musical Fund Society members broke into a marching tune. Sam stood and listened and tapped his foot and nodded his head in time. As they marched away, he lifted his hand in farewell salute.

While the Civil War raged in the States, Samuel Brannan raged on the coast. Sam was outspokenly against all Southerners and especially violent against slavery. San Francisco was itself a sharply divided camp, because the majority of its businessmen were hardheaded Yankees while all Government appointees, including the men who worked in the custom house, were Southerners who had secured their positions through the machinations of southern Senators who had held the balance of power before the war.

On the twenty-fifth of February, 1865, a rumor reached San Francisco that Charleston had been taken. Sam was so filled with glee that he gathered all his cronies and they repaired to the nearest bar and drank toast after toast to the Yankee victory. About eleven that evening they decided that it would be a good idea to fire a volley in celebration, so they went over to the old Battery at the base of Telegraph Hill and secured a cannon. This they wheeled down to a suitable spot on Montgomery Street. There was a good deal of staggering and weaving while the gun was loaded. At last Sam held the light to the fuse. The men stepped back and held their ears. The cannon roared and the celebrants gave a rousing cheer for the Northern victory. Heads popped out of near-by windows. People came running from near and far to find out what had caused the terrible explosion. Sam welcomed them with upflung arms. "We're jusht shelebrating over the fall of Charleshton," he roared.

"To hell with Charleston!" the nearest resident shouted. "You drunken fools broke every window in my house when you shot off that cannon. You'll pay for new ones, I can tell you that. Charleston, indeed!"

The next day's papers carried the story of the night's escapade alongside the war news. Charleston was still safe in Southern hands. Sam grew a little touchy at any reference to Charleston in the days that followed, for he was ultimately forced to pay out $2500 for the broken glass and other concussion damage his premature celebration had caused.

In the spring Sam took ship for New York, and from there to Europe. He was going to fetch his family home. They had been away for eight years, during which he had seen them only on the flying trips he had taken abroad.

He met his family in Geneva. The girls had been in school there ever since they had come to Europe, but Sammy had been in schools in both France and England. Sam wasted no time in telling them all what he had come for. Ann Eliza's lips grew set and at last she spoke sharply.

"I'm sorry, but we are not going back to the States."

Sam looked at her in surprise. "I said that I came to take my family home, and that's exactly what I'm going to do," he said grimly.

Ann Eliza rose abruptly from her chair. The children were scattered about the room; Sammy was slumped in a chair, his legs swinging idly over its arms while he languidly smoked a long Turkish cigarette. The girls were huddled together on the sofa, watching their parents with wide eyes. They spoke French better than English, and Sam could hear them whispering between themselves in this strange-sounding language. He felt like a foreigner among them.

"We are not going back to San Francisco," Ann Eliza said. "I've spent eight years here with the children so that they could get good educations. Now they have culture and charm, and if they stay here they will be admitted into the best homes and will have position and wealth when they marry."

Sam snorted angrily. "I'm getting damned sick and tired of your foolish notions. Our younguns are Americans, the children and grandchildren of pioneers. I want them to come home to America where they can learn to be proud of what America means. It's a young country, but it's the greatest country in the world. I don't want them to grow up talking and acting like foreigners and forgetting the kind of people they sprung from. I'd a whole lot rather have my girls marry plain American businessmen than foreigners who will marry them for their money. At least the Americans will work for them and act like men, and not like a bunch of lily-livered dudes. And Sammy—look at him, lolling around like a damned female! This is not what I wanted my younguns to grow into. It's time I took a hand and see that they come down to our level where they belong."

"I will not go back to San Francisco," Ann Eliza insisted. "The people there are simply awful. I used to think it would be nice to be a society leader there. Now I know that the women who make up the most exclusive society are either former washerwomen or the daughters of saloon-keepers. There's not an ounce of real culture in the whole town."

"Who are you to get uppity about your neighbors?" Sam asked. "Your Ma was running a boardinghouse when I married you."

Ann Eliza glared at him. "That's right, be vulgar. Let your children see how crude and uncouth you can be."

"Oh, they won't understand me," he said angrily. "I talk American. All they understand is monkey talk."

Ann Eliza waved her hands like a Frenchwoman and shrugged, "It's certain that you want to prove to them that you are not a gentleman and couldn't be if you wanted to."

"To hell with you and your put-on airs! I say that we are all going back to San Francisco and live like any decent family ought to, and that's just what I mean."

"And I say that I will not go back there. Now what are you going to do about it?"

"I'm going to take the next ship back home. You can come with me and have the best that money can buy, or you can stay here and starve to death, because when I get on that ship I'll never send you another cent as long as I live. You can come home and make a home for me or stay here and starve. It's up to you."

Ann Eliza sent the children from the room. She argued with Sam for hours, but when the argument ended Sam had won. At last she gestured wearily. "All right, I'll go back because you're forcing me to. I'll hire servants to keep your house and for the sake of the children we'll pretend we are happily married, but I can tell you this, Sam Brannan, I'll never live with you as a wife again."

Sam put his face close to hers. "You'll never get the chance. I can have my pickings of beautiful women, young or old, and I've done right well by myself so far. If you think I want you back after all the water that's run under the bridge, you're crazy."

"That suits me," she spat at him. "But just you start any scandals or try to make me a laughing-stock like you did once before, and I'll take half your fortune and I won't have to pretend to be a wife any longer. Just put that in your pipe and smoke it!"

"Well, at least we've dug through the veneer enough to find out that what you want from me is money and nothing else. It's a relief to be honest once in a while, don't you think?"

She glared at him for a long moment. "Sometimes I hate you, Sam Brannan," she said, and swept out of the room.

Chapter XXVI

THE BRANNAN FAMILY took rooms at a hotel until the new house which Sam was having built at 930 Clay Street should be finished.

Joseph Winans, who was associated with Sam in the Pacific Bank as well as being a bondholder—as Sam was—in the Napa Valley Railroad, had become so enamored of the new house Sam had under construction that he wanted to buy the lot next to it and put up an identical one. Sam did not want to sell, but he agreed to build an identical house and lease it to the Winans family for as long as they might wish to stay. And thus it was that the Winans home was being built at 926 Clay Street.

Sam went up to Calistoga as soon as he could after his return from Europe, to see how the Napa Valley Railroad was progressing. He found that it was completed to Napa from Vallejo, at a cost to the county of $10,000 a mile. Sam was most desirous of having the road extended to Calistoga, and agreed to advance several hundred thousand dollars toward such a purpose if the county would finance the rest. This was agreeable to the county authorities, providing Sam would furnish the depot at Calistoga.

Sam consulted with the construction engineer. "If the road is extended to Calistoga, how long would it take to build it?" Sam asked.

"At the rate we have been going, about two years."

"That's all right," Sam said. "Come on, get in my rig and I'll drive you up to Calistoga. I want you to show me where the logical place for the depot will be."

The man climbed into Sam's buggy. "That won't be hard," he grinned. "The survey is already done, like you ordered before you went to Europe."

When the two men reached the village of Calistoga the engineer pointed out the place where the road would end. A church foundation was already on the ground. Sam went to the minister of the church and paid him the price of the lot, plus the cost of the work already done. The depot thus came to be built upon a church foundation.

When Sam returned to San Francisco he found Ann Eliza critical of everything and everybody. She had received a few invitations to swank affairs but refused to go, saying that she would not associate with new-rich scrubwomen and brothel-keepers. Few of her former friends remained in the city and those who did were not wealthy enough to suit her snobbish tastes; she left them strictly alone. The wives of Southern office-holders had been in disgrace with the Yankees since the beginning of the war, and this left Ann Eliza with no one to meet socially. She seemed a little more content when they moved into the new house, with all the new furniture imported from New York, but afterward she grew bored and restless again. She would not unbend even to Sarah Winans, for she considered Sarah too gaudy in dress and too anxious to be seen in public places. The fact that Sarah was not above an intrigue put her beyond the pale with Ann Eliza, and her gambling was déclassé in the extreme. Mary Ann Carpenter would have been acceptable to her aunt, had she been less under her younger sister's influence.

At dinner in the new house one evening, Ann Eliza waited for the Chinese cook—who was also serving the meal—to leave the room before she burst out, "Sam, I've simply got to go back to Europe, or at least New York. I can't stand it here. There's nothing to do and nowhere to go. The children can't find anyone suitable for them to associate with. This is a horrible place."

"How about Fanny Ralston and her set? They seem like nice people."

"Oh, she's all right but she's awfully stuck up. I don't get along with her, what with the airs she tries to put on. I won't let her patronize me, and if she can't patronize me she doesn't want to associate with me."

Addie, Sam's oldest daughter, now eighteen, spoke her mind: "The girls here in town are awfully crude, Papa. None of them speak French or have ever seen a decent opera. And Cousin Sophie, that horrible little cousin of ours, had the nerve to come over this afternoon. It's a good thing I saw her through the window before she rang the bell. I told our maid, Celeste, to tell her we weren't home."

Before Sam could reply the lovable Fanny, beautiful in her full-blown sixteen years, giggled. "Papa, you'll die when I tell you what happened. Addie hid on the upper landing and peeked when Celeste went to the door. I would have gone and let Sophie in, but I didn't want to make Addie out a liar. Addie must have made a noise because Sophie looked up the stairs and then she looked Celeste right in the eye and she said, 'Tell that dirty old Addie that when she ain't home, she hadn't ought to hide behind the banisters. I can see her.' And she turned and walked right down the steps with that little pug-nose of hers 'way up in the air."

"And where were you all the time this was going on?" Sam asked.

"Hiding behind the drawing-room curtains."

Sam glared down the table at Addie. "That's about the stinkingest trick I ever heard of anybody playing, Addie. Sophie Brannan is your cousin, the daughter of my own brother John, and she's one of the nicest little girls that ever lived. She's just as good as you are, any old day in the week. Your mother will go over to Aunt Mary's house tomorrow and apologize for the way you acted and invite Sophie to come again. And when she does come you better be in and you'd better be nice to her, or I'll show you what a hair-brush is for."

Ann Eliza spoke quickly. "Now, Sam, don't lose your temper. I wasn't here or it wouldn't have happened. I'll drive over tomorrow and apologize. But I must admit that I don't like Mary Brannan any better than Addie likes Sophie."

Sam put down his knife and fork with an ominous look. Young Sammy had finished eating and was just lighting one of his long cigarettes. "Listen, all of you. I've got something to say. I think your mother made a God-awful mistake when she took all of you to Europe and had you educated there. It's not done you a damned bit of good and it has done a hell of a lot of harm. You're about the good-for-nothingest outfit I ever saw. There's not a sweet or lovely thing about any of you, except maybe Fanny. Your Ma has tried to educate all the homely virtues out of you, such as humility and kindness and consideration for the feelings of other folks, and she's succeeded on all of you except Fanny. And thank God for her! But the rest of you think you are little tin gods. You're not! Remember that all you are and all you've got comes to you because your father is a rich man.

You've not done a thing for yourselves, ever. You'd better take heed because I can take it away from you as easy as I can hand it out. You better come down to earth and start treating other folks decent, or I'll make you sorry."

Ann Eliza arose quickly. "Sam, I simply will not sit here through another of your tantrums."

"Sit down," Sam roared and pounded the table with his knife-handle. She looked at him a moment and then sat down stiffly on the edge of her chair.

"You need to hear this as much as they do," he said grimly. He pointed his knife at Sammy who sat blowing clouds of smoke. "Look at my son," he said sarcastically. "Sam Brannan, Jr., he is called. He's a milksop tied to his mother's apron string. If there's one manly thing about him, I'd like to see it. If he's the result of a European education, I thank God that I was educated in a little town in Maine and got my degree from the university of hard knocks. At least I can get out and cope with the world and make some headway. Sammy, if you ever had to get out and earn your daily bread, you'd starve to death."

"Oh, I say now, Father, old thing! Aren't you carrying things a bit to the extreme?"

Sam arose quickly and threw down his napkin. "I'm going down town and get a drink. I've had about all of this atmosphere I can stand." He flung out of the house.

As the months rolled on, Sam Brannan gradually attained a tolerance for the continental attitude of his family. The children, being adaptable, endured him without too much protest. Ann Eliza, however, grew steadily further away from Sam and all that he represented. The love she had once borne him had changed to utter distaste which was revealed in every word and gesture. She lived under the same roof with him in order to make the world believe that the Brannan family was a united one, but privately Sam Brannan and his family had nothing in common—not even a tolerant affection. Fanny was the only one of the four children who liked her father, but even she found him uncouth and at times hard to live with because of his determination to dominate everyone with whom he came in contact. He was much like a bad little boy who has tantrums in order to enforce his will, and though Fanny was fond of him as a person, she did weary of being forced to give in to him always.

On Christmas Eve of 1867, Sam went to the front door to open it to the first ring; for weeks he had planned a great family reunion for that evening.[98] Ann Eliza had opposed his wish to have a family party, but when she found that he would have it in spite of her she gave in, although ungraciously. She did not like Sam's family, and as much as it was possible to do so she kept her children away from them. When Sam opened the door he found his sister Mary Ann and Alexander, her husband, waiting on the stoop. "Come on in," Sam boomed and put his arms around Mary Ann and kissed her on the cheek. They went past him into the hall and he was about to close the door when he recognized the Carpenter carriage just drawing up. He waited for William and young Mary Ann to come in. Mary Ann herded her three children before her.

"Glad you could come, Doc," Sam said to Dr. Carpenter.

"I hope I can get a mouthful of turkey before somebody has a baby and sends for me," the doctor replied. Sam closed the door behind them and helped the children to remove their wraps.

It was a happy evening for Sam. His brother John's widow came with the two youngsters, Sophie and John Brannan, Jr.; and then the Winans family came over from next door, with Joseph, Jr., and Lily. Sarah was expecting a third child. The last to arrive were Ezra and his wife. Although Ann Eliza was the hostess, she did not come to welcome her guests but left the honors to Sam. She appeared at last in the dining room door and said that she was giving Wong instructions and would be out later. They all knew that she was using this as an excuse to keep out of sight. It was only when the dinner was served that she came to take her place at the foot of the long table. Sam lifted the carving-knife and fell to the work of cutting up the huge bird. "Fill up," he bellowed as he passed the plates down the table. "This is the first time in my life I've ever had so many of my family together and I want you all to have a good time. I'm sure sorry that Aleck is sick and not able to bring his family. But we'll send his presents over to him tomorrow."

The guests lingered over the table for the better part of an hour. When they drifted into the front parlor, Sam herded them around the Christmas tree. There were presents for every one on the tree or under it, and the children were so excited that they could not be controlled. Sam sat back watching them with a contented look. "I like younguns," he said to his sister Mary Ann. "I wish my own were small again. I'll be glad when they start having younguns of their own for the fun we'll have."

"Yes, having grandchildren is almost like being young and starting a family over again," she said, smiling gently as she watched her own grandchildren. When the atmosphere had quieted somewhat Sam sat back in his plush rocking-chair and called across the room to his oldest daughter. "Get up there on the stool, Addie, and play us a tune," he suggested. Addie languidly shook her head.

"I don't feel like playing, Papa," she said petulantly.

Sam leaned forward and pointed towards the piano. "I paid two thousand dollars for that rosewood piano and had mother-of-pearl insets put back of the keyboard so it would be extra fancy, but do I ever get to hear any music from it? No! Everytime I ask one of you girls that had fancy French music teachers to play me a tune you're too tired, or not in the mood, or just plain too damned ornery. How about you, Fanny? Are you in the mood?"

She shook her head. "I would play, Papa, but I'm out of practice."

Sam looked at the youngest girl. "Well, then, Lizzie, suppose you show us all what you can do."

"I don't want to," she said firmly, "and my name is not Lizzie. It's Lisa."

"Lisa, my foot. You're just like your Ma, full of a lot of fool notions. All right, don't play, any of you! Sophie will get up on the stool and show you all up, won't you, Sophie?" Primly the half-grown Sophie arose and went over to the Haines-Cumming instrument. She twirled the stool, and when it was adjusted to her satisfaction she sat down. "What will you have, Uncle Sam?"

" 'Daughter of the Regiment.' That's my favorite tune," he said. She played all the music he requested, while he sat back and tapped his toe in time to the rhythm. When she had finished she gave a "so-there" look to her cousins and went back to sit beside her mother. Fanny went into the hall and returned a moment later with a big package which she placed in her father's lap. "This is my present to you, Papa," she explained. Sam was as excited as a child as he unwrapped the large square bundle. When he lifted it out, he discovered that it was a Swiss music box. Eagerly he set it on the table and looked for the way to wind it up.

"It has records, Papa. You can play half a dozen different tunes on it," Fanny explained and showed him how it worked. Sam was delighted with it. The box was destined to go with him wherever he went for many years, and any guest of his was bound sooner or later to hear the repertoire.

Sam was so engrossed in the gift that he did not notice when the two young men—his son and young John Brannan—left the room. Ann Eliza, who had stepped out into the kitchen for a few minutes, returned. "Where's Sammy gone?" she demanded of Sam.

"I don't know," he said. Sarah answered for him.

"Why, they went out just a minute ago. I saw them go down the front steps. They're probably going out to hunt up some girls and get into some devilment."

"Oh, Sam!" Ann Eliza exclaimed angrily, "I told that boy not to go out tonight. You know what a wild place San Francisco is on any holiday. I just know that they'll go and get drunk and get into heaven knows what kind of trouble!"

Mary Brannan, young John's mother, arose agitatedly. "Jack's got a wild streak in him. I've been having a hard time trying to hold him down. Go after them, Sam, and bring them home."

Sam turned away from his music box to smile at them. "Still trying to keep two young men tied to your apron strings, ain't you? You ought to be ashamed. Sammy is twenty-two and Jack's not much younger. It's time they got out and acted like men for a change. What if they do chase the girls? What if they do get drunk? At least they'll be learning about life, and that's something that every man has to learn sooner or later; the sooner they do it the better it is, say I."

Ann Eliza snapped a reply. "No one asked you what you think about it. Go get those boys and bring them home and make them behave themselves. This is Christmas Eve and they ought to be home where they belong."

Sam looked at her coldly. "You've come near making a molly-coddle out of Sammy. If it hadn't been for me you'd have succeeded. Now that he's beginning to act like a natural, normal young man you start throwing fits. I hope he does get drunk. I hope he does a lot of other things that any red-blooded man would want his son to do. I won't try to stop him—and, by God, I won't let you!"

"You are not going to speak to me that way," Ann Eliza said coldly, and she turned and swiftly left the room. The guests looked embarrassed but Sam laughed. "Come on, you folks, and listen to this tune. It's mighty pretty. It's called 'The Londonderry Air.'" While they were gathered around the little box Sam put his arm around Mary Brannan's shoulder and gave her a quick squeeze. "Don't worry about Jack. He'll be all right." She tried to smile but it was evident that she was greatly worried.

Sam went out to the hall closet to get a cigar from his coat pocket, and when he turned around he found Sarah at his elbow. She drew him into the alcove under the stairs.

"Sam, I want to borrow some money," she said abruptly.

"How much?"

"Ten thousand dollars."

"Sorry. I can't spare that much. What in God's name do you need so much for?"

"To pay my gambling losses."

Sam was exasperated. "Sarah, I've given you more than ten thousand dollars in the last year. First it's a few hundred and then it's a thousand. I've not kept track of how much I've handed over to you, but I'll bet it's more than ten thousand. I can't afford to do it. Every time you make a touch you promise that it will be the last—that you won't gamble any more—and then in a few weeks it's the same old story again. Well, by God, I'm through. I won't help you again. Joseph might just as well know what you're up to. Maybe he can make you stop."

Sarah began to cry. "Joseph is liable to do most anything if he finds out how much gambling I've done. He found out once or twice about small debts and he gave me hell. He's so honest and conscientious that he can't even bear the thought of speculating. I don't dare let him know. Why, he'd go absolutely crazy. There's no telling what he might do."

"Well, that's your lookout," Sam replied. "I've been telling you for years that it would catch up with you sometime. If you will dance you have to be prepared to pay the piper. I simply can't afford to carry you any more. Joseph will have to know eventually, so why not now?"

"I promise I'll stop if you'll just see me through this time. Now that I'm in the family way I've got to be spared any worry. If you don't give me the money I'll be so frantic that I'll mark the baby."

"Bosh, Sarah! You can't work that old whizzer on me. If you want to mark your baby, that's up to you. I can't give you that much money and that's final."

Sarah no longer pretended to be sad or soft. She looked coldly at Sam. "I'm not asking you for money, Sam. I'm demanding it. You'd better give it to me or you may be sorry."

Sam smiled sardonically. "You're not scaring me, Sarah Winans. You won't talk. You don't dare. If Joseph Winans knew as much about you as I do, he'd cut your throat."

There was a muffled exclamation and they turned to find Ann Eliza confronting them.

"This has been a very interesting conversation, right from the start. I was just inside the linen closet when you came out here. I've heard every word. There are several things I would like to have explained. I think Joseph would probably like to hear them, too. If you will come into the privacy of my sewing room, I think we will all understand each other better."

"I'm not going in your sewing room or any other room," Sam exclaimed passionately. "I'm no schoolboy to be ordered around."

Sarah staggered to a chair in the hall and sank into it. "I think I'm going to faint," she said. Ann Eliza walked to the parlor door, opened it a crack, and called in a high voice to Joseph Winans to come out. A moment later he appeared. Sam gathered up his hat and coat and started for the front door. Ann Eliza intercepted him. "If you walk out of that door without explaining everything I suspect to Joseph and me, I will file suit for divorce the day after Christmas and I will name your own niece as corespondent."

Sam looked at her in consternation. "You wouldn't dare!" he said.

"Don't tempt me," she said. He put down his hat and coat and meek as a child followed his wife into the little room which opened off the hall. Joseph had stood watching the three of them with a puzzled look and then as he began to understand he walked towards his wife, took her by the arm, assisted her forcibly but gently to her feet, and propelled her into the sewing room. The door closed.

Ann Eliza and the children left for an extended stay in New York. Sam's sister, Mary Ann Badlam, and her husband came to live with Sam so that he would have some one to keep house for him. Although the papers carried the story that Ann Eliza was leaving for a tour, there was much gossip in San Francisco. Gradually it came to be known in the better homes around the city that Joseph and Sarah Winans were no longer speaking to each other. They lived in the same house, ate at the same table, and supervised the care of their children, but they never spoke a word directly to each other—never were they to speak again, one to the other, so long as they lived. There were those who said that the estrangement between Joseph and his wife had some relation to the departure of Ann Eliza Brannan, and there were many speculations as to what the underlying reason might be. But no one, other than the four involved, knew the answer.

Sam began to drink steadily and heavily. Friends who had been intimate with him for years and who admired him for his loyalty and generosity, began now to drift away from him. Sam, like his father, was erratic when in his cups; and he was in his cups most of the time. He noticed that some of his business associates were beginning to avoid him, and that he was never invited to their homes any more. He felt hurt. Perhaps if he left town for a time he could get hold of himself, find new interests, and when he came back he could re-establish his old friendships. He took a boat for Los Angeles.

Book Four

Chapter XXVII

THE SPRAWLING little Spanish town which was Los Angeles was a relief to jangled nerves after the rush and roar of San Francisco. For a day or so Sam was at loose ends, and then he heard that the estate of Abel Stearns was for sale. Instantly he became interested. He might be able to make a business deal which would net him a nice profit, and have something to occupy his mind at the same time. He rode a horse over a goodly portion of the one hundred and seventy thousand acres which belonged to the Stearns heirs, and found it to be rich and fertile soil. The rancho covered the greater part of what was to become known as Los Angeles County. Stearns had been an American who had married into a wealthy Spanish-California family, and now that he was dead his children did not wish to cut up the land but wanted to sell it in a piece and divide the money for its sale between them. Sam eventually bought it. He hired an agent and directed him to cut the rancho up into small farms and to throw these farms on the market so that the hordes of land-seekers who were beginning to come into this semitropical region could have a place to settle.[94] Sam lost interest after a few weeks and left the business to his agent. He sailed for home, stopping in San Francisco only long enough to check over his business affairs with young Aleck, and then headed for Calistoga, where he could rest alone for a time.

Sam got off the stage at Calistoga late in the afternoon and went into the grocery store. The proprietor, McDowell, called a cheery greeting. "See you won your case over the sawmill. The Sheriff was in a few days ago and said as how he guessed you could take possession any time now." A customer named Swift turned and recognized Sam.

"Hello, Brannan," he said and paused. Then he spoke rapidly. "The Sheriff might have told McDowell you could take possession of your mill, but he didn't know what he was talking about. A feller named Snyder took the mill over yesterday. Claims that the feller that owned it, Buck, owes him money and he's taking the mill in payment."

"Oh, he did, did he? Well, I guess I got a thing or two to say about that. I loaned Buck money on that mill, and I got a mortgage on it. And according to McDowell here, the courts have decided that my claim is just. So I guess Mr. Snyder will have to be moving, pronto."

"I wouldn't be too sure about that, Brannan. This Snyder is a tough hombre."

"Well, I'll soon find out," Sam said grimly, and turning he went out of the store, walked two blocks west, and turned north, following the street which paralleled the creek. Swift came running to catch up with him and they walked together.[95] When they came to the edge of the mill grounds they turned off the highway and approached the building, which was about seventy feet from the street, set back in the shade of a giant oak on the side of the stream. They had progressed about ten feet when Snyder, from inside the mill, called through the window, "What do you want, Brannan?"

"I want this mill and I want it right now," Sam bellowed.

"You can want and be damned," Snyder said.

"It's mine by due process of law," Sam reminded the man. "If you want it, take your case to court and get it in the proper manner."

"Not me. I got it now and possession is nine points of the law. I got it and I'll keep it."

"Like hell you will!" Sam retorted. "I'll be back in the morning with the sheriff and if you're still there, God help you!"

Sam stopped walking and spoke to Swift. "Let's go back now. It's getting too dark to see, and these bastards may make trouble tonight. I'll run him out of there in the morning."

As they started back toward the highway someone in the mill shouted, "Give it to the son-of-a-bitch!"

There was a volley from a rifle. Sam half turned and then he felt a burning sensation in his side. He reached blindly for Swift, calling out, "I'm shot!" There was a second volley from inside the mill. Both men fell to the ground. Two passers-by came running from the street and dragged the injured men to the roadside. They found Sam unconscious, his face bloody. His coat was riddled with shot and there were eight holes in his back. The most dangerous wound was in the neck, for the bullet had entered from the right rear and had passed out in such a way that his Adam's apple was injured. One ball had passed through Sam's right arm about four inches above the elbow, and another had entered the hip and passed from right to left of the spine. A stretcher was quickly made up of tree branches and coats, and Sam was removed to the hotel and Dr. Rowell called. Swift was taken to his home. He had several superficial wounds.

Dr. Rowell examined Sam carefully before he reported to those waiting anxiously to hear whether he would live or die.

"Gentlemen, I doubt that he will pull through this. The bullet which passed near his spine may leave him paralyzed for the rest of his life, even if he survives the other wounds. It will be a miracle if he lives."

The next morning Mary Ann Badlam arrived to nurse her injured brother. The doctor was a little more encouraging to her.

"He may live. He has a magnificent body and plenty of vitality in spite of the fact that he has drunk too much lately. He may pull through, but if he does he will be crippled all the rest of his life."

"Sam would rather die than be a cripple," she said passionately.

A week later Sam was well enough to sit up. On the eighth of May, 1868, a reporter from the *Alta California* found him puttering about in his vineyard. As they talked, numerous workmen went about their tasks in the far-flung vineyards and in the nursery, where mulberry trees were being grown. Sam, although weak, was very much interested in what they were doing, and often interrupted his conversation to call out an order to one or another of his laborers. He looked well, although he had lost considerable weight. He left the next day in his own carriage for San Francisco, Mary Ann riding beside him and Alexander driving. When they arrived, Sam kept to his bed for several days. He was miserable and restless. Some of the bullets were still lodged in his body and they caused him much pain. When he tried to walk he was very lame in his left hip. He read an article about the attack upon him in the Calistoga paper, and at the last paragraph he roared with anger, so that Mary Ann came running to quiet him.

"What it says here is true. Those dirty bastards that have drifted into Napa Valley lately have done everything they could to cause me trouble. I'll run them all out of there before I'm through if they're not careful."

"What does it say?" Mary Ann asked, and picking up the paper she read:

> It [the attack on Sam] is the same spirit of lawless malignity which destroyed nearly a thousand head of French and Spanish Merino sheep, imported at immense expense by Mr. Brannan which were driven, in the night, over a high precipice at the upper end of Napa Valley, sometime since, because they riled the source of a stream which afforded water to parties below.

Mary Ann clucked and shook her head. "It's a dirty shame, that's what it is!"

"I'll get even with those fellers sooner or later, but this Snyder is the first one I'll take care of. The sheriff has already got him out of the mill for me. But I'll horsewhip him within an inch of his life when I get well."

But Sam was destined never to recover fully from his hip injury, and Snyder put a great distance between them.

By September Sam was well again, although partially paralyzed in his left hip; he had to walk with a cane. But his old zest for life had returned and he was filled with energy and plans for the future.

Calistoga and Napa had planned a big celebration for the opening of the railroad which would extend on from Napa to the resort. Sam, who had been the moving spirit behind the project, insisted upon making the celebration important. He chartered a ship to carry three thousand people from San Francisco to Vallejo. The Odd Fellows Lodge came out en masse with its band, playing lively tunes all the way up the bay on the boat. At Vallejo, Sam greeted them as they disembarked. Then all the celebrants got on the train, which was trimmed with flags and bunting, and rode to Napa. There the mayor stood on a high temporary platform to await them. Everyone got off the train, the mayor gave a speech, Sam cut the ribbon which would allow the engine to pull forward onto the new track, and the train was ready to proceed. The crowds poured back into the cars, new participants in the festivities from Napa and the surrounding country got on also, and the train rode out through beautiful country toward Calistoga. The magnificent new depot which Sam had had erected was trimmed with the gayest of flags. Carriages and hacks awaited the visitors, and all who could crowd into them rode up to the resort. The rest walked the short distance and found the scenery well worth a short walk.

Sam took his place on the balcony of the swimming-bath house and made a speech welcoming everyone. Over near the race track, Sam's cooks were preparing whole carcasses of beef and pig. People drifted about the grounds to see the fountains, the museum, the aviaries, and the horses and track, while children skated around the rink on the hill. Most of the young people took a swim in the pool, and at lunch they lined up along the lengthy tables to eat their fill.

This was to be Sam's last magnificent gesture, for his business ventures were not making the money they once had, and he was no longer young, nor did he feel well. The more his hip bothered him, the more he drank to kill the pain. He took little interest in his business, leaving it entirely in young Aleck's hands. He spent money recklessly, Sam did, just as he had for many years, and although his nephew kept warning him that he could no longer afford to do so, Sam brushed away his words and went his stubborn way. Young Aleck was worried, and at last he set down an ultimatum to Sam.

"Uncle Sam, I'm going to quit working for you if you don't buckle down and take more interest in things. A good many times, when there are important business decisions for you to make, you're nowhere to be found or else you're drunk. I do the best I can, but after all I can't decide one thing and then have you come along and decide another way. If it was my own business I'd know what to do and I'd do it, but since it's yours I have to do what you want, and I don't always know what that is. You're spending money too fast. We've not got it coming in any more."

Sam laughed. "You sound like Lizzie used to. Now stop nagging me. I'm still a rich man. I can afford to lose a little."

"You may be rich in land, but you're not rich in ready cash. And it's getting harder all the time to turn your land into cash. We've got taxes to pay, and interest, and a thousand and one little debts.

You've got to retrench, Uncle Sam, or you'll wake up one of these days and find yourself a poor man."

"Suppose you let me worry about that. You go on doing the best you can, Aleck. You're a good businessman and I trust you."

Aleck shrugged helplessly. "Well, you can't say I haven't warned you," he said.

Sam still had a hunger for land. He went over into Steptoe Valley in Nevada to buy agricultural land near Mineral City, and he bought silver mines in the Robinson District. Then he built sawmills to make timbers for the mines, which he paid to have developed; and also quartz and smelting mills. Then he found he had to build roads to get his ore out. But the last fact he discovered was that he could not make enough on his investment to repay him for what he had put in. He tired of this venture after a year or so and let it lie idle.

In May of 1869 the California Pacific Railroad bought out the Napa Valley road. Sam and Joseph Winans both had large sums invested in bonds of the road, and when it went to the larger company they lost their entire investment.

Chapter XXVIII

THE YEAR 1870 turned out to be a nightmare year for Sam Brannan. Ann Eliza returned from the East with their grown children and started suit for divorce.[96] The hearing came on before Judge J. Morrison in the Fourth District Court. She asked for a divorce and half of the community property. Sam pleaded that he could not give this in cash. He could give it in property. But Ann Eliza did not want property; she wanted cash. Sam's answer stipulated [97] that he owned property worth $600,000; that he had an income of $5,000 a month but was indebted in the sum of $400,000; that the greater part of his debts was secured by mortgages on his real estate; and that his income was absorbed by payments on interest. He explained that the money he had been giving Ann Eliza for her support, and for the support of their children, came from outside operations or from borrowing. Ann Eliza listened to his story and then had her attorney issue an injunction so that Sam could dispose of no property until such time as her claims were granted. Upon Sam's plea, Judge Morrison modified the injunction so that Sam could carry on his business.

Sam decided that it was high time he began to look into his business situation. He sat down and went over the books with Aleck. He was aghast to discover how much of his once great fortune he had dissipated. Aleck pointed out some salient facts. "You've sunk a half a million dollars on the Calistoga resort," he pointed out. "You'll never even make it pay its own way for one season. The second year after you opened the place you put a manager in charge. When he left he took all the profits and half the good furnishings—or at least as much as he could carry away in a coach. Then the next year you leased it out, like you've been doing ever since, but the lessees usually take out more than is put in. When it needs repairs or upkeep we have to take care of it. So that's the first white elephant you've got on your hands. You sunk thousands in Nevada and we'll never take anything out of there again. You spent hundreds of thousands on railroads in this

state, and all you've got to show for it is a few shares of stock in the
Central Pacific Company."

"Well, now that I need it, I guess maybe the Central Pacific better
pay me some dividends," Sam said.

On June 21, 1870, through his attorneys M. G. Cobb and "Beast"
Ben Butler,[98] of New Orleans fame in the recently concluded Civil
War, Sam entered suit against the Central Pacific Railroad to get a
return on his investment. This was the forerunner of suits brought by
other principal stockholders of the Central Pacific to force payment of
dividends. It was considered blackmail by the Big Four.

Sam made no secret of the fact that he considered the organizers
of the Central Pacific as nothing better than bandits. His Cause of
Action claimed that the Big Four had set out to build a railroad for
one purpose only: to get rich, and rob everyone with whom they came
into contact in order to do so.

Named as defendants were the Central Pacific and each of its
founders; subsidiary companies such as Wells, Fargo and Company;
subsidiary railway companies which the Central Pacific had swallowed
up; and even banker D. O. Mills, who was assisting the railroad four
by helping them to hide their sharp practices. The action was brought
in behalf of Sam and several others who had bought initial stock. It
set forth that the professed capital stock amounted to $8,500,000,
divided into 85,000 shares at $100 each. Samuel stated that he had
himself duly subscribed and paid for 200 shares at the nominal par
value in November of 1864.

Sam pointed out that Stanford, Huntington, Hopkins, and Crocker
had each subscribed to 150 shares on the day of incorporation, which
had been June 27, 1861, and that they had then pledged themselves
to pay in cash, on that day, 10 per cent of each subscription. But Sam
believed, and was informed, that they had not on that day or any
other day paid any money of their own into the venture, but had
used only such monies as other investors had paid in. He claimed that
the defendants, by secret devices, had elected themselves a majority
of directors, and by so doing were able to control the project so that
only they profited, while all other stockholders lost. He listed the
various acts of Congress, acts of the separate counties, acts of the
states, and acts of cities, which had given money and land to the Big

Four without apparent return. He summarized their subsidies and grants from such sources, and claimed that they had thus received $156,825,360.

Sam's complaint further claimed that instead of constructing a railroad with the money they had so dishonestly gained, the organizers had, in order to defraud the stockholders, set up a separate construction under the name of C. Crocker and Company to build the road to Sacramento. The complaint said:

> The price and rates for building said railroad and telegraph line were exorbitant, at the rate of 200% over and above actual and reasonable cost and the materials, furniture and equipment furnished in the name of said C. Crocker & Co.; whereby the defendants did appropriate to their own use and did vote to themselves under the practice of being directors of said Central Pacific large sums of money, to-wit; $7,000,000 over and above the actual cost.

Sam went on to mention the Contract and Finance Company which the founders had later created to build the road on to Promontory, Utah; which company sublet the work "at prices more than 1000% below the prices which said Central Pacific undertook to pay Contract and Finance Company." And, of course, the Big Four pocketed the difference.

Sam said that Wells, Fargo and Company had watered its capital stock, increasing it from $10,000,000 to $15,000,000, to accommodate the railroad four, in return for the exclusive right of transporting express over the road.

Sam claimed that he and other stockholders had repeatedly demanded dividends on their stock, or, if this was not to be had, at least an accounting of the disposition of earnings, assets, and subsidies. This the Big Four had refused to give, claiming that the company was making no profits. Yet in the face of this statement, four men who had possessed less than $100,000 apiece now had fortunes which ran into millions. Sam declared that the defendants could have, at any time of late, declared a dividend of $50,000,000, divided it among the stockholders, and still have had left a large sinking fund and a surplus in the hands of the treasurer.

Sam's complaint said that the defendants had procured, from his attorney, the first draft of the complaint, and having read it had resorted to skullduggery to outwit him. They had transferred to

D. O. Mills and Company 3000 shares of capital stock issued by the City and County of Sacramento, and 2500 shares issued by Placer County, with the understanding that the Mills Company would hold it and vote it as the Big Four dictated, until such time as it would be convenient for them to have it turned back to them.

Sam said that he believed that the defendants did not have in their combined possession more than $250,000 over and above what they had misappropriated from the Central Pacific. In conclusion he asked that an injunction be placed against each of the defendants to prevent them from disposing of anything; that an actual account of the cost of production be immediately made public; that the defendants be forced to surrender all stocks or bonds of the railroad held by them openly or in secret.

Before a hearing could be had publicly, Leland Stanford called upon Sam in his office at No. 3 Masonic Hall.[99] They conferred for an hour. At the end of that time Sam surrendered his stock—$20,000 worth—for $100,000 in cash. All the suits brought by other stockholders who followed Sam's example were settled by the Big Four that year in the same manner. Stock which had cost the Central Pacific $100 a share was bought back at $400 and $500 a share.

Years later when the Senate of the United States investigated graft in railroad building, Commissioner Anderson asked Leland Stanford why Samuel Brannan had brought this suit against the railroad. "We considered it one of our blackmail suits," Stanford replied.

Anderson pressed him for details. "I want to ask you when suits of this character were brought, what inducing motive was it that caused you gentlemen to pay the large sums of money at the rate of four hundred and five hundred a share, which were paid for the adjustment of these suits, instead of compelling the party to go to his proof and show the exact state of facts to the whole world?"

Stanford squirmed. "We were building other roads and did not wish these suits to go on and spoil our credit." [99]

Sam, on the day he received cash for his shares, did not question the motive. He was too glad to get his money returned at a profit.

Although he had dropped the Central Pacific suit, he was not so lucky where Ann Eliza was concerned. In July she had another hearing. No settlement was made, and the next hearing was set for September. In August, while this was pending, Charles Bohn filed suit against Sam for assault and battery and claimed $10,000 damages. Sam had struck the man in the face during a fight in a bar.[100] He settled the case out of court.

On the twenty-ninth of September Ann Eliza's motion for alimony and counsel fees was submitted.[101] The divorce was granted, but Sam appealed the judgment for alimony.

While the final hearing was pending, Sam decided to forestall any further action on the part of Ann Eliza. He gave away to his relatives a great portion of the Calistoga estate. Cottages were given to Mary Ann Badlam, to young Mary Ann Carpenter, to Sarah Winans, to young Aleck and each of his children, to Ezra, and to the widow of Sam's brother John.

In October Sam was sued for $372.62, which was the balance due on a note he had co-signed for H. Edgerton. Sam sighed at the dishonesty of men when he handed the money for the note to the clerk of the Fourth District Court, for he had just a week previously paid out more than a thousand dollars on a note he had endorsed for Smith Clark.

In December the final hearing came before the court on Sam's appeal. The judgment was rendered: Sam had to turn over in cash, to Ann Eliza, one half the value of their community property.[102] Sam left the court and returned to his office. Young Aleck looked at him sadly when Sam broke the news to him.

"This will break you, Uncle Sam."

Sam sighed heavily. "I need a drink," he said. "Go over the books and see what can be done."

"No, Uncle Sam. You've got to stay and help me figure this out. Most of my time is taken up lately with my work as Supervisor of the Sixth Ward. When the people elected me to the job last fall they expected me to work. I've not got time to try to pull you out of this hole."

Sam sat down. They went carefully over the books. When they were done, Sam knew that he had come to the end of his resources unless he found some new way to make money. He got up and put on his high hat. "I'm going down to the Russ House and get roaring drunk. I never thought a woman would be the finish of me, especially my wife." He went out and slammed the door.

Chapter XXIX

IT WAS WITH a sense of resentment that Sam signed the papers which turned the Express and Armory buildings into cash, in order to help raise the almost half million dollars which had been awarded to Ann Eliza. The only building he had left was the Masonic Building, and it was heavily mortgaged. All the bulk of Sam's vast land holdings went under the hammer, until all he had left was the farm at Nicholaus and the Calistoga resort.

For the next ten years he collected the rents from Masonic Hall, sold a lot now and then in a real estate deal, and made something every summer from Calistoga, but he was no longer able to live on a lavish scale. Mary Ann kept house for him at the residence on Clay Street, which was no longer a show place but was beginning to look run down. Sam spent his mornings in his office but in the afternoons he was usually to be found at one or another of the bars.

Ann Eliza and Sam's alienated children had gone East after the divorce and Sam heard nothing from them. Young Aleck was devoting his time to his own job and to politics, in which he had a future.

In 1873 the Comstock burst upon a willing world and started an orgy of gambling such as San Francisco had never seen before. Sam did not gamble, but he did try to make something out of his Nevada lands; to no avail. Sarah Winans caught the Comstock fever and speculated with every penny she could obtain. Joseph, by refusing to give her money and refusing to approve any credit to her, had kept her from obtaining enough money to do any great amount of gambling, but still she could speculate with small amounts, and this she did with the connivance of her sister, Mary Ann, who was now a widow and had come to live with the Winans. Joseph welcomed Mary Ann and her two children, for Mary Ann was a good housekeeper and took over the responsibility which should have been Sarah's. Now that

Sam was often hard pressed for funds he could no longer help them much, though he did give them fifty or a hundred dollars when he had it to spare.

In 1875 William Ralston, Sam's erstwhile friend, walked into the ocean one afternoon to solve his financial worries. Sam was shocked at the news.

For three years young Sam had been in business as a commission merchant with money he had evidently secured from his mother. Now that he was thirty and in business, his mother and the three girls maintained a residence in San Francisco. At first they had lived in a rather pretentious place, but Sam heard indirectly that Ann Eliza, upon Sammy's advice, had invested heavily in mining stock in Nevada; apparently it proved worthless, for in the last year she had moved to a less expensive house.

In 1876 the Musical Fund Society summoned Sam to a meeting at which its members wished to do him honor.[103] It was the first day of August and Sam was on his way to Pioneer Hall for the meeting. He detoured down to the wharf to collect a small bill so that he would have some change in his pocket. Having secured the money, he started up the wharf to the street. At the corner he saw a young woman get out of her carriage and come down the wharf toward the office of the steamship company. She was walking toward him and he was close to her before he recognized his daughter Fanny. He stopped uncertainly, not sure whether she would speak or pass him by. As soon as she recognized the aging man she stopped short. "Why, Papa," she exclaimed. "This is a surprise!"

Sam's hip was uncommonly lame this afternoon. He felt old and tired, but never discouraged. "Yes," he smiled. "It's been a long time since I saw any of you. How have you been?"

"All right, I guess." Her face clouded and she looked sadly up at her father, who drooped just a little now. The lame hip made him seem older than his face looked. Sam waited for her to speak, for she seemed to have something on her mind.

"Papa, I wish we could have lived different than we did. So many times lately I've wished that we could have grown up in the same house with you here in San Francisco. I don't think Mama's idea of taking us to Europe to be educated was too good. We learned foreign ways during our formative years, and now that we are grown and have to live here it's a disadvantage. When we came back home to live, I was awfully happy. I guess I'm more like you than the others, because I always seemed to understand you better than Mama. I liked you better to live with. I can even sort of understand why you did some of the things you did, although I sort of wish you'd never done them. After we left and went East, Mama was always bitter against you and she said things that I wish I'd never heard. I've never been really happy since then, not until lately anyway."

"What did she say?" Sam asked tensely.

"I can't tell you. But they were pretty horrible. She was very bitter about you, and she hates Cousin Sarah like fury."

Sam spoke the hatred that had been piling up within him for years against Ann Eliza. "Your mother is a narrow, contracted woman that no man could live with. I've done things I regret, and maybe there were times when I treated her shabby-like, but if she'd been patient like other wives are, I'd have come to heel in time and we could have lived out our days contented, and given our children the kind of home life they was entitled to. I've got the wild Brannan blood in me that makes us hard to live with sometimes. My father had it, too, but my mother was patient and put up with it, and she raised her family in a united home. Of course, Ma wasn't panting to get her hands on a lot of Pa's money and she could be contented with simple things. That has been your Ma's undoing. She is at heart a greedy, selfish, mean woman who got the swelled head, and from what I see from a distance it looks like she's come near ruining the lives of all you children. Sammy's never married. I guess he'll never even amount to much as a man. And Addie's about twenty-six now and she's not married. How about you?"

Fanny smiled suddenly. "I'm on my way to buy a ticket on the steamship to New York. I'm going to get married next month."

"That's fine!" Sam exclaimed. "Who's the feller?"

"Howard Schuyler of New York City. We're all going back for the wedding."

Sam looked at her radiant face for a long moment. "I hope you'll be very happy. You deserve a good husband," he said, and he meant it. They chatted for a few moments more and then Sam went on up to the Hall of Pioneers. He was met at the door by Judge Hall, who led him up to the platform. The meeting was officially opened by the playing of the "Sam Brannan March" which had been especially composed for the occasion by Professor Spadini. When the march was finished, Judge Hall arose and addressed the audience. "We are happy to be gathered here today to do honor to our most illustrious pioneer, Samuel Brannan, who arrived in Yerba Buena just thirty years ago today." Then he launched into a eulogy of Sam Brannan, and among other things he said, "The very incipient and the most successful steps leading to the construction of the Central Pacific Railroads were inaugurated by this grand old pioneer, Sam Brannan." When the Judge had finished, Captain Swasey rose and listed all the wonderful enterprises Sam Brannan had started in San Francisco and in California. After the close of the meeting Sam had a good time reminiscing with his old friends of the Pioneer Society.

On the tenth day of August a nominating convention met in the Masonic Hall,[104] and during a recess one of the members came into Sam's office.

"Mr. Brannan, we are considering nominating you to Congress. Would you come in and give a little talk to our delegates to help them decide?"

"I'd be glad to," Sam said and went limping into the Hall.

"If you nominate me to this office," Sam promised his listeners, "I will work for several reforms. I am in favor of the city owning all its own gas and water works. I want to urge all the people to work to keep the Chinese out of here. The Central Pacific is bringing in cheap Chinese labor by the thousands to build their railroad, and if it don't stop we are going to have a serious labor situation. White men are getting tired of being thrown out of work so that coolies can have their jobs. These white men have a decent standard of living to maintain and wives and children to support. They can't compete against coolie labor. If we don't soon pass laws to prevent rich corporations from importing this Chinese labor, we are going to have some race wars in our midst. We've got to make a fight now with the ballot-box or fight later with guns."

The convention shouted itself hoarse when he had finished his talk. But its members decided he was too radical to be nominated.

In 1877 the Masonic Hall was sold to satisfy the mortgage. The farm at Nicholaus was next to go. All that Sam had left was the Calistoga resort, but late in the year it, too, went under the hammer. It was auctioned off to Sam's old enemy, Leland Stanford. All that remained of it was the cabins which belonged to Sam's various relatives.

In 1879 Sam took stock of his resources. All he had left was the Clay Street house in which he lived. Sam went down to the office of the Odd Fellows Lodge and stated his position. He asked that the lodge give back to him the land on Mission Street which he had once donated as a cemetery, but which was now valuable business property which paid the lodge good revenues. The officers said they would take his plea under advisement. The lodge voted down the proposition.

When word came to Sam that he could hope for no help from the lodge, he had just one ace in the hole left. "I'll write to Mexico and see if the Government won't pay me back the sixteen thousand dollars and more that I advanced to help them in their fight against Maximilian."

Mary Ann sniffed. "Well, you can ask them, but knowing governments the way I do, I don't think they'll give you back anything." She went out to fetch in the evening paper and when she came back she laid it in Sam's lap.

"Look what it says there on the first page," she said and pointed to an article. "It says the Mansion House at Calistoga has burned to the ground. Wonder how Stanford will like living there now." Sam chuckled. After all, there was such a thing as poetic justice. But at the same time there was a feeling of sadness that one more of his dreams had gone up in smoke.

On September 2, 1879, he addressed a letter to the Mexican Government setting forth the fact that he had put up the sum of $16,695.87 to outfit the Brannan contingent and to keep it in action in Mexico against the forces of Maximilian; that he was now destitute and would appreciate the return of his initial investment.

For months he awaited a reply. He had to close his office because he could no longer pay the rent, and he formed the habit of sitting by the bay window in the front parlor and watching for the postman to bring a letter. For three months he waited. In December of 1879 a letter arrived from the Secretary of State of Mexico. Sam's petition had been denied.

Chapter XXX

EARLY IN 1880, Sam took his problem to Aleck, who was now tax assessor for the City and County of San Francisco, with offices at 22 City Hall.

"Aleck, I've got a hunch that if I go down to Mexico City and press my claim in person I might get results. Will you lend me the money for boat fare?"

"I guess I can, Uncle Sam, but I don't have any hope for you getting any money from there." He was thoughtful for a moment. "It's too bad you wouldn't listen to me when I used to warn you of what you were heading for. If you'd have quit drinking then and tended to business you'd still be rich."

"It's no use saying, 'If you'd done this or if you'd done that,'" Sam flared. "It's too late for that kind of talk."

"Yes, I see it is," Aleck agreed. "You're just one of those fellers that will never learn. I know it don't seem nice for you to have me throw it up to you, but I'm talking to you now for your own future good. Give up this constant drinking of yours and you'll be able to make a comeback. Stay here in San Francisco, and stay away from saloons. If you do, there are a dozen men in town that you could go to work for."

Sam shook his head. "I guess it's too late for that, too, nephew. I can't quit. I've tried but I can't. This game leg of mine gets to hurting, and the only relief I get is from taking a few good shots of whiskey."

"It may make you feel better for a little while, but it's making your paralysis worse."

"Yes, booze does a lot of things to me, all bad, but I guess we'll be pals as long as I live. Now quit your preaching and make me out a check so that I can go south. When they grant my claim I'll pay you back."

Alexander wrote him the check. Then he shook hands with Sam

and wished him well. "Write often, Uncle Sam. We'll be anxious to know how you are. If you need more money, write, but don't ask unless you have too. A family takes an awful lot of money, and now that I've got Ma and Pa to support I'm having a hard time making ends meet."

"Don't worry, Aleck. I won't ask for anything I don't absolutely have to have. And whatever you give me is just a loan."

"We hope so," Aleck said, smiling, and followed him to the door.

So Sam sailed down to Mexico and took passage for Mexico City and hired a Mexican attorney to present his claim. Manuel Penichi, former member of the Mexican Congress from Yucatan, got up another petition which he presented in person to the Secretary of Public Works. General Carlos Pacheco, Secretary of Public Works, granted the claim in 1880. Sam was awarded great acreage in Sonora, which must be surveyed and colonized within two years if Brannan was to retain title to it. President Juarez concurred in the grant. Immediately Sam began to make plans for laying the foundation of another great fortune.

He sent invitations to all the Associated Press members in California to come to Mexico to dine at the Tivoli del Elisea at 1 P.M. on the Fourth of July to celebrate his new good fortune.[105] None of them came, nor did Sam expect them, but his invitation gave him newspaper publicity, which was what he had to have if he was to get his land colonized by Americans within two years.

On the strength of his land grant, Sam was able to raise enough money to pay his and Don Manuel Penichi's fare to New York to interest capital in the Mexican colonization scheme. Eventually George Ripley played host at a dinner given in Sam's honor. Sam gave a rousing talk to the prospective stockholders, and they in turn advanced him a sum of money so that he could start a survey and advertise in United States papers to attract colonists to the land. Penichi's presence gave assurance to the Americans that the Mexican Government's proposition was bona-fide. The Sonora City and Improvement Company was incorporated under the laws of the State of New York.

Sam returned to Mexico by way of San Francisco.[106] He saw many of his old friends and all his relatives except Ann Eliza and his family, who were living, Mary Ann told him, in the old Ralston mansion on Second Street and taking in boarders. The *Daily Alta* sent a reporter around to interview Sam at the Winans residence. He wrote that "Colonel Sam Brannan, sojourning for the past 18 months in the City of Mexico, returned to this city by the southern transcontinental route. Colonel Brannan is visiting with Judge Winans at 926 Clay Street." The next night the Honorable Frank Soule, Judge Winans, General Castro, Judge Freelon, the Honorable J. W. Harker, and several other old friends entertained him at dinner at the Palace Hotel. Sam was filled with enthusiasm for his new venture and told them all his hopes and plans. He returned to Mexico City the next day.

On August 1, 1881, the *Sacramento Union* published an editorial about Sam's new land venture, and it described the valley of Sonora which Samuel was trying to colonize as "rich and capable of producing two crops a year and to supply plenty of water. The oranges grown there are superior to those of Florida." But in closing the editorial pointed out that "the Mexican authorities foresaw the danger of placing Brannan in possession of the grant by making an official survey and cunningly avoided it by raising a question of legal obstacles."

The Mexican Government in making the Sonora land grant to Sam had made no grant at all. The officials knew that the land was tenanted by the Yaqui Indians and that Samuel would never be allowed to make a survey or colonize the land. Sam, realizing none of this, went on with his great plans. He rode a horse over part of his domain, and in a letter to John Ricketson dated October 11, 1881, said, "There are worse Indians in San Francisco than in Sonora." He had not been molested by them as yet and spoke in ignorance. In closing he added, "I was in the saddle one month and twenty days, which shows how vast my acres are. I believe that with the proper inducements Americans and Mexicans can be coaxed to colonize this land."

There can be no doubt that the land was wonderful. The grant was situated in the northern and eastern portions of the State of

Sonora and contained 1,687,585 acres, which were divided into two sections. The larger section was situated in the districts of Arizpe and Moctezuma, and contained 1,335,837 acres of agricultural, grazing, and timber lands. The other was in the district of Sahuaripa and contained 351,748 acres of fair grazing land with some small valleys which could be farmed. But the greatest value of the land was in the immense basin of anthracite coal which lay under it.[107]

Sam worked the rest of the year trying to get things organized so that a surveying crew could be sent out. He lived in Guaymas, Mexico, where he soon became a familiar figure to the natives. He became acquainted with the widow Carmen de Llaguno, who had been a child-bride and was now the mother of a married daughter also named Carmen.[108] Sometime in 1882 Sam married the attractive Mexican matron, which caused considerable gossip in Guaymas for the bride was in her early thirties and Sam was sixty-three and lame. Carmen, however, had braved public opinion to marry Sam, for it was said that he was a rich as well as eccentric American businessman. She had even braved the wrath of the priest, for he had refused to marry a non-Catholic to a Catholic, and since one could not marry in Guaymas without a priest it had been necessary for the impetuous lovers to take the stage down to Tucson in the Territory of Arizona to have a civil ceremony performed.

While still a newlywed, Samuel was supervising the preparations for a survey of the Sonora grant. Sam had learned by this time that he would have to deal with the Yaqui Indians before he could either survey or colonize the land, and so, when everything was ready, he decided to take a trip inland to consult the chief of the tribe and get his consent to allow a survey. In a letter to Aleck written on August 18, 1882, Sam said:

> I leave today by water for the Yakie River on a visit to the Chief, in company with the second chief, will be gone about 6 days, if I don't lose my scalp. My wife don't like for me to go. Her father was kild by order of an old chief when there to make a treaty with them, when she was a young girl. She is now 35.
>
> I have one letter to write to Mexico while Carmelita is packing up—and I am off in three hours with a fair wind and will be there sometime tomorrow.
>
> Wife sends love to all the family and I join in the same.
>
> Your Uncle
>
> My hand pains me terribley writing since daylight, now one o'clock.[109]

Samuel sailed up the river to see the chief. Arrived at the spot where tribal headquarters were located, Sam left the boat, and accompanied by the Yaqui who had come with him he walked up to the house occupied by the chief. The chief came out and waited for him. Sam limped forward with a smile and outstretched hand. The proud old man looked at Sam with glowering eyes. Then abruptly he raised his arm and pointed his finger towards the river. He said the only word of English he knew: "Git!" Samuel got.

Sam found himself faced with difficulties. In spite of the fact that he had sent out thousands of dodgers and handbills and had advertised in papers all over the United States and Mexico, he had by the end of 1881 interested not a single settler. He was trying to get a survey started in spite of the Yaquis, but was having small success. Men simply would not go out on the land carrying instruments, knowing that a group of Yaquis might kill them at any moment. Sam heard from Aleck that representatives of the New York company had come to San Francisco and sold stock in the company to every friend and relative he had. Sam was pleased that these old friends and all his relatives believed in him enough to invest money in his scheme. It was to be several months before he learned that the New York company was made up of men who wanted quick money and had no interest in Sam or his schemes; for, once they had secured thousands of dollars as investments, they quietly disappeared. Sam wrote to the company offices when more money was needed to push the survey, only to be notified by the New York post office that the offices were closed and the officers absconded. This was a blow which went deep. Sam lost his cheerfulness for a time and almost decided to give up his dreams of a new fortune.

It was during this period, in 1883, that two Mormon missionaries visited Guaymas, and in their travels came in contact with Sam. They wrote to the *Deseret News*, the Mormon newspaper, an account of their meeting with Samuel, and described him as living in "squalid penury and wretchedness." In commenting upon their statement an editorial recalled that Parley P. Pratt had once predicted that Sam would live to see the day when he would want for a dime to buy a loaf of bread.

On March 21, 1883, Sam wrote to Aleck from Guaymas:

Sunday 64 years old was my birthday and I spent the day at home and thank
you for your kind wishes until you are better paid. I do not look for youth but to
fill my destony.

Ship my portrait and the portrait of my father which your mother has without the signature of the Consul and it will come duty free.[110]

Samuel's marriage was not working out satisfactorily. Although
poverty had forced him to give up steady drinking, he was still erratic
and quick-tempered, and Carmen had little patience with him when
she discovered that he was not rich. After a particularly violent quarrel about his lack of money, Carmen packed up her things and
departed to live with her daughter in Mexico City.

Sam was not sorry to see her go. Perhaps he would have a little
peace and quiet at home in the little hut where he was forced to live.
However, rheumatism settled in his lame hip and he missed having
someone to wait on him when he could not get about. He grew so ill
in June that he had friends bring him pencil and paper and drew up
his will. It read:

In the name of God, Amen!
I declare all my former Wills null and void this day.

1. I bequeath and give to my son, Samuel Brannan, one dollar, and to my oldest
    daughter Adelade Brannan, one dollar, my third and youngest daughter
    Lizzie Brannan, one dollar. The reason that I bequeath so small a sum is that,
    I gave to their mother at the time of my divorce from her, a large fortune of
    over one half millions of dollars and she took charge of the children and alien-
    ated them from me and I since learned that she has squandered it away in
    gambling in mining stocks, which I am sorry to hear.
2. I give and bequeath to John Ricketson, now residing in Guaymas, one half of
    all my property in New Guaymas or Point Arena, Mexico, in Block No. 9.
    The other half to Alexander Badlam, Junior, my nephew, the oldest son of
    my sister, Mary Ann Badlam, now residing in San Francisco, Calif. U.S.A.
3. To share and share alike, in one half to each of my ten Mexican claims of
    land and railroad franchise or moneys, Ricketson paying one half the land cost
    me in New Guaymas, eight hundred dollars.
4. They, Ricketson and Badlam, paying all my honest debts and my funeral
    expenses, to be levied on my property in Block No. 9 Guaymas, Mexico, they
    to prosecute all of these claims against Mexico, not paid.
                                                    SAMUEL BRANNAN.
    dated: June 28, 1883.

Sam did not mention Fanny in his will, for he knew that she was well provided for.

John Ricketson was an American married to a Mexican woman. He was Sam's partner in the real estate business at Guaymas

Mrs. Ricketson came in to take care of Sam and soon he was up and about again. A signed contract arrived at this time from the Mexican Government, giving him two years more to prove his title to the Sonora land grant. The parties to the contract were General Carlos Pacheco on one side and Manuel Penichi, representing Brannan, on the other. Article 1 of the new contract stipulated that Pachecho authorized Mr. Samuel Brannan to survey (provided no other party had a better right thereto) up to seventy-five thousand hectares of public lands situated to the west of the River Yaqui between Comoripa and Sahuaripa in the State of Sonora. Sam smiled sardonically when he read the parenthetical note. "They think they're making damned sure I won't get that land," he told Ricketson, "but I'll survey it in spite of the Yaqui Indians and I'll colonize it, too, in spite of them. I'll control that land yet, or know the reason why."

When Samuel read Article 8 he felt a little dubious of his ability to comply. It set forth that Samuel was authorized to colonize the land within the term of five years, with five hundred families. Three-fourths of the colonists must be of Spanish origin. The others could be American. By signing the contract Samuel bound himself to place on the Sonora land at least fifty families within the first two years. "All I can do is try," he said to John Ricketson as he signed his name.

Sam made every effort to coax settlers to his land. He advertised that they could have homesteads for nothing if they would just come and live on these lush lands in a semitropical paradise. But still the shadow of the Yaqui Indians loomed large. The Mexicans would take no chances—they would not have settled on Yaqui lands if Sam had paid them to do so; and Americans were far away and would not believe the fabulous stories they read in the papers.

Sam would have starved if Alexander had not kept sending him supplies and money, but this was a drain that Alexander could ill afford.

Late in 1884 Samuel organized a new company to promote the Sonora land. This was called the Sonora Land Company. Notices were sent to all the American and Mexican newspapers and again dodgers were sent out to attract settlers. Alexander paid the cost of printing the handbills, but no settlers came. Then Sam began to try to sell stock in his company. He advertised for agents, but none were forthcoming. This scheme, like all the others, came to naught.

Although Sam was now entirely dependent upon his nephew, he was still filled with grandiose plans for the future.

Samuel's belief that he could make money in Mexico finally dwindled away and he left Mexico to go to Nogales, in the Territory of Arizona, in the hope that he could find some way to make a living. He wrote to Alexander constantly, and even though he had left Mexico he did not give up the idea that he might still, by some miracle, be able to prove title to the Sonora land. He kept urging Alexander to try to interest various rich San Franciscans in the plan, even to Leland Stanford. But Stanford, like the others, saw no merit in the scheme and would put no money in it.

In March of 1885 Aleck forwarded Sam two shirt bosoms, in accordance with a request from his uncle, with collars attached; one lawn, one rep. The neck size was fifteen inches. "Also one grey shirt mixed with a little red, side pockets sack coat." The waist was forty-one inches, the leg thirty-one and one-half inches, and chest forty-two, which reveals that Sam at sixty-six years of age was six feet in height, fairly heavy about the waist, with still a powerful chest.

In a letter to Aleck he wrote, "You bet no scrub of a woman will ever break me if I once get up again." And in closing he added, "Tell Stanford if you see him that he ought to be in my fix about a month for fun but I don't care. If he will lend me ten thousand dollars for one year he can charge what interest he pleases or have one-half of what I make."

But Stanford would advance no money to his old enemy.

In the fall of 1885 Sam took the stage down to Tucson to write up the election returns for the little paper there. He said that the stage fare from Nogales to Tucson cost him seven dollars.

Two years passed, during which his hopes were raised again and again as various individuals came to look over his lands and talked of financing him. But no one ever did. Sam often went hungry, for young Aleck was burdened now with his father and mother as well as his own growing family, and also with the erratic Sarah Winans and Mary Ann Carpenter and their children. The estates left by the two women's husbands had been rapidly frittered away. It was utterly impossible for him to send any further funds to Sam. Even if Sam had been on good terms with his own son, it would have profited him nothing, for young Sammy had failed in business and was panning ore at the head of the Yaqui River on some of the Sonora land which his father had given him. He made enough to live on but not enough to help either his father or his mother, who was now living with her youngest daughter Lisa, who had married a man named Gjessing. Ann Eliza's fortune had long since disappeared.

In describing his poverty to Aleck, Sam wrote: "What a pleasure it is to be poor; you ought to see my den; one room 4 trunks and 2 chairs and the walls are adobe with a dirt roof and when it rains I get the benefit of it. Office and bed are room in one, no fire all winter and yet I am as happy as a Clam in a crow's nest, for I have got the world by the Cahonies and don't care a damn."

There was one kind of business Sam decided he could make a living from. He would sell pencils. He wrote to Aleck requesting that several dozen be sent to him. When they arrived he wrote:

Nogales, Arizona, June 5, 1887.

DEAR ALECK:

The pencils have arrived. They are splendid. Everybody wants them. Sam Brannan buys them!

The more I think of it, the more I want to go to San Francisco. I think I can make a bigger fortune than ever, if the climate suits me and Stanford carries out his project to build the road from there to Fort Euma and connect with the S. P. I want to get there as soon as I can. What do you know about the road being built? And who is down there that I know? Stanford had better bought property there than Calistoga.

Then Sam went out, using a cane to help his injured hip, and sold the pencils from door to door or standing on street corners. He made enough that way during the next few months to pay his fare to San Francisco.

The *Morning Call* of San Francisco noted on November 1, 1887, that "Samuel Brannan arrived in this city from Mexico yesterday on the steamer *Newbern*."

Samuel visited with his relatives for the next two weeks, mostly staying at Aleck's home. His dream of making a new fortune in San Francisco soon went glimmering when he saw how the city had changed since he had left it. This was a bustling metropolis which had no time for a lame old man. Men whom he had once befriended crossed the street to keep from speaking to him, and Sam felt hurt, knowing that they avoided him for fear he might ask for money. "I would never do it, though," he told Aleck in the evening. "I've never got so hard up yet that I've had to beg. I've sold pencils to make a living, but I've not begged."

Sam did not feel well in San Francisco. The fog and rain chilled him to the bone and the rheumatism came back into his lame hip. Two weeks after he arrived in San Francisco he made ready to leave for the south. H. H. Bancroft, the historian, called upon Sam the day he was to leave.

"Mr. Brannan, I wish that you would write a personal account of your life, especially emphasizing the history of California since you arrived."

"I'd sure like to do it, Mr. Bancroft," Sam replied, "but that would take time. I've got to find some way to make a living and I'm afraid I won't have much time for tinkering around writing history."

Bancroft smiled easily. "Oh, but I would be glad to pay you for such a history. You write it first and name the price and whatever it is, within reason, I'll gladly pay."

So Sam promised that he would write a personal history for Bancroft. "But I want you to promise me that you will not publish it while I live," he stipulated.

"Agreed," said Bancroft.

Sam set sail for San Diego. He took up residence in a cheap little tent house on the edge of a creek, and while it rained and he was tied to his bed a goodly portion of each day, Sam began to write his history of California. A cloudburst swelled the creek one night and Sam had to get up and hobble to higher ground as best he could with his lame leg. The tent and all its furnishings were swept away, and Sam's history never was completed.

The story has been told, and repeated in many newspapers, that Sam Brannan received a cash settlement of forty-nine thousand dollars from the Mexican Government in return for some bonds he had supposedly purchased, and that with this money he returned to San Francisco, paid up all his debts, and lived out his last days in affluence and in perfect health. Nothing could be further from the truth.

In San Diego Sam tried first one way to make a living and then another. None of them were successful. He tried to set himself up as a dealer in real estate, but he had no capital and was doomed to failure before he started. He wrote to Aleck constantly, and he harped upon the idea that he might be able to sell his Mexican lands to someone; but this, of course, was but the stubborn hope of an old man.

Aleck could not support Sam and yet he felt the keenest sympathy for the battle-scarred old warrior. It was he who appealed to the Occidental Lodge of the Odd Fellows to do something for their most illustrious charter member. A committee was appointed by the lodge in May of 1888 to create a fund from net revenues to maintain and support Sam. When the small pittance they allowed reached Sam, it came as a welcome surprise. He was able to move into a little apartment above a store and to hire a woman to come and clean up once a week for him.

It was in May that he wrote to Aleck:

Will you see if you can find the portrait of my father which was painted by Charles Granger, and take care of it for me. He is taken standing and dressed for winter coming out of the house (it is as I saw him) and as near perfection as need be. . . . He was nature's noble man and his wife also.

That fall Sam moved to Escondido, thirty miles north of San Diego. The great Mexican land deal was not abandoned; merely put aside for a while until Sam could get on his feet financially. He felt that Escondido would offer him a chance to rehabilitate himself. The old land hunger still gnawed at his vitals. If he could buy a little piece of land and start a farm in this semitropical country, he would soon be financially independent. He wrote glowingly of the possibilities there to Aleck and begged him to come down and see for himself.

Aleck did finally come. When he returned to San Francisco he sent four hundred dollars to Sam, with which to buy land. Sam acknowledged receipt of this money and promptly bought acreage within the city limits of Escondido. Then he wrote to his nephew to tell him what he had done and added, "The morning you left I felt pretty bad. Perhaps you would call that the blues. I never had them." This was in November of 1888.

His health was poor that winter, and he could not get about when it rained. Magdalena Moraga, a Mexican woman, came to keep house for him.[111] She was a quiet woman who went about her work with little to say. Sam talked to her almost constantly, for he was hungry for companionship. She listened to him but made no comment, only her great black eyes showing that she heard and was interested.

In April, when the sun grew warm, he was able to hobble around outside a little. But early in May he fell ill with inflammation of the bowels. Magdalena nursed him faithfully. One morning he seemed a little better and she propped him up with pillows. He was in great pain, but he seemed to want to talk of other days, when he had been rich and sought after. He told her of how rich he had been, but she looked at him stolidly, unbelieving. Toward noon he grew tired.

"Take the pillows away and let me lay down," he said. She did so. "Now go get me my Swiss music box and put the 'Londonderry Air' on. It always makes me think of my little Fanny. She's married to a rich man now. I wish I could see her again."

As the tune played out, Sam nodded his head in time to it. When it was finished he closed his eyes. That night he died—on May 14, 1889, just two months after his seventieth birthday.

No mourner but Magdalena followed him to the cemetery lot in San Diego, where his body lay in a vault for several months until Aleck was able to bring money to have it interred.

The *Evening Bulletin* in San Francisco, like other San Francisco newspapers, took note of his passing:

His money having disappeared and all his schemes come to naught, Brannan came over the line to San Diego, sick and despondent, seeking health. A friend of the writer of these lines who saw the unfortunate man shortly before he passed away, says he was paralysed in his left side and looked gaunt and haggard, but there was something of the old nerve and spirit that had carried him through his long and arduous career in California still remaining. He was dressed in the light pajama-fashioned cotton clothing of the ordinary Mexican paisano, and wore a large sombrero; the costume looked more comfortable (the climate considered) than elegant.

"Come, Amigo, we will drink to the memory of old times in California. I did the State some service when I lived there. You cannot deny that."

And that was the man who once had an income of $1,000 a day!

Notes

1. All information for this chapter and others dealing with Sam's early life was either gathered from the Brannan family records or told to the writer by Sophie Brannan Haight, a daughter of his brother John Brannan. She is now dead.
2. *Doctrinal Church History* (L.D.S. Library, Salt Lake City), II, 327, gives proof that the Badlams were members of the Church, for it mentions a sum of money given to Joseph Smith by Alexander Badlam, Sr. On p. 204 is a notation that Alexander Badlam was ordained a Seventy. When Alexander moved to the Coast he was appointed to do whatever missionary work he could, for the Church Journal History (MS, Church Library) May 28, 1855, p. 1, says: "Elder Alexander Badlam, who labored in California and seemed to be particularly interested in the Chinese, wrote a lengthy letter under date of May 28, 1855, to Elder George A. Smith, in which he gave a description of some of the manners, habits and customs of the Chinese for whom he had conceived a most friendly interest."
3. As related by Sophie Brannan Haight.
4. *Times and Seasons*, V, 388.
5. "Twenty Years Later," *Sacramento Daily Union*, Sept. 11, 1866.
6. Parley P. Pratt, *Autobiography*.
7. *Sacramento Daily Union*, Sept. 11, 1866.
8. Frank Alfred Golder, *March of the Mormon Battalion*, p. 37.
9. *Times and Seasons*, VI, 1037.
10. *Ibid.*, VI, 1043.
11. Church Jour. Hist., Jan. 12, 1846.
12. *Times and Seasons*, Jan. 15, 1846.
13. Church Jour. Hist., Jan. 26, 1846.
14. *Times and Seasons*, VI, 1126.
15. *Ibid.*
16. William Glover MS. John Eager MS. Augusta Joyce Crocheron, *Representative Women of Deseret*, p. 102.
17. Eager MS.
19. *Millennial Star.* Newspaper published at London, England. IX, 39.
20. Eager MS.
21. *Ibid.*
22. Glover MS.
23. Sacramento Daily Un., *loc. cit.*

24. Crocheron, *loc. cit.*
25. J. H. Brown, *Reminiscences and Incidents*, p. 31.
26. "Filings from an Old Saw," *Golden Era*, 1850–1854.
27. Brown, *op. cit.*, p. 39.
28. Glover MS.
29. *Ibid.*
30. George H. Tinkham, *History of Stanislaus County.*
31. *San Jose Pioneer*, June 16, 1877.
32. Zoeth Skinner Eldredge, *The Beginnings of San Francisco*, p. 520.
33. *Millennial Star*, IX, 306.
34. *San Jose Pioneer Record*, June 23, 1877.
35. George R. Stewart, *Ordeal by Hunger.*
36. *Millennial Star*, IX, 305.
37. William Clayton's Journal, in Church Jour. Hist.
38. *Ibid.*
39. Orson F. Whitney, *History of Utah*, Vol. I.
40. Clayton, *op. cit.*
41. *Ibid.*
42. Utah Early Records. MSS., Bancroft Library.
43. *Ibid.*
44. H. H. Bancroft, *Inter-Pocula.*
45. Glover MS.
46. *Ibid.*
47. Bancroft, *History of California*, V, 677.
48. Sutter's Fort Diary. MS., Bancroft Library.
49. William Heath Davis. *Seventy-five Years in California.*
50. William Warren Ferrier, *Ninety Years of Education in California, 1846–1936*, p. 19.
51. *Oakland Tribune*, Knave Section, Feb. 28, 1937.
52. Henry Bigler's Diary. MS., Bancroft Library.
53. *Ibid.*
54. *John A. Sutter Diary* (Grabhorn Press, San Francisco, 1932)
55. Sutter's Fort Diary.
56. *Ibid.*
57. William T. Sherman, *Memoirs*, I, 67.
58. James Peter Zollinger, *Sutter.*
59. *A History of California Newspapers*, ed. Douglas C. McMurtrie (reprinted from *Sacramento Daily Union*, Dec. 25, 1858.)
60. Julian Dana, *The Sacramento*, p. 219.
61. Bancroft, *Inter-Pocula*, p. 609.
62. Thompson and West, *History of Sacramento County*, p. 51.
63. Peter Burnett, *Recollections and Opinions of an Old Pioneer*, p. 298.
64. Thompson and West, *op. cit.*, p. 46.
65. Z. S. Eldredge, *op. cit.*, p. 573.

66. W. H. Davis, *op. cit.*
67. Peter J. Deloy, *History of Sutter and Yuba Counties.*
68. Utah Early Records. MS., Bancroft Library.
69. Bancroft, *Inter-Pocula,* p. 346.
70. Bancroft, *Popular Tribunals,* p. 78.
71. Deloy, *op. cit.,* p. 268.
72. Thompson and West, *op. cit.*
73. Theodore H. Hittell, *History of California,* III, 345.
74. Zollinger, *op. cit.,* pp. 296–307.
75. Hittell, *op. cit.,* Vol. III.
76. *Daily Alta California,* May 4, 1850.
77. Frank Soule, *Annals of San Francisco,* p. 567.
78. Hittell, *op. cit.,* III, 357. See also Soule, *op. cit.,* p. 340.
79. Bancroft, *Popular Tribunals,* p. 206.
80. Parley P. Pratt, *Journal of the Pacific Mission.* MS. in my own collection.
81. John Adam Hussey, "New Light upon Talbot H. Green," *California Historical Quarterly,* Mar. 1939.
82. Sophie Brannan Haight.
83. *Daily Alta California,* May 22, 1853 (Sunday).
84. Don C. Wiley, in *San Francisco Examiner,* Dec. 31, 1936.
85. Fred Talbot, *Cassell's Railways of the World,* III, 523. See also Bancroft, *History of California,* on the development of railways.
86. Sophie Brannan Haight.
87. Franklin D. Walker, *San Francisco's Literary Frontier,* p. 217.
88. Slocum and Bowen, *History of Napa County,* p. 326.
89. Sophie Brannan Haight.
90. *Daily Alta California,* Nov. 3, 1869.
91. Zoeth S. Eldridge, *History of California,* V, 431.
92. Samuel Smiles MS., Bancroft Library. Written when Brannan was 63.
93. Sophie Brannan Haight.
94. Oscar T. Shuck, *Representative Men of the Pacific,* p. 457.
95. *Napa County Record.* Slocum, Bowen and Co., p. 328.
96. *The Golden Era,* June 12, 1870.
97. *Daily Alta California,* June 10, 1870.
98. Railroad Pamphlet. Bancroft Library.
99. *Report of the U.S. Pacific Railway Commission* (Executive Documents of the Senate of the United States for the first session of the Fiftieth Congress), page 73.
100. *Daily Alta California,* Aug. 27, 1870.
101. *Ibid.,* Sept. 29, 1870.
102. Brannan's own words in his Will, written June 28, 1883. Brannan papers in coll. of Mrs. Maude Pettus.
103. *Daily Alta California,* Aug. 1, 1876.
104. *Ibid.,* Aug. 11, 1876.

105. *San Jose Pioneer*, Aug. 28, 1880.
106. *Daily Alta California*, Apr. 30, 1881.
107. Brannan papers in coll. of Mrs. Maude Pettus.
108. Letter from American Vice Consul A. F. Yepis, written to author from Guaymas, Sonora, Mexico, May 13, 1937.
109. Brannan letters to Alexander Badlam, Junior. Coll. of Mrs. Maude Pettus.
110. All the letters and papers referred to in this and the last chapters are in the coll. of Mrs. Maude Pettus.
111. George Barron, formerly Curator of the Golden Gate Museum, is authority for this statement. He mentions a visit to Brannan made at the time.

Bibliography

Ayers, Col. James J., *Gold and Sunshine* (Boston: Badger, 1922).

Bancroft, Hubert H., *History of California, 1542–1890* (7 vols., San Francisco: History Co., 1890).

—— *History of Utah, 1540–1887* (San Francisco: History Co., 1891).

—— *History of the Pacific States:* vols. xxx, *California Inter-Pocula*, xx-xxxii, *Popular Tribunals* (San Francisco: History Publishing Co., 1886, 1887).

Bigler, H. W., Diary of a Mormon in California. MS., Bancroft Library— Bigler's version of the gold discovery, which is accepted by all authorities.

Brannan, Samuel *vs.* Central Pacific Railroad. Pamphlet in Bancroft Library.

Brown, J. H., *Reminiscences and Incidents of "the Early Days" of San Francisco* (1845–1850) (San Francisco: Mission Journal, 1886).

Buck, Franklin A., *A Yankee Trader in the Gold Rush* (Boston: Houghton Mifflin, 1930).

Buffum, E. G., *Six Months in the Gold Mines* (Philadelphia: Lea & Blanchard, 1850).

Burnett, Peter H., *Recollections and Opinions of an Old Pioneer* (New York: Appleton, 1880).

California Blue Book of 1932. Compiled under direction of Frank C. Jordan (State Printing Office).

California Historical Society Quarterly (San Francisco). All files.

California State Library, MSS., Brannan files.

Clayton, William, Journal MS., Latter Day Saints Library, Salt Lake City.

Cleland, Robert Glass, *History of California: The American Period* (New York: Macmillan, 1922).

Crocheron, Augusta Joyce, *Representative Women of Deseret* (Salt Lake City: Graham, 1884).

Cross, Ira B., *Financing an Empire: History of Banking in California* (Indianapolis: Clarke Publishing Co., 1927).

Dana, Julian, *The Man Who Built San Francisco* (New York: Macmillan, 1936).

—— *The Sacramento* (New York: Farrar & Rinehart, 1939).

Dana, Richard H., *Two Years Before the Mast* (Boston: Houghton, 1911).

Doctrinal Church History, MS., Latter Day Saints Library, Salt Lake City.

Davis, William Heath, *Seventy-five Years in California* (San Francisco: Howell, 1929).

Delay, Peter J., *History of Yuba and Sutter Counties* (Historic Record Co., L. A. 1924).

Dunlap, Florence McClure, Thesis, University of California, 1928.

Eldredge, Zoeth Skinner, *The Beginnings of San Francisco* (San Francisco: Author, 1912).

—— History of California (5 vols., New York: Century History Co., 1915).

Ferrier, William Warren, *Ninety Years of Education in California, 1846–1936.* (Berkeley: Author, 1937).

Gillespie, Charles V., MS., Bancroft Library.

Glover, William, MS., Bancroft Library.

Golder, Frank Alfred, *March of the Mormon Battalion from Council Bluffs to California* (New York: Century Co., 1928).

Golden Era (weekly newspaper), files of 1853–54.

Harpending, Asbury, *The Great Diamond Hoax*, ed. James H. Wilkins (San Francisco: J. H. Barry, 1913).

Haswell, Charles H., *Reminiscences of an Octogenarian of New York* (New York: Harper, 1895).

Hittell, John S., *A History of the City of San Francisco and Incidentally of the State of California* (San Francisco: Bancroft, 1878).

Hittell, Theodore H., *History of California* (4 vols., San Francisco: Stone, 1885–1897).

Jacobsen, Pauline, "Story of Sam Brannan," *San Francisco Bulletin*, May 20, 1916.

Journal History of the L.D.S. Church. MS. in Church Library.

Larkin Letters, MS. at Bancroft Library.

McMurtrie, Douglas C., *History of California Newspapers* (New York: Plandome Press, 1929).

Millennial Star. Mormon newspaper published at London, England.

Myers, Gustavus, *History of the Great American Fortunes* (3 vols., Chicago: Kerr, 1914).

Napa County History (San Francisco: Slocum, Bower & Co., 1881).

Napa Sketch Book (San Francisco: S. Meneffee).

Newspapers:
> *Calistoga Tribune.*
> *Alta California.*
> *The Californian.*
> *California Star.*
> *Deseret News*, Salt Lake City.
> *Oakland Tribune* (knave section).
> *Oakland Enquirer.*
> *Placer Times.*
> *Sacramento Union.*
> *San Francisco Bulletin.*
> *San Francisco Examiner.*
> *San Francisco Herald.*
> *San Francisco Morning Call.*
> *San Jose Pioneer.*

Overland Monthly, June, 1889 (San Francisco).

Palmer, L. L., *History of Napa and Lake Counties* (San Francisco: Slocum, Bowen, 1881).

Phillips, Catherine Coffin, *Portsmouth Plaza, the Cradle of San Francisco* (San Francisco: J. H. Nash, 1932).

"Pioneer Days in San Francisco," *Century Magazine*, Feb., 1892.

Pratt, Parley P., *Autobiography*, ed. by his son (Chicago: Pratt Bros., 1888).

—— Journal of Pacific Mission, MS. in author's possession.

Rensch, Hero Eugene, Rensch, E. G., and Hoover, Mildred, *Historic Spots in California: Valley and Sierra Counties* (Stanford, Calif.: Stanford Univ. Press, 1933).

Rider, Fremont, *California: A Guide-Book for Travellers* (New York: Macmillan, 1925).

Royce, Josiah, *California* (American Commonwealth Series). (Boston: Houghton, 1886.)

Sacramento County History (San Francisco: Thompson and West, 1880).

San Francisco City Directories (1851 to 1880).

San Francisco Police Gazette.

"San Francisco's Famed Cliff House," *P. G. & E. Progress*, Apr., 1937 (San Francisco).

Scherer, James A. B., *The First Forty-niner* (New York: Minton, Balch, 1925).

Sherman, Gen. W. T., *Memoirs* (New York: Appleton, 1887).

Shuck, Oscar T., *Representative and Leading Men of the Pacific* (San Francisco: Bacon & Co., 1870).

Soule, Frank, *Annals of San Francisco* (New York: Appleton, 1855).

Southern Pacific. Report of U.S. Pacific Railway Commission—Executive Documents of the U.S. Senate, 50th Congress. Washington: Government Printing Office, 1888.

Stanislaus County History, George H. Tinkham (Historic Record, Los Angeles, 1921).

Stewart, George R. *Ordeal by Hunger* (New York: Holt, 1936).

"Story of Samuel Brannan," *Improvement Era*, July, 1936 (Salt Lake City).

Sutter County History (Oakland, Calif.: Thompson and West, 1879).

Sutter's Fort Diary of Events from 1845 to 1848, kept by Swasey, Bidwell, Looker, and Sutter. Copy in Bancroft Library.

Sutter, John A., *Diary* (San Francisco: Grabhorn Press, 1932).

——*Personal Reminiscences.* MS., Bancroft Library.

Talbot, Fred A., *Cassell's Railways of the World* (London: Waverly, 1925).

Times and Seasons. Official Mormon newspaper published at Nauvoo.

Todd, Charles Burr, *Story of the City of New York* (New York: Putnam, 1892).

—— *In Olde New York* (Albany: McDonough, 1907).

Trubody MS., Bancroft Library.

Unbound documents—Records of Early California. MSS., Bancroft Library.

Walker, Franklin D., *San Francisco's Literary Frontier* (New York: Knopf, 1939).

Whitney, Orson F., *History of Utah* (4 vols. Salt Lake City: Cannon, 1892).
Williams, Mary Floyd, *History of the San Francisco Committee of Vigilance of 1851* (Berkeley: University of California Press, 1921).
Zollinger, James Peter, *Sutter* (New York: Oxford University Press, 1939).

GENERAL READING

Burton, Sir Richard F., *City of the Saints* (London: Longman, Green, 1861).
Evans, John Henry, *Joseph Smith: An American Prophet* (New York: Macmillan, 1933).
Kelly, Charles, and Birney, Hoffman, *Holy Murder: The Story of Porter Rockwell* (New York: Minton, Balch, 1934).
Linn, William A., *Story of the Mormons* (New York: Macmillan, 1902).
Stenhouse, T. B. H., *Rocky Mountain Saints* (New York: Appleton, 1873).
Tyler, Daniel, *A Concise History of the Mormon Battalion in the Mexican War* (Salt Lake City, 1881).

Passenger List of the Ship

BROOKLYN

Addison, Isaac (wife and daughter)

Aldrich, Silas (died at sea) accompanied by wife Prudence, son Jasper, and daughter

Atherton, William and wife

Austin, Julius C. Wife and 3 children

Brannan, Samuel. Wife and child

Buckland, Alondus L. D. Mother, Hannah D. Buckland

Bullen, Newell. Wife and 3 children

Burr, Charles C. Wife and child

Burr, Nathan. Wife

Cade, John (possibly Kincaid) and wife

Clark, Sophia P.

Combs, Abram. Wife and 3 children

Corwin, Mrs. Fanny M. (Brannan's Mother-in-Law)

Eager, John

Eager, Lucy. 2 daughters

Eager, Mary (one of the daughters)

Eager, Thomas

Ensign, Elias (died at sea)

Ensign, Miss Eliza (died at sea)

Ensign, Jerusha. Son

Evans, William. Wife and 4 children

Fisher, Joseph R.

Fisher, Mary Ann

Fowler, Jerusha. 4 children (A child of John (?) Fowler died at sea)

Glover, William. Wife and 3 children

Goodwin, Isaac. Wife (died at sea) and 6 children

Griffith, Jonathan. Wife and 2 children

Hamilton, Mrs. Mary. (Perhaps children)

Haskell, A. G.

Hayes, Jacob

Hicks, Joseph
Horner, John M. Wife
Hyatt, Elisha. Wife and son
Ira, Cyrus (or Irea)
Joyce, John. Wife and 2 children
Jones, Mrs. Isabella
Kemble, Edward C.
Kittleman, George
Kittleman, John
Kittleman, Sarah
Kittleman, Thomas
Kittleman, William. Wife and 6 children
Knowles, Richard. Wife
Ladd, Samuel (or Johnson)
Lane, Emmeline A.
Leigh, Isaac. Wife (or Lee)
Light, James. Wife and child
Lovett, Angeline M.
McCue, Patrick. Wife and 4 children
Marshall, Earl. Family
Meder, Moses A. Wife, Sarah D., and child
Mowry, Barton. Wife and 2 sons
Mowry, Origin. Family
Mowry, Rinaldo
Moses, Ambrose. Wife and 4 children
Murray, Miss Mary
Narrimore, Edwin (died at sea)
Narrimore, Mercy M. and child
Nichols, Joseph. Wife and child (died at sea)
Nutting, Lucy
Oakley, Howard
Pell, E. Ward. Wife and 2 daughters
Petch, Robert. Wife and 2 children
Philips, John
Pool, Peter
Pool, Mary
Pool, Elizabeth
Read, Christiana
Read, Hannah T. (Jimison?) and child
Reed, John

Reed, Rachael
Robbins, Isaac R. Wife and 2 children
Robbins, John R. Wife and 2 children (both died at sea)
Rowland, Henry (Roulan or Rollins) and daughter
Rowland, Isaac
Savage, Eliza
Scott, James
Sirrine, George W.
Sirrine, John J. Wife and child
Skinner, Horace A. Wife and child
Smith, Amelia
Smith, Orrin. Wife and 6 children
Smith, Robert. Wife and 2 children
Snow, Zelnora S.
Sparks, Mary. Family
Sparks, Quartus. Wife and child
Stark, Danied. Wife and 2 children
Still, George. Wife and 3 children
Stivers, Simeon
Stout, William. Wife and child
Stringfellow, Jesse A.
Thompkins, Thomas. Wife and 2 children
Ward, Frank (not a Mormon)
Warner, Caroline. 3 children
Winner, George K. Wife and 6 children (one child died at sea)

Members of the *Brooklyn* company who remained faithful, most of whom went to Deseret:

Prudence Aldrich, son Jasper, and daughter—Bountiful, Utah
Julius Austin—Bear Lake, Utah (a locality, not a town)
Alondus Buckland—Bountiful, Utah
Newell Bullen—Richmond, Utah
Charles Burr—Burrville, Utah
John Cade (or Kincaid)—Salt Lake Valley
Sophia Clark—Ogden, Utah
Abram Combs—Beaver, Utah
John Eager—Salt Lake Valley
Thomas Eager—Oakland, Calif.
William Evans—Centerville, Utah
Mary Fisher—San José, Calif.

William Glover—Farmington, Utah
Isaac Goodwin—Cache, Utah
John Kittleman—Salt Lake Valley
William Kittleman—Centerville, Utah
Richard Knowles—Salt Lake Valley
Samuel Ladd (or Johnson)—St. George, Utah
Mrs. Ambrose Moses and daughter Clarisa—Salt Lake Valley
Rinaldo Mowry and mother—Kaysville, Utah
Lucy Nutting—Lehi, Utah
John Philips—Beaver, Utah
Peter Pool—Smithfield, Utah
Christiana Read—Cache, Utah
Isaac Robbins—Provo, Utah
John Robbins—Salt Lake City, Utah
Eliza Savage—Salt Lake City, Utah
James Scott—Salt Lake Valley (disfellowshipped but later reinstated)
George Sirrine—Mexico
Amelia Smith—Salt Lake Valley
Robert Smith—Sandy, Utah
Zelnora Snow—Farmington, Utah
Daniel Stark—Payson, Utah

Members of the *Brooklyn* company as listed above were taken from a list made by William Glover in 1884, available at Bancroft Library. The towns listed were in Deseret which later became the Territory of Utah but are listed as they are now in the state of Utah.

Members of the *Brooklyn* company who apostatized or were disfellowshipped:

Isaac Addison—returned east before 1847.
Lucy Eager went to Monterey, California in 1847. Previous to this she kept a store in Yerba Buena for a short time. Mary and Arabella became apostates.
John Joyce apostatized; deserted his family when he went to the gold mines.
Sarah Kittleman married E. P. Jones, who was not a Mormon, and after leaving their San Francisco Hotel went to Kentucky.
Ambrose Moses disfellowshipped; lived at Mission Dolores for a time. One of his daughters married Eustachio Valencia and was the first

Mormon to be buried at the Mission. Her children were taken to Utah and raised in the Mormon faith by Ambrose Moses' wife.

Barton Mowry apostatized and later became a Spiritualist.

E. Ward Pell disfellowshipped; remained in San Francisco.

Orrin Smith disfellowshipped; remained in Honolulu.

Quartus Sparks disfellowshipped by Parley P. Pratt for abuse of his family and drunkenness.

Members of the *Brooklyn* company who remained faithful but did not go to Deseret:

William Ensign (son of Jerusha)—San Francisco

Joseph Fisher—California

Jerusha Fowler—California

Jonathan Griffith—California

Jacob Hayes—California

John Horner—Washington Corners, now known as Irvington, California. He built a meeting-house at Washington Corners and preached there. He was a very successful farmer.

Cyrus Ira—California

George Kittleman—San Francisco, Calif.

Thomas Kittleman—San Francisco, Calif.

Albert Lee (son of Isaac Leigh or Lee)—San Francisco

Joseph Light—California

Angeline Lovett—San Francisco (with her husband, Thomas Kittleman).

Earl Marshall—joined Horner's colony at Washington Corners.

Patrick McCue—California

Origin Mowry—East Shore farmer.

Joseph Nichols—California

Howard Oakley—California

Robert Petch—California

George Still—California

Simeon Stivers—Washington Corners, joined Horner's colony.

William Stout—Santa Cruz, California

Jesse Stringfellow—San Jose, California

George Winner—San Francisco; became a river pilot on the Sacramento

INDEX

LaVergne, TN USA
05 October 2009
159976LV00002B/89/A